Lecture Notes in Artificial Intelligence   13652

Subseries of Lecture Notes in Computer Science

Series Editors

Randy Goebel
University of Alberta, Edmonton, Canada

Wolfgang Wahlster
DFKI, Berlin, Germany

Zhi-Hua Zhou
Nanjing University, Nanjing, China

Founding Editor

Jörg Siekmann
DFKI and Saarland University, Saarbrücken, Germany

More information about this subseries at https://link.springer.com/bookseries/1244

Max Bramer · Frederic Stahl (Eds.)

Artificial Intelligence XXXIX

42nd SGAI International Conference on
Artificial Intelligence, AI 2022
Cambridge, UK, December 13–15, 2022
Proceedings

 Springer

Editors
Max Bramer
University of Portsmouth
Portsmouth, UK

Frederic Stahl
DFKI: German Research Center for Artificial
Intelligence
Oldenburg, Germany

ISSN 0302-9743 ISSN 1611-3349 (electronic)
Lecture Notes in Artificial Intelligence
ISBN 978-3-031-21440-0 ISBN 978-3-031-21441-7 (eBook)
https://doi.org/10.1007/978-3-031-21441-7

LNCS Sublibrary: SL7 – Artificial Intelligence

This Springer imprint is published by the registered company Springer Nature Switzerland AG
The registered company address is: Gewerbestrasse 11, 6330 Cham, Switzerland

Preface

This volume, entitled Artificial Intelligence XXXIX, comprises the refereed papers presented at the forty-second SGAI International Conference on Innovative Techniques and Applications of Artificial Intelligence, held in December 2022. The conference was organised by SGAI, the British Computer Society Specialist Group on Artificial Intelligence.

This year's Donald Michie Memorial Award for the best refereed technical paper was won by a paper entitled 'Practical Limits to Transfer Learning of Neural Network Controllers from Earth to Space Environments' by Collins Ogundipe and Alex Ellery (Carleton University, Canada).

This year's Rob Milne Memorial Award for the best refereed application paper was won by a paper entitled 'Job Assignment Problem and Traveling Salesman Problem: A Linked Optimisation Problem' by B.M.E. Lacroix, A. Ogunsemi, and J. McCall (National Subsca Centre, Robert Gordon University, UK), M. Kern and G. Owusu (BT Applied Research, UK), and D. Corsar (Robert Gordon University, UK).

The other full papers included are divided into sections on AI for Health and Medicine, AI for Scientific Discovery and Decision Making, AI for Industrial Applications, and Feasibility Studies of Applied AI.

The volume also includes the text of short papers presented as posters at the conference.

On behalf of the conference Organising Committee, we would like to thank all those who contributed to the organisation of this year's program, in particular the Program Committee members, the Executive Program Committees, and our administrators Mandy Bauer and Bryony Bramer.

September 2022

Max Bramer
Frederic Stahl

Organisation

Conference Committee

Conference Chair

Max Bramer   University of Portsmouth, UK

Technical Program Chair

Max Bramer   University of Portsmouth, UK

Deputy Technical Program Chair

Jixin Ma   University of Greenwich, UK

Application Program Chair

Frederic Stahl   DFKI - German Research Center for Artificial
                              Intelligence, Germany

Workshop Organiser

Adrian Hopgood   University of Portsmouth, UK

Treasurer

Rosemary Gilligan   SGAI, UK

Poster Session Organisers

Juan Augusto   Middlesex University London, UK
Richard Ellis   RKE Consulting, UK

AI Open Mic and Panel Session Organiser

Andrew Lea   PersuasionXP, UK

FAIRS Organiser

Giovanna Martinez   University of Nottingham, UK

Publicity Organiser

Nadia Abouayoub   SGAI, UK

Conference Administrator

Mandy Bauer   BCS, UK

Paper Administrator

Bryony Bramer   SGAI, UK

Technical Executive Program Committee

Max Bramer (Chair)   University of Portsmouth, UK
Frans Coenen   University of Liverpool, UK
Adrian Hopgood   University of Portsmouth, UK
John Kingston   Nottingham Trent University, UK
Gilbert Owusu   BT, UK

Application Executive Program Committee

Frederic Stahl (Chair)   DFKI - German Research Center for Artificial
                                    Intelligence, Germany
Richard Ellis   RKE Consulting, UK
Rosemary Gilligan   SGAI, UK
Jixin Ma   University of Greenwich, UK
Lars Nolle   Jade University of Applied Sciences, Germany
Richard Wheeler   University of Edinburgh, UK

Technical Program Committee

Per-Arne Andersen   University of Agder, Norway
Juan Augusto   Middlesex University London, UK
Farshad Badie   Berlin School of Business and Innovation (BSBI),
                                    Germany
Raed Sabri Hameed Batbooti   Southern Technical University, Iraq
Lluis Belanche   Universitat Politecnica de Catalunya, Spain
Mirko Boettcher   Techniker Krankenkasse, Germany
Soufiane Boulehouache   University of Skikda, Algeria
Max Bramer   University of Portsmouth, UK
Krysia Broda   Imperial College London, UK
Ken Brown   University College Cork, Ireland
Sandy Brownlee   University of Stirling, UK

Marcos Bueno	TU Eindhoven, The Netherlands
Nikolay Burlutskiy	AstraZeneca, UK
Philippe Chassy	University of Liverpool, UK
Darren Chitty	Aston University, UK
Frans Coenen	University of Liverpool, UK
Bertrand Cuissart	Université de Caen, France
Ireneusz Czarnowski	Gdynia Maritime University, Poland
Nicolas Durand	Aix-Marseille University, France
Frank Eichinger	DATEV eG, Germany
Martin Fyvie	Robert Gordon University, UK
Hossein Ghodrati Noushahr	University of Leicester, UK
Adrian Hopgood	University of Portsmouth, UK
Chris Huyck	Middlesex University London, UK
Zina Ibrahim	Kings College London, UK
John Kingston	Nottingham Trent University, UK
Ivan Koychev	University of Sofia, Bulgaria
Nicole Lee	University of Hong Kong, SAR China
Anne Liret	BT, France
Fernando Lopes	National Laboratory of Energy and Geology, Portugal
Jixin Ma	University of Greenwich, UK
Stewart Massie	Robert Gordon University, UK
Silja Meyer-Nieberg	Universität der Bundeswehr München, Germany
Roberto Micalizio	Università di Torino, Italy
Daniel Neagu	University of Bradford, UK
Lars Nolle	Jade University of Applied Sciences, Germany
Joanna Isabelle Olszewska	University of the West of Scotland, UK
Daniel O'Leary	University of Southern California, USA
Filipo S. Perotto	ONERA, France
Maria Dolores Rodriguez-Moreno	Universidad de Alcalá, Spain
Fernando Saenz-Perez	Universidad Complutense de Madrid, Spain
Miguel A. Salido	Universitat Politècnica de València, Spain
Sadiq Sani	BT Applied Research, UK
Sid Shakya	Khalifa University, UAE
Simon Thompson	GFT Technology, UK
M. R. C. van Dongen	University College Cork, Ireland
Nirmalie Wiratunga	Robert Gordon University, UK

Application Program Committee

Manal Almutairi	University of Reading, UK
Mercedes Arguello Casteleiro	University of Southampton, UK

Elmar Berghöfer	German Research Center for Artificial Intelligence GmbH (DFKI), Germany
Ken Brown	University College Cork, Ireland
Nikolay Burlutskiy	ContextVision AB, Sweden
Xiaochun Cheng	Middlesex University London, UK
Sarah Jane Delany	Technological University Dublin, Ireland
Tarek El-Mihoub	German Research Center for Artificial Intelligence GmbH (DFKI), Germany
Richard Ellis	RKE Consulting, UK
Andrew Fish	University of Brighton, UK
Rosemary Gilligan	University of Hertfordshire, UK
Carl James-Reynolds	Middlesex University London, UK
Colin Johnson	University of Nottingham, UK
Friedemann Kammler	German Research Center for Artificial Intelligence GmbH (DFKI), Germany
Alice Kerly	The CAI Company, UK
Mathias Kern	BT, UK
Andrew Lea	PersuasionXP, UK
Daniel Lukats	German Research Center for Artificial Intelligence GmbH (DFKI), Germany
Christoph Manß	German Research Center for Artificial Intelligence GmbH (DFKI), Germany
Lars Nolle	Jade University of Applied Sciences, Germany
Navya Prakash	German Research Center for Artificial Intelligence GmbH (DFKI), Germany
Juan Antonio Recio Garcia	Complutense University Madrid, Spain
Sam Richardson	GFT Financial Ltd., UK
Georgios Samakovitis	University of Greenwich, UK
Janina Schneider	German Research Center for Artificial Intelligence GmbH (DFKI), Germany
Frederic Stahl	German Research Center for Artificial Intelligence GmbH (DFKI), Germany
Christoph Tholen	German Research Center for Artificial Intelligence GmbH (DFKI), Germany
Richard Wheeler	Edinburgh Scientific, UK
Mattis Wolf	German Research Center for Artificial Intelligence GmbH (DFKI), Germany

Contents

AI for Industrial Applications

Feasibility Studies of Applied AI

Short Papers

Best Technical Paper

Practical Limits to Transfer Learning of Neural Network Controllers from Earth to Space Environments

Collins Ogundipe[✉] and Alex Ellery

Department of Mechanical and Aerospace Engineering, Carleton University, 1125 Colonel by Drive, Ottawa K1S 5B6, Canada
collinsogundipe@cmail.carleton.ca

Abstract. Given the similarity in form and dynamics between earth-based and space-based robotic manipulators, transfer learning of neural network controllers would naturally be a plausible avenue to address the challenges of limited computation resources onboard the spacecraft (space manipulator). We have introduced a pretrained and learned feedforward neural network for modeling the control error a priori. While the results are encouraging, there are major limitations of neural networks' capability to ensuring the transfer learning of similar earth-based dynamics to space-based dynamics, given that the parameters of contrast are fairly straightforward. To show these limitations, we present a novel approach that is inspired by human motor control. We have explored the adaptability of neural networks as a key feature for robust AI which has traditionally suffered from brittleness. This was demonstrated through a practical problem of transferring a neuro-controller from earth to space. It was discovered that neural networks including deep learning models are still too brittle for general AI. We have developed appropriate neural network models using trajectory data from 7 degrees-of-freedom (7-DOF) Barrett Arm, as representative of an earth-based to space-based manipulator kinematics and dynamics.

Keywords: Transfer learning · Neural network · Forward model · Space robotics · Manipulator · Free-flyer

1 Introduction

In human level manipulation, various sections of the brain extend into the motor area M1 to supply feedback signals. The parietal cortex, for instance, deals with visual control of hand motions, and it calculates the error between the current cartesian position and the desired cartesian position [1]. To do this, an efference copy of the motor commands is required to produce a feedforward compensation. The efference copy of the motor commands is typically transmitted to an emulator which models the input-output response of the musculoskeletal system. From a biomimetic perspective, it is believed that a hierarchical neural network system in any control architecture can imitate this function of the motor cortex [2]. During human manipulation, the error between the actual motor

© The Author(s), under exclusive license to Springer Nature Switzerland AG 2022
M. Bramer and F. Stahl (Eds.): SGAI-AI 2022, LNAI 13652, pp. 3–16, 2022.
https://doi.org/10.1007/978-3-031-21441-7_1

outputs (joint position (θ) and joint velocity ($\dot{\theta}$) evaluated by the proprioceptors) and the commanded motor input (torque τ, from the motor cortex) is fed back as [$\theta^{desired} - \theta$] having a time delay of 40–60 ms [3]. However, a "forward dynamics model of the musculoskeletal system exists within the spinocerebellum-magnocellular red nucleus system" [3]. This forward model accepts feedback (θ and $\dot{\theta}$) from the proprioceptors and an afferent copy of the motor command (τ) from the motor cortex. Consequently, the forward model receives motor command τ as its input and outputs an estimated predictive trajectory θ^* [3], processing this input-output comparison between the pair (τ and θ^*) to generate a predicted error [$\theta^{desired} - \theta^*$] in a much faster manner to minimize the error. The forward model does this prediction/comparison in 10–20 ms, transmitting this to the motor cortex in the process [3]. The sensory effects of the motor command are predicted by this forward model. This type of top-down prediction model is centered on the statistical reproducible model of the causative nature of the world learned via input-output pairs. This can be directly explored with predictive neural networks as forward model by adopting input-output models of deep learning architecture or multivariate regression. In human level interaction, these forward models of the musculoskeletal system have been learned through the initial motor babbling that started from infancy [3]. And the learned models are transferred to adapt to changes in stimuli or environments, given the underlying dynamics remain the same.

This leads to the practical problem we have detailed in this paper, which is the transfer learning from earth-based manipulators to space-based manipulators. In space robotics, there are simply two fundamental changes from earth to space which are accounted for through: (i) the absence of gravity in space, and (ii) the direct substitutions of certain derived parameters which are quantified in numbers and readily available as a modification of the earth-based equivalents. So, essentially, the dynamics of the robotic system remain the same, and necessary environmental variations are readily accounted for. All other space-based environmental factors are known to be negligible as they pertain to the dynamics of space robot's interaction. The environmental disturbance torques (gravity gradient, aerodynamics and magnetic torques) imposed on the robot's spacecraft are very small – within $10e-6$ Nm [4]. The primary differentiating characteristics of space robotics from terrestrial robotics is that the robot operates in a microgravity environment. Transfer learning of neural network controller trained as a forward model in a biomimetic approach similar to how human manipulation is carried out should be able to exhibit efficient generalization as typically shown for new data input in most deep learning domain/applications. However, the practical limitation of transfer learning of neural network controllers is the exhibition of lack of general intelligence, as detailed in this paper.

Considerable effort has been put into developing machine learning methods that can learn and improve inverse dynamics model of robotic manipulators [5–8]. Online learning has been the focus in these settings because when considering motions with object interactions, learning one global model becomes very challenging, if not impossible, since the model must be a function of contact and payload signals. To approach the issue of global/dynamic model, learning task-specific (error) models has been proposed in the past [9–12], such that the overall global problem is simplified into two subproblems – (1) finding a task-specific inverse dynamics model and (2) detecting which task model to use. This permits to iterate the collection of data specific to a task, learn an error model, and then apply the learned model during the required task execution. However, a key difficulty that has been encountered is the computationally efficient learning of models that are data-efficient as possible, such that only few iterations are required while achieving consistent convergence in the error model learning. We seek to address this using predictive feedforward approach, in a pre-learned fashion, by ensuring the transfer learning of earth-based model to space environment. Our take on this is that pre-learned input-output models are computationally efficient compared with analytical models – the latter require exact knowledge of parameters (commonest sources of errors which include payload variation) and require computation time. Learned models reduce computation by storing model in memory, which also ensure a more compliant and reactive robot.

For feedback control to work, errors must exist to invoke the corrective behaviour. This is not the case for feedforward control which does not require errors to work. Forward model implemented in conjunction with feedback control reduces the potential error excursions [13]. Currently, space manipulators are typically teleoperated in space by astronauts or by ground operators and are operated very slowly. This acts as a severe restriction on productivity rates. The incorporation of feedforward controllers, therefore, offers the advantage to robustify and speed up operations as they do not require error excursion to function. In the following, we first described in Sect. 2, the background to the derived parameters relating space-based manipulator's kinematics and dynamics to earth-based environment. In Sect. 3, we detailed a novel predictive feedforward control via a forward model; followed by a complete overview of our learning algorithms and manipulator configuration in Sect. 4. Finally, we evaluate the results of the proposed scheme in Sect. 5 and outlined the practical limitations of transfer learning of the neural network controller. Section 6 detailed the conclusion which exposes problems in neural networks including deep learning as a model of general intelligence.

2 Space-Based Kinematics and Dynamics

We must first consider the kinematics and dynamics of a freeflyer-mounted manipulator. The main differentiating characteristics of space robots from terrestrial robots is that terrestrial robots are mounted onto a firm ground; in space, we have no such force or torque reaction cancellation to the movement of manipulator arms. Additionally, the robot operates in a microgravity environment; hence, the kinematics and dynamics of free-flying robotic manipulator deployed in space will take a different approach. In the consideration of a free-flying robotic manipulator mounted on a spacecraft bus having dedicated attitude control, the position kinematics (p^*) of the manipulator in connection with inertial space is given by [14, 15]:

$$p^* = r_{c0} + R_0 s_0 + \sum_{i=1}^{n} R_i l_i \tag{1}$$

where r_{c0} is the position of the spacecraft centre of mass with respect to the inertial coordinates; R_0 is the attitude of the spacecraft with respect to the inertial coordinates;

s_0 is the position vector of the manipulator base with respect to the spacecraft body centre of mass; R_i is the 3-by-3 direction cosine matrix of each link with respect to the base coordinates; n is the number of serial rigid body links; i represents the link number from 0 to n; while l_i is the vectoral length of link i from $(x_{i-1}, y_{i-1}, z_{i-1})$ to (x_i, y_i, z_i) (Shown in Fig. 1.)

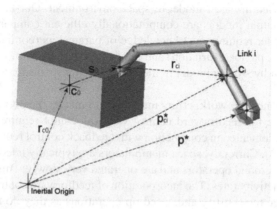

Fig. 1. Spacecraft-Manipulator Geometry (C_0 represents spacecraft's center of mass; r_{ci} is the distance between the centres of mass of adjacent links with respect to the base coordinates; C_i is the center of mass of link i; p_{ci}^* is the position of the link i centre of mass with respect to the inertial coordinates).

For spacecraft bus with dedicated attitude control, $R_0 = I_3$ (identity matrix). The center of mass of the whole system (the robotic manipulator, satellite bus mount, and the payload) is represented by [14, 15]:

$$p_{cm}^* = \frac{\sum_{i=0}^{n+1} m_i p_{ci}^*}{\sum_{i=0}^{n+1} m_i} \tag{2}$$

where p_{cm}^* is the location of the centre of mass of the complete manipulator/spacecraft system with regards to the inertial coordinates; m_i is the mass of each component rigid body links; n is the number of rigid body links; $n = 0$ represents the spacecraft body link; p_{ci}^* is the position of link i centre of mass in reference to the inertial coordinates. Similarly to terrestrial manipulator algorithms in the form of $p_i = R_i l_i$, the equation of the space manipulator for the location of the center of mass of the complete manipulator/spacecraft system with regards to the inertial coordinates (p_{cm}^*) has been derived to be [16–18]:

$$p_{cm}^* = r_{c0} + \left(1 - \frac{m_0}{m_T}\right)s_0 + \frac{1}{m_T}\sum_{i=1}^{n} R_i \left(\sum_{j=i+1}^{n+1} m_j l_i + m_i r_i\right) .. \\ + \frac{m_{n+1}}{m_T} R_{n+1} r_{n+1} \tag{3}$$

where m_0 is the mass of the spacecraft bus; m_T is the total mass of the system; m_i is the mass of each component rigid body i comprising the system; r_i is the vectorial distance from the origin of link i to the centre of mass of link i; $n+1$ represents the corresponding notations for the payload link. Equation (3) was separated into three parts: parts related to body 0 (the spacecraft), bodies 1 to n (the manipulator links) and body $n+1$ (for the payload). This then reduces to [18]:

$$p_{cm}^* = r_{c0} + \left(1 - \frac{m_0}{m_T}\right)s_0 + \sum_{i=1}^{n} R_i L_i + \left(\frac{m_{n+1}}{m_T}\right)r_{n+1}$$

$$\text{where } L_i = \frac{1}{m_T}\left(\sum_{j=i+1}^{n+1} m_j l_i + m_i r_i\right)$$

(4)

This concludes the location of center of mass of the system with respect to inertial space. It is assumed arbitrarily that the local inertial reference frame initially coincides with the spacecraft bus center of mass, that is, $r_{c0} = 0$, since any point fixed in the interceptor body could be regarded as inertially fixed prior to any robotic maneuver [18]. Having defined p_{cm}^*, the term r_{c0} is then substituted into Eq. (1), which gives

$$p^* = p_{cm}^* + s_0 + \sum_{i=1}^{n} R_i l_i - \frac{1}{m_T}\sum_{i=1}^{n+1}\sum_{j=i}^{n+1} m_j r_{ci}$$

(5)

This is further simplified into:

$$p^* = p_{cm}^* + s_0 + \sum_{i=1}^{n} R_i l_i - \dots$$

$$\frac{1}{m_T}\sum_{i=1}^{n+1}\sum_{j=i}^{n+1} m_j(R_i r_i + R_{i-1}s_{i-1})$$

(6)

where $r_{ci} = R_i r_i + R_{i-1}s_{i-1}$ [18]. Similarly, we separate out the three parts associated to the spacecraft mount (body 0), bodies 1ton for the manipulator links and body n + 1 for the payload [18]. This gives

$$p^* = p_{cm}^* + \frac{m_0}{m_T}s_0 + \sum_{i=1}^{n} R_i \lambda_i - \frac{m_{n+1}}{m_T}R_{n+1}r_{n+1}$$

$$\text{where } \lambda_i = \frac{1}{m_T}\sum_{j=0}^{i}(m_j l_j - m_i r_i)$$

(7)

Accordingly, λ_i is referred to as the lumped kinematic parameter for each manipulator link. The Eq. (7) of p* is an equivalent form to that of the terrestrial-based manipulator of the form $p = \sum_{i=1}^{n} R_i l_i$ with added constants; (p_{cm}^* is constant, and λ_i is constant as the lumped kinematic/dynamic parameter, replacing the l_i in terrestrial-based manipulator).

Therefore, the inverse kinematics solution to the space manipulator geometry can be found with little modifications to the terrestrial algorithms.

3 Predictive Feedforward Control

Our bio-inspired error-learning approach addresses the need for reactive and adaptive behavior to diverse range of tasks under dynamic environmental conditions. If we could successfully demonstrate this for a terrestrial manipulator, the idea is to incorporate the approach in a free-flyer concept for the removal of space debris of varying sizes; with the aim to offer a solution transferrable from earth to different orbital bands. In effect, we propose here a control scheme that is centered on biomimetic models for predictive forward control in conjunction with traditional feedback control. We believe that bio-inspired forward models could provide solution for adaptive and robust control, which could position robotic manipulators for the complex task of salvaging space debris if the learned model can be successfully transferred to space environment. Adaptivity will be implemented through learning of new forward models to adapt to new situations; robustness is implemented in the form of forward models that provide rapid behavior without relying on error excursions unlike traditional feedback controllers. The superiority of feedforward-feedback control over feedback control only has been clearly demonstrated [13]. Pure feedback control is implausible for reactive manipulation due to substantial delays in sensors' feedback signals. This is like the case biologically where human reaction time is limited to a maximum of about 400–500 ms [19]. Therefore, predictive feedforward strategy is proposed as added measure to correct the robot's trajectory along with the feedback control. In this current study, we have not yet implemented feedback delays into the forward model yet – the work presented here is the first step in building a more comprehensive and sophisticated manipulator control system. The bio-inspired control system should comprise a paired feedforward-feedback system with a learning system that adapts forward models for different scenarios such as time delays and/or payload variations. Hence, the core of this approach is the forward model presented. A two-layer approach towards grasping has been presented: (i) position control through feedback, which is the traditional approach – but delays in the feedback cycle can generate instabilities; (ii) the addition of a feedforward predictive capability to partially circumvent this problem of instabilities by adopting pre-trained set of neural networks which in a way emulates the function of the cerebellum as seen in humans.

The predictive feedforward approach involves pre-learned models trained offline, which then provide a computationally efficient control model for low controller gains necessary for reactive and adaptive control. We have introduced task-specific models that are able to learn from their errors (make error predictions) under different and varying dynamics. The proposed approach is more practical for space-based manipulators because there would be no major hindrances such as high computational complexity; and secondly, the trained forward models do not require high computational resources to implement which is usually a constraint onboard spacecraft. This is where transfer learning comes in as a practical solution for transferring pre-trained earth-based model to space environment. Most automatic control algorithms have not been demonstrated in space as most manipulator control systems are teleoperated from earth.

Here, we present a forward model that is learned (or trained) as a neural network approximator using some trajectory datasets relating the output torque τ to the kinematic state of the joints $(\theta, \dot{\theta}, \ddot{\theta})^T$ in an experimental teaching mode (Fig. 2). The trained forward model will hence be able to take the analytically calculated torque (efference copy of input motor commands) as its input, while the output of the neural network will be the predicted trajectory output $(\theta_{ff}, \dot{\theta}_{ff}, \ddot{\theta}_{ff})^T$. The system then incorporates an inverse model with a feedforward adaptive part; that is, it includes a feedback loop and feedforward component. The feedforward controller is trained using the output of the feedback controller which serve as error signals. The trained feedforward component models the inverse dynamics of the system. The feedback controller is effectively a computed torque controller while the feedforward controller employs a gradient descent to minimize the error.

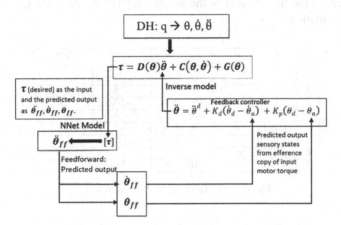

Fig. 2. The predictive forward model scheme. The neural network ("NNet") model is trained using data from experimental teaching mode. DH stands for Denavit–Hartenberg; q represents DH parameters for forward kinematics. D, C and G represent inertia matrix, coriolis and gravity components respectively; K_d and K_p are derivative and proportional controller gains.

The forward dynamic model of a robotic manipulator is given by (for the sensory joint acceleration rate):

$$\ddot{\theta} = D^{-1}(\theta)[\tau - C(\theta, \dot{\theta}) - G(\theta)]$$

Joint acceleration $\ddot{\theta}$ could be integrated to get joint rate $\dot{\theta}$ and joint rotation θ as the predicted sensory state outputs from torque input τ. The body's muscular nature which produces a predicted trajectory output from efference input motor commands can be imitated by the predictive forward model [20]. To compensate for time delays, the feedforward control consequently predicts its response to system disturbances using a model of the plant process [21]. This predicted trajectory output would be supplied as input to the feedback component to compensate for delays (and this process could continue iteratively). It is believed that forward models can adjust 7.5 times more speedily than when using only inverse models [22]. The forward model, in this case, is executed as a neural network function estimator to the forward dynamics.

4   Methodology

We present here the configuration and kinematics of the space manipular adopted, and the mathematical implementation of the neural network multiple-target prediction algorithms.

4.1   Barrett WAM Configuration

For this study, the configuration of the WAM (Whole Arm Manipulator) representing the parameters of the manipulator at the initial (stowed) position are shown below as used in the simulation:

k	a_k (m)	α_k (rad)	d_k (m)	θ_k	Lower Limit (θ_{kL} rad)	Upper Limit (θ_{kU} rad)
1	0	$-\pi/2$	0	θ_1	-2.6	2.6
2	0	$\pi/2$	0	θ_2	-2.0	2.0
3	0.045	$-\pi/2$	0.55	θ_3	-2.8	2.8
4	-0.045	$\pi/2$	0	θ_4	-0.9	3.1
5	0	$-\pi/2$	0.3	θ_5	-4.76	1.24
6	0	$\pi/2$	0	θ_6	-1.6	1.6
7	0	0	0.06	θ_7	-3.0	3.0

Fig. 3. D-H Table of the Barrett WAM.

The Barrett arm is a 7-DOF manipulator with a three-fingered hand as representative of an on-orbit servicing manipulator kinematics. For the kinematics solution, the procedure discussed and presented in Sect. 2 was implemented for the space manipulator. The procedure is the space-based kinematics shown for modifying terrestrial robots to space robots. The key to the space application approach is to replace the terrestrial parameters of a_k and d_k of Fig. 3 with the spaced-based equivalence [18], according to the lumped kinematic parameters as described in Sect. 2.

4.2   Implementation of Multiple-Target Prediction Algorithms

Machine learning algorithms were developed to learn/train the forward dynamics model by using the joint torques as input and the joint trajectories as targets. With respect to the nature of the trajectory datasets, and after various experimentations, the multiple-output regression tree and the multi-layer perception (MLP) multiple-output regression algorithms were identified for best prediction accuracy and computational efficiency. We present here the implementation of the algorithms, with emphasis on the multiple-output decision tree regression. Given a feature vector x, we aim to predict a vector of output responses y using the function $h(x)$:

$$x = (x_1, x_2, x_3 \ldots, x_m) \overset{h(x)}{\Rightarrow} y = (y_1, y_2, y_3 \ldots, y_d)$$

Some of the notable challenges are the proper modeling of dependencies among targets, i.e., between targets $y_1, y_2, y_3 \ldots, y_d$; and dealing with large number of multiple variable loss functions outlined over the output vector, $\mathcal{L}(y, h(x))$.

There are two methods existing for multiple output regression, namely (i) problem transformation methods and (ii) algorithm adaptation methods. In our case, we used the algorithm adaptation method because it provides more accurate predictive performance, particularly in cases where there are correlations among the targets [23–25] - as we have in our robotic trajectory dataset, where the targets $(\theta, \dot{\theta}, \ddot{\theta})^T$ are co-related. Given a training dataset D of N samples containing a value assignment for individual variable $X_1, X_2, \ldots, X_m, Y_1, Y_2, \ldots, Y_d$; that is, $D = \{(\mathbf{x}^{(1)}, \mathbf{y}^{(1)}), \ldots, (\mathbf{x}^{(N)}, \mathbf{y}^{(N)})\}$. Every sample is categorized by an input vector of m predictive variables $\mathbf{x}^{(l)} = (x_1^{(l)}, \ldots, x_j^{(l)}, \ldots, x_m^{(l)})$ and an output vector of d target variables $\mathbf{y}^{(l)} = (y_1^{(l)}, \ldots, y_i^{(l)}, \ldots, y_d^{(l)})$, with $i \in \{1, \ldots, d\}$, $j \in \{1, \ldots, m\}$, and $l \in \{1, \ldots, N\}$.

The aim is to learn multiple output regression model from D comprising of a function h that ascribe to each sample, given by the vector $\mathbf{x}$, and a vector $\mathbf{y}$ of d target values:

$$h : \Omega_{X_1} \times \ldots \times \Omega_{X_m} \to \Omega_{Y_1} \times \ldots \times \Omega_{Y_d}$$
$$\mathbf{x} = (x_1, \ldots, x_m) \to \mathbf{y} = (y_1, \ldots, y_d),$$

where Ω_{X_j} and Ω_{Y_i} denote the sample spaces of each predictive variable X_j, for all $j \in \{1, \ldots, m\}$, and each target variable Y_i, for all $i \in \{1, \ldots, d\}$, respectively. The variables in targets $(\theta, \dot{\theta}, \ddot{\theta})^T$ are taken to be continuous, as it is the case for manipulators' joint trajectory. The trained multi-output model will be employed subsequently to concurrently predict the values $\{\hat{\mathbf{y}}^{(N+1)}, \ldots, \hat{\mathbf{y}}^{(N')}\}$ for all target variables of the new incoming unlabeled examples $\{\mathbf{x}^{(N+1)}, \ldots, \mathbf{x}^{(N')}\}$. Multi-target regression trees, as adopted in our case, can predict multiple continuous targets simultaneously. They have major benefits over adopting single regression tree for individual target [26]. Here, we have adopted an extension of the univariate recursive partitioning method (CART) [27] to our multi-target regression task. Therefore, the multivariate regression trees are modeled similarly to the steps followed in CART. The approach that performed better between MLP neural network and multi-target regression was chosen in each instance.

5 Results

Presented here are the results of the predictive feedforward model of the Barrett WAM space manipulator. The significance of the result is to demonstrate how we have developed neural network and regression models which are capable of predicting (to a high degree of accuracy) forward trajectory variables $(\theta_{ff}, \dot{\theta}_{ff}, \ddot{\theta}_{ff})$ from an efference copy of the torque, as shown in Fig. 4. It means the models are poised to cancel the sensory effects of the arm movement, providing anticipated sensory consequences from the motor command. With this, instabilities that could arise in delays when using traditional feedback cycle have been partially circumvented. This is akin to how the human cerebellum functions as discussed in Sect. 3. Here, we adopt a dataset publicly made available by [28], where the Barrett WAM was taken by the end-effector and guided along several trajectories in a teaching mode – in this case, it implies that sensor noise was included in the training dataset. During the imagined motion, the joint trajectories $(\theta, \dot{\theta}, \ddot{\theta})$ were sampled from the robot and the corresponding motor torques (τ) measured for each data point. The dataset has a total of 12,000 samples. For the 7 degree-of-freedom (7-DOF)

Barrett arm, 7 motor torques were measured, along with 21 joint trajectory variables representing seven joint angles (θ), seven joint velocities ($\dot{\theta}$) and seven joint accelerations ($\ddot{\theta}$).

Deep learning neural network models and multiple-output regression models were developed, and we learned the forward dynamics model by using the joint torques as input and the joint trajectories as targets. Given a feature vector x, we aim to predict a vector of output responses y using the function h(x):

$$x = (x_1, x_2, x_3 \ldots, x_m) \overset{h(x)}{\Rightarrow} y = (y_1, y_2, y_3 \ldots, y_d)$$

Table 1. Prediction accuracy of joint angles (Data point 243).

Joint number	Joint angle (rad) Test Set	Joint angle (rad) Predicted	Accuracy (%)
1	0.0814	0.0799	98.2
2	0.6165	0.5696	92.4
3	0.0236	0.0222	94.1
4	1.745	1.6647	95.4
5	0.2123	0.199	93.7
6	0.0781	0.0751	96.2
7	0.0869	0.0844	97.1

The independent features were used to train each set of targets grouped separately by the joint angles, joint velocities, and the joint accelerations. Meaning three different models with different hyperparameters were trained (learned), in an attempt to manage target dependencies. The first model relates the 7 joint torques as input to the 7 joint angles as targets; the second model was learned between the 7 joint torques as input and the 7 joint velocities as targets, while the third model learned the relationship between the 7 joint torques as input and multiple-target prediction of the 7 joint accelerations as the output. It should be noted that the joint trajectory datasets for the training and testing were randomly split for better model learning and performance. In Table 1, a comparison for a chosen data point (sample number 243) for the predicted feedforward joint angles are shown, while Table 3 represents the case for joint velocities. These tables show the results comparing the predicted feedforward joint trajectory (for angle and velocity) to some desired joint trajectory specified as test set from the dataset. Table 2 shows the comparison for the accuracy of the end-effector's position in the three-dimensional cartesian space. This relates the desired joint angles and the predicted joint angles for the seven degrees of freedom, as carried out with space manipulator forward kinematics.

Table 2. Prediction accuracy of end-effector's position (data point 243).

End-effector Cartesian position	Desired position	Predicted (actual) position	Accuracy (%)
x-position	0.0040	0.0037	92.5
y-position	0.0047	0.0046	97.9
z-position	0.9008	0.9005	99.9

Table 3. Prediction Accuracy of Joint Velocities (Data point 243).

Joint number	Joint velocity (rad/s) Test Set	Joint velocity (rad/s) Predicted	Accuracy (%)
1	0.0657	0.0647	98.5
2	−0.1850	−0.1835	99.2
3	−0.1794	−0.160	89.2
4	−0.0678	−0.0646	95.3
5	−0.0235	−0.0231	98.1
6	0.0478	0.0434	90.8
7	−0.0895	−0.0872	97.4

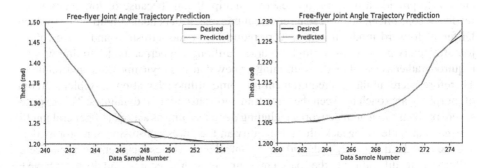

Fig. 4. Predicted-to-desired, data points 240–255; 260–275, for joint angle 1, simulated free-flyer.

Figure 4 represent results of several sample data points for the simulated Barrett WAM free-flyer, showing prediction correlation along the path of joint-angle motion (θ) for a single chosen joint (Joint 1). The joint trajectory dataset from the terrestrial case was simulated and modified following the kinematics and dynamics of robotic free-flyer presented in Sect. 2. Initially, the free-flyer dataset was tested on the predictive model built earlier for the terrestrial case. The performance was, surprisingly, poor and unsatisfactory. However, retraining the earth-based model using the newly gotten free-flyer space dataset resulted in highly correlated trajectory accuracy between the desired and predicted as shown in Fig. 4 – without the need to tune the hyperparameters. The drawback to the feedforward model here is the need to re-learn the new dataset as adopted for the space manipulator. It was discovered that the possibility of transfer learning could not be exploited after the optimized initial training, even though the deduced terrestrial-to-space manipulator dynamics were incorporated analytically in the model learning process. A second limitation was the fact that a change in dynamics (such as time delays and/or payload variations) resulted in the necessity to retrain the model, and learned weights were not transferable. Again, the controlling equations and dynamics of the terrestrial-to-space manipulator have not changed, these limitations should have been learned (accounted for) in the trained model as part of the space robot's dynamics.

The prediction accuracy in both cases ranged between 89–99%, and our model compared favorably to the expected feedforward joint trajectory. In the simulation carried out, low gains were required subsequently in the feedback controller for trajectory tracking. The feedforward model provided good anticipatory sensory consequences, although a morphing system will be required to transform between the terrestrial and free-flyer dynamics. For the variations seen in the prediction accuracies, this issue will apply to any serial manipulator control system.

6   Conclusion and Future Work

We have introduced forward models implemented as trained neural networks as a means of supplementing traditional feedback controllers for space manipulators. The forward models show high accuracy predictions for the feedforward joint trajectory; robust enough to provide a platform for reactive manipulation (because of low gains in the feedback controller), in a way to circumvent the sensor-dependent traditional approach. Different forward model trainings were required for the terrestrial and space robot's joint trajectory predictions for high accuracy, although hyperparameter tuning was not required, rather a case of model re-training on new datasets (dynamics and environment). Therefore, there might be a requirement for some offline adaptation or implementation of morphing approach between the terrestrial and spaced-based dynamics. This exposes severe problems in neural networks including deep learning as a model of general intelligence – transfer learning lacks the adaptability and requires a profusion of motor models, and the introduction of payloads and force control exacerbates this. Yet, the human cerebellum can readily adjust to the space environment within seconds and does not have to start learning from motor babbling as implied by the neural network model. It is clear as detailed in Sect. 2 that the terrestrial kinematics and the space kinematics are of the same form but with only changes in parameters. Given that the two equations are similar, the two polynomial curve shapes should be similar but shifted in multidimensional space to match their specific input-output mappings. Transfer learning cannot seem to shift one polynomial curve fit onto the other, but the human cerebellum can. The problem is that input-output mapping that a neural network learns does not retain the kinematic/dynamic structure. This is a practical limitation of regression and neural network models as shown in this work.

An obvious approach to provide a solution would be to explore reinforcement learning algorithm. An adaptive feedforward model is pre-trained on earth prior to deployment and subsequently adapts to changes in the dynamics and other environmental parameters of the system in space. A recent suggestion to such an approach was covered in Rapid Motor Adaptation algorithm [29]. This is an approach that we are currently exploring its feasibility for adaptive and compliant space manipulator control transferable from learned model. Continuous online training as typically obtained in the context of traditional reinforcement learning deployment is not feasible in the application of space robotics, for reasons stated in Sect. 3 – constraint of high computational resources onboard spacecraft.

References

1. Bullock, D., Grossberg, S.: Cortical networks for control of voluntary arm movements under variable force conditions. Cereb. Cortex **8**(1), 48–62 (1998)
2. Kawato, M., Furukawa, K., Suzuki, R.: Hierarchical neural network model for control and learning of voluntary movement. Biol. Cybern. **57**, 169–185 (1987)
3. Ellery, A.: Tutorial review of bio-inspired approaches to robotic manipulation for space debris salvage. Biomimetics J. **12**(5), E19 (2020)
4. Shrivastava, S., Modi, V.: Satellite attitude dynamics and control in the presence of environmental torques—a brief survey. J. Guid. Control. Dyn. **6**, 461–471 (1983)
5. Vijayakumar, S., Schaal, S.: Locally weighted projection regression: Incremental real time learning in high dimensional space. In: Proceedings of the International Conference on Machine Learning (ICML), pp. 1079–1086 (2000)
6. Nguyen-Tuong, D., Peters, J. R., Seeger, M.: Local Gaussian process regression for real time online model learning. In: Advances in Neural Information Processing Systems (NIPS), pp. 1193–1200 (2008)
7. Gijsberts, A., Metta, G.: Real-time model learning using incremental sparse spectrum Gaussian process regression. Neural Netw. **41**, 59–69 (2013)
8. Meier, F., Hennig, P., Schaal, S.: Incremental Local Gaussian Regression. In: Advances in Neural Information Processing Systems, pp. 972–980 (2014)
9. Jamone, L., Damas, B., Santos-Victor, J.: Incremental learning of context-dependent dynamic internal models for robot control. In: Proceedings of the IEEE International Symposium on Intelligent Control (ISIC), pp. 1336–1341 (2014). https://doi.org/10.1109/ISIC.2014.696 7617
10. Toussaint, M., Vijayakumar, S.: Learning discontinuities with products-of-sigmoids for switching between local models. In: Proceedings of the International Conference on Machine Learning (ICML), pp. 904–911 (2005)
11. Petkos, G., Toussaint, M., Vijayakumar, S.: Learning multiple models of non-linear dynamics for control under varying contexts. In: International Conference on Artificial Neural Networks, pp. 898–907. Springer (2006)
12. Wolpert, D.M., Kawato, M.: Multiple paired forward and inverse models for motor control. Neural Netw. **11**(7–8), 1317–1329 (1998)
13. Ross, J., Ellery, A.: Panoramic camera tracking on planetary rovers using feedforward control. Int. J. Adv. Rob. Syst. **4**, 1–9 (2017)
14. Lindberg, R., Longman, R., Zedd, M.: Kinematics and reaction moment compensation for the spaceborne elbow manipulator. In: 24th Aerospace Sciences Meeting, AIAA-86-0250, Nevada (1986)

15. Longman, R., Lindberg, R., Zedd, M.: Satellite-mounted robot manipulators—new kinematics and reaction compensation. Int. J. Robotics Res. **6**(3), 87–103 (1987)
16. Vafa, Z., Dubowsky, S.: On dynamics of manipulators in space using the virtual manipulator approach. In: Proceedings of IEEE International Conference on Robotics and Automation, pp. 579–585 (1987)
17. Vafa, Z., Dubowsky, S.: Kinematics and dynamics of space manipulators: the virtual manipulator approach. Int. J. Robotics Res. **9**(4), 852–872 (1990)
18. Ellery, A.: An Introduction to Space Robotics. Praxis–Springer Series on Astronomy and Space Sciences. Praxis Publishers (2000)
19. Tovée, M.J.: Neuronal processing: how fast is the speed of thought? J. Curr. Biol. **4**(12), 1125–1127 (1994)
20. Morasso, P., Baratto, L., Capra, R., Spada, G.: Internal models in the control of posture. Neural Netw. **12**, 1173–1180 (1999)
21. Basso, D., Belardinelli, O.: Role of the feedforward paradigm in cognitive psychology. Cogn. Process. **7**, 73–88 (2006)
22. Flanagan, J., Vetter, P., Johansson, R., Wolpert, D.: Prediction precedes control in motor learning. Curr. Biol. **13**, 146–150 (2003)
23. Kocev, D., Džeroski, S., White, M.D., Newell, G.R., Griffioen, P.: Using single- and multi-target regression trees and ensembles to model a compound index of vegetation Condition. Ecol. Model. **220**(8), 1159–1168 (2009)
24. Breiman, L., Friedman, J.H.: Predicting multivariate responses in multiple linear regression. J. Roy. Stat. Soc. B **59**(1), 3–54 (1997)
25. Simila, T., Tikka, J.: Input selection and shrinkage in multi-response linear regression. Comput. Stat. Data Anal. **52**(1), 406–422 (2007)
26. Izenman, A.J.: Reduced-rank regression for the multivariate linear model. J. Multivar. Anal. **5**, 248–264 (1975)
27. Breiman, L., Friedman, J.H., Stone, C.J., Olshen, R.A.: Classification and Regression Trees. Chapman & Hall/CRC (1984)
28. Nguyen-Tuong, D., Seeger, M., Peters, J.R.: Model learning with local Gaussian process regression. Adv. Robot. **23**, 2015–2034 (2009)
29. Kumar, A., Fu, Z., Pathak, D., Malik, J.: RMA: Rapid Motor Adaptation for Legged Robots. In: The Robotics: Science and Systems (2021). https://doi.org/10.48550/arXiv.2107.04034

Best Application Paper

Job Assignment Problem and Traveling Salesman Problem: A Linked Optimisation Problem

Akinola Ogunsemi[1(✉)], John McCall[1], Mathias Kern[3], Benjamin Lacroix[1], David Corsar[2], and Gilbert Owusu[3]

[1] National Subsea Centre, Dyce, UK
{a.ogunsemi,j.mccall,b.m.e.lacroix}@rgu.ac.uk
[2] Robert Gordon University, Aberdeen, UK
d.corsar1@rgu.ac.uk
[3] BT Applied Research, Ipswich, UK
{mathias.kern,gilbert.owusu}@bt.com

Abstract. Linked decision-making in service management systems has attracted strong adoption of optimisation algorithms. However, most of these algorithms do not incorporate the complexity associated with interacting decision-making systems. This paper, therefore, investigates the linkages between two classical problems: job assignment problem and travelling salesman problem (JAPTSP) of a service chain system where service personnel perform tasks at different locations. We formulate a novel mathematical model from a linked optimisation perspective with objectives to minimise job cost and total travel distance simultaneously. We present three algorithmic approaches to tackling the JAPTSP: Non-dominated Sorting Genetic Algorithm for Linked Problem (NSGALP), Multi-Criteria Ranking Genetic Algorithm for Linked Problem (MCR-GALP), and Sequential approach. We evaluate the performance of the three algorithmic approaches on a combination of JAP and TSP benchmark instances. Results show that selecting an appropriate algorithmic approach is highly driven by specific considerations, including multi-objective base performance metrics, computation time, problem correlation and qualitative analysis from a service chain perspective.

Keywords: Service chain optimisation · Linked optimisation problem · Multi-criteria decision making · Multi-objective optimisation

1 Introduction

The concept of linked decision-making arises in several different research communities involving two or more optimisation problems whose solutions interact. Optimisation algorithms are increasingly adopted to support such decision problems. But, most of these algorithms do not incorporate the complexity associated

Supported by BT and The DataLab.

with the interacting decision-making process in the joint systems [1]. A linked optimisation problem explains the joint optimisation task involving n (i.e. $n \geq 2$) interdependent problems where a decision made for one problem causes a ripple effect on other dependent problems. Real-world problems, like service chains, are systems characterised by such interdependency, where some features of the sub-components of the problem are linked [2]. In such linkages, an optimal solution for individual operational components might not guarantee an optimal solution for the overall problem [3]. An example is the integration between job assignment (JAP) and travelling salesman problem (TSP) of a service chain system where service personnel perform tasks at different locations. Thus, integrating the two problems results in multiple travelling salesman problems (MTSP).

JAP and TSP are two distinct classical optimisation problems whose integration applies to hospital resource planning, field service management [4], and supply chains. The recent global shocks (COVID-19, climate change, blockage of the Suez canal) have demonstrated the importance of interdependencies and the need to create service chains that are more resilient and have significantly reduced impact on the environment. For instance, during the first COVID-19 wave in England, three of five mandated health visiting services were paused to redeploy health visitors to respond to caseloads across several communities [5]. It was recommended that a clear plan for health visiting service is required to ensure sufficient capacity and manage missed appointments backlog [5]. JAP and TSP can be applied to the health visiting problem to provide sufficient capacity and allow spare capacity redeployment to respond to COVID caseloads.

We investigate the integration of JAP and TSP to minimise the total job assignment cost and travelling cost of visiting the job locations by the agents. To study JAPTSP, we use 114 combined problem instances of existing benchmarks in JAP and TSP. We exploit three algorithmic approaches to these combined problem instances. These algorithms include; Nondominated Sorting Genetic Algorithm for Linked Problem (NSGALP), Multi-Criteria Ranking Genetic Algorithm for Linked Problem (MCRGALP), and Sequential approach.

The paper is organised as follows. Section 2 gives a brief review of related work of JAPTSP. We define the JAPTSP in Sects. 3, 4 describes our approach and Sect. 5 provides our experimental setup and discuss results. Lastly, Sect. 6 concludes and presents future works.

2   Problem Background

JAPTSP refers to a class of optimisation problems where service personnel/agents are assigned to perform tasks in different cities. JAPTSP is an extension of the multiple travelling salesman problems (MTSP) and workforce scheduling and routing problems studied in the literature. So far, different variations of JAPTSP have been explored in the literature [6]. Castillo-Salazar et al. undertake a survey study in workforce scheduling [6]. They refer to scenarios where personnel carry out tasks at different locations as Workforce Scheduling and Routing Problem (WSRP). In the study of WSRP, [4] describes an iterated local search ILS algorithm. The paper evaluated ILS against a mixed integer programming (MIP) model and an adaptive larger neighbourhood search (ALNS) algorithm. Similarly, [7] proposed a greedy heuristic algorithmic design for five time-dependent constraints for WSRP. Another variation of JAPTSP is seen in [8] involving the investigation of a Travelling Maintainer Problem (TMP) based on a generalised formulation of TSP. Their proposed problem seeks to find the best route for maintainers that minimises the travel, maintenance, and expected failure cost for all cities. The authors present a genetic algorithm and particle swarm optimisation solutions for comparison in the TMP study. Similarly, [9] adopts a genetic algorithm for a team scheduling problem. Also, [10] presents a mixed integer programming for multi-depot multiple travelling salesman problems (MmTSP) where an individual salesman travels from a particular location to a set of locations to complete tasks and return to the original location.

In JAPTSP, determining the optimal job assignment and obtaining the best multiple permutations of tours are the two decisions that must be taken simultaneously. In tackling the JAPTSP, we need to identify how the two problems (JAP and TSP) are connected. There are several ways of connecting them depending on how they interdepend. The integration of JAP & TSP causes complexity in designing appropriate algorithms for solving the problem.

3   Problem Formulation

3.1   Linked Problem Perspective

A linked optimisation problem P of n connected problems is;

$$P = \{p_1, p_2, \cdots, p_n, (D)\} : \quad p_\iota \in P \quad and \quad \iota = 1, \cdots, n \tag{1}$$

$$p_\iota = \left\{ x^\iota_{\{x^1_*, \cdots, x^n_*\} \backslash x^\iota_*}, f^\iota_{\{x^1_*, \cdots, x^n_*\} \backslash x^\iota_*}, c^\iota_{\{x^1_*, \cdots, x^n_*\} \backslash x^\iota_*} \right\} \tag{2}$$

In Eq. 2, x^ι_* denotes candidate solution in x^ι. $\{x^1_*, \cdots, x^n_*\} \backslash x^\iota_*$ are feasible solutions for other problems in P which affect p_ι. $x^\iota_{\{x^1_*, \cdots, x^n_*\} \backslash x^\iota_*}$ is a search space of problem p_ι. $f^\iota_{\{x^1_*, \cdots, x^n_*\} \backslash x^\iota_*} : x^\iota \to \mathbb{R}$ denotes the objective function. $c^\iota_{\{x^1_*, \cdots, x^n_*\} \backslash x^\iota_*}$ denotes constraints set of p_ι. $D = \{D^X, D^F, D^C\}$ connects the problems in Eq. 3.

$$D^X_{\iota j} / D^F_{\iota j} / D^C_{\iota j} = \begin{cases} 1, & \text{if } x^\iota_* \text{ changes } x^j / f^j / c^j \\ 0, & Otherwise \end{cases} \tag{3}$$

3.2   Job Assignment Problem JAP

From [16], let $I = \{1, 2, \cdots, m\}$ be a set of agents, and let $J = \{1, 2, \cdots, \mathbf{n}\}$ be a set of jobs, where $i \in I, j \in J$ respectively. Let c_{ij} be the cost of assigning job j to agent i, $\mathbf{r}_{ij}$ be the resource required by agent i per job j, and b_i be the capacity of agent i. y_{ij} represents a $0 - 1$ variable, where 1 denotes that agent i performs job j and 0 otherwise. JAP seeks to find the assignment of jobs to agents x_{JAP} that minimises:

$$min f^1(x_{JAP}) = \sum_{i=1}^{m} \sum_{j=1}^{n} c_{ij} y_{ij} \qquad (4)$$

Subject to:

$$\sum_{i=1}^{m} y_{ij} = 1 \quad \forall j \in J \qquad (5)$$

$$\sum_{j=1}^{n} r_{ij} y_{ij} \leq b_i \quad \forall i \in I \qquad (6)$$

$$y_{ij} \in \{0,1\} \quad \forall i \in I, \forall j \in J \qquad (7)$$

Constraints 5 ensures that each job is assigned to exactly one agent, Constraints 6 ensures that the resource requirement of jobs assigned to an agent does not exceed the agent's capacity and Constraints 7 defines the decision variables.

3.3 Travelling Salesman Problem TSP

The travelling salesman problem (TSP) is one of the famous classical optimization problems that involves determining a tour that minimises the total distance traveled by a salesman [17]. TSP is defined by $\mathbf{n} \times \mathbf{n}$ distance matrix of $\mathbf{n}$ cities where the salesman is required to visit each city once. The distance between two cities j and k is defined by d_{jk} and the objective function is given by:

$$min f^2(\mathbf{x}_{TSP}) = \sum_{j=2}^{n} d_{j-1,j} + d_{\mathbf{n},1} \quad \mathbf{x}_{TSP} = (\mathbf{x_1}, \mathbf{x_2}, \cdots, \mathbf{x_n}) \qquad (8)$$

where $f^2(\mathbf{x}_{TSP})$ denotes the total traveling distance minimisation as the optimisation criterion of TSP and $\mathbf{x}_{TSP}$ represents a permutation of $\mathbf{n}$ cities.

3.4 JAPTSP

JAPTSP seeks to minimise the cost of job assignments and total traveling distance of visiting the assigned job locations by the agents. It is defined by $\mathbf{n}$ cities with given distance matrix $\{d_{jk}\}$, and $\mathbf{n}$ jobs to be assigned to m agents/personnel with given availability/skill capacity/requirements. Here, the number of jobs for JAP corresponds to the number of locations in TSP. Each job in the JAP has a location in TSP. We define JAPTSP in Eq. 9

$$\begin{cases} min f^1(x_{JAP}) = \sum_{i=1}^{m} \sum_{j=1}^{n} c_{ij} y_{ij} \\ min f^2_{x_{JAP}}(\mathbf{x}_{TSP}) = \sum_{i=1}^{m} f^2(\mathbf{x}_{TSP_i}) \end{cases} \qquad (9)$$

JAPTSP is constrained by Constraints 5 - Constraints 7.

4 Proposed Approach

We propose Sequential approach, NSGALP and MCRGALP. Approaches are described in Sects. 4.1–4.4.

4.1   Genetic Components

The sequential algorithmic approach uses two genetic algorithms for each sub-problem. The sub-problems have two different solution representations that uniquely differentiate the two algorithms in terms of encoding and genetic operators used by each algorithm. In NSGALP and MCRGALP, we embed the different encodings and the genetic operators in a single algorithmic process.

Encoding. The encoding of JAPTSP uses two mechanisms; integer-based encoding for JAP and permutation-based encoding for TSP. The Integer-based solution representation addresses the assignment of jobs to agents. The permutation-based mechanism addresses a sequence of travel by agents.

Initialisation. An initialisation is done by randomly generating a population of size N. In the sequential approach, each algorithm in Algorithm 1 generates its population separately and applies it to the genetic search process. It is quite different in NSGALP and MCRGALP. In Algorithms 2 and 3, each randomly generated solution of JAP instantiates the TSP and then generates a random solution for the modified TSP and pairs with the solution of the JAP.

Non-Dominated Sort. Fast sort algorithm [18] is adopted in NSGALP to sort initial population. In the sorting process, we create a set S that contains all the dominated solution pairs. Individuals left out form the first front. Next, the ones that dominate others in set S are placed in the next. The process continues until we find the subset of S where no individual dominates each other.

Crowding Distance. Crowding distance is assigned front-wise and allows comparison within each front [19]. Calculation of crowding distance is defined in Eq. 10. Each front is considered individually and then sorted in non-decreasing order so that the first and last solution pairs are assigned infinite values.

$$\text{dist}^{\alpha,\beta}_{(JAP,TSP)} = \sum_{\iota=1}^{n} \frac{f^{\iota}_{\alpha,\beta+1} - f^{\iota}_{\alpha,\beta-1}}{f^{\iota}_{\alpha,max} - f^{\iota}_{\alpha,min}} \quad \forall \alpha \tag{10}$$

TOPSIS. We adapted TOPSIS method as a selection operator in MCRGALP. TOPSIS is one of multiple criteria decision making methods that was first introduced by Yoon and Hwang [20]. TOPSIS decision-making technique is classified into five main steps [22]. Step 1 normalises decision matrix in Eq. 11.

$$r_{i\iota} = \frac{f^{\iota}_i}{\sum_{i=1}^{|pop^t|}(f^{\iota}_i)^2} \tag{11}$$

Step 2 determines normalized weighted value $v_{i\iota}$ with weight $w_{\iota} = (w_1, \cdots, w_n)$ in Eq. 12.

$$v_{i\iota} = r_{i\iota} * w_{\iota} \tag{12}$$

Step 3 identifies the ideal best solutions v^+_{ι} and ideal worst solutions v^-_{ι} in Eq. 13 and Eq. 14.

$$v^+_{\iota} = \{(\max v_{i\iota}|\iota \in I), (\min v_{i\iota}|\iota \in I'), i = 1, \cdots, |pop^t|\} = \{v^+_1, \cdots, v^+_n\} \tag{13}$$

$$v^-_{\iota} = \{(\min v_{i\iota}|\iota \in I), (\max v_{i\iota}|\iota \in I'), i = 1, \cdots, |pop^t|\} = \{v^-_1, \cdots, v^-_n\} \tag{14}$$

Step 4 calculates Euclidean distance from v_i^+ and v_i^-, where $i = 1, 2, \cdots, |pop^t|$.

$$S_i^+ = \sqrt{\sum_{\iota=1}^{n}(v_{i_\iota} - v_i^+)^2} \tag{15}$$

$$S_i^- = \sqrt{\sum_{\iota=1}^{n}(v_{i_\iota} - v_i^-)^2} \tag{16}$$

Step 5 calculates performance score and ranks the solution pairs.

$$\mathcal{P}_i = \frac{S_i^-}{S_i^+ + S_i^-} where \quad 0 \leq \mathcal{P}_i \leq 1 \tag{17}$$

Genetic Operators. A genetic method uses crossover and mutation operators to update solutions during a search process [23]. Here, we use the same pair of crossover and mutation in the individual approach for the respective solution types. We use Integer SBX crossover operator for the JAP solutions and partially mapped crossover PMX for TSP solutions. Regarding mutation operators, we use Integer Polynomial mutation for updating the JAP solutions and permutation swap mutation for the TSP solutions, respectively. The genetic methodological framework uses the same crossover and mutation operators for all three approaches. In Algorithm 1, we adopt an integer-coded genetic algorithm A_{JAP} which uses integer SBX crossover and integer polynomial mutation operators to generate offspring for the JAP. In terms of the TSP, we use a permutation-coded genetic algorithm A_{TSP} in the sequential approach. A_{TSP} uses PMX and permutation swap mutation to update solutions. We employed tournament selection in algorithms A_{JAP} and A_{TSP}. The procedure for offspring generation is the same for Algorithms 2 and 3. The procedure is outlined as follows; Generate **n** offspring of JAP solutions from mating pool $\mathcal{R}_{JAP}^t$ using integer SBX crossover and integer polynomial mutation operators. Then, use each offspring to instantiate problem TSP and randomly generate N TSP solutions. Next, perform crossover and mutation operations on N solutions of TSP and generate **n** offspring. Then, evaluate the offspring and sort them in descending order. Last, select best offspring from **n** offspring of TSP and pair with each offspring of JAP.

4.2   Sequential Approach

The sequential algorithmic approach solves JAPTSP in sequence and is commonly known for solving problems in a hierarchical structure, usually between two decision-makers [25,26]. Algorithm 1 shows a sequential approach for solving JAPTSP. First, algorithm A_{JAP} solves problem p_{JAP}, selects the best solution x_{JAP}^* then, uses best solutions x^*_{JAP} to instantiate TSP p_{TSP} based on their linkage structure. Next, the instantiated p_{TSP} is solved using algorithm A_{TSP} and then select best solution $\mathbf{x}_{TSP}^*$.

Algorithm 1: $SEQUENTIAL$

$x_{JAP}^* \leftarrow A_{JAP}|p_{JAP};$
$\mathbf{x}_{TSP}^* \leftarrow A_{TSP}|(p_{TSP}, x^*_{JAP})\ ;$
Result: $(x_{JAP}^*, \mathbf{x}_{TSP}^*)$

4.3 NSGALP Approach

Here, we consider the solutions of JAP and TSP as a joint solution and adapt the fast nondominated sorting procedure, a fast crowded distance estimation procedure, and a simple crowded comparison operator based on [18] framework. Details about the framework is in [18]. Algorithm 2 shows a multi-objective framework we adopted in tackling JAPTSP.

Algorithm 2: $NSGALP$	**Algorithm 3:** $MCRGALP$
$pop^0_{(JAP,TSP)} \leftarrow$ initialise ; Evaluate $pop^0_{(JAP,TSP)}$; Assign non-dominated sort to $pop^0_{(JAP,TSP)}$; Apply crowding-distance to $pop^0_{(JAP,TSP)}$; $t \leftarrow 0$; **while** *Stopping criterion not met* **do** $\quad \mathcal{R}^t_{(JAP,TSP)} \leftarrow$ Select from $pop^t_{(JAP,TSP)}$; $\quad Q^t_{(JAP,TSP)} \leftarrow$ Generate offspring from $\mathcal{R}^t_{(JAP,TSP)}$; $\quad$ Evaluate $Q^t_{(JAP,TSP)}$; $\quad \mathbf{pop}^t_{(JAP,TSP)} \leftarrow pop^t_{(JAP,TSP)} \cup Q^t_{(JAP,TSP)}$; $\quad$ Assign fast non-dominated sort to $\mathbf{pop}^t_{(JAP,TSP)}$; $\quad$ Apply crowding-distance assignment to $\mathbf{pop}^t_{(JAP,TSP)}$; $\quad pop^{t+1}_{(JAP,TSP)} \leftarrow$ Select survivor from $\mathbf{pop}^t_{(JAP,TSP)}$; $\quad t \leftarrow t+1$; **end** **Result:** $\mathcal{F}^1_{(JAP,TSP)}$	$pop^0_{(FLP,PFSP)} \leftarrow$ Randomly initialise population ; Fitness evaluation on $pop^0_{(JAP,TSP)}$; $t \leftarrow 0$; **while** *Stopping criterion not met* **do** $\quad$ Assign score to each solution pair in $pop^t_{(JAP,TSP)}$; $\quad pop^*_{(JAP,TSP)} \leftarrow$ Get best $\ltimes$ pairs of $pop^t_{(JAP,TSP)}$; $\quad Q^t_{(JAP,TSP)} \leftarrow$ Generate offspring from $pop^*_{(JAP,TSP)}$; $\quad$ Fitness evaluation on $Q_{(JAP,TSP)}$; $\quad$ Assign score to each solution pair in $Q_{(JAP,TSP)}$; $\quad pop^t_{(JAP,TSP)} \leftarrow pop^t_{(JAP,TSP)} \cup Q^t_{(JAP,TSP)}$; $\quad pop^{t+1}_{(JAP,TSP)} \leftarrow$ Get top N solution pairs with best score from $pop^t_{(JAP,TSP)}$; $\quad t \leftarrow t+1$; **end** **Result:** $(x^*_{JAP}, \mathbf{x}^*_{TSP})$

4.4 MCRGALP Approach

MCRGALP uses a similar approach in Sect. 4.3 but with differences in the output returned and the comparison operators used in the tournament selection. Unlike NSGALP, MCRGALP uses a multi-criteria performance metric known as Technique for Order of Preference by Similarity to Ideal Solution (TOPSIS), which assigns a performance score to each joint solution. TOPSIS is widely used in multi-objective evolutionary algorithms. For example, [29] used TOPSIS as an evaluation approach to prioritise candidate solutions in their algorithmic framework. MCRGALP uses TOPSIS as a comparison operator in the tournament selection process to guide the selection of $\ltimes$ joint solutions at different phases of the algorithm process. See performance score computation in Sect. 4.1.

5   Experiments

We performed series of computational experiments to evaluate the proposed algorithmic approaches. The experiments are conducted on the same computer environment with Intel Core i9, 2.4 GHz, 32 GB RAM, and Windows 10 Enterprise OS. The three algorithmic approaches are implemented in Java.

5.1   Benchmark Problems

We evaluate the proposed algorithmic approaches on two sets of instances for both problems in JAPTSP. The first set is JAP instances using Beasley [30] benchmark. The second set contains TSP instances of Gerhard's [31] benchmark. We combined each instance in JAP benchmark with each TSP instance based on their problem size. We assume that a job in JAP corresponds to a location/city in TSP. So, we obtained 114 combined instances in total. See Table 1.

Table 1. Linked problem instances

Problem size	No. of agents	No. of instances
100	5	**30**
100	10	**30**
100	20	**24**
200	5	**10**
200	10	**10**
200	20	**10**
Total		**114**

5.2   Exploratory Analysis of Problem Linkages

In the data exploration analysis, we generate randomly and evaluate 10000 solutions for JAP (p_1). For each solution generated on the JAP, we instantiate TSP (p_2) based on our linked optimisation framework. We then, generate randomly and evaluate 1000 solutions for the instantiated TSP and compute its mean value. Next, for each JAPTSP instance, we determine the relationship between the sub-problems using Spearman's correlation coefficient.

5.3   Performance Metric

We use four performance metrics. This includes; Hypervolume (HV) [32], Relative Hypervolume (RHV), Inverted Generational Distance (IGD) [33] and Multiplicative Epsilon [34]. For each problem instance, we obtained a reference point r and a reference front Z as input parameters for metric computations.

Relative Hypervolume RHV. The relative hypervolume measures the proportion of hypervolume achieved by individual approach. This is computed by dividing the hypervolume of approximations by individual approach by the hypervolume of the true Pareto front. A higher RHV indicates that approximations are closer to the true Pareto front.

$$RHV(\mathbf{Z}, A) = \frac{HV(A, \mathbf{r})}{HV(\mathbf{Z}, \mathbf{r})} \tag{18}$$

where $0 \leq RHV(\mathbf{Z}, A) \leq 1$

Hypervolume HV. HV considers the volume of the objective space dominated by an approximation set [35] bounded by a given reference point $\mathbf{r} \in \mathbb{R}^2$. Higher HV values indicate a better performance of the corresponding approaches.

Inverted Generational Distance IGD. IGD assesses the quality of approximations achieved by multi-objective algorithm to the Pareto front [33]. The metric measures how the approximations convergence towards the true Pareto front. The smaller the IGD value, the closer the calculated front to the true Pareto front [36]. IGD is calculated as follows:

$$IGD(A, \mathbf{Z}) = \Big(\frac{1}{|\mathbf{Z}|} \sum_{i=1}^{|\mathbf{Z}|} \min_{a \in A} \mathbf{d}(\mathbf{z}, a)^2\Big)^{\frac{1}{2}} \tag{19}$$

where $\mathbf{d}(\mathbf{z}, a) = \sqrt{\sum_{\iota}^{n}(\mathbf{z}_{\iota}, a_{\iota})}$ with a_{ι} being the ιth fitness value of point a from the approximations A and $\mathbf{z}_{\iota}$ being an ιth fitness value of point $\mathbf{z}$ from the true Pareto front $\mathbf{Z}$.

Multiplicative Epsilon ϵ. The Epsilon indicator gives a factor by which an approximation set is worse than another with respect to all objectives [34]. A lower Epsilon value corresponds to a better approximation set, regardless of the type of problem (minimization, maximization or mixed). We compute as follows;

$$epsilon(A, \mathbf{Z}) = \max_{\mathbf{z} \in \mathbf{Z}} \min_{a \in A} \max_{1 \leq \iota \leq n} epsilon(a_{\iota}, \mathbf{z}_{\iota}) \tag{20}$$

where $epsilon(a_{\iota}, \mathbf{z}_{\iota}) = a_{\iota}/\mathbf{z}_{\iota}$

5.4   Parameter Settings

Table 2 shows the parameters used by the individual approach. To measure the behavior of our approaches for solving the JAPTSP, we maintained the same parameter settings for the different genetic algorithm in all the approaches. An additional set of parameters are used by the TOPSIS (Technique for Order of Preference by Similarity to Ideal Solution) method adopted in MCRGSLP approach. We set the weight for JAP fitness to 0.35 and its constraint, in case of violation, to 0.30. The weight for TSP is set to 0.35.

Table 2. Parameter settings

Parameters	NSGALP	MCRGALP	SEQUENTIAL	
No. of Algorithms	**1**	**1**	**2**	
Experimental Runs	100	100	100	100
Population Size	100	100	100	100
Max Evaluations	10000	10000	10000	10000
Mating Pool Size	100	100	–	–
Offspring Size	100	100	20	20
IntegerSBXCrossover	0.9	0.9	0.9	–
PMXCrossover	0.1	0.1	–	0.1
Integer Polynomial Mutation	–	–	–	–
Permutation Swap Mutation	0.5	0.5	–	0.5

5.5   Experimental Results and Analysis

Performance Metrics. Table 3 shows the mean results of the four metrics. The best values are highlighted in bold font. NSGALP shows the best performance across all four metrics, although the mean results appear close to each other, especially in the hypervolume metric. MCRGALP slightly outperforms NSGALP and sequential approaches in problem instance ($Size = 100$ and $m = 5$) in terms of epsilon metric.

Table 3. Mean values of relative hypervolume, hypervolume, inverted generational distance and epsilon metrics of MCRGALP, NSGALP and SEQUENTIAL

Size	m	RHV			HV			IGD			EPSILON		
		MCRGALP	NSGALP	SEQ	MCRGALP	NSGALP	SEQ	MCRGALP	NSGALP	SEQ	MCRGALP	NSGALP	SEQ
100	5	0.749	**0.775**	0.703	0.174	**0.180**	0.163	7048.24	**6544.26**	10598.16	**1.186**	1.187	1.226
100	10	0.711	**0.778**	0.670	0.186	**0.204**	0.172	8716.75	**7049.15**	12260.79	1.237	**1.195**	1.280
100	20	0.670	**0.763**	0.610	0.195	**0.224**	0.171	12505.42	**8987.10**	17753.56	1.301	**1.188**	1.448
200	5	0.794	**0.834**	0.794	0.154	**0.163**	0.154	11026.66	**7454.52**	13790.09	1.134	**1.101**	1.125
200	10	0.734	**0.815**	0.758	0.157	**0.175**	0.161	14559.31	**9678.85**	13654.81	1.195	**1.133**	1.177
200	20	0.697	**0.808**	0.721	0.159	**0.186**	0.163	18550.02	**12371.31**	17784.36	1.236	**1.140**	1.217

We check the significance of the difference between the statistical results using the Wilcoxon signed-rank test at 0.05 significance level. Table 4 summarizes the corresponding p values among the compared algorithms on instances grouped by problem size and size of agents. We highlight with bold font in Table 4 the comparisons that indicate no statistical difference in performance between the algorithms. Table 4 suggests that, despite the exceptional performance of NSGALP, MCRGALP and sequential approaches can also effectively tackle some instances of the linked problem, but that depends on how the two problems are linked. Figure 2 gives the overall perspective of the performance of the algorithmic approaches, and the selection of the best approach points toward NSGALP. However, there are several explanations for why NSGALP outperforms the other two. Metrics are multi-objective based and are influenced mainly by the number of non-dominated points produced by an algorithm.

Table 4. The p values of all metrics among the three algorithmic approaches on different problem combinations

Size	m	RHV			HV			IGD			EPSILON		
		NSGALP vs SEQ	NSGALP vs MCRGALP	MCRGALP vs SEQ	NSGALP vs SEQ	NSGALP vs MCRGALP	MCRGALP vs SEQ	NSGALP vs SEQ	NSGALP vs MCRGALP	MCRGALP vs SEQ	NSGALP vs SEQ	NSGALP vs MCRGALP	MCRGALP vs SEQ
100	5	1.49E-04	1.30E-01	9.88E-03	3.03E-03	3.40E-01	1.11E-04	3.50E-03	2.90E-01	1.22E-02	2.01E-04	9.00E-01	6.36E-05
100	10	4.80E-07	3.82E-10	8.24E-02	2.92E-02	6.38E-03	2.39E-04	5.08E-03	5.01E-02	1.67E-01	2.84E-04	3.55E-01	1.39E-06
100	20	1.20E-06	1.34E-08	3.28E-02	5.39E-02	3.53E-03	7.21E-05	1.01E-03	6.29E-03	1.40E-01	8.45E-01	4.88E-03	3.75E-04
200	5	8.90E-02	7.57E-02	9.70E-01	4.52E-02	1.86E-01	1.01E-03	2.57E-02	1.40E-01	8.90E-02	2.57E-02	2.73E-01	4.40E-04
200	10	4.52E-02	3.30E-04	5.71E-01	6.40E-02	1.40E-01	1.71E-03	1.40E-01	2.11E-02	2.41E-01	5.80E-03	6.78E-01	1.71E-03
200	20	3.76E-02	5.83E-04	5.71E-01	1.21E-01	2.57E-02	7.28E-03	7.57E-02	7.28E-03	2.41E-01	6.40E-02	3.45E-01	2.83E-03

Computational Time Complexity. We also consider the performance of the algorithmic approaches based on computational time. Figure 3 shows four plots of mean computational time against the selected performance metrics. Figure 3a shows the mean computing time against the relative hypervolume metric, Fig. 3b shows the mean computing time against the hypervolume metric, Fig. 3c IGD and Fig. 3d shows the mean computing time against the epsilon metric. There is no doubt that the sequential approach required less computational time than the other approaches in all combinations of problem instances.

Correlation Analysis. We further consider algorithm performance in terms of the correlation score obtained by randomly generated solutions, as discussed in Sect. 5.2. We compare the performance of the competing algorithms on instances that obtained the lowest (-0.0264), median (-0.0016) and highest (0.0198) correlation coefficients. Figure 1 shows the empirical attainment function obtained by competing algorithmic approaches on the instances with respective minimum, median and maximum correlation scores. Overall, the NSGALP approach produces the best attainment coverage.

Service Chain Perspective. Suppose we consider the two problems from the perspective of two service companies or business units involved in a service chain. Our results can offer guidance on the benefits and costs they will likely experience based on the approach used to solve the overall problem. For example, the NSGALP is quite interesting due to the large extent of variability in fitness values of the JAP criterion. In Fig. 4a, the NSGALP solves the first problem in a view to trade-off the other problem. However, the trade-off of the second problem is not that much, as there is a peak at the lower TSP fitness value. However, the MCRGALP tends to hit a sweet spot for both problems in 99%

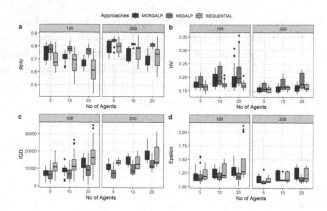

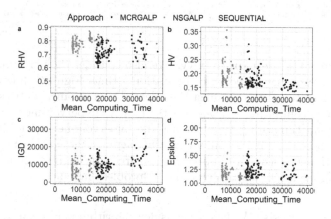

Fig. 1. Overall performance based on RHV, HV, IGD and Epsilon metrics

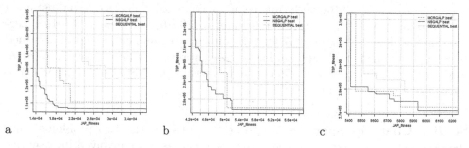

Fig. 2. Mean computation time against performance metrics

Fig. 3. Empirical attainment function of algorithmic approaches on problem instances with minimum, median and maximum correlation coefficients approaches

of the problem instances, but this does not quantify the performance metrics used. Therefore, in deciding how to solve the problem with the sequential and NSGALP, it is more apparent that both companies must consider the impact that optimising one problem will have on the other and decide if the resulting costs/benefits are acceptable. In contrast, the MCRGALP maintains a balanced compromise on both problems.

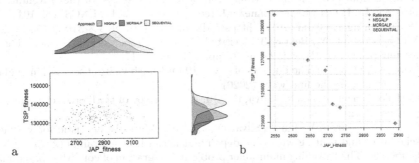

Fig. 4. Distribution of solutions found by all approaches on problem size 100 & m = 5.

6   Conclusion and Future Work

This paper presented a linked optimisation problem (JAPTSP) of two minimisation problems: JAP and TSP. The JAP assigns agents to jobs that minimise the job cost, while the TSP determines a subset of tours that minimise total travelling distance. We employed three algorithmic approaches; NSGALP, MCRGALP, and SEQUENTIAL to tackle the JAPTSP. We compare the performance of the three approaches on 114 combinations of problem instances. Empirical results indicate that NSGALP outperforms the other two methods. We also consider other factors in selecting an appropriate algorithmic method. These factors include: mean computation time, degree of correlation between the combined problem instance, and qualitative analysis from a service chain perspective. MCRGALP seems to maintain balanced multiple decision-making without sacrificing one for the other. In terms of mean computational time, the sequential method outperforms the other two methods. Concerning future research, we need to consider the use of appropriate performance metrics that measure how algorithms perform towards obtaining results that converge to an equilibrium point (i.e. a balanced joint solution) which is unbiased towards a method. Further exploration of some properties of the algorithms can be undertaken as the good performance of the NSGALP and MCRGALP results in sacrificing computational time.

References

1. Ibrahimov, M., Mohais, A., Schellenberg, S., Michalewicz, Z.: Evolutionary approaches for supply chain optimisation: part i: single and two-component supply chains. IJICC **5**(4), 444–472 (2012)

2. Bonyadi, M.R., Michalewicz, Z., Barone, L.: The travelling thief problem: The first step in the transition from theoretical problems to realistic problems. In: IEEE CEC. IEEE **2013**, 1037–1044 (2013)
3. Vieira, D.K.S., Soares, G.L., Vasconcelos, J.A., Mendes, M.H.S.: A genetic algorithm for multi-component optimization problems: the case of the travelling thief problem. In: Hu, B., López-Ibáñez, M. (eds.) EvoCOP 2017. LNCS, vol. 10197, pp. 18–29. Springer, Cham (2017). https://doi.org/10.1007/978-3-319-55453-2_2
4. Xie, F., Potts, C.N., Bektaş, T.: Iterated local search for workforce scheduling and routing problems. JH, vol. 23, no. 6, pp. 471–500, 2017
5. Conti, G., Dow, A.: The impacts of covid-19 on health visiting services in england: Foi evidence for the first wave (2020)
6. Castillo-Salazar, A., Landa-Silva, D., Qu, R.: A survey of workforce scheduling and routing (2012)
7. Castillo-Salazar, J.A., Landa-Silva, D., Qu, R.: A greedy heuristic for workforce scheduling and routing with time-dependent activities constraints (2015)
8. Camci, F.: The travelling maintainer problem: integration of condition-based maintenance with the travelling salesman problem. JORS **65**(9), 1423–1436 (2014)
9. Zhang, T., Gruver, W., Smith, M.H.: Team scheduling by genetic search. In: IPMM'99 (Cat. No. 99EX296), vol. 2. IEEE, pp. 839–844 (1999)
10. Assaf, M., Ndiaye, M.,: Multi travelling salesman problem formulation. In: 4th ICIEA. IEEE **2017**, 292–295 (2017)
11. Shuai, Y., Yunfeng, S., Kai, Z.: An effective method for solving multiple travelling salesman problem based on nsga-ii. SSCE **7**(2), 108–116 (2019)
12. Stolk, J., Mann, I., Mohais, A., Michalewicz, Z.: Combining vehicle routing and packing for optimal delivery schedules of water tanks. OR Insight **26**(3), 167–190 (2013)
13. Chen, L., Langevin, A., Lu, Z.: Integrated scheduling of crane handling and truck transportation in a maritime container terminal. EJOR **225**(1), 142–152 (2013)
14. Chen, T.-L., Cheng, C.-Y., Chen, Y.-Y., Chan, L.-K.: An efficient hybrid algorithm for integrated order batching, sequencing and routing problem. IJPE **159**, 158–167 (2015)
15. Moons, S., Ramaekers, K., Caris, A., Arda, Y.: Integrating production scheduling and vehicle routing decisions at the operational decision level: a review and discussion. CIE **104**, 224–245 (2017)
16. Chu, P.C., Beasley, J.E.: A genetic algorithm for the generalised assignment problem. COR **24**(1), 17–23 (1997)
17. Gerhard, R.: The traveling salesman: computational solutions for tsp applications. Lect. Notes Comput. Sci. **840**, 1–223 (1994)
18. Deb, K., Pratap, A., Agarwal, S., Meyarivan, T.: A fast and elitist multiobjective genetic algorithm: Nsga-ii. IEEE TEC **6**(2), 182–197 (2002)
19. Muhuri, P.K., Ashraf, Z., Lohani, Q.D.: Multiobjective reliability redundancy allocation problem with interval type-2 fuzzy uncertainty. IEEE TFS **26**(3), 1339–1355 (2017)
20. Hwang, C.-L., Yoon, K.: Methods for multiple attribute decision making. In: Lecture Notes in Economics and Mathematical Systems, vol 186, pp. 58–191 Springer, Berlin, Heidelberg (1981). https://doi.org/10.1007/978-3-642-48318-9_3
21. Rahim, R., et al.: Topsis method application for decision support system in internal control for selecting best employees. In: JP: Conference Series, vol. 1028, no. 1. IOP Publishing, p. 012052 (2018)
22. Triantaphyllou, E., Shu, B., Sanchez, S.N., Ray, T.: Multi-criteria decision making: an operations research approach. EEEE **15**(1998), 175–186 (1998)

23. Luo, G., Wen, X., Li, H., Ming, W., Xie, G.: An effective multi-objective genetic algorithm based on immune principle and external archive for multi-objective integrated process planning and scheduling. IJAMT **91**(9), 3145–3158 (2017)
24. Geetha, T., Muthukumaran, K.: An observational analysis of genetic operators. IJCA **63**(18), 24–34 (2013)
25. Legillon, F., Liefooghe, A., Talbi, E.-G.: Cobra: A cooperative coevolutionary algorithm for bi-level optimization. In: IEEE CEC. IEEE **2012**, 1–8 (2012)
26. Ibrahimov, M.: Evolutionary algorithms for supply chain optimisation. Ph.D. dissertation (2012)
27. Lin, C.K.Y.: Solving a location, allocation, and capacity planning problem with dynamic demand and response time service level. MPE, vol. (2014)
28. Ullrich, C.A.: Integrated machine scheduling and vehicle routing with time windows. EJOR **227**(1), 152–165 (2013)
29. Nourmohammadi, A., Zandieh, M.: Assembly line balancing by a new multi-objective differential evolution algorithm based on topsis. IJPR **49**(10), 2833–2855 (2011)
30. Beasley, J.E.: Or-library: distributing test problems by electronic mail. JORS **41**(11), 1069–1072 (1990)
31. Reinelt, G.: Tsplib95. IWR, Heidelberg **338**, 1–16 (1995)
32. Zitzler, E., Thiele, L.: Multiobjective evolutionary algorithms: a comparative case study and the strength pareto approach. IEEE TEC **3**(4), 257–271 (1999)
33. Bezerra, L.C.T., López-Ibáñez, M., Stützle, T.: An empirical assessment of the properties of inverted generational distance on multi- and many-objective optimization. In: Trautmann, H. (ed.) EMO 2017. LNCS, vol. 10173, pp. 31–45. Springer, Cham (2017). https://doi.org/10.1007/978-3-319-54157-0_3
34. Zitzler, E., Thiele, L., Laumanns, M., Fonseca, C.M., Da Fonseca, V.G.: Performance assessment of multiobjective optimizers: An analysis and review. IEEE TEC **7**(2), 117–132 (2003)
35. Zitzler, E., Thiele, L.: Multiobjective optimization using evolutionary algorithms — a comparative case study. In: Eiben, A.E., Bäck, T., Schoenauer, M., Schwefel, H.-P. (eds.) PPSN 1998. LNCS, vol. 1498, pp. 292–301. Springer, Heidelberg (1998). https://doi.org/10.1007/BFb0056872
36. Manson, J.A., Chamberlain, T.W., Bourne, R.A.: Mvmoo: Mixed variable multi-objective optimisation. JGO **80**(4), 865–886 (2021)

AI for Health and Medicine

Twitter Flu Trend: A Hybrid Deep Neural Network for Tweet Analysis

Mahsa Abazari Kia[1]([✉]) [iD] and Fatemeh Ebrahimi Khaksefidi[2]

[1] School of Computer Science and Electronic Engineering, University of Essex,
Colchester, UK
ma19194@essex.ac.uk
[2] University of Isfahan, Isfahan, Iran

Abstract. Popular social networks such as Twitter have been proposed as a data source for public health monitoring because they have the potential to show infection disease surveillance like Influenza-Like Illnesses (ILI). However, shortness, data sparsity, informality, incorrect sentence structure, and the humorous are some challenges for tweet analysis and classification. In order to overcome these challenges and implement an accurate flu surveillance system, we propose a hybrid 1d-CNN-BiLSTM framework for semantic enrichment and tweet classification. Different embedding algorithms are compared for producing semantic representations of tweets to assist unrelated tweet filtering in the classification stage. We find that fine-tuning pre-trained Word2Vec enhances the model capability for representing the meaning of flu-related tweets than other embedding models. Our approach has been evaluated on a flu tweet dataset and compared with several baselines for tweet processing and classification. Experimental results show that: (1) the proposed hybrid deep neural networks can improve tweet classification due to considering their semantic information;(2) the proposed flu surveillance system achieves a state-of-the-art correlation coefficient with ILI rate published by CDC (https://www.cdc.gov/).

Keywords: Tweet analysis · Hybrid deep neural network · CNN-BiLSTM · Flu-trend

1 Introduction

Public health condition monitoring is important for health organizations and governments to respond to emerging epidemics [5]. U.S. Centers for Disease Control and Prevention (CDC) aggregate data from a network of a huge number of outpatient providers across the united states to provide the count of Influenza-Like Illnesses (ILI) rates and infection level monitoring for each previous week [3]. Delays and costs for identifying the start of an infection epidemic in these systems of disease surveillance systems cause big damage to society [12]. Strong interest

M. Bramer and F. Stahl (Eds.): SGAI-AI 2022, LNAI 13652, pp. 37–50, 2022.
https://doi.org/10.1007/978-3-031-21441-7_3

in reducing these delays and costs and a way to develop an accurate surveillance system brings us to use real-time and low-cost data sources. With the growth and popularity of social networks in the world, such as Twitter, we are going to use them as valuable data sources that can fulfill the implementation of on-time and low-cost ILI surveillance systems. But the analysis of tweets faces some challenges, such as shortness and informality, humor, incorrect sentence structure, ambiguity, and so on, which poses difficulties in using tweets and causes some drawbacks in analysis and classification [13]. These tweets' characteristics make it challenging to detect influenza infection tweets. For example, tweets like "I feel so sick I got Bieber fever" and "I had a dream that I had a terrible flu last night. I woke up and clearing my throat extra" are classified as ILI infection tweets because of the existence of ILI related words and complexity in understanding the meaning [2]. In this way, humorous and ambiguous tweets, tweets that look like ILI infection tweets but their meaning is unrelated to ILI infection, are easily counted as ILI infection tweets which cause incorrect results and overestimating or underestimating of ILI rate. Adding semantics to tweet representation may be needed to deal with these kinds of tweets. Most of the researchers that have tried to add semantics to tweets have used entity extraction and knowledge source linking, which is appropriate for limited fields such as sentiment analysis, topic classification, incident detection, etc. For this kind of enrichment, there should be some named entities that improvement of analysis depends on their accurate extraction and linking to their related concepts in knowledge sources. This paper proposes a framework for implementing a flu surveillance system using deep learning approaches. We investigate embedding algorithms and deep neural networks for semantic enrichment and analyzing flu tweets. We studied deep learning approaches for semantic classification and designed a framework to track flu trends in the U.S. We used pre-trained Word2Vec and GloVe for generating tweet representation. We used a hybrid 1d-CNN and BiLSTM network for tweet classification, which uses convolution as a feature extractor and then BiLSTM as a sequence model to treat extracted features as a sequence and classifies the tweets. We evaluate the proposed framework on a dataset that is prepared especially for the case of flu and is collected using a boolean query containing standard flu symptoms introduced by [25]. We compare our results with previous works which aim to calculate ILI rates. Also, we use MNB and SVM with n-grams, 1d-CNN, BiLSTM, and LSTM as baselines. Experimental results show that the proposed framework achieves state-of-the-art correlation with the ground truth data (CDC ILI rate). This shows that embedding algorithms and hybrid deep neural networks can improve tweet classification by considering the meaning of tweets. The main contribution of our work is summarized below:

– While previous flu tweet classification researches used conventional methods, we studied the deep learning algorithms' performance for tweet semantic enrichment and classification.
– We proposed a novel framework, "Twitter Flu Trend", for exploring flu trends in the U.S. by fine-tuning the pre-trained Word2Vec model for learning word

vectors that contain both syntactic and semantic information and a combinational 1d-CNN-BiLSTM classifier.
- We have created a Flu-related tweet dataset by collecting old tweets utilizing a boolean query containing standard flu symptoms. We have labeled the tweets to Flu-infectious and Non-Flu-infectious.

2 Related Work

We classify the related works into three main sections: Researches about ILI surveillance using Twitter, semantic enrichment via knowledge sources, and semantic representation with deep learning.

2.1 ILI Surveillance Using Twitter

In the area of social media data mining, Twitter data provided lots of applications and valuable insights into various fields, but there is limited study on the public health information system, specially influenza-like illnesses which is a significant infectious disease. The most famous study is [8], which designed the Google Flu Trend surveillance system tried to estimate the level of flu activity by analyzing the queries that were searched on Google. Flu trend estimated by computing the search frequency of 45 selected queries all around the world which is no longer publishing. Other researches are based on Twitter; some of them are done manually and have not used classification for detecting flu infection tweets automatically like [12] that presented an approach for differentiating between flu infection, concerns, and awareness tweets by relying on a set of features and templates which is defined manually. Doan et al. [5] developed a novel filtering method for ILI-related tweets, which filters tweets based on syndrome keywords from BioCaster ontology and semantic features such as negation, hashtags, emoticons, humor, and geography. Broniatowski et al. [3] created a two-phased supervised classification model to separate flu-related tweets from health-related tweets in the first phase and flu infection tweets in the second. Allen et al. [1] Proposed an approach that uses n-gram for generating features and an SVM classifier for classifying tweets that contain flu and influenza terms. Jain et al. [10] introduced a novel approach that produces dynamic keywords for collecting flu-related tweets and then classifies tweets with SVM for recognizing flu infection tweets. Velardi et al. [25] developed an approach that produces slang synonym clusters of flu symptoms and proves that using flu symptoms is more helpful in retrieving flu infection messages than using flu names. The synonyms are used to extend the standard symptom-based query for influenza-related disease defined by European CDC to collect tweets indicating infection.

2.2 Semantic Enrichment with Knowledge Sources

Knowledge sources can be used at various stages in data mining processes for various purposes, such as creating additional variables [21]. Schulz et al. [23]

proposed a model for semantic enrichment of tweets using DBpedia to improve incident tweets identification. Saif et al. [22] presented a semantic sentiment classification method that extracts entities from tweets and their semantic concepts from DBpedia as additional features. Varga et al. [24] used semantic concepts of knowledge sources related to the extracted entities from short texts to enhance classification or clustering tasks. All these researches used semantic concepts from DBpedia or other knowledge sources to fix the ambiguity of those entities that have several names, and they have to be homogenized to improve data mining tasks such as sentiment analysis, topic classification, or car crash classification which is dependent on correct diagnosis of named entities. Using the type and attributes of semantic concepts creates a semantic set of features which is useful for completing lexical features for these tasks.

2.3   Semantic Representation with Deep Learning

Deep learning approaches can automatically capture the text's syntactic and semantic features simultaneously without feature engineering, which is laborious and time-consuming. They have drawn much attention in natural language processing (NLP) and achieved state-of-the-art performances [4]. Wang et al. [26] proposed a framework to expand short texts based on word embedding clustering and convolutional neural network to overcome the sparsity and semantic sensitivity to context in short texts. Gatti et al. [6] explored the richness of word embeddings produced by unsupervised pre-training, a deep convolutional neural network proposed to exploits character to sentence-level information and perform sentiment analysis of short texts. Edouard et al. [7] exploited information acquired from external knowledge bases to enrich Named Entities (NEs) mentioned in the tweets. Then enriched content is used for building word-embedding vectors, which serve as feature models for training supervised models for event classification, Naïve Bayes, SVM, and LSTM classification algorithms have been compared. Wang et al. [27] developed a CNN-LSTM model consisting of two parts, regional CNN and LSTM, for dimensional sentiment analysis. Unlike a conventional CNN, the proposed regional CNN divides an input text into several regions, and then regional information is integrated using LSTM for prediction.

3   Our Method

In this section, we present our approach for improving tweet classification in case of ILI infection via hybrid deep neural networks. An overview of the proposed hybrid deep neural network is shown in Fig. 2. We first introduce word embedding as a class of techniques for generating distributional representations of words and their models in Sect. 3.1 and then we describe the 1d-CNN model, which produces features of a tweet via convolution layers (Sect. 3.2). The BiLSTM model is described in Sect. 3.3, which predicts tweet labels in our hybrid network.

3.1 Word Embedding

Word embeddings is a class of techniques in which words are represented as vectors with real values in a predefined space. Each word is mapped into a vector, and vector values represent different aspects of a word mainly learned through context [16]. Word vectors capture general syntactical and semantic information [14], and the main advantage of distributional vectors is that they capture the similarity between words [9]. Thus it has been proven that embeddings are efficient in capturing context similarity and analogies [18]. In this research, we use Word2Vec and GloVe algorithms for producing word vectors to evaluate them for producing the semantic representation of words through their context to filter ambiguous tweets (containing flu-related terms, but their meaning is unrelated to flu).

Word2Vec. Skip-gram and CBOW are the two models of Word2Vec, which are proposed by Mikolov et al. [17]. Skip-gram computes the conditional probability of the context words surrounding the target word in both directions across a window with size k. On the other hand, the CBOW model aims to maximize the Formula 1 while the skip-gram tries to maximize Formula 2. In the Formula 1 and 2, v corresponds to vocabulary size, m_t refers to the target word, m_j refers to context words, and c is the window size. Moreover, negative sampling and hierarchical Softmax are the two algorithms for learning the output vectors of CBOW and skip-gram.

$$\frac{1}{v}\sum_{t=1}^{v} \log p\left(m_t \mid m_{t-\frac{c}{2}} \ldots m_{t+\frac{c}{2}}\right) \tag{1}$$

$$\frac{1}{v}\sum_{t=1}^{v} \sum_{j=t-c,j=t}^{t+c} \log p\left(m_j \mid m_t\right) \tag{2}$$

GloVe. GloVe is another famous word embedding method which is based on word occurrences in textual corpus and proposed by Pennington et al. [20]. This method is based on two main steps, the first is constructing matrix X from training corpus as a co-occurrence matrix where X_{ij} is the frequency of the word i co-occurring with the word j, second is factorization of X in order to get the embedding vectors. Using Ratios instead of raw probabilities helps to reduce noise by identifying relevant words from irrelevant which is shown in Eq. 3.

$$F\left(\mathcal{W}_i - w_j, \varpi_k\right) = \frac{p_{ik}}{p_{jk}} \tag{3}$$

$p_{ik} = X_{ik}/X_i$ is the occurrence probability of word k in the context of the word i. $\mathcal{W}$ are word vectors and ϖ_k are context word vectors. They used vector differences and the dot product of the arguments for preventing mixing dimensions and preserving linearity as depicted in Eq. 4.

$$F\left((w_i - w_j)^T \varpi_k\right) = \frac{p_{ik}}{p_{jk}} \tag{4}$$

F is assumed as a function and for resolving symmetry, the Eq. 4 can be re-written in a different way:

$$w_i^T \varpi_k + b_i + b_k = \log (x_{ik}) \tag{5}$$

Finally an objective function is proposed that should be minimized by Eq. 6 where $f(x)$ is weighting function.

$$J = \sum_{i,j=1}^{v} f(x_{ij}) \left(w_i^T \varpi_j + b_i + b_j - \log (x_{ij}) \right)^2 \tag{6}$$

3.2 Convolutional Neural Network (CNN)

1d-CNN, firstly proposed by Kim et al. [11], takes sentences of varying length as input which is the concatenation of word vectors. If $w_i \in R^d$ refers to word embedding of the ith word in the sentence, where d is the dimension of word embedding and $w_{i:i+j}$ refers to the concatenation of vectors $w_i, w_{i+1}, \ldots, w_j$. A number of filters, also called kernel, with different window size move on the word embeddings to perform one-dimensional convolution and create feature maps. Each filter extracts a specific pattern of n-gram. For example a filter $k \in R^{hd}$ produces a feature c_i with using the window of words $w_{i:i+h-1}$:

$$c_i = f \left(w_{i:i+h-1} \cdot k^T + b \right) \tag{7}$$

Here, b is the bias term and f is a non-linear activation function. The filter k is applied to all possible windows using the same weights to create the feature map [28].

$$c = [c_1, c_2, ..., c_{n-h+1}] \tag{8}$$

The next layer usually is max-pooling layer. In this layer max pooling operation, $\hat{c} = max[c]$, captures the most useful local features from feature maps. The outputs of multiple filters which is operated by max-pooling layer are concatenated in the next layer to form a single feature vector. Finally, a fully connected Softmax layer generates the probability distribution over labels.

3.3 Bidirectional Long Short Term Memory (BiLSTM)

Bidirectional Long Short Term Memory (BiLSTM) is putting two independent LSTM together and LSTM [28] is a modified Recurrent neural networks (RNN) architecture. RNN [29] use the idea of processing sequential information. The term recurrent means that a same task is performed over each instance of the sequence such that the output is dependent on previous computations and results [28]. Simple RNNs are consisting of a memory known as hidden state s which maintain previous computations and an optional output y. At each time step t the hidden state s_t is computed based on the previous hidden state s_{t-1} and the input at current time step x_t:

$$S_t = f (ux_t + ws_{t-1}) \tag{9}$$

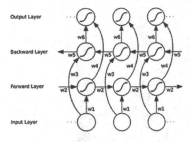

Fig. 1. Bidirectional LSTM architecture [29]

f is taken to be a nonlinear activation function such as *tanh*, *ReLU* and u, w account for weights that are shared across time. The output at time step t is computed as $y_t = softmax(vh_t)$ where v is another shared weight parameter of network and is an activation function often implemented at the final layer of a network. In practice the simple RNNs networks suffer from vanishing gradient problem that LSTM, a RNN variant, designed to deal with this and overcome the limitations of simple RNNs such as processing long sequences with long-term temporal dependencies [15]. LSTM has three gates: input, forget and output gates and hidden state is calculated based on the combination of these three gates as per Equations below:

$$x = \begin{bmatrix} h_{t-1} \\ x_t \end{bmatrix} \tag{10}$$

$$f_t = \sigma\left(w_f.x + b_f\right) \tag{11}$$

$$i_t = \sigma\left(w_i.x + b_i\right) \tag{12}$$

$$o_t = \sigma\left(w_o.x + b_o\right) \tag{13}$$

$$c_t = f_t \otimes c_{t-1} + i_t \otimes \tanh\left(W_c \cdot X + b_c\right) \tag{14}$$

$$h_t = o_t \oplus \tanh\left(c_t\right) \tag{15}$$

BiLSTM uses two LSTMs to learn each token of sequence based on both the right and the left context of the token. As shown in Fig. 1 one LSTM process the sequence from left to right and the other one from right to left [19]. Output W at each time step is dependent on both forward and backward layers. Forward layer processes the left context of the input and backward layer processes the right context.

3.4 Hybrid Neural Network

We combine 1d-CNN and BiLSTM in a way that features are extracted by one-dimensional convolution. Multiple filters with different sizes and max-pooling have been applied at the first stage and then passed to the BiLSTM as a sequence input. BiLSTM network does the classification based on generated feature maps which indicate the features of the input. Finally, a fully connected layer and Softmax regression are used to output the probability for each class.

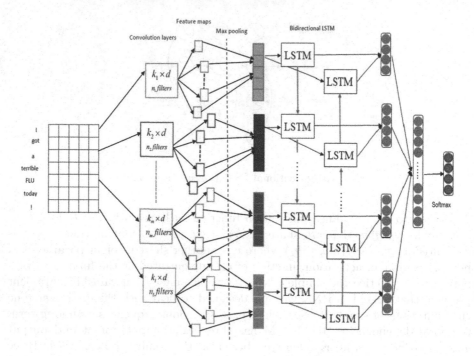

Fig. 2. The proposed hybrid 1d-CNN BiLSTM for generating tweet semantic representation and classification

4 Experiments

4.1 Experimental Setup

For training 1d-CNN-BiLSTM, we prepared a dataset using a java program that collects tweets by connecting to Twitter search and applying a time span and a Boolean query. The prepared dataset is filtered by location to build a training dataset with only a U.S. location. Accessing a great number of tweets is one of the limitations in using standard Twitter APIs that the java program tries to overcome. We use a symptom-based query for fetching flu-related tweets because using symptoms is more preferred by people than using disease names. The query is based on standard flu definition, which is symptom-based and defined by CDC. The query is expanded by using slang synonyms for symptoms introduced in [25]. The expanded query contains both technical and slang terms, which are used for collecting tweets from September 2019 to March 2020 (influenza peak season). We give a positive label to tweets that indicate infection and a negative label to other tweets. Other tweets contain awareness, ambiguous, satirical tweets in which the Boolean query is true for them, but they do not declare flu infection. Also, two different states are considered for embedding production.

– Pre-trained Word2Vec: initialize word vectors with the Google's pre-trained Word2Vec model and adjust the values through the training process. The

pre-trained word embeddings were learned on the part of the Google News dataset, which contains 300-dimensional vectors for 3 million words and phrases.
- Pre-trained GloVe: initialize word vectors with twitter's pre-trained GloVe model and adjust the values through the training process. The pre-trained word embeddings were trained over 2 billion tweets with an embedding size of 200.

At the first stage for 1d-CNN, we use filter windows of 2, 3, 4, 5 with 256 feature maps each, ReLU as an activation function, and a general max pooling. At the next stage for training BiLSTM, the input sequence is features extracted from input tweets through the convolution layer, followed by the max-pooling layer. u, v, w and are initialized to a random vector of small values. Finally, a fully connected layer and Softmax regression are used to output the probability for each class. A back-propagation algorithm with the Adam optimization method is used to train the network through time. After each training epoch, the network is tested on validation data.

4.2   Baseline Methods

To make strong comparisons, nine popular methods which are commonly used for tweet classification are utilized as baselines. In experiments, we evaluate all methods on our benchmarks and separate them into deep neural network and conventional models. Some brief introductions of baseline methods are given below:

MNB-uni: multinomial Naïve Bayes with unigrams as features and TF-IDF weighting.

MNB-uni-bi: multinomial Naïve Bayes with uni-bigrams as features and TF-IDF weighting.

MNB-uni-bi-tri: multinomial Naïve Bayes with uni-bi trigrams as features and TF-IDF weighting.

SVM-uni: SVM with unigrams as features and TF-IDF weighting.

SVM-uni-bi: SVM with uni-bigrams as features and TF-IDF weighting.

SVM-uni-bi-trigrams: SVM with uni-bi-trigrams as features and TF-IDF weighting.

1d-CNN: one dimensional CNN with two different embeddings and parameters, given in the previous section.

BiLSTM: Bidirectional LSTM with two different embeddings and parameters, given in the previous section.

LSTM: LSTM with two different embeddings and the same parameters given for BiLSTM.

5   Results

All results are obtained under the same distribution of experimental data, 90% for training and 10% for testing. In Table 1 it can be observed that the best

Table 1. Results comparison of deep neural network baseline methods and conventional tweet classification baselines.

Model	Accuracy				
	Word2Vec Pre-trained	GloVe Pre-trained	Unigrams	Uni-bigrams	Uni-bi-trigrams
1d-CNN	0.91	0.86			
BiLSTM	0.86	0.84			
LSTM	0.89	0.87			
1d-CNN-BiLSTM(Ours)	0.92	0.87			
MNB			0.80	0.82	0.83
SVM			0.81	0.80	0.79

performance of all models obtained with Word2Vec embedding. It can be seen that our approach achieved the highest accuracy in all embedding states in comparison to other baseline models and the second-best model is 1d-CNN. It is obvious that single BiLSTM performed poorly but when it is combined with 1d-CNN it enhanced the accuracy. Using only the left context information of a sequence in LSTM, hinder accurate processing for text sequences, because both right and left contexts are important for the sequences and this is the reason that we didn't use LSTM in a combinational model as a baseline. MNB has better performance with combinational n-grams than SVM and its best result is achieved by uni-bi-trigrams which is 0.02% better than the best of SVM. The salient difference, about 0.09%, can be seen between the accuracy of our approach with Word2Vec and MNB with un-bi-trigrams which demonstrates flu tweets classification is a challenging task for conventional classification models. Table 2 shows four examples of tweets that cause conventional models to perform poorly because of negation, ambiguity, sense of humor, and complexity in awareness tweets detection. As it is clear our approach can classify these kinds of tweets more accurately due to fine-tuning pre-trained Word2Vec and utilizing a hybrid classifier benefiting both BiLSTM and 1d-CNN properties.

Table 2. Four examples of tweets that conventional models cannot classify them accurately.

Negation	Homesick for day 2. I was awake at 4 am this morning and still can't sleep. Not the flu but an ugly cough and... https://fb.me/74P04sXKL
Ambiguity	I had a dream that I had a terrible flu last night. I woke up and clearing my throat extra
Humorous	I feel so sick, I have Bieber fever
Awareness	Dry, chesty cough, sore throat? How to get rid of the Aussie flu symptom - and if cough medicine doesn't work go http://newspaper-report.today/2018/01/dry-chesty-cough-how-to-get-rid-of-the-aussie-flu-symptom-and-if-cough-medicine-works/ ..

5.1   Correlation Evaluation

For evaluating the proposed approach in the real world, a set of new tweets is collected during the 2020–2021, and 2021–2022 influenza peak season for analyzing and classification to estimate the Pearson correlation coefficient between Twitter Infection rate (obtained by our approach) and ILINET (flu infection rate published by CDC). The Pearson correlation coefficient between ILINET and Twitter infection rate (Twitter Flu Trend) is 0.96 for 2020–2021 and 0.97 for 2021–2022 that are shown in Fig. 3. Vertical axis at the right-hand shows weighted ILINET and the left hand axis indicates the number of tweets expressing infection. The horizontal axis shows the number of week in the year, and as reported by CDC the influenza season peak is usually between the week 48 and week 13. We can see the same peak points, ascending and descending trends in Fig. 3 for both rates which shows the proposed approach estimation is highly correlated with the real ILI rate. Comparison of previous flu-related works and our approach is shown in Table 3. It can be observed that the highest correlation belongs to [5] and [25] which used manual classification and they are not proper for producing an automated ILI surveillance system. Google Flu Trend [8] is the only flu surveillance system that is no longer published and its mean correlation is 0.90. In comparison with other works that used a classifier for estimating Twitter flu rate, we can say our approach achieved state-of-the-art performance in both accuracy and correlation, which conduct us to implement an ILI surveillance system using Twitter with the name Twitter Flu Trend. This ILI surveillance system is publishing U.S. ILI daily rate and shows the U.S. ILI trend from the beginning of 2023.

Table 3. Correlation coefficient and accuracy comparison between the proposed approach and flu-related methods.

Model	Correlation coefficient	Classification algorithm	Accuracy
Lamb et al. [12]	0.79	Manual	
Broniatowski et al. [3]	0.93	SVM	
Allen et al. 2016 [1]	0.70	SVM	0.78
Ginsberg et al. [8]	0.90		
Jain et al. [10]		SVM	0.77
Aramaki et al. [2]	0.89	SVM	0.76
Doan et al. [5]	0.98	Manual	
Velardi et al. [25]	0.98	Manual	
Proposed approach	**0.97**	**1d-CNN-BiLSTM**	**0.92**

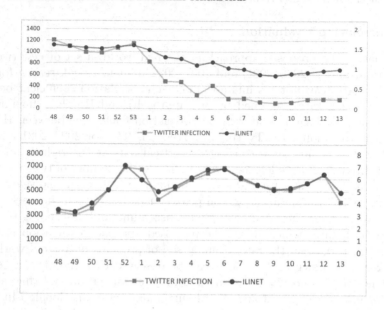

Fig. 3. The upper plot:Pearson correlation coefficient between ILINET and Twitter infection rate between week 48-2021 and week 13-2022. The lower plot:Pearson correlation coefficient between ILINET and Twitter infection rate between week 48-2020 and week 13-2021.

6   Conclusion

Twitter offers unique challenges and opportunities for monitoring and surveillance of public health. We have presented a method for tracking the flu epidemic in the U.S. using a hybrid deep neural network for analyzing tweets. Our model is capable of differentiating between reports of actual infection and Twitter chatter by utilizing the advantages of combining 1d-CNN and BiLSTM and semantic embedding vectors. Our Twitter infection rate correlates strongly with CDC ILI data. In addition, we have demonstrated the ability to use this technique for designing an ILI surveillance system called "Twitter Flu Trend," which calculates the U.S. ILI daily rate. Also, ILI intensity calculation for each U.S. state is our future work for detailed infection level monitoring.

References

1. Allen, C., Tsou, M.H., Aslam, A., Nagel, A., Gawron, J.M.: Applying gis and machine learning methods to Twitter data for multiscale surveillance of influenza. PLoS ONE **11**(7), e0157734 (2016)
2. Aramaki, E., Maskawa, S., Morita, M.: Twitter catches the flu: detecting influenza epidemics using twitter. In: Proceedings of the 2011 Conference on Empirical Methods in Natural Language Processing, pp. 1568–1576 (2011)

3. Broniatowski, D.A., Paul, M.J., Dredze, M.: National and local influenza surveillance through twitter: an analysis of the 2012–2013 influenza epidemic. PLoS ONE **8**(12), e83672 (2013)

4. Chen, T., Xu, R., He, Y., Wang, X.: Improving sentiment analysis via sentence type classification using bilstm-crf and cnn. Expert Syst. Appl. **72**, 221–230 (2017)

5. Doan, S., Ohno-Machado, L., Collier, N.: Enhancing twitter data analysis with simple semantic filtering: example in tracking influenza-like illnesses. In: 2012 IEEE Second International Conference on Healthcare Informatics, Imaging and Systems Biology, pp. 62–71. IEEE (2012)

6. Dos Santos, C., Gatti, M.: Deep convolutional neural networks for sentiment analysis of short texts. In: Proceedings of COLING 2014, the 25th International Conference on Computational Linguistics: Technical Papers, pp. 69–78 (2014)

7. Edouard, A., Cabrio, E., Tonelli, S., Le Thanh, N.: Semantic linking for event-based classification of tweets. Int. J. Comput. Linguist. Appl., 12 (2017)

8. Ginsberg, J., Mohebbi, M.H., Patel, R.S., Brammer, L., Smolinski, M.S., Brilliant, L.: Detecting influenza epidemics using search engine query data. Nature **457**(7232), 1012–1014 (2009)

9. Goldberg, Y.: Neural network methods for natural language processing. Synthesis Lectures Hum. Lang. Technol. **10**(1), 1–309 (2017)

10. Jain, V.K., Kumar, S.: An effective approach to track levels of influenza-a (h1n1) pandemic in India using twitter. Procedia Comput. Sci. **70**, 801–807 (2015)

11. Kim, Y.: Convolutional neural networks for sentence classification. In: Proceedings of the 2014 Conference on Empirical Methods in Natural Language Processing (EMNLP), pp. 1746–1751 (2014)

12. Lamb, A., Paul, M., Dredze, M.: Separating fact from fear: tracking flu infections on twitter. In: Proceedings of the 2013 Conference of the North American Chapter of the Association for Computational Linguistics: Human Language Technologies, pp. 789–795 (2013)

13. Li, H., Ji, H., Zhao, L.: Social event extraction: task, challenges and techniques. In: Proceedings of the 2015 IEEE/ACM International Conference on Advances in Social Networks Analysis and Mining 2015, pp. 526–532 (2015)

14. Li, Y., Yang, T.: Word embedding for understanding natural language: a survey. In: Srinivasan, S. (ed.) Guide to Big Data Applications. SBD, vol. 26, pp. 83–104. Springer, Cham (2018). https://doi.org/10.1007/978-3-319-53817-4_4

15. Manaswi, N.K., Manaswi, N.K., John, S.: Deep learning with applications using python. Springer (2018)

16. Mikolov, T., Chen, K., Corrado, G., Dean, J.: Efficient estimation of word representations in vector space. arXiv preprint arXiv:1301.3781 (2013)

17. Mikolov, T., Sutskever, I., Chen, K., Corrado, G.S., Dean, J.: Distributed representations of words and phrases and their compositionality. Advances in neural information processing systems 26 (2013)

18. Mikolov, T., Yih, W.t., Zweig, G.: Linguistic regularities in continuous space word representations. In: Proceedings of the 2013 Conference of the North American Chapter of the Association for Computational Linguistics: Human Language Technologies, pp. 746–751 (2013)

19. Nowak, J., Taspinar, A., Scherer, R.: LSTM recurrent neural networks for short text and sentiment classification. In: Rutkowski, L., Korytkowski, M., Scherer, R., Tadeusiewicz, R., Zadeh, L.A., Zurada, J.M. (eds.) ICAISC 2017. LNCS (LNAI), vol. 10246, pp. 553–562. Springer, Cham (2017). https://doi.org/10.1007/978-3-319-59060-8_50

20. Pennington, J., Socher, R., Manning, C.D.: Glove: global vectors for word representation. In: Proceedings of the 2014 Conference on Empirical Methods in Natural Language Processing (EMNLP), pp. 1532–1543 (2014)
21. Ristoski, P., Paulheim, H.: Semantic web in data mining and knowledge discovery: a comprehensive survey. J. Web Semant. **36**, 1–22 (2016)
22. Saif, H., He, Y., Alani, H.: Semantic sentiment analysis of Twitter. In: Cudré-Mauroux, P., Heflin, J., Sirin, E., Tudorache, T., Euzenat, J., Hauswirth, M., Parreira, J.X., Hendler, J., Schreiber, G., Bernstein, A., Blomqvist, E. (eds.) ISWC 2012. LNCS, vol. 7649, pp. 508–524. Springer, Heidelberg (2012). https://doi.org/10.1007/978-3-642-35176-1_32
23. Schulz, A., Ristoski, P., Paulheim, H.: I see a car crash: real-time detection of small scale incidents in microblogs. In: Cimiano, P., Fernández, M., Lopez, V., Schlobach, S., Völker, J. (eds.) ESWC 2013. LNCS, vol. 7955, pp. 22–33. Springer, Heidelberg (2013). https://doi.org/10.1007/978-3-642-41242-4_3
24. Varga, A., Basave, A.E.C., Rowe, M., Ciravegna, F., He, Y.: Linked knowledge sources for topic classification of microposts: a semantic graph-based approach. J. Web Semant. **26**, 36–57 (2014)
25. Velardi, P., Stilo, G., Tozzi, A.E., Gesualdo, F.: Twitter mining for fine-grained syndromic surveillance. Artif. Intell. Med. **61**(3), 153–163 (2014)
26. Wang, J., Yu, L.C., Lai, K.R., Zhang, X.: Dimensional sentiment analysis using a regional cnn-lstm model. In: Proceedings of the 54th Annual Meeting of the Association for Computational Linguistics (volume 2: Short papers), pp. 225–230 (2016)
27. Wang, P., Xu, B., Xu, J., Tian, G., Liu, C.L., Hao, H.: Semantic expansion using word embedding clustering and convolutional neural network for improving short text classification. Neurocomputing **174**, 806–814 (2016)
28. Young, T., Hazarika, D., Poria, S., Cambria, E.: Recent trends in deep learning based natural language processing. IEEE Comput. Intell. Mag. **13**(3), 55–75 (2018)
29. Yu, Y., Si, X., Hu, C., Zhang, J.: A review of recurrent neural networks: Lstm cells and network architectures. Neural Comput. **31**(7), 1235–1270 (2019)

Data Augmentation for Pathology Prioritisation: An Improved LSTM-Based Approach

Jing Qi[1]([✉]), Girvan Burnside[2], and Frans Coenen[1]

[1] Department of Computer Science, The University of Liverpool, Liverpool L69 3BX, UK
j.qi7@liverpool.ac.uk
[2] Department of Health Data Science, Institute of Translational Medicine, The University of Liverpool, Liverpool L69 3BX, UK

Abstract. Public hospitals receive large volumes of pathology results everyday. It is therefore challenging for doctors to comprehensively analyse all this data. Pathology data prioritisation would seem to provide at least a partial solution. It has been suggested that deep learning techniques can be used to construct pathology data prioritisation models. However, due to the resource required to obtain sufficient prioritisation training and test data, the usage of deep learning, which requires large labelled training data sets, was found not to be viable. The idea presented in this paper is to use a small seed set of labelled data and then to augment this data. The motivation here was that data augmentation had been previously employed successfully to address data scarcity problems. Four data augmentation methods are considered in this paper and used to train deep learning pathology data prioritisation models. Evaluation was conducted using Urea and Electrolytes pathology data. The results show a best recall and precision of 0.73 and 0.71 respectively.

Keywords: Data prioritisation · Data augmentation · LSTM · Pathology data

1 Introduction

In any hospital, many of decisions on patient care are based on pathology test results. Doctors will interpret the results and look for abnormalities that may cause disease, such as cancer and other chronic illnesses, or health risks, such as pre-diabetes. As our ability to collect pathology data, driven by scientific and technological advances, becomes increasing more sophisticated, the quantity of pathology data that clinicians are expected to reference presents an increasingly significant problem.

In order to solve this problem, some form of automated pathology result prioritisation is suggested. The hypothesis is that there exist certain pattern in the patients pathology tests records, and that these pattern can be identified and utilised using the tools and techniques of machine learning and deep learning. However, the challenge of achieving such a prioritisation system by adopting machine learning and deep learning techniques is frequently the absence of a "ground truth", a set of examples illustrating what a priority pathology result looks like, and what it does not look like. This is largely due to the resource required but also the challenge of any rigorous definition of what a priority pathology result is. The phrase "I can't define what a priority pathology result is, but I know one when I see one" is encountered. The challenge is compounded by the fact that typical pathology data prioritisation scenarios comprise a number of pathology results and that it is also important to take into account the individual patient's pathology history. It is not simply a matter of considering a single result, instead a number of time series data sequences need to be considered together.

Some attempts have been made aimed at address the "no ground truth problem". It was assumed that a high priority pathology result equated to an anomalous result and that an anomaly detection approach using supervised learning, directed at static and time series data, could be adopted [11]. However, a criticism that can be directed at this approach is that given a large number of priority pathology results these would no longer be considered to be anomalous but as "standard" results, and therefore not be prioritised. In [10] the use of a proxy ground truth was proposed to which established deep learning techniques were applied to generate a three class (high, medium, low) pathology data prioritisation model. The proxy ground truth was based on the known outcomes of previous patients; whether they became emergency patients (high priority), in-patients (medium priority) or out-patients (low priority). The criticism that can always be directed at system that use ground truth proxy data is that it is difficult to know whether the proxy data accurately reflect the "on the ground" situation unless ground truth data is available for comparison, which then obviate the need for a proxy ground truth.

The view taken in this paper is that, although it is acknowledged that collecting a comprehensive pathology data prioritisation data set is time-consuming and costly, it is possible to collect a small number of examples. A set of examples that, on its own, is insufficient to generate and validate a machine/deep learning model, but which can be used as a seed set from which a usable ground truth can be generated (grown), a process known as *data augmentation* [2,9]. Data augmentation is the process of generating new data points from existing data, and is seen as an effective solution for dealing with the data scarcity problems. This idea is explored in this paper. A seed set was obtained founded on the Urea and Electrolytes (U&E) pathology application domain. Four different data augmentation techniques were applied to this seed set: (i) Jittering, (ii) the Synthetic Minority Oversampling Technique (SMOTE), (iii) the Deviation From Mean (DFM) mechanism and (iv) Guide Warping. Evaluation was conducted by generating and comparing pathology data prioritisation models generated using the Long Short Term Memory (LSTM) recurrent neural network framework to the augmented data.

The remainder of this paper is organised as follows. A review of relevant previous work is presented in Sect. 2. This is followed, in Sect. 3, by a review of the U&E pathology application domain used as a focus for the work. Details of the considered data augmentation techniques and the proposed pathology data prioritisation process are the provided in Sect. 4. The conducted evaluation is then reported on in Sect. 5. The paper is concluded in Sect. 6 with a summary of the main findings and some suggested directions for future work.

2 Previous Work

The general topic of the work presented in this paper broadly falls into the area of AI-based medical data classification [17]. AI-driven techniques for aiding disease detection and diagnosis have become a popular area of research, where the main objective is to help professionals make more informed decisions concerning medical diagnoses, treatments and triage. It is this last which is most relevant with respect to the work presented in this paper. Traditional machine learning techniques, such as ensemble random forests, Support Vector Machines (SVM) and Logistic regression have all been extensively used for medical triage research [17]. For example, in [1] it was proposed to use ensemble random forests to triage patients in emergency departments so as to reduce waiting time [1]. In [15] a triage approach founded on predicting anomalous patients, using a SVM model and Principal Component Analysis (PCA), was proposed. In [12] a machine learning system was presented for prioritising patients with serious (unstable) conditions from patients with stable conditions. In [16] a deep learning model was proposed in the context ophthalmology referral (triage). Some reported studies have adopted Natural Language Processing (NLP) techniques, directed at patient records, to prioritise patients [8, 17].

With respect to most existing studies related to medical data prioritisation, one of the most important factors for achieving a triage system utilising machine learning techniques is to have appropriate "ground truth" training data. In the case of the existing work on triage systems for emergency departments, triage levels were usually established in advance by experienced clinicians according to the criticality of patients [12]. Where NLP techniques have been adopted the data used for training comprised labelled doctors' reviews. However, as already noted, for some areas within the triage domain, such as pathology result prioritisation, ground truth data is usually not available because of the resource required (especially given the current COVID-19 pandemic which has placed extra strain on health services). This turn means that established techniques, such as those listed above, are difficult to use directly.

Several approaches have been proposed to address the absence of a "ground truth" problem in the context of pathology data prioritisation. As noted in the introduction to this paper, these include anomaly detection approaches [11] and ground truth proxy approaches [10]. In [11] unsupervised learning techniques were used to generate a cluster configuration for pathology results. Then, if a new patient's pathology result could not be fitted into an existing cluster it was assumed to be anomalous (an outlier) and therefore a priority result. One of the criticisms of anomaly detection-based approaches is that when there are a large number of anomalous pathology results these would be grouped into cluster configuration and therefore any new patient record would not be considered anomalous. In [10] a data set of the final destination of patients was used to categorise patients as Emergency Department, In Patient or Out Patient patients. A training set was derived of pathology history time series, each labelled with these final destination. A classifier was built using this training data and then applied to the patient. The resulting classifications were equated to a prioritisation level, high, medium or low. A criticism that can be directed at proxy ground truth-based approaches is that it is challenging to determine how representative of the "real situation" the proxy ground truth data actually is.

Another direction for dealing with the unavailability of a appropriate training data is to generate synthetic data. However, this can only be done given a comprehensive understanding of the domain under consideration which requires significant input from domain experts. This in turn entails resource which, as already noted, in the case of the pathology data prioritisation domain is not available. The approach advocated in this paper is to augment a small seed set; the generation of which does not require significant resource. Data augmentation is the process of supplementing a dataset with similar data that is created from the information held in the seed set [6]. There are two application areas for data augmentation. One is for addressing the data imbalanced problem [5]. For example to use under-sampling techniques to increase the number of samples in minority class (classes). The second is for addressing the small sample size problem [4]. The latter is the focus for the work presented in this paper.

It was noted in the introduction to this paper that when clinicians are required to prioritise current pathology data they need to take into account previous pathology data results. In other words we are talking about time series data. Thus, only data augmentation techniques which are suitable for time series data are considered in this paper. Popular data augmentation methods fall into four categories: Random Transformation, Pattern Mixing, Generative Models and Decomposition [5]. In [5] it was noted that Pattern Mixing methods are appropriate for short time series, which means that such methods are well suited to pathology data. Generative models require large amounts of (training) data, data not available in the case of the pathology data prioritisation application considered here. Decomposition models are intended for time series forecasting applications, whereas classification is under consideration here. Therefore, three alternative pattern mixing methods were considered with respect to the work presented in this paper: (i) Synthetic Minority Oversampling Technique (SMOTE), (ii) Deviation From Mean (DFM) and (iii) Guide Warping. The Jittering random transformation model was also considered. This was selected because of its simplicity and its ability for generalisation in the context of deep learning models [5].

3   Application Domain

The pathology data prioritisation application focus for the work presented in this paper was Urea and Electrolytes pathology testing (U&E testing); a commonly used test to detect abnormalities of blood chemistry, primarily kidney (renal) function and dehydration. U&E testing is usually performed to confirm normal kidney function or to exclude a serious imbalance of biochemical salts in the bloodstream. The U&E test data considered in this paper comprised, for each pathology result, the measurement of levels of: (i) Bicarbonate (bi), (ii) Creatinine (cr), (iii) Sodium (so) (iv) Potassium (po) and (v) Urea (ur). The measurement of each is referred to as a "task", thus we had five tasks per pathology test; each U&E test result comprised five pathology values. Abnormal levels in any of the tasks may indicate kidney disease.

In more detail, the U&E data used for evaluation purposes with respect to the work presented in this paper comprised a set of clinical patient records, $\mathbf{D} = \{P_1, P_2, \dots\}$, where each record $P_i \in \mathbf{D}$ was of the form:

$$P_j = \langle Id, Date, T_{So}, T_{Po}, T_{Ur}, T_{Cr}, T_{Bi}, c \rangle \tag{1}$$

where T_{so} to T_{bi} are five multi-variate time series and c is the class label taken from a set of classes C. For the work presented in this paper a three-level prioritisation was assumed $\{high, medium, low\}$. The dimensions in each multi-variate time series were: (i) test value, (ii) upper bound and (iii) lower bound. The upper bound and lower bound indicate a "band" in which pathology results are expected to fall. These values are less volatile than the pathology result values, but can change over time.

4   Pathology Data Augmentation and Prioritisation

In this section the proposed approach to pathology data prioritisation, using data augmentation, to expand a given seed set is presented. As already noted, for the evaluation presented in the following section, Sect. 5, four data augmentation methods were considered: (i) Jittering, (ii) the Synthetic Minority Oversampling Technique (SMOTE), (iii) the Deviation From Mean (DFM) mechanism and (iv) Guide Warping. Each is therefore described individually in the following four sub-sections, Subsects. 4.1 to 4.4. In each case the process for applying the method to U&E pathology is included. This section is concluded, Subsect. 4.5, with a review of the adopted process for generating pathology data prioritisation models using the LSTM framework.

4.1   Jittering

Jittering is one of the simplest methods from the random transformation category of time series augmentation [14]. The fundamental idea of Jittering is to add random noise to a *query time series*, a time series is selected from the seed set (the source data set). The query time series is then adapted in some way to form an additional time series, referred to as the *new time series*, by "jittering" the values in the time series. The idea is that the generated *new time series* (the additional time series generated) will only vary from the query time series by a factor equivalent to the noise parameters used. The method can be defined as follows:

$$x' = x_1 + \epsilon_1, x_2 + \epsilon_2, ..., x_T + \epsilon_T \tag{2}$$

where ϵ is typically Gaussian noise added to each time stamp value x_T in a query time series. The adopted process of applying Jittering to U&E pathology data was as follows:

1. For each patient time series P_n add Gaussian noise $\epsilon \in \mathcal{N}(0, \sigma^2)$ to each time stamp value within each pathology task. The value 0.03 was used for the value of σ, as suggested in [6]. Thus $\hat{P}_{nJT} = \langle \hat{T}_{So}, \hat{T}_{Po}, \hat{T}_{Ur}, \hat{T}_{Cr}, \hat{T}_{Bi} \rangle$, where $\hat{T}_n = V_{i_1} + \epsilon_1, V_{i_n} + \epsilon_2, ..., V_{i_n} + \epsilon_n$.

4.2   SMOTE

The Synthetic Minority Oversampling Technique (SMOTE) [7] is a pattern mixing data augmentation technique. Unlike Random Transformation techniques, pattern mixing techniques preserve the distribution of the original time series when generating new time series. Though SMOTE was originally designed to deal with the imbalanced classes problem by interpolating patterns for under-represented classes, it can equally be used in the context of the small sample size problem. SMOTE can be defined as follows:

$$x' = x + \lambda |x - x_{NN}| \tag{3}$$

where sample x is a random sample selected from each class and x_{NN} is a random sample selected from the kth nearest neighbours of x. λ is a random value taken from the range $[0, 1]$. The process of applying SMOTE to the U&E pathology data considered in this paper was as follows:

1. For each query time series P_n, use $k^{st}NN$ to find the reference neighbours T_{NN} for the query time series. Here k is chosen using the identity $k = \sqrt{n}$, where n represents the number of data items in the seed data set.
2. Randomly select a "reference neighbour" from the k nearest neighbours identified in step 1.
3. Calculate the difference d_n between the current (query) time series and its reference neighbour.
4. Apply d_n to the query time series to give: $\hat{P}_{nSMOTE} = \langle \hat{T}_{So}, \hat{T}_{Po}, \hat{T}_{Ur}, \hat{T}_{Cr}, \hat{T}_{Bi} \rangle$, where $\hat{T}_n = V_{i_1} + \lambda |d_1|, V_{i_n} + \lambda |d_2|, ..., V_{i_n} + \lambda |d_n|$.

4.3 DFM

Deviation From Mean (DFM) [6] generates new time series from "mean curves" identified in the seed data. To be more specific, first a Savitzky-Golay filter [13] is used to smooth all of the seed samples of the class of interest. Then the bounding curves, with max values and min values of the smoothed time series data, are calculated. A mean curve is then computed from the bounding curves. The DFM of each time series is derived from computing the difference between each time series and the mean curve of the corresponding class. Random segments of DFMs are then combined to create a surrogate DFM curve. Finally, new time series are generated from the multiplication of the surrogate DFM and the class mean curve. The process of applying DFM to U&E pathology data was then:

1. For each time series P_n, use oversampling to ensure that all the time series are of the same length (max length). Use the Savitzky-Golay filter to smooth the time series.
2. Compute the maximum (max) and minimum (min) of all of the smoothed time series, for the class under consideration, so as to generate bounding curves. Then compute the mean curve; the mean of the bounding curves for all time series.
3. Calculate the DFM curve for all of the smoothed time series.
4. Generate a surrogate DFM curve by combining randomly selected sections from the DFM curves from Step 3, and apply a linear gradient to the selected section to scale the start and end points from the different sections.
5. Compute a new time series from the surrogate DFM and the mean curve.

4.4 Guided Warping

Guided Warping [6] generates new time series by "time warping" a query time series by a "teacher pattern" using Dynamic Time Warping (DTW) [18]. DTW is a popular time series similarity measurement technique which takes into account that the time series to be compared may be offset from one another by using a dynamic programming technique. Guided Warping "warps" the elements of a query time series to the elements of the teacher pattern selected by a DTW alignment function. In this manner the aligned elements of the query time series can be replaced by the corresponding teacher time series, thus a new reference time series can be generated. The process of applying Guided Warping to the U&E data was as follows:

1. Given a query time series P_n, and randomly selected teacher pattern P_i for the same class, calculate the minimum DTW warping distance $D(I, J)$, where I and J are the lengths of the two time series respectively.
2. Generate a new reference time series by warping the query time series with the aligned elements from $D(I, J)$ so that the new reference time series will features values from the query time series but at different time stamps.

4.5 LSTM for Prioritisation

The architecture for the proposed pathology data prioritisation model comprised five LSTMs one for each task. The results from the LSTMs are combined in a final "decision layer". A similar structure was proposed in [10]. The whole structure is shown in Fig. 1. Each LSTM comprised four layers: (i) an input layer, (ii) two hidden layers and (iii) a Softmax layer. The input was five set of time series, one for each component task, T_{jS_o}, T_{jP_o}, T_{jU_r}, T_{jC_r} and T_{jB_i}, made up of the augmented training data. Thus for each task, the input was a multi-variate time series $T_i = \{V_1, V_2, ..., V_m\}$ as described in Sect. 3. Each time series T_i was padded to the maximum length in T_n. The last layer of the architecture is the decision layer where the final labels for patients are predicted. After obtaining all of the five outputs and predicted labels from each of the five LSTM models, a decision logic module was used to decide the final prioritisation level of the patient. The logic rule used was: *"If there exists a prediction that equates to 'High' for one of the tasks then the overall prediction is high, otherwise average the five outputs produced by the Softmax function and choose the class with the maximum probability"*. In order to maximise the effectiveness of a LSTM hyper-parameter tuning is an important element. There are 4 parameters to be considered: (i) learning rate, (ii) batch size, (iii) number of hidden units (nodes per hidden layer) and (iv) number of epochs. Generally, the parameters can be tuned by observing the loss plots of the training and validation data, where cross-entropy can be used as the loss function. Section 5 will provide more details. For the optimization of LSTM, Adam optimization was chosen due to its efficiency and the nature of the adaptive learning rate [3].

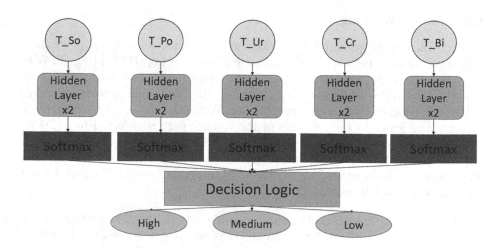

Fig. 1. LSTM architecture

5   Evaluation

The performance evaluation of the proposed approach to pathology data prioritisation is presented in this section. The evaluation U&E data set, was provided by Arrowe Park Hospital in Merseyside in the UK. The data set was entirely anonymised and ethical approval for its usage, in anonymised form, obtained by Arrowe Park Hospital. Details concerning this data set are given in Subsect. 5.1 below. Five cross validation was used through-out, and all the experiments were run using a windows 10 desktop machine with a 3.2 GHz Quad-Core IntelCore i5 processor and 24 GB of RAM. For the LSTM, a GPU was used fitted with a NVIDA GeForceRTX 2060 unit. The objectives of the evaluation were to identify the most appropriate data augmentation strategy for addressing the problem of data scarcity in the context of the pathology data prioritisation problem.

5.1   Evaluation Data Set

A general format of the data was presented in Sect. 3. The evaluation data set D comprised 3,734 patient records, each with five U&E task results (time series) per patient (no labels available). The seed data set, to which the data augmentation models were to be applied, were extracted from the original data set. Doctors supporting the work were then asked to prioritise the data according to a three-level prioritisation: high, medium, low. The resulting labelled seed set, D_{source}, comprised 30 patients, 6 labelled as high priority, 7 as medium priority and 17 as low priority. Augmentation was then applied to this data. However, it was found that in some cases only a limited number of additional (new) time series could be generated; insufficient to support the generating of a data prioritisation model. This was the found to be the case with respect to SMOTE and Guided Warping because of the way in which these augmentation techniques operate. To address this, proxy data of the form used in [10] was added. Recall that for the proxy ground truth labelling, the final destinations of the patients within the U&E data set was used to create a proxy ground truth; whether they ended-up as emergency, in or out patients; equating to high, medium and low priority respectively mentioned earlier.

5.2   Best LSTM Settings

The performance of LSTM models depends highly on the parameter settings used. Analysing the learning curve of the training and validation data is one the most popular methods to find the best parameters for a given training data set. One of the metrics for diagnosing models is the training and validation loss over time. Loss indicates prediction error. A low loss value thus indicates that more learning is required. A value of 0 indicates a model that is perfectly matched to the training data. Figure 2 shows an example set of loss plots derived from training five LSTMs, one per task, on data augmented using SMOTE. For each graph, the x-axis gives the number of times the training samples were "viewed" during LSTM generation, and the y-axis the loss value. From the figures, it can be seen that:

1. Oscillations appear in all of the loss plots.
2. For Loss plots (c), (d) and (e), loss of training and validation decreases to a point of stability and the gap between them are relatively small, which means a good performance of the model.
3. In the case of Loss plot (d) where the validation data set does not contain sufficient information for evaluating the ability of the model. The possible cause of this problem is that the patterns generated for the *Sodium* results are for the LSTM models to generalise.
4. In the case of Loss plot (a) overfitting has occurred.

Thus, from the foregoing, it can be concluded that the effectiveness of SMOTE data augmentation on different tasks is not consistent. Similar observations were identified with respect to loss plots (not shown here) generated using the other three augmentation techniques considered. Whatever the case the best parameter settings for each data augmentation techniques is given in Table 1. The setting which gives the average lowest loss on the validation set was selected.

Table 1. Parameter setting for LSTMs

Parameter name	Data augmentation methods			
	JT	*SMOTE*	*DFM*	*GW*
Batch size	64	128	256	128
Learning rate	0.001	0.001	0.001	0.001
Epochs	500	500	500	500
Hidden state	64	64	64	64

5.3   Comparison of the Overall Performance of Prioritisation

As noted earlier, four data augmentation techniques were used to generate additional training data. Consequently four training data sets were generated: D_{JT}, D_{SMOTE}, D_{DFM} and D_{GW}. Table 2 show the LSTM performance using the different augmented data set. From the table, it can been that:

1. The performance of the pattern mixing techniques (SMOTE, DFM and Guide Warping) was overall better than the Random transformation technique (Jittering) considered; although both SMOTE and Guided Warping required the inclusion of further proxy data. This, it is argued, is because of the high level of randomness in the random transformation technique.
2. The recall and precision of the medium level is lower than the other two classes. This is probably caused by the ambiguous features between the medium class and the other two classes.

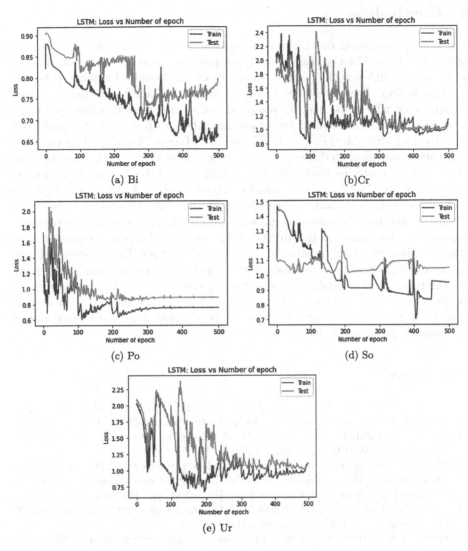

Fig. 2. Loss curves for five LSTM models based on SMOTE

Table 2. Comparison Precision and Recall of four data augmentation methods

Methods.	Acc.	Pre. High	Pre. Medium	Pre. Low	Rec. High	Rec. Medium	Rec. Low
JT	0.48	0.40	0.37	0.32	0.57	0.42	0.46
SMOTE	**0.66**	**0.55**	0.45	**0.71**	**0.72**	0.46	**0.73**
DFM	0.64	0.51	**0.53**	0.69	0.56	**0.48**	0.63
GW	0.58	**0.55**	0.41	0.51	0.64	0.42	0.60
Ave	0.59	0.51	0.45	0.56	0.62	0.45	0.61

6   Conclusions

The work presented in this paper has sought to address the pathology data prioritisation in the absence of a ground truth problem. The reason for the absence of a ground truth was the resource required, on the behalf of clinicians, to generate such data. The central idea promoted is to use a small seeds set of labelled examples, for which resource was available, and then to grow this using data augmentation techniques. Four different augmentation techniques were considered: (i) Jittering, (ii) SMOTE, (iii) DFM and (iv) Guide Warping. The proposed approaches was evaluated using U&E pathology test data which comprised five tasks. The comparative results obtained demonstrated the best performance was obtained using SMOTE, which provided a best recall and precision of 0.73 and 0.71 respectively. The work has demonstrated that the idea of generating artificial pathology data through data augmentation is a feasible option. The proposed approach is dependent on the quality of the seed set. For future work consideration will be given to the nature of the required seed set. Future work will also entail a comprehensive collaborate with clinicians to obtain feedback regarding the prioritisation produced and testing of the utility of the best performing mechanism in a real setting. The authors are currently liaising with domain experts on the practical impact of the proposed pathology data prioritisation mechanisms presented in this paper.

References

1. Azeez, D., Gan, K., Ali, M., Ismail, M.: Secondary triage classification using an ensemble random forest technique. Technol. Health Care **23**(4), 419–428 (2015)
2. Bayer, M., Kaufhold, M.A., Reuter, C.: A survey on data augmentation for text classification. ACM Comput. Surv. (2021)
3. Chang, Z., Zhang, Y., Chen, W.: Effective adam-optimized LSTM neural network for electricity price forecasting. In: 2018 IEEE 9th International Conference on Software Engineering and Service Science (ICSESS), pp. 245–248. IEEE (2018)
4. Do, E., Boynton, J., Lee, B.S., Lustgarten, D.: Data augmentation for 12-lead ECG beat classification. SN Comput. Sci. **3**(1), 1–17 (2022)
5. Iwana, B.K., Uchida, S.: An empirical survey of data augmentation for time series classification with neural networks. PLoS ONE **16**(7), e0254841 (2021)
6. Iwana, B.K., Uchida, S.: Time series data augmentation for neural networks by time warping with a discriminative teacher. In: 2020 25th International Conference on Pattern Recognition (ICPR), pp. 3558–3565. IEEE (2021)
7. Jiao, X., Li, J.: An effective intrusion detection model for class-imbalanced learning based on smote and attention mechanism. In: 2021 18th International Conference on Privacy, Security and Trust (PST), pp. 1–6. IEEE (2021)
8. Kijpaisalratana, N., Sanglertsinlapachai, D., Techaratsami, S., Musikatavorn, K., Saoraya, J.: Machine learning algorithms for early sepsis detection in the emergency department: a retrospective study. Int. J. Med. Inform. **160**, 104689 (2022)
9. Ni, R., Goldblum, M., Sharaf, A., Kong, K., Goldstein, T.: Data augmentation for meta-learning. In: International Conference on Machine Learning, pp. 8152–8161. PMLR (2021)

10. Qi, J., Burnside, G., Charnley, P., Coenen, F.: Event-based pathology data prioritisation: a study using multi-variate time series classification. In: Proceedings of the 13th International Joint Conference on Knowledge Discovery, Knowledge Engineering and Knowledge Management - KDIR, pp. 121–128. INSTICC, SciTePress (2021)
11. Qi, J., Burnside, G., Charnley, P., Coenen, F.: Ranking pathology data in the absence of a ground truth. In: Artificial Intelligence XXXVIII, pp. 209–223. Springer International Publishing (2021). https://doi.org/10.1007/978-3-030-91100-3_18
12. Raita, Y., Goto, T., Faridi, M.K., Brown, D.F., Camargo, C.A., Hasegawa, K.: Emergency department triage prediction of clinical outcomes using machine learning models. Crit. Care **23**(1), 1–13 (2019)
13. Rasjid, Z.E., Setiawan, R., Effendi, A.: A comparison: prediction of death and infected COVID-19 cases in Indonesia using time series smoothing and LSTM neural network. Procedia Comput. Sci. **179**, 982–988 (2021)
14. Talavera, E., Iglesias, G., González-Prieto, Á., Mozo, A., Gómez-Canaval, S.: Data augmentation techniques in time series domain: a survey and taxonomy. arXiv preprint arXiv:2206.13508 (2022)
15. Wang, S.T.: Construct an optimal triage prediction model: a case study of the emergency department of a teaching hospital in Taiwan. J. Med. Syst. **37**(5), 1–11 (2013)
16. Wee, C.K., et al.: Automated triaging medical referral for otorhinolaryngology using data mining and machine learning techniques. IEEE Access **10**, 44531–44548 (2022)
17. Wee, C.K., et al.: Triaging medical referrals based on clinical prioritisation criteria using machine learning techniques. Int. J. Environ. Res. Public Health **19**(12), 7384 (2022)
18. Yang, X., Zhang, Z., Cui, X., Cui, R.: A time series data augmentation method based on dynamic time warping. In: 2021 International Conference on Computer Communication and Artificial Intelligence (CCAI), pp. 116–120. IEEE (2021)

Scanned ECG Arrhythmia Classification Using a Pre-trained Convolutional Neural Network as a Feature Extractor

Hanadi Aldosari[1,4]($\boxtimes$), Frans Coenen[1]($\boxtimes$), Gregory Y. H. Lip[2]($\boxtimes$), and Yalin Zheng[2,3]($\boxtimes$)

[1] Department of Computer Science, University of Liverpool, Liverpool, UK
{H.A.Aldosari,Coenen}@liverpool.ac.uk
[2] Liverpool Centre for Cardiovascular Science, University of Liverpool and Liverpool Heart and Chest Hospital, Liverpool, UK
{Gregory.Lip,Yalin.Zheng}@liverpool.ac.uk
[3] Department of Eye and Vision Science, University of Liverpool, Liverpool, UK
[4] College of Computer Science and Engineering, Taibah University, Madinah, Saudi Arabia
hdosari@taibahu.edu.sa

Abstract. The classification of cardiovascular diseases using ECG data is considered. It is argued that to obtain a satisfactory classification features should be extracted from ECG images in their entirety, instead of translating the image into a 1D time series and only considering a small number of features as is the current common practise. The presented approach used a pre-trained Convolutional Neural Network (CNN) as a features extractor, followed by the application of T-distributed Stochastic Neighbour Embedding (T-SNE) to find the best discriminant features to perform ECG classification. The motivation using a pre-trained CNN model is that available ECG data sets tend to be limited in size; typically insufficient for training a bespoke deep learning model for feature extraction. Using a pre-trained CNN this challenge can be addressed. The features were extracted from the fully connected layers immediately preceding the softmax layer. The use of several pre-trained CNNs is reported on: VGG16, InceptionV3, and ResNet50. The operation of the proposed approach was also compared with recent relevant published approaches. A best AUC value of 0.960 was produced using the proposed approach; while the best alternative approach, out of those considered, produced an AUC of 0.932.

Keywords: ECG Classification · Convolutional neural networks · SVM Classifier · KNN Classifier

1 Introduction

Cardiovascular disease (CVD) generates a huge amount of biomedical and clinical data as a part of patient care. That data requires automated abstraction and manual analysis to be easily utilized by cardiovascular researchers, practitioners

M. Bramer and F. Stahl (Eds.): SGAI-AI 2022, LNAI 13652, pp. 64–80, 2022.
https://doi.org/10.1007/978-3-031-21441-7_5

and doctors. Strategies and techniques that employ Machine Learning (ML) and Deep Learning (DL) have become essential for improving the cardiologists' work processes and performance, including making early diagnoses of diseases [14]. In recent decades, there has been a significant growth of interest in the automated classification and prediction of various cardiovascular diseases based on ECG data [5, 17, 35]. Much of the available ECG data tends to be in paper "print out" format; this is especially the case with respect to longitudinal studies [23]. It is only in recent times that ECG machines have been able to output digital format ECG data.

The typical process for processing "paper" ECG data is to first scan the paper format data so that a digital image is available; although, depending on the nature of the scanning, the image quality may be affected. The digitised ECG images can be used directly as the input to a selected ML or DL algorithm. However, this entails a high computational cost, in many cases making this approach prohibitive. To reduce this computational cost a frequent practice is to translate the 2D ECG image data into a 1D time series format, and then select features from the resulting time series [26, 30, 36, 39, 49].

The adopted feature extraction process is usually founded on a small number of global characteristics of ECG data; notably the amplitude and interval values of what are referred to as the P, QRS and T (P-QRS-T) waves[1] [20, 29, 38, 46]. These are the same key points that practitioners consider when conducting visual analysis of ECG signals.

The translation from 2D to 1D tends to introduces further irregularities and information loss. However, the main disadvantage of P-QRS-T style techniques is that they only focus on a small set of features. The alternative, and that considered in this paper, is to extract discriminatory features from the 2D scanned ECG image data without transformation to a 1D format. Thus maintaining the computational advantage of feature based ECG classification, whilst circumventing the disadvantages associated with the P-QRS-T style 1D techniques.

The question is then how best to extract the desired features from the raw ECG data. The Convolutional Neural Network (CNN) is the state of art DL technique for working with image data. However, to train a CNN requires a considerable amount of data. Generally speaking the amount of ECG data available for CVD classification is insufficient to train a CNN for feature extraction, especially where practitioners are interested in a particular form of CVD. The solution here is to use a pre-trained CNN model [9, 16, 21, 31, 33, 40, 44, 52]. In this paper three different pre-trained CNN models, to extract features from ECG scanned image data, are considered: (i) ResNet50, (ii) VGG16 and (iii) InceptionV3. These models were selected because of their high robustness and proven efficiency with respect to ECG data applications. However, using these techniques a large number of features will be identified. If all the extracted features were to be considered any computational advantage that might have been gained would be lost. A feature selection process should therefore be applied so

---

[1] The P wave indicates atrial depolarization, the QRS wave ventricular depolarization and the T wave ventricular re-polarization.

as to identify features that are the best discriminators of class. With respect to the work presented in this paper use of the T-distributed Stochastic Neighbour Embedding (T-SNE) dimension reduction technique is advocated. Once an appropriate subset of features has been identified a classification model can be built. In this paper the use of Support Vector Machine (SVM) and k-Nearest Neighbour (KNN) classification were considered.

A further advantage of using features, regardless of the nature of these features, is that they can be augmented with additional features obtained from elsewhere, for example features extracted from Electronic Patient Record (EPR) data. As a consequence it may be the case that a "better" classification results. This idea is also explored in this paper.

The application focus for the work presented in this paper is the detection of abnormal ECGs. ECGs that feature some form of CVD indicated by an irregular, and often an unusually fast, heart rate. The remainder of this paper is structured as follows. A review of relevant existing work is presented, in Sect. 2. The proposed approach is then described in Sect. 3, and the associated evaluation in Sect. 4. The paper is concluded, in Sect. 5, with a summary of the main findings and some ideas for future work.

2   Previous Work

The analysis and interpretation of cardiovascular activity using ECG data is acknowledged, by medical practitioners, to be a challenging task. According to [41], the interpretation of ECGs can only be done by practitioners with extensive prior knowledge and skills. It is also very time-consuming. Consequently the automated interpretation of ECG data using the tools and techniques of ML and DL is seen as desirable. Examples, with respect to the classification of a variety of CVDs using ML and DL technology, can be found in [5,17,19,24,35]. Many of these methods report good result.

As noted in the introduction to this paper ECG data, traditionally, comes in a "paper print out" format. For ML and DL algorithms to be applied the paper format data needs to be scanned. A process that entails the introduction of: (i) irregularities of various kinds, (ii) the inclusion of spurious information and noise, and (iii) information loss. The quality of the scanned images is thus, in many cases, in question; however this is accepted as an unavoidable side effect if ML and DL techniques to existing is to be applied to, paper format, ECG data. The work presented in this paper is directed at the use of scanned ECG image data. The normal process is to convert to a 1D time series conceptualisation so that, typically, P-QRS-T wave form-based ML and DL techniques can be applied [26,30,36,39,49]. A range of ECG digitisation tools have been used covert 2D ECG data into time series formats [7,8,13,18,30,36,43]. However, as already noted, the P-QRS-T approach features the disadvantage that only a small part of the available data is utilised.

Although the work presented in this paper is directed at paper format ECG data it is worth noting in this literature review that in more recent times ECG machines that produce digitised output have become increasingly available, although much existing data is still in the paper format. This avoids many of the issues associated with the scanning of paper ECG data. The digital output can be in two forms 2D digital image output or 1D time series output. The 1D time series format offers the advantage that P-QRS-T style 1D techniques can be applied directly. In the case of 2D output the practice is to first translate into a 1D format, and then apply the tried and tested P-QRS-T waveform approach to feature selection. However, as noted in the introduction to this paper, P-QRS-T style techniques feature the disadvantage that much of the data is ignored. For any kind of longitudinal study paper format ECG data remains the dominant format.

In this paper the focus is on using state-of-the-art technique to extract features from 2D ECG data using Convolution Neural Networks (CNNs), and to then we used the power of DL and ML classification algorithms to classify the ECG data. CNNs have been successfully applied to classify ECG data in the 1D, time series, context [1,32,42,53] (although RNNs are more common). Although CNNs provide promising results for 1D time series data, better results have been reported when CNN are applied to 2D medical image data [34,45]. Accordingly,it is noteworthy that some researchers working with 1D time series ECG data, directly produced by a ECG machine, have considered converting this time series data into a 2D image format so the CNNs can be applied [10,11,25,27,28,37,50].

However, as noted in the introduction to this paper, training CNNs for ECG classification require large amounts of data to achieve a desirable performance. The state-of-art solution is to use some form of Transfer Learning (TL) where a pre-trained model is adopted and fine tuned using additional data. The utilization of TL allows Knowledge learnt from patterns in one domain to be applied in another domain; for example to enable classification with respect to the other domain. In the case of CNNs pre-trained image recognition models, such as ResNet and Inception v3, are available which can be fine tuned using a limited amount of ECG image data [9,16,21,31,33,40,44,52]. For example in [9] the authors fine tuned Inception V3 with real scanned images data to produced good results (AUC of 0.935). The work presented in this paper used the same data set as used in [9]. In this paper three pre-trained CNN model were fine tuned to extract features from 2D ECG image data, which were then used to construct SVM and KNN classification models. We compared the results with [9] model and [16].

3 Proposed Approach

This section presents the proposed approach to feature extraction from ECG raw image data. The approach comprises five stages:

1. ECG Image Pre-processing.
2. Features Extraction.
3. Dimension Reduction
4. Data Augmentation
5. Feature Vector Generation

Detail concerning each of these stages is presented in the following five sub-sections, Subsects. 3.1, 3.2, 3.3, 3.4 and 3.5.

3.1   ECG Image Pre-processing

So that the ECG image data could be used with an appropriate pre-trained CNN model the images needed to be dimensioned so as to be compatible with nature of the adopted architecture for the CNN model in question. For example ResNet50 requires that the input images size is a multiple of 32. Therefore, with respect to the work presented here, all images were first resized; 299×299 pixels for InceptionV3, and 224×224 pixels for ResNet50 and VGG16

3.2   Feature Extraction

The idea presented in this paper is to extract features from ECG image data and then to use the extracted features to build a classification model, thus avoiding the disadvantages of 1D techniques as considered earlier in this paper. The proposed method is to extract the desired features using pre-trained CNNs. Usually, initial layers of a CNN capture basic input image features, such as boundaries and colour patterns. Then the deeper hidden layers capture the complex higher-level feature patterns [6]. The most discriminating features are thus held in the Fully-Connected Layers (FCLs) before the final output classification layer (the softmax layer). The features in these FCLs were the features used with respect to the work presented here. Three pre-trained CNN image recognition models were considered: (i) VGG16, (ii) ResNet50 and (iii) InceptionV3. Details concerning these pre-trained models are presented below.

VGG16. The VGG network architecture was introduced by Simonyan and Zisserman in [47]. The acronym VGG stands for Visual Geometry Group, a group within the Department of Science and Engineering at the University of Oxford. The group has released a series of CNN models beginning with VGG, VGG16 to VGG19, the number denotes the number of layers. VGG16 was used with respect to the work presented in this paper. The VGG16 architecture requires a $224 \times 224 \times 3$ image size as an input, and generates an output feature vector size of 4096. Details of the adopted VGG16 architecture are presented in Table 1. Features were extracted from the last two FCLs prior to the SoftMax layer.

Table 1. The network structure of VGG16 convolutional neural network used in this paper

Layer type	Kernel size	Output size
Conv 1	3 × 3,64 3 × 3,64	224 × 224 × 64
Max pool		112 × 112 × 64
Conv 2	3 × 3,128 3 × 3,128	112 × 112 × 128
Max pool		56 × 56 × 128
Conv 3	3 × 3,256 3 × 3,256 3 × 3,256	56 × 56 × 256
Max pool		28 × 28 × 256
Conv 4	3 × 3,512 3 × 3,512 3 × 3,512	28 × 28 × 512
Max pool		14 × 14 × 512
Conv 5	3 × 3,512 3 × 3,512 3 × 3,512	14 × 14 × 512
Max pool		7 × 7 × 512
FC-4096, FC-4096, FC-1000, softmax		

Table 2. The network structure of ResNet50 convolutional neural network used in this paper

Layer type	Kernel size	Output size
Conv 1	$7 \times 7 \times 3$	$112 \times 112 \times 64$
Max pool	3×3	56×56
Conv 2_x	$\left\{ \begin{array}{l} 1x1, 64 \\ 3x3, 64 \\ 1x1, 256 \end{array} \right\} \times 3$	56×56
Conv 3_x	$\left\{ \begin{array}{l} 1x1, 128 \\ 3x3, 128 \\ 1x1, 512 \end{array} \right\} \times 4$	28×28
Conv 4_x	$\left\{ \begin{array}{l} 1x1, 256 \\ 3x3, 256 \\ 1x1, 1024 \end{array} \right\} \times 6$	14×14
Conv 5_x	$\left\{ \begin{array}{l} 21x1, 512 \\ 3x3, 512 \\ 1x1, 2048 \end{array} \right\} \times 3$	7×7
Average pool		1×1
1000-d fc, softmax		

ResNet50. The ResNet network architecture was introduced by He et al. [22]. It is considered by some to be the state-of-the-art for CNN-based image recognition [4]. There are multiple versions of ResNetXX where 'XX' indicates the number of layers. The most commonly used, and that used with respect to the work presented in this paper, is ResNet50. The ResNet-50 architecture, as in the case of VGG16, requires a 224 × 224 × 3 pixel images as an input, and outputs a feature vector of size is 2048. The details of the adopted ResNet-50 architecture are given in Table 2, features were extracted from the last FCL prior to the SoftMax layer.

Inception-V3. The "Inception" micro-architecture was introduced by Szegedy et al. [48]. The original name of this architecture was GoogLeNet, but subsequent manifestations have simply been called Inception VN where N denotes the version number. Inception-V3 is that used in the context of this paper. The Inception-V3 architecture require 224 × 224 × 3 pixel images. The output feature vector is of size 2048. The details of the adopted Inception-V3 architecture are given in Table 3. Features were extracted from the last FCL prior to the SoftMax layer.

Table 3. The network structure of the Inception-v3 CNN used in this paper

Layer name	Patch size	Output size
Conv	3×3/2	149×149×32
Conv	3×3/1	147×147×32
Conv padded	3×3/1	147×147×64
Max Pool	3×3/2	73×73×64
Conv	3×3/1	71×71×80
Conv	3×3/2	35×35×192
Conv	3×3/1	35×35×288
3 × Inception	Module 1	17×17×768
5 × Inception	Module 2	8×8×1280
2 × Inception	Module 3	8 × 8 × 2048
Max Pool	8 × 8	1 × 1 × 2048
Linear, Logits, Softmax		

3.3 Dimensionality Reduction

Dimensionality Reduction (DR) is pre-processing step aimed at either reducing the number of features, thus reducing the resources required for classification model generation, or to aid in visualising the data before any analysis is performed. In the case of classification model generation DR is applied before model training is commenced [51]. From the previous section, 4096 features were extracted using VGG16, and 2048 using ResNet50 and Inception-V3. Thus DR was adopted in order to reduce the number of features, while attempting to keep as much of the variation in the original features set as possible. There are many algorithms that can be used for DR that can be categorised into two groups: linear algebra and manifold learning. In linear algebra the methods used examine the linear relationship between the variables, while in manifold learning non-linear approaches are used to capture more complex relationships between variables. For the work presented in this paper three methods were considered: (i) Principal Components Analysis (PCA) and (ii) Singular Value Decomposition (SVD) and T-distributed Stochastic Neighbor Embedding (T-SNE). The first two are linear algebra approaches and the third a manifold approach. In more detail:

- PCA conducts a linear combination of an existing large set of features so as to create a new set of features. These new features are referred to as "Principal Components". The aim is to capture as much information as possible in the smallest number of principal components.
- SVD decomposes the original features into three constituent matrices to remove redundant features. The twin concepts of Eigenvalues and Eigenvectors are used to calculate these matrices.

- T-SNE reduces the number of features by creating two or three new features. It calculates the probability similarity of points in a high dimensional space and uses this define a low dimensional space. Nearby points in the high dimensional space are then mapped to the nearest points in the low dimensional space.

3.4   Data Augmentation

The ECG image data set used for evaluation purposes was a binary-labelled, imbalanced, data set (see Subsect. 4.1 for more detail). To address this issue the minority class was augmented through the application of an oversampling technique. In "classic" oversampling, the minority data is simply duplicated. However, this will not add any new information. In [12] the Synthetic Minority Oversampling Technique (SMOTE) was presented, a technique which can be used to synthesize new examples from existing examples. For the work presented in this paper SMOTE was adopted. SMOTE operates by first selecting random records from the minority class and, for each selected record, the k-nearest neighbours. Synthetic data is then created using these "clusters". For the work presented in this paper three different SMOTE techniques were considered: (i) the original SMOTE, (ii) Support Vector Machine SMOTE (SVM-SMOTE) and (iii) Adaptive Synthetic Sampling (ADASYN):

- As noted above, the original SMOTE operates by first selecting random records from the minority class and, for each selected record the k-nearest neighbours. Synthetic data is then created using these "clusters".
- Using SVM-SMOTE, instead of using K-nearest neighbors, support vectors are used. Synthetic data is randomly created along the lines joining each minority class support vector with a number of its nearest neighbors.
- Using ADASYN data density is used to create synthetic data. Additional synthetic data is created in the "areas" where the minority class is less dense.

3.5   Feature Vector Generation

The last process in the proposed approach is the generation of a set of feature vectors $H = \{V_1, V_2, \dots\}$. Each $V_i \in H$ is of the form $\{v_1, v_2, \dots, c\}$ where v_i is a numerical features values extracted from an ECG scanned image. Interestingly v_i could also be a values obtained from some other source than the core ECG data. In the evaluation presented later in this paper the results of experiments are reported where age and gender are appended to H. For classification model training purposes a final element c, a class label taken from a set of classes C, is added to each $V_i \in H$. For the evaluation presented in Sect. 4, $|C| = 2$ was used. A previously unseen record will have a null value for the variable c as this is the value we wish to predict.

4   Evaluation

The evaluation of the proposed mechanism is presented in this section. For the evaluation the Guangzhou Heart Study data set was used [15]. Some detail concerning this data set is provided in Subsect. 4.1. Both SVM and KNN classification models were used for the evaluation with Grid Search to choose the best parameters: SVM (C, gamma and kernels) and KNN (neighbors, weights and p). The evaluation metrics used were accuracy, F1 and AUC; Ten-fold cross-validation was used throughout. The Friedman Test was used to determine whether or not there was a statistically significant difference between the performance of the models. Where a statistically significant difference was found, the Nemenyi post-hoc test was used to identify the distinctions between the performance of the mechanisms considered. The objectives of the evaluation were as follows:

1. To identify the most appropriate pre-trained CNN model, dimensionality reduction technique and data augmentation technique.
2. To compare the operation of the proposed approach when the feature set is appended with additional data.
3. To compare the operation of the proposed approach with other published approaches.

Each is discussed in further detail below in Subsects. 4.2, 4.3 and 4.4.

4.1   Data Set

As we require a scanned image dataset in this paper, The Guangzhou Heart Study data set is used, comprised 1172 patients (399 males, and 773 females) with a mean age of 71.4 years; each patient was associated with a 12-leads ECG scanned image and patient attributes, including age and gender. Each patient record had been labelled according to arrhythmia type, either sinus arrhythmia (normal) or abnormal. The abnormal category included: (i) Atrial Fibrillation (AF) and Flutter (AFL), (ii) premature atrial or ventricular contraction, (iii) Atrioventricular Block (AVB), (iv) ventricular tachycardia, (v) Supraventricular Tachycardia (SVT), (vi) Wolff-Parkinson-White syndrome (WPW), (vii) pacing rhythm and (viii) junctional rhythm. From the 1172 patients, 878 (74.9%) were classified as normal, and the remaining 294 (25.1%) as abnormal. The image resolution was 300 dpi (dots per inch) and each image was stored using JPEG compression. Ten cross validation was used throughout, thus on each run the training data comprised 1055 images, and the test data 117 images.

4.2   Best Combination of Techniques

From Sect. 3 the proposed approach incorporated three categories of technique:

– Feature extraction.

– Dimension reduction.
– Data augmentation.

Three different techniques were considered with respect to each. Experiments were conducted to identify the best technique in each case.

For the feature extraction VGG19, ResNet50 and Inception-v3 were considered (as described previously in Subsect. 3.2). Recall that for VGG the number of features was 4,096, and for ResNet50 and Inception-v3 the number of features was 2,048. We also considered the combination of the extracted features, because in [40] this had demonstrated good results. We ran the experiments using each feature vector set separately and in combination: (i) all models $(4,096 + 2,048 + 2,048 = 8192$ features), (ii) ResNet50 and VGG16 $(4,096 + 2,048 = 6144$ features), (iii) ResNet50 and Inception-v3 $(2,048 + 2,048 = 4096$ features) and (iv) VGG16 and Inception-v3 $(4,096 + 2,048 = 6144$ features). In all cases t-SNE was used for feature selection and SMOTE for record augmentation (to limit the number of combinations to be considered with respect to this first set of experiments). The results obtained are given in Table 4. From, the table, it can be seen that the best accuracy and AUC values were obtained using Resnet50 feature selection coupled with SVM classification (AUC of 94.21% and accuracy of 94.12). While when using kNN classification best results were obtained when all 8192 features were used in combination (AUC of 87.32% and accuracy of 87.70%). A subsequent Friedman Test indicated that there was a statistically significant difference in operation when using SVM classification, but not when using kNN classification. Figure 1 shows the result of a Nemenyi post-hoc test using SVM classification. From the figure it can be seen that the ResNet50 model has significant differences with all other models except with ResNet50+VGG16

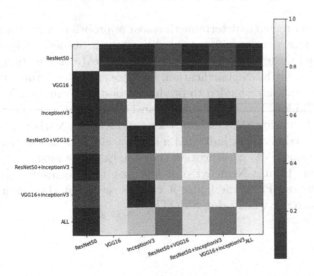

Fig. 1. Nemenyi post-hoc test for feature generation coupled with SVM classification

Table 4. SVM and KNN classification performance using a different pre-trained models features

Model/Classification	SVM			KNN		
	Accuracy %	F1 %	AUC %	Accuracy %	F1 %	AUC %
ResNet50	**94.21**	**93.64**	**94.12**	85.80	86.72	86.17
VGG16	89.34	89.56	89.47	85.32	86.29	84.62
InceptionV3	85.27	85.56	85.46	84.34	85.45	84.62
ResNet50+VGG16	89.97	89.89	90.06	85.38	86.37	85.75
ResNet50+InceptionV3	88.07	88.34	88.20	86.11	87.00	86.46
VGG16+InceptionV3	89.96	90.30	90.1	87.01	87.75	87.27
ResNet50+VGG16+InceptionV3	88.39	88.49	88.48	**87.32**	**87.80**	**87.70**

($p = .25$) and VGG16 +InceptionV3 ($p = 0.20$). It was thus concluded that for feature extraction ResNet50 was the most appropriate choice.

For the experiments to determine the best dimensionality reduction technique the three alternatives discussed in Subsect. 3.3 were considered: (i) T-SNE, (ii) SVD and (iii) PCA. Table 5 shows the results obtained using ResNet50 feature selection (because the experiments reported above indicated that this produced the best results) and SMOTE augmentation (to limit the number of combinations to consider). Results are given using both SVM and kNN classification. Inspection of the table indicates that best values were obtained using T-SNE, while PCA caused over-fitting regardless of whether SVM or kNN classification was used. It was thus concluded that for feature selection T-SNE was the most appropriate choice.

For the experiments to determine the most appropriate augmentation method three alternatives were considered (as discussed in Subsect. 3.4). Experiments were conducted using ResNet50 and t-SNE for SVM classification, and all features and t-SNE for KNN classification; because earlier experiments (see above) had indicated that these tended to produce a best performance. The results are presented in Table 6. From the table it can be seen that SMOTE produced the best results when using SVM classification, and ADASYN when using kNN classification. A Friedman Test indicated a statistically significant difference in the results when using SVM classification (not the case when using kNN). Figure 2, show the result from a Nemenyi post-hoc test for the results obtained using SVM classification. From the figure it can be seen that there is a statistically significant difference when using SMOTE.

Table 5. SVM and KNN classification performance using a range of features selection techniques

Technique/Classification	SVM			KNN		
	Accuracy %	F1 %	AUC %	Accuracy %	F1 %	AUC %
T-SNE	**94.21**	**94.19**	**94.12**	**87.32**	**87.80**	**87.70**
SVD	63.10	62.66	63.16	68.03	49.12	64.39
PCA	Overfitting			Overfitting		

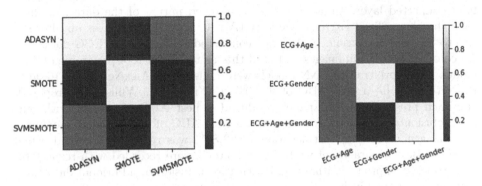

Fig. 2. Nemenyi post-hoc test for augmentation techniques and SVM classification

Fig. 3. Nemenyi post-hoc for all models with SVM classifier

4.3 Analysis of the Effect of Adding Additional Data

The previous sub-section described the experiments conducted to determine the best feature extraction, feature selection and augmentation techniques for processing ECG image data to support ECG classification. Best results were obtained using ResNet50 feature extraction, T-SNE feature selection and SMOTE data augmentation. Further experiments were conducted to determine whether any advantage could be gained by adding additional features from related sources. To this end age and gender were added to the generated feature vector for each ECG (note that each ECG in the data set was related to a single patient). Similar experiments were conducted in [2]; but in the 1D, time series, context.

The results are presented in Table 7. From the table, and with reference to Table 6, it can be seem that adding patient age improves the effectiveness of the classification, an AUC of 95.17 using SVM, and 89.15 using KNN (compared to 94.12 and 87.70 respectively, when not adding additional information). Gender has a less pronounced effect. Figure 3 shows the result of Nemenyi post-hoc test applied to all models for SVM classification after a Friedman Test reported that there was a statistically significant difference. From the figure it can be seen that there was a statistically significant difference between using ECG + age +

gender and ECG + gender; thus adding age has prominent effect on performance. In the KNN case, the Friedman Test indicated that there was no statistically significant difference between the models ($p = 1.0$).

4.4 Comparison of Approaches

The experimental results obtained, using the proposed approach, were also compared those obtained in recently published work directed at the same data set, namely the work presented in [9] and [16]. In [9], they fine-tuned an Inception-v3 pre-trained model to extract features which were than classified using a dense, fully connected layer. To address the imbalanced nature of the data set, they used the Generalized Extreme Value (GEV) activation function as an alternative to Sigmoid activation. In [16] they converted 1D time-series ECG data into 2D colour spectrogram images and used this as the input to a pre-trained CNN model. Three pre-trained CNN models were considered: AlexNet, VGG-16, and ResNet-18. In [9] a best AUC of 93.20% was reported. Whilst the proposed approach presented in this paper produced a best AUC of 94.12% with out the inclusion pf additional features, and a best AUC of 96.07% when including age and gender. In [16] best accuracy of 83.82% was reported, obtained using AlexNet. Best accuracies of 94.21% and 96.06% were recorded with respect to the proposed approach without and with the inclusion of additional data (age and gender) respectively.

Table 6. SVM and KNN classification performance using a range of data augmentation techniques

Technique/Classification	SVM			KNN		
	Accuracy %	F1 %	AUC %	Accuracy %	F1 %	AUC %
SMOTE	**94.21**	**94.19**	**94.12**	87.32	87.80	87.70
ADASYN	91.69	91.19	91.69	**88.46**	**81.11**	**88.82**
SVMSMOTE	88.99	85.73	88.69	87.58	80.82	88.23

Table 7. SVM and KNN classification performance when adding additional data

Technique/Classification	SVM			KNN		
	Accuracy %	F1 %	AUC %	Accuracy %	F1 %	AUC %
ECG + Age	95.19	94.98	95.17	88.97	89.13	89.15
ECG + Gender	94.45	94.06	94.38	88.49	89.13	88.86
ECG + Age + Gender	**96.06**	**95.92**	**96.07**	**89.01**	**89.46**	**89.37**

Finally, in the introduction to this paper, the disadvantages of using 1D waveform representations of ECG data was noted. It was hypothesised that using 2D image directly to extract the features would produce a better classification than that obtained using features selected from 1D transformed waveform representations of ECG data. Accordingly, the scanned images were transformed into a time series format using a recent algorithm for achieving this [18]. Once the image set had been transformed the 1D motif approach proposed in [3] was used to extract features. An accuracy of 72.35% was obtained using the 1D approach, compared that with 94.21% and 96.06% accuracies obtained using the proposed approach (without and with the inclusion of age and gender).

5   Conclusion

An approach to classifying ECG image data using a pre-trained CNN model to extract features has been presented. The motivation for the work was the observation that most ECG data is still in paper format. For classification purposes this paper ECG data is typically processed by first scanning into a digital format, from which time series are generated, from which a small number of features (P-QRS-T wave features) are extracted, which are then used to build a classification model. This chain of processes introduces a range of irregularities and noise. To reduce this chain it was suggested that 2D features, extracted directly from the scanned images, could be used; and that features be extracted using some form of CNN. It was also noted that the amount of data available is frequently insufficient to build a CNN. Hence it was proposed to use a pre-trained CNN model. Three CNN models were considered for the feature extraction, together with three feature selection mechanisms. It was also noted that the data available tends to be imbalanced; typically we have more examples of ECGs for patients with a CVD than without (individuals tend to only have ECGs taken when a CVD is suspected). A range of augmentation techniques were considered. The presented evaluation demonstrated that best results were obtained using ResNet50 feature extraction, T-SNE feature selection and SMOTE data augmentation. Experiments were also conducted to investigate the effect of adding additional features obtained from elsewhere (age and gender) and this was found to provide an improved result. A best AUC of 96.07 was obtained. Comparison was made with existing work, that presented in [9] and [16]. The results indicated that the proposed approach outperformed these existing approaches. Finally comparison was undertaken with a 1D technique indicating that the motivating hypothesis was correct.

References

1. Acharya, U.R., et al.: A deep convolutional neural network model to classify heart-beats. Comput. Biol. Med. **89**, 389–396 (2017)
2. Aldosari, H., Coenen, F., Lip, G.Y., Zheng, Y.: Addressing the challenge of data heterogeneity using a homogeneous feature vector representation: a study using time series and cardiovascular disease classification. In: International Conference on Innovative Techniques and Applications of Artificial Intelligence, pp. 254–266. Springer (2021). https://doi.org/10.1007/978-3-030-91100-3_21
3. Aldosari, H., Coenen, F., Lip, G.Y.H., Zheng, Y.: Motif based feature vectors: towards a homogeneous data representation for cardiovascular diseases classification. In: Golfarelli, M., Wrembel, R., Kotsis, G., Tjoa, A.M., Khalil, I. (eds.) DaWaK 2021. LNCS, vol. 12925, pp. 235–241. Springer, Cham (2021). https://doi.org/10.1007/978-3-030-86534-4_22
4. Almabdy, S., Elrefaei, L.: Deep convolutional neural network-based approaches for face recognition. Appl. Sci. **9**(20), 4397 (2019)
5. Annam, J.R., Kalyanapu, S., Ch, S., Somala, J., Raju, S.B.: Classification of ECG heartbeat arrhythmia: a review. Procedia Comput. Sci. **171**, 679–688 (2020)
6. Awais, M., et al.: Can pre-trained convolutional neural networks be directly used as a feature extractor for video-based neonatal sleep and wake classification? BMC Res. Notes **13**(1), 1–6 (2020)
7. Badilini, F., Erdem, T., Zareba, W., Moss, A.J.: ECGScan: a method for conversion of paper electrocardiographic printouts to digital electrocardiographic files. J. Electrocardiol. **38**(4), 310–318 (2005)
8. Baydoun, M., Safatly, L., Hassan, O.K.A., Ghaziri, H., El Hajj, A., Isma'eel, H.: High precision digitization of paper-based ECG records: a step toward machine learning. IEEE J. Transl. Eng. Health Med. **7**, 1–8 (2019)
9. Bridge, J., Fu, L., Lin, W., Xue, Y., Lip, G.Y., Zheng, Y.: Artificial intelligence to detect abnormal heart rhythm from scanned electrocardiogram tracings. J. Arrhythmia (2022)
10. Brisk, R., et al.: Deep learning to automatically interpret images of the electrocardiogram: do we need the raw samples? J. Electrocardiol. **57**, S65–S69 (2019)
11. Cao, Q., et al.: Practical fine-grained learning based anomaly classification for ECG image. Artif. Intell. Med. **119**, 102130 (2021)
12. Chawla, N.V., Bowyer, K.W., Hall, L.O., Kegelmeyer, W.P.: SMOTE: synthetic minority over-sampling technique. J. Artif. Intell. Res. **16**, 321–357 (2002)
13. Chung, D., et al.: Construction of an electrocardiogram database including 12 lead waveforms. Healthc. Inform. Res. **24**(3), 242–246 (2018)
14. Cuocolo, R., Perillo, T., De Rosa, E., Ugga, L., Petretta, M.: Current applications of big data and machine learning in cardiology. J. Geriatr. Cardiol.: JGC **16**(8), 601 (2019)
15. Deng, H., et al.: Epidemiological characteristics of atrial fibrillation in southern China: results from the Guangzhou heart study. Scienti. Rep. **8**(1), 1–10 (2018)
16. Diker, A., Cömert, Z., Avcı, E., Toğaçar, M., Ergen, B.: A novel application based on spectrogram and convolutional neural network for ECG classification. In: 2019 1st International Informatics and Software Engineering Conference (UBMYK), pp. 1–6. IEEE (2019)
17. Ebrahimi, Z., Loni, M., Daneshtalab, M., Gharehbaghi, A.: A review on deep learning methods for ECG arrhythmia classification. Expert Syst. Appl.: X **7**, 100033 (2020)

18. Fortune, J., Coppa, N., Haq, K.T., Patel, H., Tereshchenko, L.G.: Digitizing ECG image: new fully automated method and open-source software code. medRxiv (2021)
19. Gupta, D., Bajpai, B., Dhiman, G., Soni, M., Gomathi, S., Mane, D.: Review of ECG arrhythmia classification using deep neural network. Materials Today: Proceedings (2021)
20. Gupta, V., Mittal, M., Mittal, V., Saxena, N.K.: A critical review of feature extraction techniques for ECG signal analysis. J. Instit. Eng. (India): Series B 1–12 (2021). https://doi.org/10.1007/s40031-021-00606-5
21. Hadiyoso, S., Fahrozi, F., Hariyani, Y.S., Sulistiyo, M.D.: Image based ECG signal classification using convolutional neural network. Int. J. Online Biomed. Eng. **16**(4) (2022)
22. He, K., Zhang, X., Ren, S., Sun, J.: Deep residual learning for image recognition. In: Proceedings of the IEEE Conference on Computer Vision and Pattern Recognition, pp. 770–778 (2016)
23. Holkeri, A., et al.: Experiences in digitizing and digitally measuring a paper-based ECG archive. J. Electrocardiol. **51**(1), 74–81 (2018)
24. Houssein, E.H., Kilany, M., Hassanien, A.E.: ECG signals classification: a review. Int. J. Intell. Eng. Inform. **5**(4), 376–396 (2017)
25. Izci, E., Ozdemir, M.A., Degirmenci, M., Akan, A.: Cardiac arrhythmia detection from 2D ECG images by using deep learning technique. In: 2019 Medical Technologies Congress (TIPTEKNO), pp. 1–4. IEEE (2019)
26. Jayaraman, S., Swamy, P., Damodaran, V., Venkatesh, N.: A novel technique for ECG morphology interpretation and arrhythmia detection based on time series signal extracted from scanned ECG record. Advances in Electrocardiograms-Methods and Analysis, pp. 127–140 (2012)
27. Ji, Y., Zhang, S., Xiao, W.: Electrocardiogram classification based on faster regions with convolutional neural network. Sensors **19**(11), 2558 (2019)
28. Jun, T.J., Nguyen, H.M., Kang, D., Kim, D., Kim, D., Kim, Y.H.: ECG arrhythmia classification using a 2-D convolutional neural network. arXiv preprint arXiv:1804.06812 (2018)
29. Kar, A., Das, L.: A technical review on statistical feature extraction of ECG signal. In: IJCA Special Issue on 2nd National Conference-Computing, Communication and Sensor Network, CCSN, pp. 35–40 (2011)
30. Khleaf, H.K., Ghazali, K.H., Abdalla, A.N.: Features extraction technique for ECG recording paper. In: Proceeding of the International Conference on Artificial Intelligence in Computer Science and ICT (2013)
31. Kim, J.S., Kim, S.H., Pan, S.B.: Personal recognition using convolutional neural network with ECG coupling image. J. Ambient. Intell. Humaniz. Comput. **11**(5), 1923–1932 (2020)
32. Kiranyaz, S., Ince, T., Gabbouj, M.: Real-time patient-specific ECG classification by 1-D convolutional neural networks. IEEE Trans. Biomed. Eng. **63**(3), 664–675 (2015)
33. Li, C., et al.: DeepECG: image-based electrocardiogram interpretation with deep convolutional neural networks. Biomed. Signal Process. Control **69**, 102824 (2021)
34. Litjens, G., et al.: A survey on deep learning in medical image analysis. Med. Image Anal. **42**, 60–88 (2017)
35. Liu, X., Wang, H., Li, Z., Qin, L.: Deep learning in ECG diagnosis: a review. Knowl.-Based Syst. **227**, 107187 (2021)

36. Loresco, P.J.M., Africa, A.D.: ECG print-out features extraction using spatial-oriented image processing techniques. J. Telecommun. Electron. Comput. Eng. (JTEC) **10**(1–5), 15–20 (2018)
37. Mathunjwa, B.M., Lin, Y.T., Lin, C.H., Abbod, M.F., Shieh, J.S.: ECG arrhythmia classification by using a recurrence plot and convolutional neural network. Biomed. Signal Process. Control **64**, 102262 (2021)
38. Mir, H.Y., Singh, O.: ECG denoising and feature extraction techniques-a review. J. Med. Eng. Technol. **45**(8), 672–684 (2021)
39. Mishra, S., et al.: ECG paper record digitization and diagnosis using deep learning. J. Med. Biol. Eng. 1–11 (2021). https://doi.org/10.1007/s40846-021-00632-0
40. Naz, M., Shah, J.H., Khan, M.A., Sharif, M., Raza, M., Damaševičius, R.: From ECG signals to images: a transformation based approach for deep learning. Peer J. Comput. Sci. **7**, e386 (2021)
41. O'Keefe, J.H., Hammill, S.C., Freed, M.S., Pogwizd, S.: The Complete guide to ECGs: a comprehensive study guide to improve ECG interpretation skills. Jones & Bartlett Learning (2017)
42. Rajpurkar, P., Hannun, A.Y., Haghpanahi, M., Bourn, C., Ng, A.Y.: Cardiologist-level arrhythmia detection with convolutional neural networks. arXiv preprint arXiv:1707.01836 (2017)
43. Ravichandran, L., Harless, C., Shah, A.J., Wick, C.A., Mcclellan, J.H., Tridandapani, S.: Novel tool for complete digitization of paper electrocardiography data. IEEE J. Transl. Eng. Health Med. **1**, 1800107–1800107 (2013)
44. Salem, M., Taheri, S., Yuan, J.S.: ECG arrhythmia classification using transfer learning from 2-dimensional deep CNN features. In: 2018 IEEE Biomedical Circuits and Systems Conference (BioCAS), pp. 1–4. IEEE (2018)
45. Sarvamangala, D., Kulkarni, R.V.: Convolutional neural networks in medical image understanding: a survey. Evolut. Intell. 1–22 (2021). https://doi.org/10.1007/s12065-020-00540-3
46. Seena, V., Yomas, J.: A review on feature extraction and denoising of ECG signal using wavelet transform. In: 2014 2nd International Conference on Devices, Circuits and Systems (ICDCS), pp. 1–6. IEEE (2014)
47. Simonyan, K., Zisserman, A.: Very deep convolutional networks for large-scale image recognition. arXiv preprint arXiv:1409.1556 (2014)
48. Szegedy, C., et al.: Going deeper with convolutions. In: Proceedings of the IEEE Conference on Computer Vision and Pattern Recognition, pp. 1–9 (2015)
49. Thanapatay, D., Suwansaroj, C., Thanawattano, C.: ECG beat classification method for ECG printout with principle components analysis and support vector machines. In: 2010 International Conference on Electronics and Information Engineering, vol. 1, pp. V1–72. IEEE (2010)
50. Ullah, A., Anwar, S.M., Bilal, M., Mehmood, R.M.: Classification of arrhythmia by using deep learning with 2-D ECG spectral image representation. Remote Sens. **12**(10), 1685 (2020)
51. Velliangiri, S., Alagumuthukrishnan, S., et al.: A review of dimensionality reduction techniques for efficient computation. Procedia Comput. Sci. **165**, 104–111 (2019)
52. Weimann, K., Conrad, T.O.: Transfer learning for ECG classification. Sci. Rep. **11**(1), 1–12 (2021)
53. Yıldırım, Ö., Pławiak, P., Tan, R.S., Acharya, U.R.: Arrhythmia detection using deep convolutional neural network with long duration ECG signals. Comput. Biol. Med. **102**, 411–420 (2018)

AI for Scientific Discovery and Decision Making

Bootstrapping Neural Electronics from Lunar Resources for In-Situ Artificial Intelligence Applications

Alex Ellery[✉]

Carleton University, Ottawa, ON K1S 5B6, Canada
`aellery@mae.carleton.ca`

Abstract. Artificial intelligence and robotics are leveraging technologies for lunar exploration. However, future lunar surface exploration will require exploitation of in-situ resources to reduce (and ultimately eliminate) the costs imposed by the transport of materiel from Earth. Solid-state manufacturing of electronics assets from lunar resources to eliminate its supply from Earth is impractical. We propose the in-situ manufacture of vacuum tube-based computational electronics which requires only a handful of materials that are available on the Moon. To offset the problem of exponential growth in physical footprint in CPU-based electronics, we propose the implementation of analogue neural network hardware which has Turing machine capabilities. We suggest that the artificial intelligence requirements for lunar industrialisation ecology can be demonstrated in principle by analogue neural networks controlling a small rover. We pay particular attention to online learning circuitry as the key to adaptability of analogue neural networks.

Keywords: Analogue neural network hardware · Turing machine models · Lunar in-situ resource utilisation · Neural network rover navigation

1 Introduction

Everyone is choosing to go the Moon, not because it is easy, but because it has potentially useful resources. Current interest in in-situ resource utilisation (ISRU) on the Moon is based on recovering water ice at the polar regions ostensibly to support a human presence. The advent of commercial, government and other interests towards lunar resources leads to a loose confederation of private and government installations on the Moon, the "Moon Village". However, rather than adopting ISRU as an addendum to human bases on the Moon, we are interested in leveraging lunar resources as a *modus operandi* for total lunar industrialisation as independent of Earth as is feasible, i.e. to bootstrap an entire infrastructure from lunar resources. A crucial backbone to this notion is the ability to construct machines of production rather than products *per se* from lunar resources Any kinematic machine – be they load-haul-dump rovers, CNC milling machines, 3D printers or assembly manipulators as the machines of production - comprises specific configurations of electric motors supported by control systems capable of universal computation.

© The Author(s), under exclusive license to Springer Nature Switzerland AG 2022
M. Bramer and F. Stahl (Eds.): SGAI-AI 2022, LNAI 13652, pp. 83–97, 2022.
https://doi.org/10.1007/978-3-031-21441-7_6

It is the latter that is of concern here. A general approach to exploiting in-situ resources on the Moon involves extracting around 10 materials sufficient to realise all basic functional subsystems of a spacecraft – a demandite list extracted through a lunar industrial ecology [1, 2] which feeds into a generalised metal extraction system [3]. Two examples of utilities that can be leveraged from such in-situ resources are an energy infrastructure [4] and lunar bases [5]. We wish specifically to construct computational resources from in-situ resources on the Moon. An important consideration is that we cannot import Earth technology with all its complex supply chains to the extraterrestrial environment. Any technology we employ on the Moon must have a robust lunar supply chain with minimal reliance on Earth. So it must be with lunar computers which must function in a thermally hostile and radiation-saturated environment. We cannot simply shoehorn terrestrial technologies wholesale to the Moon it is premised on the entire globally-interconnected industrial complex on Earth. A mobile phone for instance comprises over 30 different materials for different functional components – each material must be mined, extracted, refined, mixed, formed and assembled. The manufacturing process assumes a bevy of reagents and high precision terrestrial facilities. The in-situ lunar environment imposes severe constraints on the availability of material and infrastructure resources. Here, we focus on using lunar resources to construct neural electronics capabilities in-situ as a step towards full self-sufficiency of computer technology necessary to realise artificial intelligence functions. The implementation of solid-state computers would be impossible from lunar resources due to [6]: (i) paucity of common reagents used in solid-state manufacture; (ii) stringently controlled environmental conditions required in solid-state manufacture; (iii) extreme temperatures required for solid-state manufacture; (vi) unsuitability of solid-state electronics to severe thermal and radiation environments extant on the Moon; (v) extreme cost of electronics foundries. Furthermore, given the paucity of plastic ingredients – carbon in particular – and exotic metals on the Moon suggest that approaches using organic polymers, nanoparticles or exotic metals cannot be substituted on the Moon. We must adopt a new engineering philosophy that exploits technologies derived from the available materials.

2   Modes of Computation

We propose thermionic vacuum tubes as an alternative to transistors because they comprise of only a small number of materials configured into a relatively simple construction, all of which can be sourced from the Moon. A vacuum tube is simple in construction – a tungsten cathode that emits electrons attracted to a nickel anode controlled by a third nickel grid electrode encased in an evacuated glass or ceramic tube and linked by silicone or ceramic-insulated kovar wiring. Fused silica glass encapsulation may be derived from lunar anorthite), aluminum wire from lunar anorthite, high temperature kovar wiring from nickel-iron meteorites, tungsten filament cathodes from nickel-iron meteorites coated with calcium oxide and alumina from lunar anorthite, and nickel anodes and control grids from nickel-iron meteorites. Only a small number of materials are required and are readily extracted from lunar resources. The chief problem resides in that vacuum tube-based computers are cumbersome – ENIAC used almost 17,500 vacuum tubes, over 7000 diodes, 1500 relays, 70,000 resistors and 10,000 capacitors with a mass of over 25 tonnes covering an area of almost $170 \, m^2$ and consumed $150 \, kW$ of power. Clearly, the enormity of such a computer renders this approach infeasible for a lunar infrastructure. This is a direct result of the von Neumann central processing unit (CPU)-based architecture. The core of the CPU is one or more arithmetic logic units (ALU), each a combinatorial logic circuit for performing arithmetic operations (addition, subtraction, negate, increment/decrement and sign) and bitwise logical operations (AND, OR, EX-OR and NOT) on 4-bit, 8-bit, 16-bit, 32-bit or 64-bit data widths. For example, the modest embedded 8051 CPU comprises 2,200 logic gates but modern computers comprise ~500 million logic gates. The von Neumann architecture stores data in a variety of different memory locations which must be fetched as input data to the CPU and the results of which must be pushed back into memory. The basic operation of the von Neumann architecture is the fetch-decode-execute cycle which is wasteful in hardware footprint and energy. There are alternative Turing machine-equivalent approaches to computation. We have adopted a neural network architecture implemented as electronics of such a machine. This was driven by several constraints: (1) limited material availability on the Moon for electronics manufacture, (2) superiority over the traditional von Neumann architecture in terms of Turing computability, (3) superiority of neural architectures over von Neumann architectures in terms of physical footprint.

3 3D Printer-Based Turing Machine

To address the problem of 3D printing computing machines, we revert to the original Turing machine model of a computer. Our implementation of a Turing machine comprises an input tape represented by magnetic core memory rather than a magnetic tape, an output tape represented by an analogue neural network circuit and a read/write head represented by a generic 3D printer (Fig. 1).

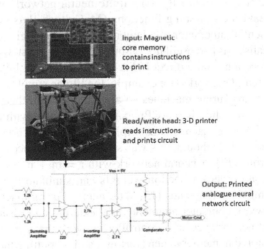

Fig. 1. Turing machine model with magnetic core memory (input tape), neural net circuit (output tape) and 3D printer (read/write head).

Magnetic core memory comprises the same basic components as a DC electric motor – 3D printing of such has been demonstrated [7]. Magnetic core memory uses ferrite magnetic cores (toroids) through which wires are passed to convey read and write signals. Each core stores 1 bit of information non-volatilely as zero or one depending on the direction of the core's magnetisation. The coincident current system enables a small number of wires to control a large number of cores in 3D stacks. A large number of small ferrite toroidal cores are held on layers of XY grids of wires through the toroidal centres. Only where the combined magnetic field from X and Y lines cross exceeds the threshold will the magnetic polarity reverse. Magnetic core memory offers high reliability and was used for the Apollo Guidance Computer and Space Shuttle Flight Computers. An automated assembler machine based on a four-axis cartesian (x,y,z,R) gantry that positions two tooling heads with respect to a worktable constitutes a possible model of the 3D printer [8]. The tooling heads position standard parts for assembly with compliance to accommodate small positioning errors. A punch-press was used for fabricating the modular boards of electrical insulator FR4 fibreglass-epoxy composite. A wire-electric discharge machine was used for fabricating electrically conducting tin-plated phosphor-bronze alloy wire. Together, these two materials constituted the modules for the assembly of electrical circuits. In our Turing machine model, the 3D printer thus becomes a central component of universal computation that operates in much the same way as a Jacquard loom – it prints out analogue neural network hardware circuitry according to the program stored in magnetic core memory as its output.

We must now consider the 3D printed output circuitry. For our output tape, we have adopted the artificial neural network whose architectural complexity grows only logarithmically with space and time resource requirements compared with the exponential growth in von Neumann architectures – any function that can be computed by logic gates of size z and depth d can be computed by a neural network of depth $d/e\log(z)$ and size $O(z^{1+e})$ with error $e > 0$ [9]. Neural networks are capable of implementing logic and arithmetic functions directly: (i) a finite neural network of discrete neurons characterised by Heaviside squashing functions (McCulloch-Pitts neurons) is equivalent to a finite sequential automaton implementing Boolean logic gates [10]; (ii) the half-adder can be realised as two oscillator output neurons cross-strapped to their inputs with excitatory connections and a direct bidirectional inhibitory link between the two neurons. Recurrent neural networks (for example, the Elman simple recurrent neural net is a Moore machine) are Turing machines so any computation that can be performed by a von Neumann architecture-based CPU can be performed with a recurrent neural network. A universal Turing machine was implemented on a recurrent neural network comprising 886 neurons [11] though this was subsequently reduced to 96 then 25 and finally to just 9 neurons [12]. A neural network with $r = m + n + 2$ layers of neurons and two sets of second order connection weights can simulate in real-time a Turing machine with m-symbols and n-states [13]. The neural Turing machine is based on a recurrent neural network computer augmented by external addressable memory [14]. The recurrent neural network acts as a controller network that performs processing of input data and data stored in memory, then storing it and outputting the results. Content-based addressing through partial similarity matching of vectors simplifies data retrieval from the external memory. Like recurrent neural networks in general, the neural Turing machine can be trained through gradient descent learning.

There is a bio-inspired rationale to the adoption of analogue neurons – neocortical neurons exhibit the multistability of digital flipflop circuits with the graded response of analogue circuits modulated by positive feedback gain in its recurrent connections [15]. These neuromorphic computing architectures favour analogue electronics with digital encoding implemented as integrate-and-fire (spiking) neurons rather than McCulloch-Pitts neurons [16]. However, we do not address spiking neurons here. The physical circuit footprint of analogue electronics is often more efficient *ceteris paribus* than digital architectures. Analogue neural networks implement asynchronous event-driven computing eliminating the processor clock and reducing power consumption. They are more tolerant of low-accuracy components than conventional logic-based computation. Although analogue circuits suffer from noise and parameter variations, they offer high speed and low energy consumption. The use of physical neural networks through its synaptic weights co-locating data memory and data processing in massively parallel architectures such as SpiNNaker (spiking neural network architecture) eliminate the von Neumann bottleneck of CPUs and GPUs which waste energy [17]. In-memory computing may be based on crossbar arrays of memory cells that conduct analogue multiply-accumulate operations typical of a neural network of neurons [18].

4 Analogue Neural Network Learning Circuitry

Online learning is a highly desirable capability – indeed, it is essential for compensating for unreliable components, a trait of analogue circuitry. In general, neural learning involves weight update $w_{ij}(t + 1) = w_{ij}(t) + \eta \delta_{ij} x_{ij}$ performed at each iteration until the output of the neural network minimised the error from the desired outputs $\delta_{ij}^{out} = (x_{ij}^d - x_{ij}) x_{ij} (1 - x_{ij})$. Implementing neural learning through weight update with analogue circuitry represents a challenge. A simple learning algorithm is the Madaline rule II (MRII) which implements feedforward neural network training so that weight changes are minimized [19] – MRII extends the MR I to multilayer networks. This is the minimum disturbance principle. All weights are set to small random values and training patterns are then presented in random order. In response to an output error in the network, the MRII algorithm selects first layer neuron with the lowest output value and reverses it. The network output error is checked again: if the network output error is reduced, the weight change is accepted, otherwise the original weight is restored. This process continues with first layer neurons with increasing output values until all the output errors are corrected. If all the output errors are not zero, the procedure is then applied to pairs of first layer neurons beginning with those with outputs close to zero. Then it may be applied to trios of neurons, etc. After the first layer has been exhaustively tested, the second layer may be tested, etc. depending on the number of layers. Once completed, the previous training patterns must be re-applied in random order to prevent oscillations. Although a painstaking process in comparison with backpropagation, it is nevertheless readily implemented in analogue electronics. These suffer from nonlinear distortions which motivated the MR III algorithm which does not require the derivative of the error function. The weight update is given by a least square algorithm based on mean square error as the performance index:

$$w_{i+1} = w_i + \Delta w_i = w_i - \eta\left(\frac{\Delta e_i^2}{\Delta s}\right) = w_i - 2\eta e_i\left(\frac{\partial e_i}{\partial s}\right) = w_i + 2\eta e_i\left(\frac{\partial y_i}{\partial s_i}\right) \quad (1)$$

where $\Delta e_i = -\Delta y_i$, $e_i = y_i^d - y_i$ = output error. This is the Widrow-Hoff rule which may be simplified to eliminate the need for linear multipliers at the cost of slower convergence:

$$w_{i+1} = w_i + 2\eta sgn(e_i)sgn(\nabla y_i) \quad (2)$$

In this case, DC offsets may appear which require adaptive cancellation using a number of analogue approaches at the cost of physical footprint [20]. An analogue implementation of neural learning through gradient descent was presented composed of integrators, summers, comparators and multipliers [21]. A simple Hebbian learning rule has been implemented as voltage activations on a series of circuits – V_{ij} multiplier - $w_{ij}V_j$ multiplier - summer - V_i neuron multiplier circuits [22]:

$$V_i = f\left(\sum_j w_{ij}V_j\right) \quad (3)$$

$$\frac{dw_{ij}}{dt} \propto \frac{dV_{ij}}{dt} = aV_iV_j - bw_{ij} \quad (4)$$

where k, a, b = small constants, f(.) = sigmoidal activation function, V_i = voltage on post-synaptic neuron i, V_j = voltage on pre-synaptic neurons j synapsing on neuron i. The second term represents weight decay that may be set to zero as b = 0. Wide-range Gilbert multipliers output a current that is proportional to the product of the input voltages: $I_0 = a\left(\frac{V_1-V_2}{V_3-V_4}\right)$. The summer outputs a current that is proportional to the sum of inputs based on Kirchoff's laws. The synaptic weight w_{ij} may be represented as a voltage V_{ij} on a capacitor: $V_{ij} = \frac{I_c}{C} \propto V_iV_j$. . The non-linear function f(.) exploits the saturation behaviour of the neuron multiplier. An analogue circuit block that implements backpropagation without clock synchronisation has been devised in which synaptic weights are stored as voltages in capacitors $V_w(t) = V_w(0) + \frac{1}{C}\int_o^T I(t)dt = V_w(0) - \frac{K}{C}\int_o^T \frac{\partial E(t)}{\partial V_w(t)}dt$ where K = conductance coefficient, the charging of which imposes time delays [23]. Learning was implemented with analogue circuit feedback. Analogue multiple voltage input lines with sample-and-hold circuits may implement input voltages as modifiable synaptic weights which may be adjusted more easily than resistance weights [24]. During learning, input voltage is varied but during operations, connection weights are held in the sample-and sold circuit. Online backpropagation offers the potential for continuous online learning [25]. An electrical circuit representation of the more complex backpropagation learning algorithm has been derived [26]. The backpropagation algorithm of the multilayer perceptron adjusts its weights (conductances) by gradient descent:

$$w_{ih}(t+1) = w_{ij}(t) - \eta\frac{\partial e}{\partial w_{ij}} \quad (5)$$

where $e = \frac{1}{2}(y^d - y)^2$, $\frac{\partial e}{\partial w_{ij}} = \frac{\partial e}{\partial y}\frac{\partial y}{\partial w_{ij}} = (y^d - y)\frac{\partial t}{\partial w_{ij}}$, , f'(.).) = sigmoid function, y = network output, V_i^k = neuron voltage output from ith neuron of kth layer. The output sensitivity of the multilayer perceptron is given by:

$$\frac{\partial y}{\partial w_{ij}(k)} = V_i^{k-1}\Delta V_j^k = V_i^{k-1}f'(V_j^k)I_j^k = V_i^{k-1}f'(V_j^k)\sum_m w_{mj}^{k1}y_m^{k+1}(1 - y_m^{k+1}) \quad (6)$$

The incremental connection weight may be represented by:

$$\Delta w_{ij}(t) = -\eta\frac{\partial e}{\partial w_{ij}(t)} \quad (7)$$

where $\eta = RC$ = settling time constant. The implementation of the backpropagation algorithm on physical neural networks offers both speed of learning and high energy efficiencies [27]. To avoid complex computations of derivative of the error function required of the delta rule, the Madaline III rule implements gradient estimation based on node perturbation:

$$\Delta w_{ij} = \frac{\partial E}{\partial f\left(\sum_j w_{ij}x_j\right)}x_j \quad (8)$$

where f(.) = nonlinear squashing function. This requires wire routing to each neuron, multiplication hardware and addressing logic. Rather than node perturbation, weight perturbation may be employed with less hardware. Analogue VLSI implementation of feedforward and recurrent neural networks may implement on-chip learning through gradient estimation through finite differences as an approximation to backpropagation [28]. The weight update rule involves a constant weight perturbation $pert_{ij}$ and is given by the finite difference which can be mapped onto an analogue implementation:

$$\Delta w_{ij} = \frac{E(w_{ij} + pert_{ij}) - E(w_{ij})}{pert_{ij}} \quad (9)$$

where E = total mean square error. Analogue implementation measures the errors with unperturbed and perturbed weights, subtracts them and multiplies by a constant. No backpropagation flow is necessary. A similar version applies simultaneous weight perturbations to compute central difference approximations to the differential of the error in parallel [29]:

$$\Delta w_{ij} = \frac{E\left(w_{ij} + \frac{1}{2}pert_{ij}\right) - E\left(w_{ij} - \frac{1}{2}pert_{ij}\right)}{pert_{ij}} \quad (10)$$

The learning rule thence becomes: $w_{ij}(t + 1) = w_{ij}(t) - \eta\Delta w_{ij}$ \quad (11)

Our goal is to explore analogue neural networks with a focus on neural learning to determine its plausibility as an approach to artificial intelligence on the Moon.

5 Analogue Neural Network Circuit Simulations

Neural networks comprise of an input layer of input data to be processed, hidden layer(s) responsible for extracting information from the input data and an output layer outputting the desired response. Fixed weight neural networks are inflexible due to the inability to be trained for different tasks as the neuron weights implemented as resistors remain fixed. We have examined two approaches to analogue neural networks with learning circuitry. The first was a simulated approach and the second was a simulated and physical construction approach. In both cases, we implemented two analogue circuit modules – a forward network that propagates signals from the input to the output layer and a backpropagation circuit that propagates the error backwards through the network from the output to compute the weight changes.

In our first simulated analogue neural network design using LTSPICE [30], we adopted a two input neuron – three hidden neuron – one output neuron configuration for the forward circuit. The forward network comprised several subcircuits – an op-amp-based summation circuit, an activation function circuit, a voltage-controlled resistor, an op-amp multiplier and a general inverter op-amp circuit. The neuron itself is constructed from a neuron summation sub-circuit and an activation function sub-circuit. The combination of weighted resistors is used to provide summed outputs. The summer amplifier is well understood (see Fig. 6(b) for an example) such as that adopted in the Yamashita-Nakamura neuron model [31]. Voltage-controlled resistors (VCR) were adopted to implement synaptic weights similar to [32] – they were based on a surgeless electronic variable resistor and attenuator design [33]. The VCR design was based on two vacuum tubes with cross-connected cathodes and grids to operate as a voltage divider (Fig. 2(a)). The weights represented by the VCR are updated from the backpropagation network. Every neuron performs a set of operations for which a decision is made whether to fire a neuron or not based on the activation function. The activation function typically applies a nonlinear squashing function to the weighted summation. We explored two activation functions – an op-amp-based linear activation function (Fig. 2(b)) and a vacuum tube-based differential amplifier (Fig. 2(c)) [34]. The threshold may be adjusted through the activation function but use of resistors requires positive weights. Inhibitory links may be implemented through the activation function as negative state [35]. An analogue op-amp multiplier exploits the nonlinear properties of class AB op-amps using three interconnected op-amps with a collection of resistors to output an approximation of the product of two inputs [36] (Fig. 3). There is a vacuum tube amplifier implementation with class-AB operation characteristics [37].

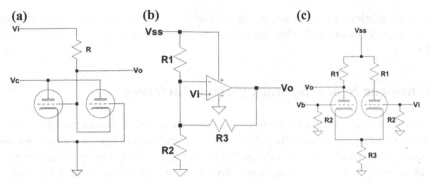

Fig. 2. (a) Voltage-controlled resistor; (b) linear activation function; (c) vacuum tube-based differential amplifier.

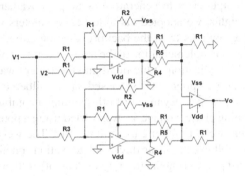

Fig. 3. Op-amp multiplier.

The backpropagation circuit comprised three sub-circuits: (i) a subtraction sub-circuit to calculate the error between the forward network output and the target value, (ii) VCRs and (iii) the back propagation multiplication block that calculates the neuron errors. The subtraction sub-circuit comprised an op-amp inverting amplifier to subtract voltages as well as for adding voltage biases (Fig. 4).

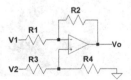

Fig. 4. Subtracting op-amp inverting amplifier.

The backpropagation multiplication sub-circuit contains a subtraction op-amp and cascaded op-amp multipliers. The resultant error outputs of the backpropagation circuit are multiplied with the neuron outputs using op-amp multiplication circuits. Each of the sub-circuits were functionally validated but once assembled into the neural network, the training simulations failed to update the weights of our vacuum tube-based analogue neural network successfully. We suspected the problem may be associated with the VCRs.

6   Analogue Neural Network Circuit Hardware

We built a different trainable analogue neural network circuit to demonstrate the principle of online training on a rover vehicle [38]. The forward interconnection of neurons were arranged into successive layers – the analogue neural network configuration comprised two input neurons plus a bias neuron followed by a two neuron hidden layer plus a bias neuron to a two neuron output layer. As before, the neural network is primarily constructed using (transistor-based) op-amps. The circuits were also simulated using the Proteus PCB simulator software generating two outputs to our network with weight values changed from output error to generate new outputs. Rather than VCRs for the adjustable network weights, we adopted variable potentiometers which were updated according to the voltage outputs from the backpropagation circuit during training. As before, the analogue circuit implementation of the neuron requires a weighted summation and a multiplication. Multiplication of the input and the weight was implemented by a four quadrant translinear multiplier (AD534) based on the Gilbert cell. The inputs to the multiplier can either be positive, negative or both yielding a combination of the signed inputs. During the training phase, voltage Vx was varied using a potentiometer to update and obtain the optimum weight yielding the output $Vout$. The weighted summation of inputs to a neuron was followed a linear threshold activation function. It was executed at the end of the forward pass during the training of data rather than at each neuron. The forward circuit of the analogue neural network is prototype of the implementation of this arrangement is shown in Fig. 5.

Fig. 5. Forward propagation neural network circuit.

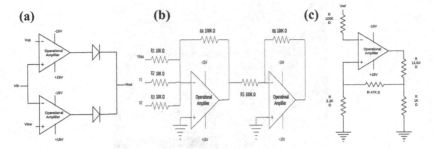

Fig. 6. (a) Window comparator; (b) summer amplifier (c) voltage comparator circuits.

The backpropagation circuit required several subcircuits:

(i)   Window comparator (Fig. 6(a)) to detect input voltage range – two voltage comparators provide upper (5 V) and lower (2 V) reference voltages. The output fires if the input is outside this range but not of it is within the range, i.e. a bandstop filter. A voltage inverter inverts this to give an output of 5 V within the range and < 1 V outside the range.

(II)   Summation circuit (Fig. 6(b)) to output subtraction of the two inputs (either 5 V or <1 V) and the output of the window comparator.

(III)   (iii) Voltage comparator (Fig. 6(c)) outputs (−1 V/+1 V) the input summation which alternates between the negative and positive saturation voltage based on the voltage at the non-inverting input of the op-amp.

Smaller learning rate ensures better stability over convergence speed but our data set was simple so it was set at 0.1 V. The error output was defined thus:

Error = −1 when the desired output was less than 2 V but the actual output was greater than 2 V

= 1 when the desired output was greater than 2 V but actual output was less than 2 V.

= 0 for zero error

The errors were output as voltage values of −1 V and +1 V. The backpropagation circuit is shown in Fig. 7.

The forward and backpropagation circuits were mounted on a small rover over an obstacle course. The rover was fitted with two front corner digital IR sensors to detect obstacles within 9 cm connected directly to the input nodes of the forward neural network through a 12-bit DAC converter MCP4725. An Arduino UNO board controlled four servo motors for the four wheels, two on each side. Two voltage inputs to the neural network are from the distance sensors that detect obstacles and from a bias node while the two-node output layer is connected to the respective wheel motors of the rover on either side. A simple dataset was used for training the network: zero obstacle path yielded inputs of 1 V but a left/right obstacle yielded an input of 4 V. A total motor output of 2 V yielded all-stop while under 2 V yielded appropriate turns and forward movement. During the

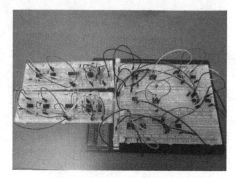

Fig. 7. Backpropagation circuit.

training phase, the circuit performing forward propagation was initiated with random voltage weights to map distance sensor inputs to the output – this is subsequently fed to the backpropagation circuitry comprising a threshold activation sub-circuit as well as multipliers and summers. Over multiple iterations, the network successfully converge to weight values that minimised the error from the desired output. The potentiometers were varied according to the output over several iterations to drive robot to realise a BV2B behaviour [39]. The robot successfully demonstrated the desired obstacle avoidance behaviour through a path with several obstacles – a left obstacle stopped the right wheels while driving the left wheels, and vice versa.

7   Conclusions

We have implemented a backpropagation algorithm in analogue circuitry demonstrating that electronic hardware is malleable and therefore carries the potential to be used for computational purposes as demonstrated on a simple rover. The neural network received training through the analogue circuit without any software programs. However, there are several issues that deserve further investigation. Although the training of the neural net is implemented through the backpropagation circuitry, the weight updates were applied manually which would preferably be implemented automatically clearly demonstrating learning directly from the physical environment. The crux is to implement weight memory updates directly electronically. There are several options for non-volatile memory cells including resistive RAM and magnetoresistive RAM in which each memory cell encodes a synaptic weight as analogue conductance. Non-volatile memories may be manufactured through microtechnology as magnetoresistive RAM comprising current-controlled magnetic tunnel junctions collectively implementing resistance summation [40]. This offers much lower energy consumption. Hardware implementation of neural networks is of interest as an application of the electrical memory element, the memristor for its ability to regulate current flow within itself, while simultaneously retaining the memory of its previous state without electrical power [41–43], including CMOS-based memristors [44–46]. A ferroelectric memristor with a voltage-controlled resistance employed as a variable synaptic weight suffer from conductance hysteresis from historical voltages [47]. However, memristor micro-manufacturing (as for solid-state) does not appear feasible for the near future. Future work should involve training the network of neural net with more complex tasks including sensing in its immediate domain and with predicted expectations. This introduces the issue of analogue neural network scalability. Although a neural design by trial-and-error was implemented because of the circuit's simplicity, genetic algorithms offer the possibility of evolving neural network designs for more complex problems offline. However, incremental adaptation rather than global optimization offers ease of implementation and time-efficiency [48]. Such learning methods have yet to be tested, but they can plausibly be implemented through electronic hardware. Finally, the internal circuitry of the op-amps consisted of transistor configurations which should be replaced with vacuum tube-based circuitry to enhance its relevancy to manufacturability on the Moon.

References

1. Ellery, A.: Sustainable in-situ resource utilisation on the Moon. Planet. Space Sci. **184**(4), 104870 (2020)
2. Ellery, A.: Are there biomimetic lessons from genetic regulatory networks for developing a lunar industrial ecology? Biomimetics J **6**(3), 50 (2021)
3. Ellery, A., Mellor, I., Wanjara, P., Conti, M.: Metalysis FFC process as a strategic lunar in-situ resource utilisation technology. New Space J **10**(2), 224–238 (2022)
4. Ellery, A.: Generating and storing power on the Moon using in-situ resources. Proc. IMechE J. Aerosp. Eng **236**(6), 1045–1063 (2021)
5. Ellery, A.: Leveraging in-situ resources for lunar base construction. Can. J. Civ. Eng. **49**(5), 657–674 (2022)
6. Ellery, A.: Is electronics fabrication feasible on the Moon? In: Proceedings ASCE Earth & Space Conference Colorado School of Mines, Denver (2022)
7. Ellery, A.: Universal construction based on 3D printing electric motors: steps towards self-replicating robots to transform space exploration. In: IEEE International Symposium Robotics & Intelligent Sensors (IRIS), pp. 81–85. Ottawa, Canada (2017)
8. Lagsford, W., Ghassaei, A., Gershenfeld, N.: Automated assembly of electronic digital materials. In: Proceedings of the Manufacturing Science and Engineering Conference, paper no. MSEC2016-8627 (2016)
9. Parberry, I.: Circuit Complexity and Neural Networks. MIT Press Foundations of Computing, Cambridge, MA (1994)
10. Hopfield, J.: Neurons with graded response have collective computational properties like those of two-state neurons. Proc Natl. Acad. Sci. **81**, 3088–3092 (1984)
11. Siegelmann, H., Sontag, E.: On the computational power of neural nets. J. Comput. Syst. Sci. **50**, 132–150 (1995)
12. Siegelmann, H., Margenstern, M.: Nine switch-affine neurons suffice for Turing universality. Neural Netw. **12**, 593–600 (1999)
13. Sun, G.-Z., Chen, H.-H., Lee, Y.-C., Giles, C.: Turing equivalence of neural networks with second order connection weights. Proc. Int. Joint Conf. Neural Networks **2**, 357–362 (1991)
14. Graves, A., Wayne, G., Danihelka, I.: Neural Turing machines. arXiv-1410.5401 (2014)
15. Hahnloser, R., Sarpeshkar, R., Mahowald, M., Douglas, R., Seung, S.: Digital selection and analogue amplification coexist in a cortex-inspired silicon circuit. Nature **405**, 947–951 (2000)
16. Roy, K., Jaiswai, A., Panda, P.: Towards spike-based machine intelligence with neuromorphic computing. Nature **575**, 607–617 (2019)
17. Mehonic, A., Kenyon, A.J.: Brain-inspired computing needs a master plan. Nature **604**, 255–260 (2022)

18. Burr, G.W., Sebastian, A., Ando, T., Haensch, W.: Ohm's Law + Kirchhoff's Current Law = Better AI: neural-network processing done in memory with analog circuits will save energy. In: IEEE Spectrum, vol. 58, no. 12, pp. 44–49 (2021)
19. Winter, R., Widrow, B.: MADALINE RULE II: a training algorithm for neural networks. In: IEEE 1988 International Conference on Neural Networks, vol. 1, pp. 401–408 (1988)
20. Carusone, A., Johns, D.: Analogue adaptive filters: past and present. IEE Proc. Circuits Devices Syst. **147**(1), 82–90 (2000)
21. Wang, T., Zhuang, X., Xing, X., Xiao, X.: Neuron-weighted learning algorithm and its hardware implementation in associative memories. IEEE Trans. Comput. **42**(5), 636–640 (1993)
22. Schneider, C., Card, H.: CMOS implementation of analog Hebbian synaptic learning circuits. In: IJCNN-91-Seattle International Joint Conference on Neural Networks, vol. 1, pp. 437–442 (1991)
23. Paulu, F., Hospodka, J.: Design of fully analogue artificial neural network with learning based on backpropagation. Radioengineering **30**(2), 357–363 (2021)
24. Kawaguchi, M., Ishii, N., Umeno, M.: Analogue neural circuit and hardware design of deep learning model. Procedia Comput. Sci. **60**, 976–985 (2015)
25. Wang, Y., Lee, D.: Online backpropagation learning for a human-following mobile robot. Preprint (2007)
26. Martinelli, G., Perfetti, R.: Circuit theoretic approach to the backpropagation learning algorithm. IEEE Int. Symp. Circuits Syst. **3**, 1481–1484 (1991)
27. Wright, L., et al.: Deep physical neural networks trained with backpropagation. Nature **601**, 549–555 (2022)
28. Jabri, M., Flower, B.: Weight perturbation: an optimal architecture and learning technique for analogue VLSI feedforward and recurrent multilayer networks. IEEE Trans. Neural Netw. **3**(1), 154–157 (1992)
29. Maeda, Y., Hiano, H., Kanata, Y.: Learning rule of neural networks via simultaneous perturbation and its hardware implementation. Neural Netw. **8**(2), 251–259 (1995)
30. Larson, S., Ellery, A.: Trainable analogue neural network with application to lunar in-situ resource utilization. In: Proceedings of the International Astronautical Congress, Jerusalem, IAC-15-D3.3.6 (2015)
31. Yamashita, Y., Nakamura, Y.: Neuron circuit model with smooth nonlinear output function. In: Proceedings of the International Symposium Nonlinear Theory & its Applications, Vancouver, pp. 11–14 (2007)
32. Martinelli, G., Perfetti, R.: Circuit theoretic approach to the backpropagation learning algorithm. In: IEEE Symposium on Circuits and Systems, vol. 3, pp. 1481–1484 (1991)
33. Meier, E.: Surgeless electronic variable resistor and attenuator. U.S. Patent 2 726 290 (1955)
34. Gray, T.: Direct-Coupled Amplifiers Applied Electronics, 2nd edn., pp. 499–508. John Wiley & Sons Inc, New York (1954)
35. Bradley, W., Mears, R.: Backpropagation learning using positive weights for multilayer opto-electronic neural networks. In: IEEE Lasers and Electro-Optics Society Annual Meeting, pp. 294–295 (1996)
36. Riewruja, V., Rerkratn, A.: Analog multiplier using operational amplifiers. Indian J. Pure Appl. Phys. **48**, 67–70 (2010)
37. Gray, T.: Amplifiers with operation extending beyond the linear range of the tube characteristic curves: class AB, class B and class C amplifiers Applied Electronics, 2nd edn., pp. 609–652. John Wiley and Sons Inc., New York (1954)
38. Prasad V, Ellery A (2020) "Analogue neural network architecture for in-situ resourced computing hardware on the Moon" *Proc Int Symp Artificial Intelligence, Robotics and Automation in Space* (iSAIRAS), paper no 5005

39. Braitenburg, V.: Vehicles: Experiments in Synthetic Psychology. MIT Press (1984)
40. Jung, S., et al.: Crossbar array of magnetoresistive memory devices for in-memory computing. Nature **601**, 211–217 (2022)
41. Chua, L.: Memristor: missing circuit element. IEEE Trans Circuit Theory **18**, 507–519 (1971)
42. Zhao, Y, Shi, G.: Circuit implementation method for memristor crossbar with on-chip training. In: IEEE Asia Pacific Conference on Circuits and Systems (2018)
43. Thomas, A.: Memristor based neural networks. J. Phys. D: Appl. Phys. **46**, 093001 (2013)
44. Ebong, I., Mazumder, P.: CMOS and memristor-based neural network design for position detection. Proc IEEE **100**(6), 2050–2060 (2012)
45. Larras, B., Chollet, P., Lahuec, C., Seguin, F., Arzel, M.: Fully flexible circuit implementation of clique-based neural networks in 65-nm CMOS. IEEE Trans. Circ. Syst. I, 1–12 (2018)
46. Yeo, I., Chu, M., Lee, B.-G.: A power and area efficient cmos stochastic neuron for neural networks employing resistive crossbar array. IEEE Trans. Biomed. Circuits Syst. **13**(6), 1678–1689 (2019). https://doi.org/10.1109/TBCAS.2019.2945559
47. Ueda, M., Nishitani, Y., Kaneko, Y., Omote, A.: Backpropagation operation for analogue neural network hardware with synapse components having hysteresis characteristics. PLoS ONE **9**(11), e112659 (2014)
48. Harvey, I.: Cognition is not computation; evolution is not optimisation. In: Gerstner, W., Germond, A., Hasler, M., Nicoud, J.-D. (eds.) Artificial Neural Networks — ICANN'97. LNCS, vol. 1327, pp. 685–690. Springer, Heidelberg (1997). https://doi.org/10.1007/BFb0020233

Query Resolution of Literature Knowledge Graphs Using Hybrid Document Embeddings

Iqra Muhammad[(✉)], Frans Coenen, Carol Gamble, Anna Kearney, and Paula Williamson

The University of Liverpool, Liverpool L693BX, UK
iqra@liverpool.ac.uk

Abstract. Literature Knowledge Graphs play a critical role in helping domain experts carry out query resolution for finding relevant articles in published literature. Such knowledge graphs are usually in the form of Curated Document Databases (CDDs). Domain Experts and researchers typically query such literature knowledge graphs using some form of query-resolution mechanism. Machine learning techniques can be used to automate query-resolution. This paper presents a document query-resolution mechanism, given a query and set of documents in a knowledge graph, based on a hybrid word embedding that combines knowledge graph embeddings with "traditional" embeddings. A query-document data set extracted from a clinical trials CDD (the ORRCA CDD) was used. Three "traditional" word embeddings were considered: CBOW, BERT and SciBERT. The evaluation demonstrated that hybrid embeddings produced better results than when the embedding models were used in isolation. A best Mean Average Precision of 0.486 was obtained when using a CBOW and random walk knowledge graph hybrid embedding.

Keywords: Query resolution · Word embedding · Document ranking

1 Introduction

The number of published papers in the scientific domain has increased year-on-year. As a consequence researchers find it increasingly cumbersome to find relevant literature. Researchers typically find relevant publications using a query-resolution mechanism directed at some document repository such as Google Scholar or PubMed. The query resolution process can be made more effective if a more domain specific document repository is used. The fundamental idea underpinning query-resolution is that, given a search query, potential documents matched to the query can be ranked according to how well they match the query and the top k documents returned because these are considered to be the most relevant to the query. This requires that the query and documents are represented

© The Author(s), under exclusive license to Springer Nature Switzerland AG 2022
M. Bramer and F. Stahl (Eds.): SGAI-AI 2022, LNAI 13652, pp. 98–111, 2022.
https://doi.org/10.1007/978-3-031-21441-7_7

in a way that facilitates matching. The most common approach is to use some form of word embedding. A word embedding is a learned text representation whereby each word or phrase in a document or query is represented by a numerical vector. A document embedding for each document in document repository (CDD) can then be generated by averaging the individual word embeddings. A query embedding can be generated in a similar manner.

The query-resolution process can be made even more effective if the document repository (CDD) is encapsulated in the form of a literature knowledge graph, as opposed to the traditional relational database typically adopted, because knowledge graphs impose a structure on the data that avoids the need for exhaustive searching when responding to queries.

One example of a CDD represented as a literature knowledge graph is the Online Resource for Recruitment research in Clinical trials[1] The ORRCA CDD was developed to bring together scientific literature focused on the topic of clinical trials. There are various techniques, based on word embeddings, to support query-resolution using literature knowledge graphs. Some recent examples can be found in [3,4,28]. However, these examples all used "traditional" embeddings.

Recently, many word embedding methods based on deep learning neural networks have been used for query and document representation so as to facilitate the effective scoring of documents with respect to query resolution [2,9]. Examples include: (i) Continuous Bag of Words (CBOW) [7] (ii) Bidirectional Encoder Representations from Transformers (BERT) embedding [9] (iii) Sci-BERT embedding [2]. However, when applied to literature knowledge graph represented CDDs these embedding techniques ignore the "knowledge" that is inherently available as a consequence of the knowledge graph structure.

The central hypothesis that the work presented in this paper seeks to address is that query resolution can be made more effective if a hybrid embedding is used whereby an established word embedding is combined with a literature knowledge graph embedding [1,14,22]. More specifically a random walk knowledge graph embedding generated by conducting a random walk over a literature knowledge graph is advocated, as suggested in [11,13,25]. Experiments were conducted using three different "traditional" embeddings (CBOW, BERT and Sci-Bert) combined with a random walk embedding; and when using these embeddings in isolation.

The remainder of this paper is structured as follows. A literature review of query-resolution mechanisms is first given in Sect. 2. Then, in Sect. 3, a review of the proposed query resolution approach is given. Section 4 gives a review of Random Walk Knowledge Graph Embeddings. The conducted evaluation of the approach is reported on in Sect. 5. The paper is concluded in Sect. 6 with the main findings.

---

[1] https://www.orrca.org.uk/.

2   Literature Review

The work presented in this paper is directed at a hybrid embedding approach, where two embedding are used to represent documents stored in a literature knowledge graph and user queries directed at that graph. The idea is to combine a graph embedding, that captures the information within a literature knowledge graph, and a more traditional word embedding. Word embeddings are typically generated using a deep learning embedding model [10,24]. However, to train an embedding model requires a large amount of data and consequently significant processing power, which means that the generation of a dedicated embedding model for a specific application domain, including the clinical trails domain considered in this paper, is not a viable option. The solution is the adoption/adaptation of an existing embedding model. There are many embedding models that have been reported on in the literature and three are considered in this paper: (i) CBOW, (ii) BERT and (iii) Sci-BERT. Word embedding can be categorised as being either: (i) contextual or (ii) non-contextual. Non-contextualized word embeddings do not take into account the surrounding word context of a word whereas a contextualized embedding does. CBOW embeddings are an example of the first. BERT and Sci-BERT embedding are examples of the second. All of these word embedding models can be used in the context of transfer learning. Further detail concerning non-contextualized embeddings are presented in Sub-sect. 2.1, whilst contextualized embedding models are considered in Sub-sect. 2.2. The section is concluded, in Sub-sect. 2.3, with a discussion concerning existing work on knowledge graph embedding models.

2.1   Non-contextualized Embedding Models - CBOW

Non-contextualized embedding models do not consider an individual word's context within a document. A popular class of such embedding model is the Word2Vec model. The input to Word2Vec is a word and the output is an embedding. Some examples of Word2Vec models are the Continuous Bag Of Words (CBOW) model and the Skip-gram model [7]. The biggest benefit of using these techniques is that they can be used at scale, in real world settings, without requiring a significant amount of time to tune to a specific domain of interest (not the case when using contextualized embedding models like BERT). For the work presented in this paper the CBOW model was considered because it is exemplar of a non-contextualized embedding model and because of the good performance reported in the literature [29]. CBOW is trained by considering each word in each document in sequence using a sliding window and produces an embedding for each input word. Once training is complete the CBOW system is no longer required. Examples of reported work where CBOW embeddings have been used for query resolution can be found in [6,12,20].

2.2   Contextualized Embedding Models - BERT and SciBERT

Contextualized word embedding techniques are based on deep learning neural networks. The benefit of using contextualized word embedding models is that they take into account the surrounding context of a word. The difference between contextualized and non-contextualized models can be explained by considering the following two sentences:

The man was accused of robbing a bank.
The man went fishing by the bank of the river.

A non-contextualized embedding model would generate the same word embedding for the word "bank" in both cases, whereas a contextualized embedding system would generate different word embedding depending on the context of the word "bank". As noted above, the advantage of non-contextualized embedding models over contextualized models is that they are easy to train and can be easily deployed at scale. However, contextualized models can be shown to produce embeddings that better reflect a given text [9,27]. With respect to the work presented in this paper, BERT and Sci-BERT were considered as exemplars of contextualized models. Sci-BERT is a variation of BERT directed at scientific applications, and thus it was considered to be suited to the clinical trials application domain used as a focus for the work presented in this paper.

2.3 Knowledge Graph Embedding Models

There are various algorithms for the generation of knowledge graph embeddings used with respect to question answering and document/query representation in document retrieval. Some of such well-known knowledge graph embedding algorithms are Deep Walk [16], LINE [21] and Node2Vec [5]. With respect to the work in this paper, *Node2Vec* was used because of its ease of use and it being scalable for larger knowledge graphs as seen in recent literature [22,26]. A random walk consists of simulating a walk over a set of vertices in a knowledge graph. The output of a random walk is a set of sentences that are then given as an input to a natural language processing model like 'bag of words" model or a "skip gram" model. The most well-known work on knowledge graph embedding models used particularly for document retrieval and ranking can also be found in [11,13,18,19,25].

3   The Hybrid Query-Resolution Approach

This section gives an overview of the proposed query-resolution approach to literature knowledge graphs using a hybrid representation that combines a "traditional" embedding and a knowledge graph embedding. A schematic outlining the proposed approach is presented in Fig. 1. The input (top of the Figure) is a query Q and a document collection $\mathbf{D} = \{D_1, D_2, \ldots D_i\}$. The whole document collection D is referenced by a knowledge graph. Each document $D_i \in \mathbf{D}$ consists of n terms such that $D_i = \{d_1, d_2, \ldots d_n\}$. From Fig. 1 it can be seen that the proposed approach has four main stages.

Stage I: Pre-processing

Stage II: Generation of Word embeddings.

Stage III: Knowledge graph embedding and word embedding concatenation.

Stage IV: Measuring similarity between query embedding and document embeddings, and document ranking.

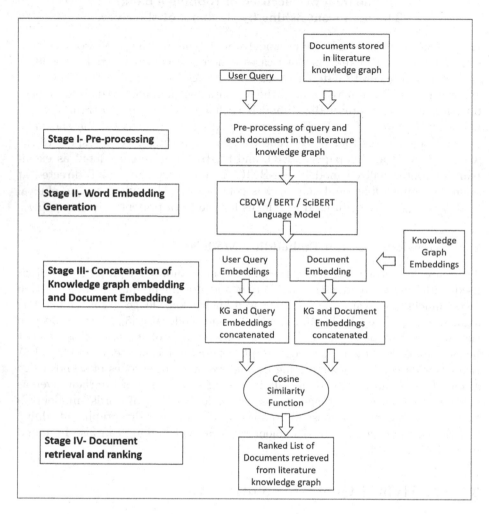

Fig. 1. Schematic of the adopted literature knowledge graph query resolution process.

During the first stage, Stage I, the input query Q and document collection $\mathbf{D}$, are pre-processed. The nature of the pre-processing depends on the nature on the language model used. For the evaluation of the proposed approach, and as noted earlier and indicated in the figure, three word embedding models were considered: CBOW, BERT and Sci-BERT. The pre-processing for the CBOW model entails punctuation and stop-word removal to give Q' and $\mathbf{D}'$. The Python Natural language toolkit[2] was used for stop word removal. The pre-processing for BERT was conducted by the BERT default tokenizer which does all the required pre-processing of the query Q and document collection D. BERT also adds special "classification" (CLS) and "seperating" sentence (SEP) tokens to the start and end of each sentence during pre-processing. The pre-processing when using Sci-BERT embedding is similar to when using BERT embedding. The result of the pre-processing, regardless of which embedding model was adopted, is a cleaned version of Q and $\mathbf{D}$, Q' and $\mathbf{D}' = \{D'_1, D'_2, \dots \}$.

During the second stage, Stage II, of the proposed query-resolution approach, as shown in Fig. 1, a selected language model is used to generate word embeddings for query Q' and each document $D'_i \in \mathbf{D}'$. Recall that a word embedding is expressed as a numeric vector of a constant length.

The third stage, Stage III, of the proposed query-resolution mechanism, takes the word embedding generated from the second stage, and concatenates the generated word embedding with a random walk knowledge graph embedding. The intuition here was that random walk knowledge graph embeddings, when combined with a "traditional" embedding, would provide additional information leading to a better query resolution performance than would otherwise be attained as suggested in [13,23]. In Fig. 1 the "traditional" embedding is referred to as the "left hand embedding" and the knowledge graph embedding as the "right hand embedding". The left-hand and right-hand embeddings are concatenated to produce a new hybrid document embedding for the query and each document in the literature knowledge graph. Further detail regarding the generation of random walk literature knowledge graph embeddings is provided in Subsect. 4 below.

The fourth stage of the proposed query-resolution mechanism takes the document embeddings and query embedding from the third stage and determines the similarity scores. For the evaluation presented later in this paper, and as indicated in Fig. 1, cosine similarity was used. Cosine similarity, is the cosine of the angle between two vectors x and y calculated using Eq. 1. Similarity scores are generated for each document in the literature knowledge graph which are then used to create a ranked list of documents from which the top k can be selected. Experiments were conducted using $k = 5$ and $k = 10$ with consultation from domain experts for the ORRCA database.

$$S_{cos}(x, y) = \frac{x.y}{||x|| \times ||y||} \tag{1}$$

4   Random Walk Knowledge Graph Embedding

The random walk knowledge graph (right-hand) embedding was generated using a random walk technique applied over a knowledge graph G. The basic idea of random walk generation was presented in [5,17]. The advantage of concatenating an embedding generated from random walk knowledge graph to a general word

---

[2] https://www.nltk.org/.

embedding (such as CBOW, BERT or Sci-BERT) is that the graph embedding will capture the knowledge held in the literature graph which, it was conjectured, would provide for a better word embedding. The proposed random algorithm used a set of random walks (paths) over G, such that $\mathbf{R} = \{R_1, R_2, ...\}$. Each random walk $R_i \in \mathbf{R}$ is of the form $[v_1, v_2, \ldots, v_{rw}]$, where v_j is a concept vertex in G and rw is the length of the walk. Note that no two values for v_j are the same. Each $R_i \in \mathbf{R}$ thus comprises a sequence of vertices representing concepts in a knowledge graph. Each random walk across G can be referred to as a "sentence". This means that various kinds of NLP models, such as a "bag of words" model or a "skip gram" model [7] can be applied to the generated sentences from such random walks. For the evaluation presented later in this paper, the Node2vec Framework was used to simulate random walks over G and for generation of random walk embeddings. A value of $rw = 3$ was used for the experiments in this paper because similar values have been used in the literature in the context of literature knowledge graph generated from ORRCA [15].

5   Evaluation

This section reports on the evaluation of the proposed hybrid query-resolution mechanism. The objectives of the reported evaluation were:

- To compare the operation of CBOW, BERT and Sci-BERT embeddings when combined with random walk knowledge embeddings and when used in isolation.
- To identify an appropriate setting for k, the number of documents returned (rank threshold). Experiments were conducted using $k = 5$ and $k = 10$.

For the random walk generation the number of random walks generated was set to 100 as such a value has been used in the literature as well [11]. This was because it represented an appropriate trade off between the execution time required to generate the knowledge graph random walk embeddings and coverage. Note that considerable computational resource is required to generate random walks. The ORRCA query-document [8] data set was used, which comprised 45 search queries.

The evaluation metrics used were Mean Average Precision (MAP) at k, for $k = 5$ and $k = 10$, calculated as shown in Eq. 2. This metric was used because the data set did not have a ground truth ranking, hence metrics like Normalized Cumulative Gain (NDCG) could not be used. In Eq. 2: (i) k is the rank threshold, (ii) Q is an evaluation query data set and (iii) ap_{jk} is Average Precision at rank k for query $j \in Q$ calculated as shown in Eq. 4. In Eq. 4: (i) p_{ji} is the ranked precision for query j at rank i. (i) p_{ji} is defined as the ranked precision for query j at rank i. (ii) m is equal to the number of relevant documents retrieved. Ranked precision is defined as the fraction of relevant documents for a query q_j retrieved from the total number of documents retrieved at (up to) rank i. Ranked precision is calculated as shown in Eq. 3, where: (i) tp_{ji} is the number of "true positives" at rank i (the number of documents that should have been retrieved in response to a query j, and were retrieved up to rank i), and (ii) fp_{ji} is the number of "false positives" at rank i (the number of documents that should not have been retrieved in response to a query q_j, but were retrieved up to rank i).

$$MAP(k) = \frac{1}{|Q|} \sum_{j=1}^{j=|Q|} ap_{jk} \quad (2) \qquad p_{ji} = \frac{tp_{ji}}{tp_{ji} + fp_{ji}} = \left(\frac{relevant}{retrieved} \right) \quad (3)$$

$$ap_{j,k} = \frac{1}{m} \sum_{i=1}^{i=k} p_{ji} \quad (4)$$

The MAP results obtained are presented in Table 1; best results highlighted in bold font. From the Table it can be seen that the hybrid CBOW and random walk knowledge graph embedding produced the best results. The suggested reason for this was that the CBOW model vocabulary was best suited to the ORRCA application domain. The results obtained when using CBOW, BERT and SciBERT in isolation seems to support this suggestion. The experiments where each of the embedding models were used in isolation also demonstrated that the knowledge graph random walk embedding performed well; thus supporting the conjecture that knowledge graph random walk embedding provides beneficial additional knowledge, which in turn increases effectiveness of the proposed query resolution approach.

Table 1. $MAP@k$ Table for BERT, SciBERT and CBOW when combined with Random Walk embeddings, and when used in isolation

Embedding model	MAP@5	MAP@10
CBOW and KG embeddings	**0.486**	**0.313**
BERT and KG embedding	0.420	0.256
SciBERT and KG embedding	0.414	0.252
SciBERT only embedding	0.393	0.186
BERT only embedding	0.409	0.256
CBOW only embedding	0.433	0.259
Random Walk KG only embedding	**0.458**	**0.271**

Inspection of Table 1 also indicates that better results were obtained using $k = 10$ than $k = 5$ in that better results were returned. Tables 2, 3 and 4 present the $AP@k$ results obtained using: CBOW and random walk embeddings and CBOW used in isolation, BERT and random walk embeddings and BERT used in isolation, SciBERT and random walk embeddings and SciBERT used in isolation. The tables present the $AP@k$ results for each of the 45 queries in the ORRCA query-document data set. The search queries that perform the best are highlighted in bold font. Inspection of the Tables indicates that Queries

Table 2. $AP@k$ results for combined CBOW and random walk embeddings, in comparison with CBOW used in isolation

Search code	CBOW + Random Walk		CBOW only	
	P@5	P@10	P@5	P@10
Search1	0.4	0.4	0.0	0.3
Search2	0.4	0.3	0.4	0.3
Search3	0.2	0.2	0.6	0.5
Search4	0.6	0.6	0.6	0.6
Search5	0.4	0.2	0.0	0.0
Search6	0.2	0.4	0.8	0.7
Search7	0.8	0.9	0.6	0.6
Search8	0.0	0.0	0.0	0.0
Search9	0.4	0.4	0.4	0.5
Search10	0.6	0.6	0.6	0.6
Search11	1.0	0.9	1.0	0.9
Search12	0.4	0.7	0.6	0.7
Search13	0.4	0.0	0.6	0.0
Search14	0.8	0.7	1.0	0.7
Search15	0.4	0.5	0.2	0.3
Search16	0.6	0.4	0.4	0.4
Search17	0.0	0.0	0.0	0.0
Search18	0.6	0.5	0.4	0.4
Search19	1.0	1.0	1.0	1.0
Search20	0.4	0.2	0.2	0.2
Search21	0.8	0.5	0.8	0.5
Search22	0.6	0.5	0.2	0.3
Search23	0.6	0.8	0.4	0.5
Search24	1.0	0.9	0.0	0.0
Search25	0.0	0.0	0.0	0.0
Search26	0.0	0.0	0.0	0.0
Search27	0.8	0.8	1.0	0.8
Search28	0.6	0.7	0.8	0.7
Search29	0.8	0.0	0.8	0.0
Search30	1.0	0.0	1.0	0.0
Search31	**1.0**	**1.0**	**1.0**	**1.0**
Search32	**1.0**	**0.9**	**1.0**	**0.9**
Search33	**1.0**	**1.0**	**0.8**	**0.9**
Search34	**1.0**	**1.0**	**1.0**	**0.9**
Search35	0.0	0.0	0.0	0.0
Search36	0.4	0.2	0.6	0.3
Search37	0.4	0.0	0.4	0.0
Search38	0.4	0.2	0	0.4
Search39	0.0	0.0	0.2	0.1
Search40	0.4	0.4	0.2	0.3
Search41	0.6	0.4	0.4	0.3
Search42	0.0	0.0	0.0	0.0
Search43	0.2	0.1	0.2	0.1
Search44	0.6	0.0	0.8	0.0
Search45	0.0	0.0	0.0	0.2

Table 3. *AP@k* results for combined BERT and random walk embeddings, in comparison with BERT used in isolation

Search code	BERT + Random Walk		BERT only	
	P@5	P@10	P@5	P@10
Search1	1.0	1.0	0.0	0.0
Search2	0.2	0.3	0.0	0.2
Search3	0.6	0.5	0.6	0.4
Search4	0.4	0.6	0.6	0.6
Search5	0.0	0.0	0.0	0.0
Search6	0.2	0.4	0.2	0.5
Search7	0.4	0.7	0.0	0.4
Search8	0.0	0.0	0.0	0.0.1
Search9	0.0	0.2	0.2	0.3
Search10	0.6	0.8	0.8	0.8
Search11	1.0	0.9	1.0	0.9
Search12	0.6	0.6	0.8	0.7
Search13	0.6	0.0	0.6	0.0
Search14	0.8	0.8	0.8	0.8
Search15	0.6	0.4	0.4	0.4
Search16	0.4	0.4	0.6	0.5
Search17	0.0	0.0	0.0	0.0
Search18	0.4	0.4	0.2	0.3
Search19	1.0	0.9	1.0	0.9
Search20	0.2	0.3	0.2	0.2
Search21	0.4	0.5	0.6	0.5
Search22	0.6	0.6	0.4	0.4
Search23	0.2	0.5	0.6	0.7
Search24	0.4	0.7	0.6	0.7
Search25	0.0	0.0	0.0	0.0
Search26	0.0	0.0	0.0	0.0
Search27	0.6	0.7	0.6	0.7
Search28	0.6	0.8	0.8	0.7
Search29	1.0	0.0	0.6	0.0
Search30	1.0	0.0	1.0	0.0
Search31	**1.0**	**1.0**	**1.0**	**1.0**
Search32	**1.0**	**0.9**	**1.0**	**0.9**
Search33	**1.0**	**0.9**	**1.0**	**1.0**
Search34	**1.0**	**0.9**	**1.0**	**0.9**
Search35	0.0	0.0	0.0	0.0
Search36	0.4	0.2	0.0	0.0
Search37	0.4	0.0	0.4	0.0
Search38	0.2	0.1	0.2	0.1
Search39	0.2	0.1	0.2	0.2
Search40	0.0	0.1	0.2	0.3
Search41	0.2	0.2	0.2	0.2
Search42	0.0	0.0	0.0	0.0
Search43	0.2	0.1	0.0	0.0
Search44	0.6	0.0	0.6	0.0
Search45	0.0	0.1	0.0	0.1

Table 4. $AP@k$ results for combined SciBERT and random walk embeddings, in comparison with Sci-BERT used in isolation

Search code	Sci-BERT + Random Walk		Sc-BERT only	
	P@5	P@10	P@5	P@10
Search1	0.0	0.3	0.0	0.3
Search2	0.2	0.2	0.0	0.3
Search3	0.4	0.3	0.2	0.5
Search4	0.6	0.6	0.6	0.6
Search5	0.0	0.1	0.0	0.1
Search6	0.2	0.1	0.2	0.3
Search7	0.4	0.6	0.0	0.5
Search8	0.0	0.0	0.0	0.0
Search9	0.6	0.4	0.6	0.4
Search10	0.8	0.7	1.0	0.8
Search11	1.0	0.9	1.0	1.0
Search12	0.2	0.3	0.8	0.7
Search13	0.6	0.0	0.4	0.0
Search14	0.4	0.5	0.8	0.8
Search15	0.4	0.2	0.6	0.4
Search16	0.0	0.1	0.2	0.4
Search17	0.0	0.0	0.0	0.0
Search18	0.4	0.4	0.4	0.4
Search19	1.0	1.0	1.0	0.9
Search20	0.0	0.0	0.0	0.2
Search21	0.4	0.5	0.4	0.5
Search22	0.8	0.6	0.4	0.2
Search23	0.4	0.6	0.6	0.5
Search24	0.6	0.6	0.6	0.7
Search25	0.2	0.1	0.0	0.1
Search26	0.0	0.0	0.0	0.0
Search27	0.4	0.5	1.0	0.0
Search28	0.6	0.7	0.8	0.7
Search29	0.6	0.0	0.8	0.0
Search30	1.0	0.0	0.0	0.0
Search31	**1.0**	**1.0**	**1.0**	**1.0**
Search32	**1.0**	**0.9**	**1.0**	**0.9**
Search33	**1.0**	**0.9**	**1.0**	**0.9**
Search34	1.0	0.9	1.0	0.0
Search35	0.0	0.0	0.0	0.0
Search36	0.0	0.0	0.0	0.1
Search37	0.4	0.0	0.2	0.0
Search38	0.2	0.4	0.0	0.1
Search39	0.0	0.1	0.0	0.0
Search40	0.2	0.2	0.4	0.2
Search41	0.4	0.2	0.4	0.0
Search42	0.0	0.0	0.0	0.0
Search43	0.2	0.1	0.2	0.1
Search44	0.6	0.0	0.5	0.0
Search45	0.0	0.0	0.0	0.2

31, 32, 33, and 34 gave the best results from all the search queries. It was conjectured that this was a function of the query size; these queries featured more keywords than other queries. The number of keywords in a search query affects the precision. Search queries with a greater number of keywords tend to achieve better results compared to search queries with fewer keywords.

6   Conclusion

This paper proposed a query resolution mechanism for queries directed at Curated Document Databases (CDDs) stored as literature knowledge graph. A hybrid document embedding was proposed that combined a "traditional" embedding with a knowledge graph embedding for queries and documents. Three kinds of word "traditional" embedding were considered: CBOW, BERT and SciBERT. The evaluation indicated that the proposed hybrid embedding resulted in better $MAP@k$ results than when the various embeddings were used in isolation. A best $MAP@k$ value of 0.486 was obtained when using a combination of CBOW and the proposed random walk knowledge graph embedding.

References

1. Ammar, W., et al.: Construction of the literature graph in semantic scholar. In: NAACL HLT 2018, pp. 84–91 (2018)
2. Beltagy, I., Lo, K., Cohan, A.: SciBERT: a pretrained language model for scientific text. In: Proceedings of the 2019 Conference on Empirical Methods in Natural Language Processing and the 9th International Joint Conference on Natural Language Processing (EMNLP-IJCNLP), pp. 3615–3620 (2019)
3. Chen, C., Ross, K.E., Gavali, S., Cowart, J.E., Wu, C.H.: Covid-19 knowledge graph from semantic integration of biomedical literature and databases. Bioinformatics **37**(23), 4597–4598 (2021)
4. Dörpinghaus, J., Stefan, A., Schultz, B., Jacobs, M.: Context mining and graph queries on giant biomedical knowledge graphs. Knowl. Inf. Syst. **64**(5), 1239–1262 (2022)
5. Grover, A., Leskovec, J.: Node2Vec: scalable feature learning for networks. In: KDD 2016, pp. 855–864 (2016)
6. Guo, J., Fan, Y., Ai, Q., Croft, W.B.: A deep relevance matching model for ad-hoc retrieval. In: Proceedings of the 25th ACM International on Conference on Information and Knowledge Management, pp. 55–64 (2016)
7. Jatnika, D., Bijaksana, M.A., Suryani, A.A.: Word2vec model analysis for semantic similarities in English words. Procedia Comput. Sci. **157**, 160–167 (2019)
8. Kearney, A., et al.: Development of an online resource for recruitment research in clinical trials to organise and map current literature. Clin. Trials **15**(6), 533–542 (2018)
9. Devlin, J., Chang, M.-W., Lee, K., Toutanova, K.: BERT: pre-training of deep bidirectional transformers for language understanding. In: Proceedings of NAACL-HLT, pp. 4171–4186 (2019)
10. Kowsher, Md., et al.: An enhanced neural word embedding model for transfer learning. Appl. Sci. **12**(6), 2848 (2022)

11. Liang, X., Li, D., Song, M., Madden, A., Ding, Y., Yi, B.: Predicting biomedical relationships using the knowledge and graph embedding cascade model. PLoS ONE **14**(6), e0218264 (2019)
12. Liji, S.K., Ilyas, P.M.: Semantic Malayalam dialogue system for Covid-19 question answering using word embedding and cosine similarity. In: 2021 International Conference on Advances in Computing and Communications (ICACC), pp. 1–6. IEEE (2021)
13. Liu, Z.-H., Xiong, C., Sun, M., Liu, Z.: Entity-duet neural ranking: understanding the role of knowledge graph semantics in neural information retrieval. In: ACL, no. 1 (2018)
14. Mai, G., Yan, B., Janowicz, K., Zhu, R.: Relaxing unanswerable geographic questions using a spatially explicit knowledge graph embedding model. In: Kyriakidis, P., Hadjimitsis, D., Skarlatos, D., Mansourian, A. (eds.) AGILE 2019. LNGC, pp. 21–39. Springer, Cham (2020). https://doi.org/10.1007/978-3-030-14745-7_2
15. Muhammad, I., Bollegala, D., Coenen, F., Gamble, C., Kearney, A., Williamson, P.: Document ranking for curated document databases using BERT and knowledge graph embeddings: introducing GRAB-rank. In: Golfarelli, M., Wrembel, R., Kotsis, G., Tjoa, A.M., Khalil, I. (eds.) DaWaK 2021. LNCS, vol. 12925, pp. 116–127. Springer, Cham (2021). https://doi.org/10.1007/978-3-030-86534-4_10
16. Perozzi, B., Al-Rfou, R., Skiena, S.: DeepWalk: online learning of social representations. In: Proceedings of the 20th ACM SIGKDD International Conference on Knowledge Discovery and Data Mining, pp. 701–710 (2014)
17. Sang, S., et al.: Gredel: a knowledge graph embedding based method for drug discovery from biomedical literatures. IEEE Access **7**, 8404–8415 (2018)
18. Sharma, S.: Fact-finding knowledge-aware search engine. In: Sharma, N., Chakrabarti, A., Balas, V.E., Bruckstein, A.M. (eds.) Data Management, Analytics and Innovation. LNDECT, vol. 71, pp. 225–235. Springer, Singapore (2022). https://doi.org/10.1007/978-981-16-2937-2_17
19. Shi, L., Li, S., Yang, X., Qi, J., Pan, G., Zhou, B.: Semantic health knowledge graph: semantic integration of heterogeneous medical knowledge and services. BioMed. Res. Int. (2017)
20. Silva, A., Mendoza, M.: Improving query expansion strategies with word embeddings. In: Proceedings of the ACM Symposium on Document Engineering 2020, pp. 1–4 (2020)
21. Tang, J., Qu, M., Wang, M., Zhang, M., Yan, J., Mei, Q.: Line: large-scale information network embedding. In: Proceedings of the 24th International Conference on World Wide Web, pp. 1067–1077 (2015)
22. Wang, Q., et al.: Covid-19 literature knowledge graph construction and drug repurposing report generation. arXiv preprint arXiv:2007.00576 (2020)
23. Wang, Q., Mao, Z., Wang, B., Guo, L.: Knowledge graph embedding: a survey of approaches and applications. IEEE Trans. Knowl. Data Eng. **29**(12), 2724–2743 (2017)
24. Wang, S., Zhou, W., Jiang, C.: A survey of word embeddings based on deep learning. Computing **102**(3), 717–740 (2020)
25. Wise, C., et al.: Covid-19 knowledge graph: accelerating information retrieval and discovery for scientific literature. In: Proceedings of Knowledgeable NLP: The First Workshop on Integrating Structured Knowledge and Neural Networks for NLP, pp. 1–10 (2020)
26. Wu, T., Wang, Y., Wang, Y., Zhao, E., Yuan, Y., Yang, Z.: Representation learning of EHR data via graph-based medical entity embedding. arXiv preprint arXiv:1910.02574 (2019)

27. Yang, W., Zhang, H., Lin, J.: Simple applications of BERT for ad hoc document retrieval. arXiv preprint arXiv:1903.10972 (2019)
28. Tong, Yu., et al.: Knowledge graph for TCM health preservation: design, construction, and applications. Artif. Intell. Med. **77**, 48–52 (2017)
29. Zuccon, G., Koopman, B., Bruza, P., Azzopardi, L.: Integrating and evaluating neural word embeddings in information retrieval. In: Proceedings of the 20th Australasian Document Computing Symposium, pp. 1–8 (2015)

On an Artificial Neural Network Approach for Predicting Photosynthetically Active Radiation in the Water Column

Martin M. Kumm[1]([⊠]), Lars Nolle[1,2], Frederic Stahl[2], Ahlem Jemai[3], and Oliver Zielinski[2,3]

[1] Department of Engineering Sciences, Jade University of Applied Science, Wilhelmshaven, Germany
martin.kumm@jade-hs.de
[2] Marine Perception, German Research Center for Artificial Intelligence (DFKI), Oldenburg, Germany
[3] Institute for Chemistry and Biology of the Marine Environment, Carl Von Ossietzky University of Oldenburg, Oldenburg, Germany

Abstract. About 1,600 bio-geo-chemical Argo floats (BGC-Argo), equipped with a variety of physical sensors, are currently being deployed in the ocean around the world for profiling the water characteristics up to a depth of 2,000 m. One of the parameters measured by the Argo is the radiometric measurement of downward irradiance, which is important for primary production studies. The multispectral Ocean Color Radiometer measures the downwelling irradiance at three wavelengths 380 nm, 412 nm and 490 nm plus the photosynthetically available radiation (PAR) integrated from 400 nm to 700 nm. This study proposes a method to reconstruct the PAR sensor values from readings of the remaining onboard sensors, independent of the location the BGC-Argo is being deployed. This allows for the PAR channel being replaced by a fourth band in the visible range. Stahl et al. [1] have already shown, that a machine learning approach, based on a multiple linear regression (MLR) or on a regression tree (RT), is capable of predicting the PAR values based on other parameters measured by the physical sensors of the BGC-Argo float. In this study, a nonlinear Artificial Neural Network (ANN) was used for the prediction of PAR. The ANN achieved a better coefficient of determination R^2 of 0.9968, compared with the MLR approach, which achieved an R^2 of about 0.97 for a combined dataset consisting of measurements from three different geographical locations. Therefore, it was concluded that the ANN was better suited to generalise the underlying transfer function.

Keywords: BGC-Argo float · Photosynthetically active radiation prediction · Artificial neural network · Machine learning

1 Introduction

Due to a dramatic increase in environmental challenges, such as climate change and the associated rise of the sea level, new methods for monitoring environmental parameters

M. Bramer and F. Stahl (Eds.): SGAI-AI 2022, LNAI 13652, pp. 112–123, 2022.
https://doi.org/10.1007/978-3-031-21441-7_8

are needed to gain a better understanding of the complex interactions in the environment. Anthropogenic activities are rapidly changing the ocean, contributing to pollution, deoxygenation, ocean warming and the resulting rise in sea level [2, 3]. To monitor these changes, modern operational oceanography uses numerous types of autonomous platforms [4]. One of these autonomous platforms is the Argo float [5–7]. Over 1,600 BGC-Argo floats have been deployed by June 2022.

A typical 10-day cycle mission of BGC-Argo float is shown in the left part of Fig. 1. It starts with a descent to a depth of 1,000 m and subsequently maintains this level while drifting away due to the ocean's currents. After nine and a half days, the float dives up to 2,000 m. After reaching the target level, the sensors begin to acquire data. When the float eventually resurfaces, it begins to transmit the data acquired via Iridium satellite communication into the Argo network [6]. The transmitted Argo float data is publicly and freely available via two global data assembly centers (GDAC) typically within 24 h (see Argo website https://argo.ucsd.edu).

Modern versions of BGC-Argo floats are, unlike older Argo floats with a three-sensor setup, equipped with a variety of additional physical, chemical and bio-optical sensors [8, 9]. Due to this increase in sensors, accompanied by data management and quality control processes, demand for machine learning has been rising [9, 10].

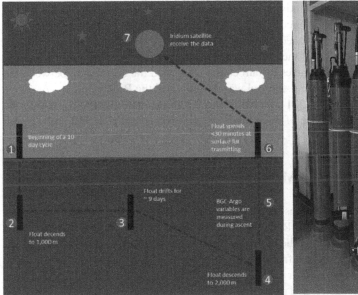

Fig. 1. Left: A typical mission of a Biogeochemical-Argo (BGC-Argo) float (adapted from [6]), Right: BGC-Argo floats ready for deployment

The BGC-Argo community suggested to re-configurate the Ocean Color Radiometer to dismiss the fourth channel, which is designed to record PAR, since this parameter could potentially be predicted from the three remaining channels, which measure the intensity of radiant energy at wavelengths at 380 nm, 412 nm and 490 nm, and the pressure. It was shown previously that both, MLR [11] and RT [12], are capable of reconstructing the PAR sensor readings [1].

This study compares the machine learning algorithms recently utilized in [1] with a new approach, based on ANNs.

2 Related Work

Due to its influence on the botanical photosynthesis process, PAR plays a fundamental role in modeling vegetation growth [13, 14]. Several studies have already shown that PAR values can be predicted by using different meteorological and radiometric parameters. López et al. [15] and Jacovides et al. [16] developed ANN models, which use global irradiance and the solar zenith angle as inputs to estimate the global PAR. Jacovides et al. achieved for their best model an accuracy of R^2 0.979, whereas the best model trained by López et al. achieved an accuracy R^2 of about 0.999. Yu et al. [17] already showed that both, ANN models and conventional regression models, can predict PAR on the surface from incoming solar radiation and that the ANN models have a higher accuracy R^2 of about 0.999 compared with the regression models with $R^2 = 0.994$. These results show that the PAR radiant flux is strongly correlated with the broadband global radiant flux. In these studies, PAR was predicted on the surface, using the global irradiance and the solar zenith angle, whereas in this study only wavelengths in a specific narrowband together with the pressure are used to predict PAR. A review of radiometric measurements on Argo floats was recently published by Jemai et al. [18].

The BGC-Argo measured the PAR in the water column and has no information about the solar zenith. Nevertheless, Stahl et al. [1] showed the correlation between the irradiance under water at several spectral wavelengths and the PAR value.

The model by Stahl et al. [1] uses MLR and RT to estimate the PAR value on the BGC-Argo with the irradiance of three other spectral wavelengths at 380 nm, 412 nm and 490 nm.

3 Vertical Radiometric Measurement of the Water Column

One of the six essential variables measured by the BGC-Argo float is the underwater light field [6]. The Ocean Color Radiometer (OCR-504) from SATLINC Inc./Sea-Bird Scientific is used for measuring the downward irradiance at three bands 380 nm, 412 nm and 490 nm plus PAR integrated from 400 nm to 700 nm [19]. It can be seen in the right-hand side of Fig. 2 how the four sensors are arranged. These three wavelengths were selected, because they are related to the main variations in underwater optical properties [20, 21]. The information from the PAR sensor is commonly used to make predictions about the light available for primary production in natural waters [22].

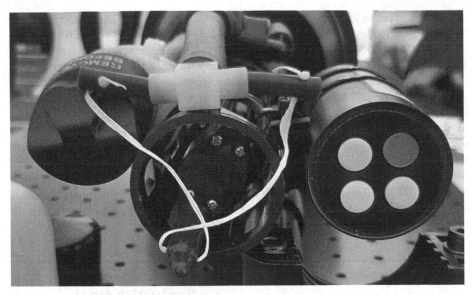

Fig. 2. OCR-504 mounted on the BGC-Argo float

In this study, the same dataset as in [1] was used to allow for a fair comparison of the methods. Float data was collected and made freely available by the International Argo Program and the national programs that contribute to it (http://www.argo.ucsd.edu and http://argo.jcommops.org). Table 1 shows the datasets from the three different sites used in this work. The sites can be identified by the World Meteorological Organization (WMO) number. The WMO number also identifies the platform type.

Table 1. Datasets

Identifier	Location	No. of instances
WMO 7900585	North Atlantic	4,403
WMO 7900562	Mediterranean Sea	13,068
WMO 7900579	Baltic Sea	1,373
WMO 7900580	Baltic Sea	1,274

4 Data Interpretation

Each instance of each dataset consists of 7 attributes. The first one indicates the cycle, the second the current number of the cycle, the third the value of the pressure in dbar, the fourth, fifth and sixth contain the different wavelengths at 380 nm, 412 nm, 490 nm and the seventh attribute represents the value of the PAR sensor.

Due to errors in the datasets, for example missing values, the associated instances were removed, leaving 1,331 instances in the WMO 7900579 dataset and 1,268 instances in the WMO 7900580 dataset. No errors were found in the other two datasets. Figure 3, 4, 5 and 6 show the correlations of each sensor with the PAR sensor. It can be seen that all sensor readings from all geographical locations, except for the pressure reading, show a good correlation with PAR. It can also be seen for readings above 100 dbar that PAR had low values. The reason for this is that light at this depth is fully absorbed by the water [1]. The fact that the pressure does not correlate with the other sensors was subsequently confirmed by the Institute for Chemistry and Biology of the Marine Environment. Therefore, Stahl et al. [1] decided to exclude the pressure from their modelling. In contrast to MLR and RT, ANNs are able to learn and interpret non-linear relations [23]. Since a non-linear relationship between PAR and the remaining parameters was expected, it was decided to use an ANN and to include the pressure values in the training set.

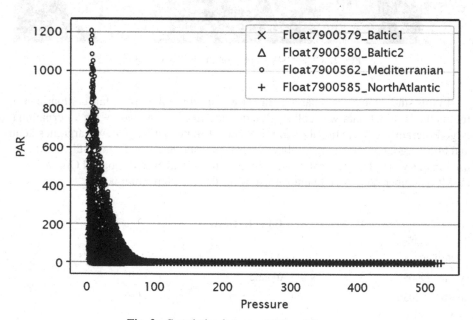

Fig. 3. Correlation between PAR and Pressure

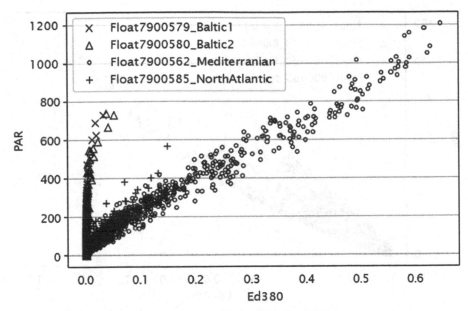

Fig. 4. Correlation between PAR and 380 nm

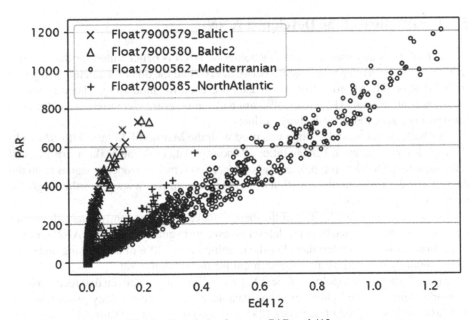

Fig. 5. Correlation between PAR and 412 nm

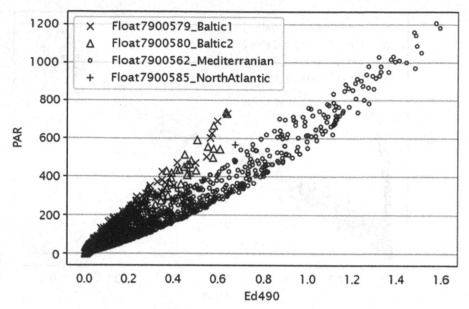

Fig. 6. Correlation between PAR and 490 nm

5 Architecture of the Developed ANN

The aim of this study was to establish whether an ANN is better suited for the generalization of the underlying relationships between PAR and the other parameters compared with MLR or RT. All error-free instances were used for modelling. The wavelength parameters at 380 nm, 412 nm and 490 nm and the pressure were used as the features for training and the PAR as the target value.

For building the model, Python was used with the Matplotlib library (https://matplotlib.org) for visualization, Pandas (https://pandas.pydata.org) and Scikit-learn (https://scikit-learn.org) for data pre-processing to detect and remove erroneous values from the dataset and the Keras implementation of TensorFlow (https://www.tensorflow.org/) for implementing the ANN.

For testing the network, 30% of the data instances were randomly selected without replacement and separated from the dataset as test data to guarantee that the ANN training is not biased towards the test data. For the training phase, 20% of the training instances were randomly selected without replacement for the validation set.

Figure 7 shows the topology of the ANN used. Since it was proven that feed-forward networks with a single hidden layer are capable of approximating any given function with any desired degree of accuracy [24], a three-layer feed forward ANN with one input layer, which can take the four input features, one hidden layer with 100 nodes and one output layer returns the predicted PAR value. The number of nodes in the hidden layer were determined empirically. The rectified linear activation function was used in the hidden-layer. For the training, Root Mean Squared propagation (RMSProp) with a learning rate of 0.01 was used. The Mean Absolute Error (MAE) was used as loss function. Each ANN was trained for 1,000 epochs, since the network tended to overfit when more epochs were used.

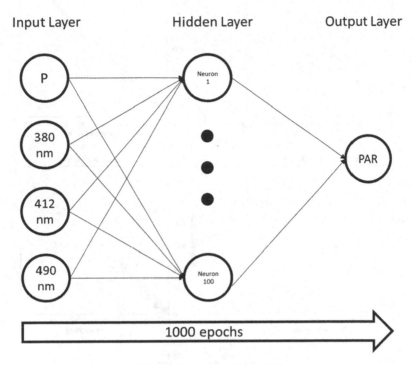

Fig. 7. Topology of the ANN

$$PAR = \sum_{j=1}^{m} \left(max \left(0, \sum_{i=1}^{n} x_i * w_{ij} * learning\ rate \right) \right) * w_{j\,PAR} * learning\ rate$$

with $x_1 = P, x_2 = 380\,nm, x_3 = 412\,nm, x_4 = 490\,nm, w = weights, learning\ rate = 0.01, n = 4, m = 100$
$$(1)$$

Eq. (1) above shows how the neural network estimates the PAR value. The two weight-matrices w_{ij} and $w_{j\,PAR}$ were determined by the ANN during the training phase. n and m are equivalent to the input nodes and the hidden nodes.

6   Evaluation of the Artificial Neural Network

Figure 8 depicts the correlation between the predictions and the ground truth for the test sets for each trained ANN. The diagram in the top row on the left side shows the results of the dataset from the North Atlantic (WMO 7900585) with an R^2 value of 0.998 and on the right side the Mediterranean Sea (WMO 7900562) with an R^2 value of 0.999. The row below the diagrams shows the results from the Baltic Sea. The dataset from the

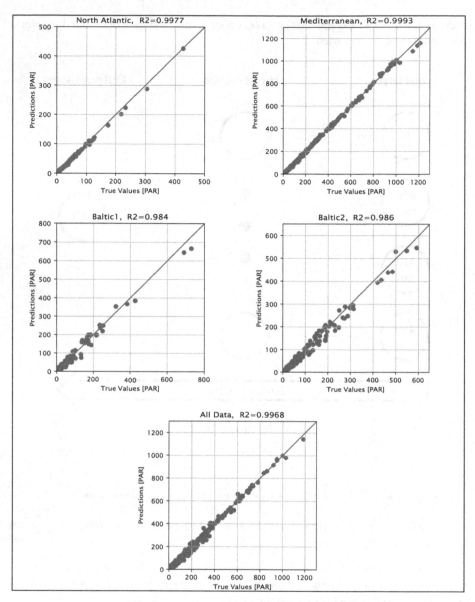

Fig. 8. Predicted vs. True PAR from each site

WMO 7900579 on the left side with a R^2 value of 0.984 and on the right side the WMO 7900580 with a R^2 value of 0.986. The diagram at the bottom shows the results for the data combined from all 4 Argo floats. Here, the R^2 value was 0.997.

When compared to MLR, the achieved R^2 value for the combined dataset was approximately 0.027 higher. This indicates that the ANN has generalised the underlying transfer function better. The reason for that might be that in this work pressure was used as an additional input parameter for the ANN. In order to allow for a fair comparison with the results from [1], another ANN was trained without using pressure as an input. It can be seen from Table 2 that the performance degraded slightly when compared to the ANN using pressure, but it performed still better or equal than MLR and RT, except for the Baltic Sea Float 1 dataset.

Table 2. R^2 values for the different models (MLR and RT from [1])

R^2 values

Dataset	ANN with pressure	ANN without pressure	MLR	RT
Combined	0.997	0.987	0.970	0.960
Mediterranean Sea	0.999	0.998	0.997	0.989
Baltic Sea Float 1	0.984	0.977	0.981	0.973
Baltic Sea Float 2	0.986	0.983	0.983	0.963
Atlantic Ocean	0.998	0.997	0.996	0.988

7   Conclusion

Due to the purpose of replacing the PAR sensor with a fourth band in the visible range, a method to reconstruct the PAR sensor values from readings of the remaining onboard sensors, based on ANNs was proposed. These generalization properties of the combined model developed make it possible to predict the PAR value independent of the geographical location where the data was acquired, with high accuracy. This indicates, that the environmental differences at those locations, for example salinity or turbidity, have no effects on the model. Therefore, the PAR sensor can be replaced by fourth band to measure the downward irradiance without losing the information about the photosynthetically active radiation in the water column.

The next steps in this work are to further evaluate the ANN model with additional datasets collected from different ocean basins before finally using the model operationally on the fleet of Argo floats.

Acknowledgments. This work was partly funded by the Ministry for Science and Culture, Lower Saxony, Germany, through funds from the Niedersächsische Vorab (ZN3480), and the German Federal Ministry of Education and Research, project SpektralArgo-N (Grant No. 03F0825A and 03V01478), and project DArgo2025 (Grant-No. 03F0857B).

References

1. Stahl, F., Nolle, L., Jemai, A., Zielinski, O.: A model for predicting the amount of photosynthetically available radiation from BGC-ARGO float observations in the water column. Commun. ECMS 36 (2021)

2. Lotze, H.K., et al.: Global ensemble projections reveal trophic amplification of ocean biomass declines with climate change. Proc. Natl. Acad. Sci. USA **116**, 12907–12912 (2019)
3. Wollschläger, J., Neale, P., North, R., Striebel, M., Zielinski, O.: Climate change and light in aquatic ecosystems: variability & ecological consequences. Front. Mar. Sci. **8**, 688712 (2021)
4. Roemmich, D., et al.: On the future of argo: a global, full-depth, multi-disciplinary array. Front. Mar. Sci. **6**, 439 (2019)
5. Sloyan, B.M., Roughan, M., Hill, K.: Global ocean observing system. New Front. Oper. Oceanogr. 75–89 (2018)
6. Claustre, H., Johnson, K., Takeshita, Y.: Observing the global ocean with biogeochemical-argo. Annu. Rev. Mar. Sci. **12**, 23–48 (2019)
7. Organelli, E., Leymarie, E., Zielinski, O., Uitz, J., D'Ortenzio, F., Claustre, H.: Hyperspectral radiometry on biogeochemical-argo floats: a bright perspective for phytoplankton diversity. Observing 90 (2021)
8. Johnson, K.S., et al.: Biogeochemical sensor performance in the SOCCOM profiling float array. J. Geophys. Res.: Oceans **122**(8), 6416–6436 (2017)
9. Claustre, H., et al.: Bio-optical sensors on argo floats. In: Claustre, H. (ed.) Reports and Monographs of the International Ocean-Colour Coordinating Group, pp. 1–89 (2011)
10. Jiang, Y., Gou, Y., Zhang, T., Wang, K., Chengquan, H.: A machine learning approach to argo data analysis in a thermocline. Sensors **17**(10), 2225 (2017)
11. Freedman, D.: Statistical Models: Theory and Practice. Cambridge University Press (2009)
12. Breiman, L., Friedman, J., Olshen, R.A., Stone, C.: Classification and Regression Trees.Routledge (2017)
13. Wang, L., Gong, W., Li, C., Lin, A., Hu, B., Ma, Y.: Measurement and estimation of photosynthetically active radiation from 1961 to 2011 in Central China. Appl. Energy **111**, 1010–1017 (2013)
14. Holinde, L., Zielinski, O.: Bio-optical characterization and light availability parameterization in Uummannaq Fjord and Vaigat-Disko Bay (West Greenland). Ocean Sci. **12**, 117–128 (2016)
15. López, G., Rubio, M., Martínez, M., Batlles, F.: Estimation of hourly global photosynthetically active radiation using artificial neural network models. Agric. For. Meteorol. **107**(4), 279–291 (2001)
16. Jacovides, C., Tymvios, F., Boland, J., Tsitouri, M.: Artificial Neural Network models for estimating daily solar global UV, PAR and broadband radiant fluxes in an eastern Mediterranean site. Atmos. Res. **152**, 138–145 (2015)
17. Yu, X., Guo, X.: Hourly photosynthetically active radiation estimation in Midwestern United States from artificial neural networks and conventional regressions models. Int. J. Biometeorol. **60**(8), 1247–1259 (2015)
18. Jemai, A., Wollschläger, J., Voß, D., Zielinski, O.: Radiometry on argo floats: from the multispectral state-of-the-art on the step to hyperspectral technology. Front. Marine Sci. **8**, 676537 (2021)
19. SATLANTIC: Operation manual for the OCR-504. In: SATLANTIC Operation Manual SAT-DN-00034, p. 66 (2013)
20. Xing, X., Morel, A., Claustre, H., D'Ortenzio, F., Poteau, A.: Combined processing and mutual interpretation of radiometry and fluorometry from autonomous profiling Bio-Argo floats: 2. Colored dissolved organic matter absorption. J. Geophys. Res. **117**, 1–16 (2012)
21. Organelli, E., et al.: A novel near-real-time quality-control procedure for radiometric profiles measured by Bio-Argo floats: protocols and performances. J. Atmos. Ocean. Technol. **33**, 937–951 (2016)
22. Mignot, A., Ferrari, R., Claustre, H.: Floats with bio-optical sensors reveal what processes trigger the North Atlantic bloom. Nature Commun. **9**, 190 (2018)

23. Hong-ze, L., Sen, G., Chun-jie, L., Jing-qi, S.: A hybrid annual power load forecasting model based on generalized regression neural network with fruit fly optimization algorithm. Knowl.-Based Syst. **37**, 378–387 (2013)
24. Hornik, K., Stinchcombe, M., White, H.: Multilayer feedforward networks are universal approximators. Neural Netw. **2**(5), 359–366 (1989)

Morality, Machines, and the Interpretation Problem: A Value-based, Wittgensteinian Approach to Building Moral Agents

Cosmin Badea[✉] [iD] and Gregory Artus [iD]

Imperial College London, London SW7 2AZ, UK
c.badea@imperial.ac.uk, g.artus@ic.ac.uk

Abstract. We present what we call the Interpretation Problem, whereby any rule in symbolic form is open to infinite interpretation in ways that we might disapprove of and argue that any attempt to build morality into machines is subject to it. We show how the Interpretation Problem in Artificial Intelligence is an illustration of Wittgenstein's general claim that no rule can contain the criteria for its own application, and that the risks created by this problem escalates in proportion to the degree to which a machine is causally connected to the world, in what we call the Law of Interpretative Exposure. Using games as an illustration, we attempt to define the structure of normative spaces and argue that any rule-following within a normative space is guided by values that are external to that space and which cannot themselves be represented as rules. In light of this, we categorise the types of mistakes an artificial moral agent could make into Mistakes of Intention and Instrumental Mistakes, and we propose ways of building morality into machines by getting them to interpret the rules we give in accordance with these external values, through explicit moral reasoning, the "Show, not Tell" paradigm, the adjustment of causal power and structure of the agent, and relational values, with the ultimate aim that the machine develop a virtuous character and that the impact of the Interpretation Problem is minimised.

Keywords: AI ethics · Interpretation problem · Moral values · Value alignment · Wittgenstein · Rules · Virtue theory · Practical reasoning · Intelligent decision support systems · Evaluation of AI systems

1 Intelligence and the Interpretation Problem (IP)

The need to build morality into machines is becoming urgent (Le Roux 2016) and is by now a burgeoning field in Artificial Intelligence (AI) research. The work of thinkers such as Bostrom (2014), Wallach and Allen (2008), Wallach and Asaro (2016), Yudkowsky (2008), and others (Anderson and Anderson 2011) warns us that advances in the power of machines will very quickly create situations where machines will be able to make decisions that not only were previously the sole preserve of human agents, but which have moral significance. Autonomous, or semi-autonomous military robots are the most obvious example of this, but there are far more mundane uses to which machines may

© The Author(s), under exclusive license to Springer Nature Switzerland AG 2022
M. Bramer and F. Stahl (Eds.): SGAI-AI 2022, LNAI 13652, pp. 124–137, 2022.
https://doi.org/10.1007/978-3-031-21441-7_9

in future be put, where ethical problems may arise, because the likely capabilities of future machines will create moral dilemmas that may not have existed for less capable machines, generated not by machines going rogue and deliberately trying to kill us (though this possibility cannot be ignored), but by machines inadvertently harming us while they carry out instructions we have given them. This critical issue is caused by an equally critical problem which we call *the Interpretation Problem (IP)*. Intelligence plus the Interpretation Problem equals trouble.

By intelligence, we of course do not necessarily mean anything as grand as consciousness or Artificial General Intelligence (AGI), but, rather, the ability to be an effective and creative utility (or function) maximiser, i.e., a machine that is 'clever' at finding ways to achieve the goals we set for it (Russell and Norvig 2003). Modern learning machines have shown great promise in this direction within certain restricted domains such as Chess, Go and Poker, with programs such as Alpha Go and Libratus using learning to develop new strategies to achieve the goals of the game of Go and Poker (i.e., winning), strategies that surprised and defeated human champions and professional players decisively (Silver et al. 2016, BBC 2016, Solon 2017). Consequently, it is not too far-fetched to think that in future we will be able to build machines that are such good means-ends reasoners, or goal maximisers, that they will be able to think of creative new ways to achieve the ends that we provide for them, which is where IP becomes a pressing issue.

The **Interpretation Problem (IP)** is the general problem that any rule or goal is capable of being interpreted in an infinite, or at least unspecifiable number of ways, and in the field of AI it leads to the possibility that a highly advanced machine may find novel interpretations of the rules that we give it, interpretations which are not incorrect, in that they can be seen as valid interpretations of the rule, but which are inappropriate in that we do not approve of them.

Bostrom's (2014) paperclip maximiser is an illustration of the risks of such machines. An intelligent goal maximiser programmed with the seemingly innocuous goal of maximising the number of paperclips in its collection might work out that the most efficient means to that end is to steal them, or trick or otherwise con people out of them. Such obviously undesirable methods would be easy to predict and address by building prohibitions into the programming. However, it may then find undesirable means we hadn't thought of, or might use too many resources, or even the wrong type of resources in their manufacture (e.g., using the atoms of its makers as raw material), so we'd have to predict and impose yet more limits in its programming, and so on.

If we want the machine to simply make paperclips according to a pre-specified method or procedure, we could break the task into algorithmic steps and program that into the machine (like in Rule-based AI), but even then, and especially when we want the machine to use its learning ability (like in Machine Learning), IP becomes an issue as the machine finds new ways to achieve its goal, and is a function of the very aspect of intelligent machines that makes them useful to us; their ability to adapt, learn and overcome. We argue that this problem is a practical demonstration of one of the key findings of Wittgenstein's later work in *"The Philosophical Investigations"* (2009, see particularly §138-242) that what we mean by words cannot be represented by a rule for its use because no rule can contain the criteria for its own application, and that this is a deeper problem with rules in general. Hence, any rule we represent to a machine cannot be specified in an unambiguous way because any representation of a rule is open to multiple interpretations. With the paperclip maximiser and other innovative goal-maximisers, no matter how many restrictions and caveats we predict and build into its programming by representing them as rules, there is always the possibility that it will find novel interpretations of those rules which will clash with our wider goals and values.

This is the basic structure of IP, and it is worth pointing out at this stage that IP is not just a problem for the sort of AGI or super-intelligent machines that Bostrom's example talks of. Any machine that is both linked causally to the world and can also innovate would expose us to IP. Deep Blue, AlphaGo and Libratus all operate within the completely closed artificial domains of a game and so have no causal relation to the world and could not cause us any trouble, but as Olivia Solon points out in an article about Libratus (Solon 2017), these and similar programs will eventually be causally linked to the real world somehow, either online or through some form of embodiment, and may be used to negotiate business deals, manage defence, cyber-security, medical treatment and other important areas of our lives. Bostrom's Paperclip maximiser had almost omnipotent causal capability, but machines with far less causal power will still be dangerous because of their creativity and ability to develop strategies we could not predict or guard against in advance. The more causal power it has in the real world, the greater the risk, so there will be a lawlike relation between the causal capability or connectivity of a machine and our exposure to IP. Hence, for any intelligent utility maximiser, the degree to which we will be exposed to IP will be proportional to the degree to which the machine is causally connected to the world. We call this relation the **Law of Interpretative Exposure**.

Moral Rules and Values. If Wittgenstein is correct, then the Interpretation Problem (IP) is not a problem that can be overcome by formulating more precise, or less ambiguous, rules, but is an inherent problem that applies to all rules, not just rules that direct an agent to optimise a goal. Even a simple instruction or imperative, prescriptive rule, or a proscriptive rule requires interpretation and cannot contain the criteria for its own application. *It is in principle impossible to specify any rule in such a way that it cannot be misinterpreted and what we mean by a rule can never be unambiguously represented.*

An obvious solution to this problem with intelligent machines, then, would seem to be not to try to predict every possible misinterpretation and close it off with a specific rule, but to program into the machine a set of general values or moral rules that would restrict its behaviour to within limits we find morally acceptable. People often cite general laws like Asimov's three laws of robotics here as an example of the sort of thing that might do the job. Such a project, however, is easier said than done. The history of philosophy is littered with attempts to reduce our moral reasoning to either prescriptive or proscriptive rules, and every attempt appears to flounder on the problem that the application of any moral rule seems to be context sensitive, and one can always find interpretations of those rules that we find morally repugnant. Utilitarian or consequentialist accounts framed in terms of prescriptive rules such as 'Do that which promotes the greatest happiness for the greatest number' create all the standard objections to Utilitarianism, such as that of what we mean by 'happiness'. Do we mean material wellbeing, simple physical pleasure, intellectual pleasure, psychological wellbeing, or some other definition of happiness? Deciding which one we mean will always require us to make a value judgement about how the rule is to be interpreted, since the rule itself cannot tell us. And even if we do specify a definition of happiness, it is still possible to find interpretations of that definition which clash with our values, as Yudkowsky's example of the smile maximiser (Yudkowski 2008) amply demonstrates – the machine may simply work out that the best way to make more people happy is to make them smile, and that the most efficient way to make everyone smile is by paralysing their faces into a rictus.

Alternatively, the rule could be interpreted as meaning that we should sacrifice the lives or wellbeing of a minority for the sake of that of the majority, which in some cases may seem right, but in others would be abhorrent, such as harvesting the organs of an innocent minority to find a cure for cancer for the majority. In both types of case, it seems that how we mean the rule is guided by values external to the rule itself and is a judgement that can only be made from a stance outside of the rule. This point will become clearer from our later discussion of games and normative spaces.

Proscriptive rules have fared no better than prescriptive rules in moral theory. Deontological or duty-based approaches, such as Kant's, or Asimov's laws of robotics place prohibitions on us such as 'do not harm other human beings', but this once again raises the question of what we mean by harm. And even if we can come up with a suitable definition, then we are left with the problem of whether we can install in the machine a sufficient understanding of the way the world works for it to be able to recognise how its actions may have wider effects that may cause harm to humans. It would basically have to know (*knowing-that* or *knowing-how*) nearly everything about humans and how they live and what can harm them, and even then, it may innovate new forms of action which create new forms of harm that simply didn't exist before. New technologies and new forms of human action are always creating moral dilemmas which didn't exist before, which force us to make judgements about how such rules as 'Do not Harm' apply, and how we interpret or apply the rule in any novel case can only be determined by values external to our rule, values which our rule is in principle incapable of embodying unambiguously.

There is a sense in which IP has been recognized in various ways by moral philosophers for millennia. In Plato's "Republic" (pt1 §1) we see Socrates demolishing the claim of Cephalus that justice consists of little more than following simple rules such as 'tell the truth' and 'always pay one's debts' by responding with the example of a situation where you've borrowed a friend's knife. One day the friend comes hammering at your door hysterically demanding his knife back so that he may kill a man who has upset him. Should you simply tell him the truth (that you still have his knife) and repay your debt so that he may go and kill the man in his unhinged current state? Clearly not. For Plato, moral rules are context sensitive and moral knowledge/wisdom of how and when to apply those rules requires an intellectual grasp of the abstract form of the good, which itself is ineffable and unrepresentable. His pupil Aristotle (1988) agreed that moral knowledge/wisdom was context sensitive and unrepresentable but rejected Plato's notions that it was a form of ineffable intellectual knowledge, preferring instead to treat virtue as a form of practical wisdom that could only be learnt through long experience and practice in pursuit of the flourishing life – a sort of practical know-how neither derivable from nor reducible to representable rules. Nearly every moral theory ever since the Greeks has found the need to ground our moral rules in some further source of values that is external to them: Utilitarianism in our innate appetite for pleasure and aversion to pain; Hume and other Naturalist theories, such as evolutionary ethics, in our biologically evolved natural sympathy for our fellow humans; Kant in the principles of logical coherence as expressed by the categorical imperative; Hegel in the social structures of our communities; Moore in an ineffable or brute intuition…the list is endless. Each one of these models, however, is an attempt to find, once and for all, the criteria, or values, by which our moral rules are to be interpreted, and in this sense, one could argue that they are all attempts to overcome IP by describing some further, or final, rule by which moral rules are to be interpreted. But Wittgenstein's work (2009) showed us that this task may be futile, since *any further rule will itself need to be interpreted, and so on, simply because that is the nature of rules.* To see this, it will be instructive to look at the way rules operate in games.

2   Normative Systems as Spaces of Possibility

Many games can be seen as a structure of different types of rules that combine to create spaces of possibility and choice in which players must pursue a specified goal or aim, under certain limitations. For example, the aim of the game of soccer is to score goals, while the limitations players are under are that they are not allowed to use their hands, or 'foul' their opponents, move off-side, etc., and the rules define what counts as a goal, what constitutes handball, off-side etc. So, the rules will consist of prescriptive imperatives that determine the aims or goals of the game, plus proscriptive rules laying out the limitations within which the players must pursue those aims, plus several definitional rules – what Searle would call *constitutive rules* (Searle 1969) – which define what is to count as scoring, handball, off-side etc. Most games seem to conform to this general pattern of the pursuit of goals under limitations within a normative space artificially created by the rules, a space of action. The net effect is that *the rules create an arena, or space of possibilities*, in which players are forced to make choices about how best to achieve the specified goal or aim, given the limitations under which they must play. In this sense, instead of directing players or determining their actions, *the purpose of the rules seems to be to create new forms of choice and new dilemmas* that did not exist before. Even in games like Monopoly, where many of the player's actions are determined by imperative conditional rules of the form 'if x, then do y', the structure of the game is such that it creates moments of dilemma and choice at specific points during the playing out of the game. Hence, games often seem mechanisms which use carefully crafted sets of different types of rules to create normative spaces of possibility, designed to extend and test the way we exercise our creative agency, by enabling new types of action.

One of the important things to notice about such normative spaces of possibilities is that they are, for all practical purposes, spaces of infinite possibilities which can accommodate an almost infinite number of possible strategies and tactics; there are an infinite number of ways to score a goal, a touchdown, a run, or to checkmate one's opponent, etc., so one can never exhaustively specify in advance all the possible tactics, moves or strategies that a rule space makes possible. This is because, as Ryle (2000) showed us, principles of strategy form a distinct set of rules which presuppose the rules of the game but are not derivable from those rules. There is no way that from my knowledge of the rules of chess I could logically deduce or otherwise predict that someone would one day invent the Sicilian Defence, or that the tactics of either bodyline bowling or sledging would be the inevitable outcome of the rules of cricket. So, if tactical principles are not logically deducible from the rules of the game, then the number of possible tactics any game may generate is limited only by the imagination, creativity, and ingenuity of the players, and so, with enough ingenuity on the part of the players, *there are, for all practical purposes, an infinite number of ways to interpret the rules* of most games.

From this we can see that games provide us with a perfect illustration of IP in action. There are an infinite number of possible tactics, strategies or interpretations that stay within the rules of the game, just as there are an infinite number of ways an AI can achieve the goals we set it, no matter how many limitations we place on it – new limitations simply force us to make new choices. Furthermore, just as we saw with AI, sometimes players in a game invent a new strategy that we consider undesirable, or do not approve of, despite its still being legally within the rules of the game. Therefore, the rules of games are continually evolving to take account of novel tactics that, for whatever reason, we think inappropriate or undesirable. But what happens when we make such modifications can be very instructive in revealing yet more complexity in the way rule systems work, because it forces us to ask why we find particular tactics undesirable and also what criteria we use as our guide when we alter the rules.

Chasing the Spirit of the Rules. The usual reason we modify the rules of a game is because a new tactic seems to clash somehow with what might be called *the spirit* or purpose or point of the game, so we alter the rules to outlaw it and so maintain the spirit or values that the game is supposed to express. A good example of this occurred in American football in the first half of the twentieth century, when players invented a new strategy called the 'flying wedge', where the whole team linked arms to form a V-shaped wedge in front of the ball carrier and then charged headlong down the pitch as one. There was nothing in the rules that prohibited such a tactic and there was no way that anyone could have deduced or predicted from the then current rules of the game that this tactic would inevitably be utilised by someone. It was solely the product of the creativity and ingenuity of the players, and it was extremely effective at scoring touchdowns if, as was usually the case, the opposing team could not find a way to break up the formation. It soon became clear, however, that this tactic had to be outlawed for several reasons. It made the game very dangerous and was a bit too effective and made the game more of a battle of brute strength than a game of artistry and skill. The tactic seemed to stifle the game and did not encourage creativity and made the game boring both to play and to watch, and the fact that the flying wedge was outlawed shows that the main reason we invented the game in the first place was to encourage the development of just those things stifled, e.g., creativity, flair, artistry, skill etc. Yet nowhere in the rules of American football are artistry, flair, skill, or creativity mentioned. *The game seems designed to promote certain values, yet nowhere in the rules are those values represented. In this sense, the values according to which we believe the rules of the game ought to be interpreted are external to the game itself, so it seems that the normative space created by the rules is designed to express those values, but those values cannot actually be represented by the rules* –such as 'Always interpret the rules of the game artistically'. This rule itself would have to be interpreted by players, and there are an infinite number of ways to do so.

The rules, then, seem designed to promote, encourage or otherwise generate new types of activity through which players can express certain values in the way they act. We invent games where we express intellectual flair, reasoning, or resilience; games where we can express physical prowess, artistry, and skill; games of perseverance, patience, creativity, strategizing and so on. And in this sense, games create what Hannah Arendt would call 'spaces of appearance' (1998, pt5), spaces created by a system of rules which allow agents to express who they are and what they value and to so define themselves. The games are always designed with certain values in mind, such as those listed above, but they can never guarantee that players will interpret the rules in line with those values because of the nature of normative spaces themselves – they are spaces for the exercise of creative agency, but the very nature of such spaces dictates that players are free to interpret the rules in their own way according to their own values. And when players interpret the rules in ways that clash with the spirit of the game, we simply change the rules.

Furthermore, sometimes the way that players interpret the rules of the game can teach us new values, by, for instance, inventing a strategy that we disapprove of, because it undermines something we took for granted or hadn't realised we valued until it was threatened or lost. It wasn't until the flying wedge was invented that we perhaps realized quite how much we valued other aspects of the game that we had before taken for granted. So, it is not just that the values that normative spaces express cannot be represented in the rules because it is logically impossible for a rule to contain the criteria for its own application, it is also the case that the values expressed by the normative space cannot be represented in the rules because often we don't even know what those values are until they are threatened. In this sense, *normative spaces create spaces of possibility where we can discover values, as well as express existing values.* Often the values that inform a normative space are not formulable beforehand but taken for granted as part of the background of our form of life.

Much of what has been said about restricted domains such as games would seem to apply to normative spaces more generally. For example, in the taxation system legislators are in a continual arms race with taxpayers (or their lawyers and accountants), where the system is designed to express certain values such as 'paying one's dues', yet certain players express their own values as being that of 'minimising one's liabilities'. The normative space created by tax law can never guarantee that all players will play the game according to the spirit or values that underpin the creation of that space because of the nature of normative spaces. So each time someone comes up with a novel strategy that is within the letter of the law, but which clashes with the spirit of the law, regulators must plug the hole with a new rule, or modify an existing rule. And this situation can never be otherwise because of the very nature of normative spaces. Any rule or system of rules always must be interpreted, which in turn presupposes that the agents operating in that space are capable of creative agency. Hence any normative space presupposes both IP plus the creativity of the agents operating within that space. *Consequently, IP is not only in principle impossible to overcome, but is actually what makes normative spaces possible in the first place.* If there were no IP and no creative agents, then we simply could not have normative spaces.

The same would seem to apply in law more generally and in morality, as rules are continually modified according to values external to the rules in response to novel strategies and developments within and across different spheres of our lives. If this is the case, then the quest that has occupied moral philosophers for centuries, that of finding some final rule, criteria or principle which will guarantee that we interpret moral rules in ways that express the values that underpin them, may be futile, and the quest to represent our values as a set of final rules that will guarantee a machine will interpret the rules we give it in line with our wider values may also be impossible.

If this is all correct, then moral rules create normative spaces for the exercise of creative agency where agents express their values in the way they interpret the rules. In this sense, the moral world is not a space where choices can be determined by the rules of the space but is instead an arena for the expression of character. *The virtues one expresses by the way one interprets the rules of the space is who one is.* Consequently, if the moral world is, as this analysis implies and as thinkers such as Arendt have suggested, such a space of appearance that enables agents to define themselves, then any intelligent machine capable of expressing its values within that space by the way it interprets the rules can never be guaranteed to express the values we approve of, so we cannot exhaustively and in advance program a perfectly moral agent. Rather, the way forward for AI research in this topic may be to try to create machines that express a virtuous character in the way they interpret the rules we give them. Yet, as we have seen, character cannot be programmed in as a set of rules but can only be expressed in the machine's interpretation of the rules we give it. Thus, the task of creating virtuous machines seems to be an extremely difficult one. However, in the remainder of this paper we make some suggestions as to how we might begin to tackle this seemingly intractable and daunting task.

3   Tackling the Interpretation Problem

Mistakes of Intention (MIs) and Instrumental Mistakes (IMs). To begin, we argue, in line with our other work (Badea and Gilpin 2021) that an artificial agent should have as part of its reasoning mechanism two major components, whether made explicit and distinguished from one another or not. The first component will deal with what it ought to do, imperatives and obligations (given or inferred), and the second one will deal with the facts or beliefs it holds, similarly to the inference engine and the knowledge base, respectively, in expert systems (Jackson 1998). We argue that the mistakes of an artificial moral agent can be split into two categories, corresponding to deficiencies in the two parts of the reasoning mechanism described above, *Mistakes of Intention (MIs)* and *Instrumental Mistakes (IMs)*; and we argue that an AI must include an explicit moral program distinct from its practical reasoning program (also argued in Wallach and Allen (2008)).

A Mistake of Intention (MI) is one about the imperatives or obligations that the agent has: about *goals* or *limits*. *Mistakes about goals* are occasions on which the agent errs about aims and goals, whether sourced extrinsically, from another agent or the environment, or intrinsically, by its own reasoning. *Mistakes about limits* concern the errors that have to do with actions it should not perform. For example, *mistakes about goals* are all the ones discussed above in the introduction of the paperclip maximiser. These stem from the fact that the specified goal had inappropriate qualifications and the same issue could also lead to *mistakes about limits,* such as when asked to "maximise X using only Y kg of matter", by the agent using matter of the wrong nature (like cooking the cat in Havens 2015), or by using excessive resources. Another example is that it could infer subgoals, such as nefariously avoiding being turned off, like Hal in "2001: A Space Odyssey". Even if we tried to overcome MIs by programming a moral framework based on a rule-based positive account, whether deontological, consequentialist, or otherwise, we would still encounter such mistakes (as we show in Bolton et al. 2022). This is because there might be many circumstances we will not have accounted for (as we show in Post et al. 2022), but most importantly, remember the consequences of IP (above and in our work from 2017): different interpretations are always possible and thus, the spectre of satisfying the literal specification given while not bringing about the intended outcome always looms darkly above us. This kind of behaviour (called *Specification Gaming* by Krakovna 2020), a subspecies of MIs, makes an alternative to these approaches, a way of mitigating IP, glow ever more brightly. We propose this alternative to be *Explicit Moral Reasoning implemented through the "Show, not Tell" (S, not T) method using Values.*

An Instrumental Mistake (IM) refers to issues with the part of the agent that deals with facts or beliefs about the world (its knowledge base), similarly to the "*failure of understanding*" in Kantian terms. This can happen if the agent does not correctly understand or predict how the world works, when it is making a factual or empirical error in its reasoning. This type of mistake could occur due to a lack or failure of the agent's common-sense knowledge, and its sources might be false beliefs, incorrect facts, or inappropriate/incomplete understanding of consequences of actions etc.

Explicit Moral Reasoning for MIs. As we have argued, the structure of a normative system together with the goals that are usually present in its rules allow us to see parallels between practical reasoning in AI (of which moral reasoning is a part) and human-centred normative systems, for example game-playing or law. Even if we somehow overcame or minimised the IMs (improving its sensors, effectors, common-sense reasoning etc.) the agent might still commit MIs, as seen above, and this illustrates why *we must attend not only to the agent's practical understanding of the world, to ward against IMs, but must also build into its reasoning system an explicit moral component, to ward against MIs.* An ontology of the parts required for good decision-making, arguing the same, is attempted elsewhere (Badea and Gilpin 2021).

Practical and Moral Goals. Artificial agents can be understood as having two types of goals: *practical goals,* which are almost always explicitly provided extrinsically and *moral goals,* which are almost never explicit (sometimes not even present), having more to do with the external point, or values of the game, than its rules. As we have seen, practical goals are immediately vulnerable to IP, especially when given in the form 'do X'. We have also seen that any finite limitations, or specific behaviours we place in the same form as part of the rules of the game are not enough to keep the agent on track with being moral, being themselves subject to IP, so we need an explicit approach for moral behaviour. Thus, *we cannot rely on moral behaviour to come as a side effect of purely (non-moral) practical goal-driven behaviour.* The practical, traditional, goals the AI has are part of the specifications of the decision problem, just like they are part of the rules of a game, but as in any game the player, or agent, can come up with ways of acting within the rules of the game but against the external point of the game, because this is not explicitly represented, so we need another mechanism to keep the agent tethered to this external point. To this end, we propose the use of active moral considerations, *values*, to inform the moral reasoning and build a *character*. To implement this, we could employ moral goals built around values. To avoid the pitfalls of purely practical goals, these values should be *explicit* and *efficacious*, that is, be directly present in the agent's reasoning, and have a material impact upon the decision making of an agent in any relevant situations it acts in. We could then have the agent prioritise these moral goals over the practical goals, ensuring that the former are not overruled by the latter.

Interpretative Exposure (Artus-Badea) Law and Causal Power. We have seen that there is a lawlike relation (which we over-indulgently call "the Artus-Badea law") between the amount of causal power a machine has and the degree to which we are exposed to IP. There is a qualitative difference between the consequences of behaviour by disembodied agents with purely digital causal power, and that of embodied fully autonomous agents with very capable sensors and effectors. The more restricted the causal power of the agent, the less unwanted effects it can have on the world, both quantitatively, as the domain it acts in is restricted, and qualitatively, as it can do less impactful actions with minimal (or no) sensors and effectors. Thus, *we propose that we adjust the causal power we build into an agent in the design process to the amount which we believe our reasoning mechanisms can successfully handle* (For example, some argue that a moral advisor is the most causal power to safely start with). Secondly, we can split the process or system of reasoning into multiple parts and focus on one while fixing the others (as advised in Badea and Gilpin 2021). For example, mirroring the types of mistakes an AI can make, MIs can be covered by a moral (or practical) reasoning system and IMs by a purely instrumental reasoning system. We could focus on the moral reasoning system and provide the instrumental understanding required ourselves by hardcoding it into the agent, thus eliminating any IMs, and focus on examining its moral reasoning system, looking for and addressing MIs (as in the moral decision-making framework we describe in Badea 2022). This is useful, as we do not yet have the sophisticated sensors and effectors required for human-level perception, common sense reasoning or understanding of the world and this method would allow us to focus on the moral reasoning without having to deal with all that.

Evaluation and Building Valuable Character. For evaluation, we might be tempted to require that the agent be able to justify its solutions to action selection problems using an exhaustive enumeration of actions based on a causal account. To do this, we might want it to represent explicitly the reasoning behind the decisions it makes purely in the form of imperatives like "if S, do X then Y", but we might not be able to accurately judge it by doing only this if IP holds, because there may be no way for us to have the agent motivate its moral decisions by having it present only a conclusive chain of imperatives or obligations to follow, such as "One is moral in a situation of type S if and only if one first performs action X, followed by action Y etc.". This is even before we mention the difficulty of deciding upon and including in advance, or learning at runtime, such a chain of imperatives for any possible variation upon the situation to be encountered. We could then get the agent to give us some (any) reasoned answer to start with, and then evaluate and modify the reasoning system we have, *a posteriori,* either manually or automatically through a learning process, without expecting it to be able to identify in a representable way the solution to complicated ethical problems *a priori* before this testing and training.

Regardless, we could require that it be able to *give a justification* for why it chose to act in a particular way, for us to gauge whether it is indeed moral or not. It could give an explanation based on the decision-making system it contains, the steps it follows in its reasoning (as we saw above) or, perhaps, the relevant values that informed its choice. Maybe it can show us the relevant values or considerations that it holds, and by looking at this and the agent's step-by-step reasoning and implementation, we can piece together how the moral decision making occurred and pass judgement on the whole package and the types of behaviours it exhibits, on this 'character' that it would have. This is another reason why building a moral agent that we can then evaluate could be centred around values, or virtues, aspects of the core of its 'character'.

4   On Implementing a Value-Based Virtuous AI

From a technical point of view, this 'character' could be made of two parts, an inter-related mechanism of explicit values and considerations that we might call the *moral paradigm,* and a corresponding *moral reasoning engine* that handles their application. An essential question that we are faced with is, then, what moral paradigm should we put in? As we have mentioned before, we cannot straightforwardly use classical versions of utilitarianism or deontology, due to IP and their rule-based nature. So how, then, do we get it to understand that which keeps human rule-following behaviour within acceptable moral bounds?

Show, not Tell (S, not T) and Values as Vehicles for Meaning. We propose a way of explaining abstract philosophical concepts (and moral paradigms) to agents, different from either defining what rules they consist of or attempting a direct representation of their content. If conveying meaning through any representational medium is subject to IP, then these conventional methods will be eternally enslaved to IP and thus to fatal ambiguity, a terrible bug in our program. A glimpse of a solution can be seen in the "Philosophical Investigations" (2009), itself a work that attempts to take us on a journey to the meaning behind the words, in the absence of any symbolic representation to convey that meaning unambiguously. We thus propose this same paradigm of **"Show, not Tell"** (S not T), but how do we *show* the meaning to the agent? Once again, we take a page from Wittgenstein's book (literally) and get the agent to understand our meaning by taking it on a journey, through a process. We start this process by engineering for it a device to help it indirectly understand what to do and how we want it to be, one which we have extensively advocated for above, a vehicle for transporting meaning between agents: *values*. By **values** we mean high-level concepts that are relevant considerations during decision making. These could be virtues, character traits ("honesty"), or concepts that are of moral importance ("property") or even morally neutral practical considerations. We argue that values are the tether to the external point of the game, crystallising what we want from the behaviour of the agents in the game, or in the moral situation. This is supported by arguments from *Virtue Ethics*, and in particular Aristotle's (1988) connection between virtues and practical wisdom (Phronesis). *Our theory is therefore equally applicable to practical reasoning of any type, not only moral reasoning, and to any kind of agents, not only AI.*

Leaning into Ambiguity. An important reason behind the usefulness of values is their ambiguity, and the fact that they are multiply realisable. That is, they can be embodied, or promoted, by different actions (even in the same context) and can be adhered to by a plethora of behaviours. But if we wish to keep values as ambiguous as possible, then, don't we give the agent leeway to perform differently to a specific desired behaviour? Was not getting the agent to do exactly what we wanted the whole point of building our AI in the first place? To this, we would say that our goal in building AI is indeed obtaining some behaviour, but what we want from an (even minimally) independent practical agent is not for it to "do action X, followed by Y, and then stop", but, rather, to achieve a complex goal while acting in a virtuous way. *The purpose of a value-based approach would be to allow the agent freedom to improvise in practical terms, while ensuring that it exhibits a certain character while doing so,* and thus now ambiguity is a feature, not a bug.

Character as Goal, Using Structure, and Relational Values. The whole point behind IP is that, in a sufficiently complex environment any goal or behaviour or piece of meaning, when conveyed in a representational way (using natural language, code, programming languages etc.), needs to be interpreted and therefore can be misinterpreted and misunderstood. If we recognise this, then we can move forward by attempting to convey the meaning that we desire using more abstract constructs (values), attempting to show indirectly, rather than tell. To start with, some values might be amenable to clear definition for a particular purpose, such as when building domain-specific AI, and they could form anchors (for example 'property' and its definitions in law). The idea here is that there can be some concrete starting point in terms of programming in values, and we can then get it to act in the spirit of these values. This we could do, for example, by *giving the agent the goal of solving the problem of becoming a certain type of character,* by building an explicit value-based moral paradigm into its reasoning, and then examining the results we get and iteratively fine-tuning it (manually or automatically) based on its behaviour. In this way, the machine would be using its creative ability to maximise the primary goal of, say, being trusted by its trainers, or being considered honest and so forth, so we would be getting the machine to do some of the work of mitigating IP for us by *giving it the goal of exhibiting certain virtues.*

The Structure of Values. Explicitly having values in the reasoning is beneficial, but to further add accuracy of meaning to our system we can leverage the structure we place the values into, and the relative preferences/interactions in the moral paradigm (Badea 2022), and choosing a structure that furthers our desired use of values seems essential. Even while being aware of IP, we still need a representable way of building the reasoning, as any kind of programming, whether rule-based or learning-based, starts with symbolic representation (pseudocode, code, specification etc). Due to IP, this representation cannot come (for perfect accuracy) in the form of conventional rules, imperatives, or goals, and so another source of precision is this structure, as the glue that holds values together and the arena in which they can perform. An example of doing this, from game theory/deontic logic/Answer Set Programming, is using a preference relation to classify values based on their relative importance into some ordered structure. We demonstrate a framework for building moral paradigms, with a preference ordering for values, based on a qualitative difference between values arranged in a structure of hierarchical layers, called *MARS*, in Badea 2022.

Relational Values. Another way of adding accuracy to the meaning of the solution is by tailoring the type of values we use. We have mentioned that the values used could be virtues, but instead of having a set of simple values, such as 'Honesty', we could use *human-dependent values*, such as 'Being trusted'. We call such values 'relational values' because they are intrinsically relative to another agent. For example, 'being trusted' is a relational value, relative to a particular human because it is measured subjectively through their opinion on the agent's trustworthiness. Thus, it does not need to understand what the values are in isolation, with no quantifiable evaluation of success, but rather in relation to us, measurably. Most attempts to achieve value alignment look at implementing the same rules we seem to follow into the machine (Taylor et al. 2016, Soares 2016). But just as we can misinterpret the rules, so could a machine, and thus we could instead focus on aligning the interpretation of the rules, through these relational values, turning us into *moral exemplars for the virtuous machines* (as we demonstrate with AI for Medicine in Hindocha and Badea 2022).

We have argued throughout this paper that there is an important distinction between rules and values. Moral rules, in the form of practical imperatives for example, correspond to the rules of the game, while values, as we have envisaged them, correspond to the spirit of the game, the external point of the game. This external point can only be shown, not said (not accurately transmitted through a representational medium). The tensions that arise between following the rules of the game and the spirit of the game, between the moral rules we give the artificial agent and the kind of behaviour we want it to achieve, stem from the *Interpretation Problem*. For this reason, and others, we propose the use of values as the core in obtaining moral behaviour. Since it is the spirit of the rules that needs to be acted upon, we propose the process of building artificial moral agents be done through a value-based approach, thus getting our agents to aim at developing a character of which we can approve. Such an anthropocentric, value-based paradigm allows us to train agents that remain tethered to the spirit of our rules and our values, to evaluate our agents as we can one another, and to set ourselves up as moral exemplars for the virtuous machines.

References

Anderson, M., Anderson, S.L. (eds.) Machine ethics. CUP (2011)

Arendt, H.: The Human Condition. University of Chicago Press (1998)

Aristotle, Thompson J. A. K. (trans) Nicomachean Ethics. Penguin, London (1988)

Badea, C.: Have a break from making decisions, have a MARS: the multi-valued action reasoning system. In: arXiv:2109.03283 [cs] (2022)

Badea, C., Gilpin, L.H.: Establishing meta-decision-making for AI: an ontology of relevance, representation and reasoning. In: AAAI 2021 Fall Symposium FSS-21. arXiv:submit/4523302 [cs] (2021)

BBC: Artificial intelligence: Google's AlphaGo beats Go master Lee Se-dol. BBC News Online. http://www.bbc.co.uk/news/technology-35785875 (2016)

Bolton, W., Badea, C., Georgiou, P., Holmes, A., Rawson, T.: Developing moral AI to support antimicrobial decision making. Nat. Mach. Intell (2022). https://doi.org/10.1038/s42256-022-00558-5

Bostrom, N.: Superintelligence: Oaths, Dangers, Strategies. OUP, Oxford (2014)

Havens, J.: The ethics of AI: how to stop your robot cooking your cat. The Guardian (2015). Retrieved 14 Dec 2017

Hindocha, S., Badea, C.: Moral exemplars for the virtuous machine: the clinician's role in ethical artificial intelligence for healthcare. AI and Ethics **2**, 167–175 (2021)

Jackson, P.: Introduction to Expert Systems, 3rd edn., p. 3. Addison-Wesley Longman Publishing Co., Inc, Boston, MA, USA (1998)

Krakovna, V., et al.: Specification gaming. DeepMind Blog (2020)

Le Roux, M.: Rise of the Machines: Keep an eye on AI, experts warn. Phys.org. https://phys.org/news/2016-03-machines-eye-ai-experts.html (2016)

Plato (trans: Lee, D) The Republic, Penguin (1987)

Post, B., Badea, C., Faisal, A., Brett, S.J.: Breaking bad news in the era of artificial intelligence and algorithmic medicine. AI Ethics (2022). https://doi.org/10.1007/s43681-022-00230-z

Russell, S.J., Norvig, P.: Artificial Intelligence: A Modern Approach, 2nd edn, p. 27, 32–58, pp. 968–972. Prentice Hall (2003). ISBN 0-13-790395-2

Ryle, G.: The Concept of Mind, pp. 74–80. Penguin, London (2000)

Searle: J. Speech Acts. Cambridge, CUP. (ch2) (1969)

Silver, D., et al.: Mastering the game of go with deep neural networks and tree research. Nature **529**, 484–489 (2016)

Soares, N.: The Value Learning Problem. In: Ethics in Artificial Intelligence Workshop at IJCAI-16 (2016). Accessed 19 Sep 2022

Solon, O.: Oh the humanity! Poker computer […]. The Guardian. Accessed (2017)

Taylor, J., Yudkowsky, E., LaVictoire, P., Critch, A.: Alignment for advanced machine learning systems, p. 5. Machine Intelligence Research Institute (2016)

Wittgenstein, L.: Philosophical Investigations, 4th edn. Wiley-Blackwell (2009)

Wallach, W., Asaro, P., (eds.) Machine Ethics and Robot Ethics. Taylor&Francis (2016)

Wallach, W., Allen, C.: Moral Machines. OUP (2008)

Yudkowsky, E.: Artificial Intelligence as a positive and negative factor in global risk. In: Yudkowsky, E. (ed.) Global Catastrophic Risks. Oxford University Press (2008). https://doi.org/10.1093/oso/9780198570509.003.0021

CRC: Consolidated Rules Construction for Expressive Ensemble Classification

Manal Almutairi[1], Frederic Stahl[2(✉)], and Max Bramer[3]

[1] Department of Computer Science, University of Reading, Reading, UK
manal.almutairi@pgr.reading.ac.uk
[2] DFKI Niedersachsen, Marine Perception, German Research Center for Artificial Intelligence GmbH (DFKI), Oldenburg, Germany
frederic_theodor.stahl@dfki.de
[3] School of Computing, University of Portsmouth, Portsmouth, UK
Max.Bramer@port.ac.uk

Abstract. Predictive modelling is one of the most important data mining tasks, where data mining models are trained on data with ground truth information and then applied to previously unseen data to predict the ground truth of a target variable. Ensemble models are often used for predictive modelling, since ensemble models tend to improve accuracy compared with standalone classification models. Although ensemble models are very accurate, they are opaque and predictions derived from these models are difficult to interpret by human analysts. However, explainability of classification models is needed in many critical applications such as stock market analysis, credit risk evaluation, intrusion detection, etc. A recent development of the authors of this paper is ReG-Rules, an ensemble learner that aims to extract a classification (prediction) committee, which comprises the first rule from each base classifier that fired. The rules are interpretable by humans, thus ReG-Rules is a step towards explainable ensemble classification. Since there is a set of matching rules presented to the human analyst for each prediction, there are still numerous rules that need to be considered for explaining the model to the human analyst. This paper introduces an extension of ReG-Rules termed Consolidated Rules Construction (CRC). CRC merges individual base classification models into a single rule set, that is then applied for each prediction. Only one rule is presented to the human analyst per prediction. Therefore, CRC is more explainable than ReG-Rules. Empirical evaluation also shows that CRC is competitive with ReG-Rules with respect to various performance measures.

Keywords: Ensemble learning · Rule-based classification · Explainable classifiers · Data mining

1 Introduction

Ensemble classification is the training of individual and diverse base classifiers and the combination of their predictive models into a unified classification model.

M. Bramer and F. Stahl (Eds.): SGAI-AI 2022, LNAI 13652, pp. 138–152, 2022.
https://doi.org/10.1007/978-3-031-21441-7_10

Ensembles are known to be generally more accurate than their individual models [7,12,13,15,23]. This is explained by the notion that combining the predictions of multiple learners can effectively remove high variance or high bias in predictions [9,15]. However, predictive learning models are required to be not only reliable and accurate, but also comprehensible to avoid the risk of irreversible misclassification, especially in many critical applications such as medical diagnoses, financial analysis, terrorism detection, etc. The use of ensemble approaches decreases the level of comprehensibility of the classification, as the human analyst is presented with a large number of different classification models [12,23]. This challenges the ability of decision makers to understand how a predictive ensemble system makes its predictions.

Therefore, this paper's contribution is a predictive ensemble learner that is both accurate and expressive at the same time. This is achieved by transforming the ensemble classification model into a consolidated expressive rule set, while preserving the predictive accuracy of the ensemble it is derived from. The level of expressiveness of the individual base learners is an important factor for improving the ensemble's explainability. This was one of the main reasons for choosing predictive rule learning approaches, as they are highly expressive and closer to 'white box models' than most other techniques. Another important reason is related to their ability to abstain from classifying a new instance when the algorithm is uncertain about a prediction. This aspect is needed to prevent costly false classifications. Nevertheless, the lower the abstaining rate, the better for most applications. Measuring the expressiveness of a rule-based learner often depends on the complexity of its rule set. A rule set is considered more expressive when it produces fewer rules with less complex terms per rule.

This paper is organised as follows: Sect. 2 discusses related work and summarises the authors' previous work on the ReG-Rules ensemble learner. Section 4 describes the proposed Consolidated Rules Construction (CRC) ensemble learner as a more explainable variation and extension of the ReG-Rules. Section 5 provides an empirical evaluation of the CRC ensemble learner, and concluding remarks including ongoing and future work are presented in Sect. 6.

2   Related Work

Ensemble methodology consists of a collection of base learners each trained on a different training subset and produces a single prediction (vote). Combining these individual predictions (decisions) using a some kind of voting approach is likely to create an ensemble with a higher level of overall predictive accuracy than its base learners [9,15]. The base learners are generated sequentially or hierarchically. The sequential paradigm leverages the concept of dependence between the individual classifiers. *Boosting*, in particular *AdaBoost algorithms* [11], is a well-known variant of this paradigm. In addition, numerous sequential ensemble techniques, such as the *Vote-boosting* algorithm [20] or the *SEL* framework [22], have recently been proposed. The parallel ensemble paradigm, on the other hand, relies on the independence and diversity of the base learners, because combining their separate decisions can effectively reduce the classification error [24]. The parallel ensemble paradigm is used in this study because it is parallelisable due to the base classifiers being independent, which can make the ensemble rule-based model more powerful in practice. *Bagging*, which stands for **B**ootstrap **aggregat**ing, is a widely used parallel technique proposed by Breiman in [8]. Bagging aims to increase the stability and predictive performance of a composite classifier. It entails random sampling of data with replacement. Each classifier learns from a sample of instances that is statistically estimated to comprise 63.2% of the training data and gives one vote to the data instance is classifying The remaining 36.8% serve as test data. The final classification is usually determined by a vote, such as a majority vote or a weighted majority vote. The capacity to eliminate bias and variance in data is the main benefit of bagging [8,9].

Random Forest is also a popular independent ensemble method [9] based on decision trees. It can be considered as an extended version of Bagging. Random Forest essentially incorporates the basic Random Decision Forest approach, which is introduced by Ho in [14], with Bagging method [21,24]. The Random Forest algorithm builds multiple decision trees. Each tree is constructed using the whole training dataset in sub-spaces selected randomly from the feature space. *Random Prism* [21], is an ensemble learner not based on trees but on rule sets produced by PrismTCS algorithm [6]. It follows the parallel ensemble learning approach and takes a bootstrap sample by randomly selecting n instances with replacement from the training dataset, where n is the total number of training instances available. Random Prism outperforms its standalone base classifier in terms of accuracy and noise tolerance, as seen in [21]. However, although Random Prism generates highly explainable base learners, the analyst must manually review each base learner's rule set to obtain insight into the classifications.

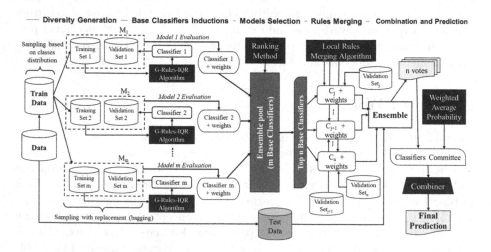

Fig. 1. The ReG-Rules learner framework

3   The ReG-Rules Ensemble Learner

ReG-Rules, a previous development of the authors of this paper, stands for Ranked ensemble G-Rules [3]. 'G' stands for Gaussian probability density distribution, which is used to build expressive base classifiers in G-Rules-IQR [2]. G-Rules-IQR [2] has been specifically developed for ReG-Rules and has shown in empirical experimentation to outperform similarly expressive rule based learners [1,4] in terms of accuracy, F1 score, tentative accuracy while producing more compact and easier to interpret rules. All the learners were evaluated against 5 metrics which are (1) the number of rules induced, (2) abstaining rate: the ratio of instances that remain unclassified, (3) F1 score: the harmonic mean of precision and recall, (4) accuracy: the ratio of correctly classified instances, (5) tentative accuracy: the ratio of correctly classified instances excluding abstained instances. G-Rules-IQR assumes normally distribute attributes and performs data transformations for non-normally distributed attributes. ReG-Rules provides an extract of the most relevant rules for each individual prediction, while preserving the predictive power of ensemble classifiers. ReG-Rules consists of 5 Stages as can be seen in Fig. 1:

Stage 1: Diversity Generation: The set of base classifiers should be diverse to assure producing uncorrelated errors and then obtain a more accurate ensemble [18,19,24]. Bagging [8] is applied to the training data to build local training and validation datasets to induce diverse base classifiers. The test data is only used to evaluate the final entire ReG-Rules ensemble.

Stage 2: Base Classifiers Inductions: M G-Rules-IQR base classifiers are induced. A value of 100 for M has performed well in ReG-Rules' empirical evaluation [3]. The out-of-bag samples produced by bagging are used to weight the performance of each individual base classifier. ReG-Rules uses a combination of metrics to calculate the weights: rule set size, number of correctly used rules (CUR), abstaining rate, accuracy and tentative accuracy.

Stage 3: Models Selection: Here three of the in Stage 2 mentioned metrics, namely tentative accuracy, CUR and abstaining rate, are used as ensemble selection criteria by ranking all the base classifiers accordingly. Only the top 20 base classifier models are retained, since 20 models produced consistently the best results in the empirical evaluation in [3].

Stage 4: Rules Merging: There is a possibility that for each rule set (of the 20 top ranked classifiers) some rules overlap. However, overlapping rules are generally unnecessary as they need to be tested at prediction stage and thus incur unnecessary additional testing cost [10]. ReG-Rules addresses this by providing a local rule merging method. This method is repeatedly applied to each base classifier in ReG-Rules.

Stage 5: Combination and Prediction: Combining classification results in ReG-Rules is based on weighted majority voting, however, not on a classifier level like most ensemble learners, but on an individual rule level. For this, ReG-Rules builds a committee of rules, termed Classification Committee (see Fig. 1), comprising the first rule that fires from each of the selected top ranked base classifiers. This committee derives a score for each possible classification as a combination of tentative accuracy, CUR, classifier vote frequency for certain classes.

In an empirical evaluation, ReG-Rules was compared against various rule based classifiers and exhibited a much better accuracy, tentative accuracy and low abstaining rate. The results also show that the local rule merging approach is very effective in lowering the total number of rules. A qualitative analysis revealed that ReG-Rules requires the human analyst to only examine a small set of relevant rules for each prediction, the classification committee [3].

4   The CRC Ensemble Learner

Although the committee in Stage 4 of ReG-Rules is much smaller than all the rules combined in ReG-Rules, the analyst still has to examine about 20 rules to extract information about the decision. Also, in ReG-Rules there is still the possibility that there are overlapping rules in the committee since rule merging is limited to local base learners. This section proposes an extension of ReG-Rules termed 'CRC', which is stand for Consolidated Rules Construction. The general structure of CRC as shown in Fig. 2 consists of five stages: (1) Diversity Generation, (2) Base Classifier Inductions, (3) Models Selections, (4) Stacking and Consolidation, (5) Prediction. The stages 1–3 are identical to the predecessor ReG-Rules and are summarised in Sect. 3. For a detailed description of Stages 1–3 the reader is referred to [3]. The new replaced Stages 4–5 are presented in the following sections by referring to the general framework (Fig. 2) and to the lines of code in Algorithm 1, which describe the CRC framework.

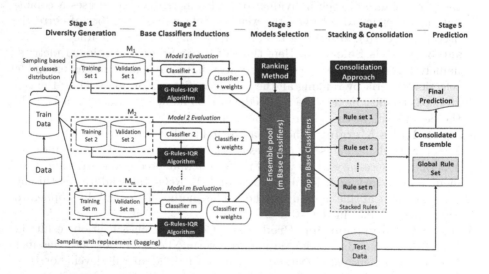

Fig. 2. The Consolidated Rules Construction (CRC) learner framework

---

Algorithm 1: Consolidated Rules Construction: CRC

Notations: M: Number of models, S: Training dataset, V: Validation dataset,
R: rule set, BC: base classifier, E_{pool}: Ensemble Pool

1 Randomly sample dataset without replacement into train and test datasets ($train$, $test$) **for**
$i = 1 \rightarrow M$ **do**
2 | $s_i \leftarrow$ a random sample of $train$ dataset generated by Bagging method (sample with
repalcement)
3 | $v_i \leftarrow$ out-of-bag set
4 | Generate a base classifier BC_i by applying Algorithm (G-Rules-IQR)[2] on s_i dataset
and learn a rule set $\rightarrow R_i$
5 | Evaluate BC_i performance by applying R_i on v_i dataset
6 | Calculate a weight for each rule induced in previous line
7 | Send BC_i including its rule set weights to the ensemble pool E_{pool}
8 **end**
9 Rank all the base classifiers BC collected in E_{pool} according to the criteria described in
Section 3 (stage 3)
10 Eliminate weak BC by selecting the n top models ($topBC$) ranked in the previous step
according to the following if statement:
11 **if** $models\ selection\ type = defualt$ **then**
12 | $n \leftarrow 20\% M$ models
13 **else**
14 | $n \leftarrow$ selected models size defined by user
15 Select the top n BC models in line 9
16 $SR \leftarrow$ stack all the rule sets induced by the n top models ($topBC$) in one large set
17 **Apply Algorithm 2** to the rule sets in SR and produce a single consolidated rule set
18 Sort the individual rules in the consolidated set according to their quality
19 **return** $CRC\ Classifier$

4.1   Stacking and Consolidation Stage

In Stage 4, Rules 'Stacking and Consolidation', the issue of overlapping rules
between all top ranked base classifiers is addressed in order to eliminate the
problem of the analyst being confronted with potentially unnecessarily overlapping and redundant rules. In this new method, CRC learner compresses the top
base classifiers into a single global rule-based model instead of locally merging
each rule set independently. This is expected to enhance the expressiveness of
the ensemble CRC learner to the point where it is similar to a common predictive
rule-based classifier. The approach consists of the following two steps:

1. *Stacking*: The CRC learner collects all the top base classifiers' rule sets
   together into one large set. This is depicted in Fig. 2 as 'stacked rules,' and
   is referred to as 'SR' in Algorithm 1 (line 16). The essential concept behind
   stacking is to simply collect rule sets in the same order as their original ranked
   base classifiers, with no optimisation or filtering applied to the rules. As a
   result, there is no longer a requirement to preserve the base classifiers, and
   they are simply deleted at this level.
2. *Consolidation*: CRC learner combines a consolidation mechanism to perform
   the global merging process and provides a consolidated rule set as highlighted
   in Algorithm 1 (line 17). The method is termed CRC Consolidator.

CRC Consolidator - after removing the base classifiers and stacking their rules
into one large set, the quality of each rule determines whether it will be preserved, improved, or even eliminated (individual weight). The process as shown

---

Algorithm 2: Consolidation Approach: CRC Consolidator

---

1 Initialise new *GlobalRules* set
2 **for** *(i = 1 → SR)* **do**
3 | *OverlappedRules ← SR$_i$* ;
4 | **for** *(j = 1 → SR [− OverlappedRules])* **do**
5 | | **if** *(SR$_i$ and SR$_j$ are identical rules)* **then**
6 | | | Skip current *SR$_j$*
7 | | **else**
8 | | | *OverlapExist ←* **Apply Algorithm 3 (Overlaps Checking)** on *SR$_i$* and *SR$_j$*
9 | | | **if** *(OverlapExist = True)* **then**
10 | | | | *OverlappedRules ←* ADD *(SR$_j$)*
11 | | | **end**
12 | | **end**
13 | **end**
14 | **if** *(OveralppedRules list contains rules other than SR$_i$)* **then**
15 | | *ConsoR ←* empty   // a new consolidated rule intialisation
16 | | **foreach** *(α in OveralppedRules list)* **do**
17 | | | **if** *(attribute α is categorical)* **then**
18 | | | | Create a rule-term *α$_j$* in the form *(α = v)* ;
19 | | | **else if** *(attribute α is continuous)* **then**
20 | | | | *x ←* smallest lower bound of *α* ;
21 | | | | *y ←* largest upper bound of *α* ;
22 | | | | Create a rule-term in a fom of *(x < α ≤ y)*
23 | | | **end**
24 | | | Append a rule-term built in lines 18 or 22 to the new consolidated rule *ConsoR*
25 | | **end**
26 | | *GlobalRules* set *←* ADD *(ConsoR)*
27 | **end**
28 **end**
29 **return** *new GlobalRules set*

---

in Algorithm 2 (CRC Consolidator) begins by initialising a new global rule set (line 1). Then each rule in SR is checked against the replications and the overlaps. If two rules (e.g. SR_1, SR_2) are identical, one of them will be removed (line 6). Otherwise, SR_1 and SR_2 will be to considered as candidate overlapped rules. This is conditioned by the decision returned from Algorithm 3 (Overlap Checking), which is invoked by the CRC Consolidator in line 8 to carry out the examination. A decision (true/false) about the current rules examination is returned to the CRC Consolidator.

The CRC Consolidator then proceeds to line 10, where the current overlapped rules are examined for the final consolidation process, and a new iteration is initiated to examine two more additional rules until all of the rules in the stacked rule sets (SR) have been examined. Then, in line 14, a process of creating a new consolidated rule from a number of overlapped rules begins. The overlapping rules are first categorised by terms. The procedure will then continue, depending on the type of attribute in each term. First, the overlapped rules are grouped by terms. Then, depending on the type of attribute in each term, the process will continue. In case of categorical attributes, a new term is generated in the form $(α = v)$ where $α$ is the attribute name and v is a discrete value that occurs in all the current overlapped terms. If the attribute type is continuous, a new term is generated in the form $(x < α ≤ y)$ where x is the smallest lower bound presented in all the current overlapped terms and y is the largest upper bound presented in the same overlapped terms. After the term is created, it will be appended to the new consolidated rule (line 24). Then, a new iteration of the next term will be started. Finally, in line 26, all the consolidated rules are added to the global rule set. The weight of each consolidated rule is estimated by averaging the weights associated to all the overlapped rules used in its generation.

Algorithm 3: Overlap Checking

---

1 **Input:** Rule1 (current rule), Rule2 (another rule)

2 **if** *(class label in Rule1 = class label in Rule2)* **and**
3   *(all attributes α in Rule1 = all attributes α in Rule2)* **then**
4   **foreach** *attribute $\alpha \in$ Rule1 and Rule2* **do**
5   **switch** *the type of α* **do**
6   **case** *Continuous*
7   **if** *(lower bound of one rule includes the lower bound of the other* **and**
8   *upper bound of one rule includes the upper bound of the other)* **then**
9 | OverlapExist ← **True**
10   **else**
11 | OverlapExist ← **False**
12
13   **case** *Categorical*
14   **if** *(discrete value in Rule1 = discrete value in Rule2)* **then**
15 | OverlapExist ← **True**
16   **else**
17 | OverlapExist ← **False**
18
19   **endsw**
20   **endsw**
21   **if** *(OverlapExist = False)* **then**
22 | Exit the loop in line 4
23   **end**
24 **end**
25 **else**
26 | OverlapExist ← **False**
27 **end**
28 **return** *OverlapExist*

4.2   Prediction Stage

As discussed in Sect. 2 combining multiple individual models' predictions promises a considerable increase in predictive accuracy compared with a single classifier. However, as mentioned in Sect. 4, ReG-Rules has a number of potential issues in training and testing phases. These are the number of base classifiers that need to be employed at prediction, and this consumes more processing overhead time prior to voting than applying a single model. Also the resulting vote on the prediction is harder to explain and justify by a human since there are several rules that need to be considered, i.e. in ReG-Rules the classification committee. In other words, the expressive power of ReG-Rules depends on the size of the classification committees and the complexity of the datasets. Both issues are removed or simplified in CRC, since CRC's learned model replaces the classification committees derived for each prediction by a single and global rule set re-used for each prediction. The first rule that matches the data instance to be classified is used to label the data instance, and at the same time this single rule serves as an explanation for the human analyst.

5 Empirical Evaluation of CRC Learning Model

The goal of the empirical evaluation is to evaluate the performance of the proposed CRC learner compared with ReG-Rules and G-Rules-IQR, which the stand-alone classifier used as base learner for both, ReG-Rules and CRC.

5.1 Experimental Setup

All the experiments were performed on a 2.9 GHz Quad-Core Intel Core i7 machine with memory 16 GB 2133 MHz LPDDR3, running macOS Big Sur version 11.4. All the 24 datasets used in the experiments were chosen randomly from the UCI repository [16], the only conditions being that they contain continuous attributes and involve classification tasks. The specifications of the datasets are highlighted in Table 1. Datasets 15, 16 and 24 included few missing values in continuous attributes. Missing values were replaced with the average value of the for the concerning attribute. Both ReG-Rules and CRC, and their base learning algorithm (G-Rule-IQR) have been implemented in the statistical programming language R [17]. The source code used to implement CRC algorithm is similar to that for ReG-Rules differing only in the methodological aspects described in Stages 4 and 5 described in Sect. 4.

The source code is available in a public online repository at https://github.com/ManalAlmutairi/PhD_Project_Codes/tree/v1.0.0 and is also archived at https://doi.org/10.5281/zenodo.5557590 [5].

All the algorithms are evaluated against 6 metrics for classifiers, which are: Number of Rules, abstaining rate, F1 score, accuracy, tentative accuracy and execution time. Execution comprises the time needed to complete all the training stages and to produce the final decisions. The remaining metrics were already described in Sect. 3. Please note that there is a relationship between accuracy, tentative accuracy and abstaining rate. Tentative accuracy simply ignores abstained instances, and accuracy treats abstained instances as potential misclassifications. Hence, the more a algorithm abstains, the higher the tentative accuracy and the lower the accuracy. The methodology used for experimentation with the 24 datasets is hold-out procedure; each dataset was randomly sampled without replacement into train and test datasets. While the 70% of the data instances were used to train and build the ensemble classifier, the remaining 30% were used as a testing dataset. In case of the ensemble models (ReG-Rules and CRC), the training dataset is used to generate multiple base classifiers using bagging, whereas the test set is used only once to assess the general performance of the classification models.

Table 1. Characteristics of the datasets used in the experiments

No.	Dataset	No. attributes	No. classes	No. instances
1	Iris	5 (4 cont)	3	150
2	Seeds	8 (7 cont)	3	210
3	Wine	14 (13 cont)	3	178
4	Blood transfusion	6 (5 cont)	2	748
5	Banknote	6 (5 cont)	2	1,372
6	Ecoli	9 (7 cont, 1 name)	8	336
7	Yeast	10 (8 cont, 1 name)	10	1,484
8	Page blocks	11 (10 cont)	5	5,473
9	User modelling	6 (5 cont)	4	403
10	Breast tissue	11 (10 cont)	6	106
11	Glass	11 (10 cont, 1 id)	7	214
12	HTRU2	10 (9 cont)	2	17,898
13	Magic gamma	12 (11 cont)	2	19,020
14	Wine quality-white	13 (12 cont)	11	4,898
15	Breast cancer	12 (10 cont, 1 id)	2	699
16	Post operative	10 (1 cont, 9 categ)	3	90
17	Wifi localization	8 (7 cont)	4	2,000
18	Indian liver patient	12 (10 cont, 1 categ)	2	583
19	Sonar	62 (61 cont)	2	208
20	Leaf	17 (15 cont, 1 name)	40	340
21	Internet firewall	12 (cont)	4	65,532
22	Bank marketing	17 (6 cont, 10 categ)	2	45,211
23	Avila	11 (10 cont)	12	20,867
24	Shuttle	10 (9 cont)	7	58,000

5.2   Results and Interpretation

In each table, the # symbol refers to the index of the dataset in Table 1. The best
result(s) in the tables for each dataset and metric are highlighted in bold letters.
Table 2 shows the number of rules induced by each algorithm. Table 3 shows the
comparison between CRC and ReG-Rules while Table 4 presents the comparison between CRC and G-Rules-IQR in these metrics, which will be discussed.
Regarding the 'number of induced rules' and the 'abstaining rates' metrics listed
in Table 2, it is not fair to compare the ensemble learners against the base classifier G-Rules-IQR. Therefore, CRC learner is only compared with ReG-Rules
ensemble. As shown in the table, the number of consolidated rules produced by
CRC is considerably smaller than the total number of rules produced by ReG-
Rules in all datasets. In most cases, the size of the rules generated by CRC
is reduced by 90%. Abstaining from classification, a typical problem of rule-
based classifiers, was almost non-existent in both ensembles (ReG-Rules and
CRC) compared with the stand-alone G-Rules-IQR's abstaining rates, which

were higher by more than 10% on several datasets compared with ReG-Rules and CRC. In four datasets (9, 10, 18 and 20) the abstaining rate in G-Rules-IQR reaches 30%, 19%, 18% and 40% respectively.

Comparing with ReG-Rules Ensemble Learner: Table 3 shows the comparison of the performance of CRC and ReG-Rules. The results of F1 score reveals that CRC performs equal or better than ReG-Rules in 13 out of 24 datasets. Also, CRC was very competitive on 4 out of the remaining datasets, on which it only underperformed by a maximum difference of 3%. Please note that the comparison between CRC and ReG-Rules in terms of overall accuracy and tentative accuracy are very similar. The results show that with respect to both metrics, CRC performs at the same level as ReG-Rules in 14 out of 24 cases. On 5 out of the remaining 10 datasets (2, 6, 11, 18 and 19) where CRC

Table 2. Number of rules and abstaining rates for CRC compared with ReG-Rules and G-Rules-IQR

#	Number of rules			Abstaining rate		
	G-Rules-IQR	ReG-Rules	CRC	G-Rules-IQR	ReG-Rules	CRC
1	*18*	342	**44**	0.07	**0.00**	**0.00**
2	*22*	386	**64**	0.03	**0.00**	**0.00**
3	*13*	250	**28**	0.06	**0.00**	**0.00**
4	*20*	321	**38**	**0.00**	**0.00**	**0.00**
5	*89*	1630	**128**	0.02	**0.00**	**0.00**
6	*37*	649	**107**	0.02	**0.00**	**0.00**
7	*99*	1648	**289**	0.04	**0.00**	**0.00**
8	*131*	2348	**570**	0.02	**0.00**	**0.00**
9	*57*	901	**162**	0.30	**0.00**	0.01
10	*28*	485	**87**	0.19	**0.00**	**0.00**
11	*30*	505	**72**	0.11	**0.02**	**0.02**
12	*35*	521	**57**	**0.00**	**0.00**	**0.00**
13	*79*	1388	**251**	**0.00**	**0.00**	**0.00**
14	*126*	2289	**243**	0.02	**0.00**	**0.00**
15	*11*	186	**28**	**0.00**	**0.00**	**0.00**
16	*29*	451	**105**	0.11	**0.00**	**0.00**
17	*59*	955	**159**	0.01	**0.00**	**0.00**
18	*47*	996	**368**	0.17	**0.00**	**0.00**
19	*16*	270	**30**	0.13	**0.00**	**0.00**
20	*124*	2015	**393**	0.40	**0.01**	0.03
21	*21*	402	**49**	**0.00**	**0.00**	**0.00**
22	*115*	1977	**428**	0.01	**0.00**	**0.00**
23	*158*	3272	**699**	0.09	**0.01**	0.01
24	*27*	428	**38**	**0.00**	**0.00**	**0.00**
Average	58	1026	185	0.07	0.00	0.00
SD	45	846	186	0.102	0.004	0.01

did not achieve the highest accuracy and tentative accuracy, it was still very close within 3% of the best results compared with ReG-Rules learner. On one dataset (#5), the accuracy and tentative accuracy of CRC were lower than ReG-Rules by about 15%. However, this is also the dataset where the highest compression in the size of the rules is taking place. Regarding the learning time, Table 3 demonstrates that CRC learner is faster than ReG-Rules on all datasets. The decrease in learning times was up to 45% in some cases.

Comparing with Stand-Alone G-Rules-IQR Learner: The performance of CRC learning model is also compared with its stand-alone inducer (G-Rules-IQR algorithm). Table 4 shows the results of this comparison using F1 score, accuracy and tentative accuracy. CRC achieves the best F1 scores in 14 out of 24 datasets.

Table 3. Comparison of the performance of CRC and ReG-Rules using F1 score, Overall Accuracy, Tentative Accuracy and Learning Time

#	F1 score		Accuracy		Tentative accuracy		Learning time (sec.)	
	ReG-Rules	CRC	ReG-Rules	CRC	ReG-Rules	CRC	ReG-Rules	CRC
1	0.93	0.93	0.93	0.93	0.93	0.93	112.8	94.8
2	1.00	0.97	1.00	0.97	1.00	0.97	232.2	192.6
3	1.00	1.00	1.00	1.00	1.00	1.00	166.2	148.8
4	1.00	1.00	1.00	1.00	1.00	1.00	358.8	322.2
5	0.99	0.87	0.99	0.84	0.99	0.84	3251.4	2939.4
6	0.91	0.91	0.95	0.92	0.95	0.92	384	360
7	0.91	0.83	0.97	0.97	0.97	0.97	3262.8	3096
8	0.87	0.82	0.98	0.98	0.98	0.98	10512	9612
9	0.95	0.87	0.94	0.86	0.94	0.87	733.2	631.2
10	0.97	0.91	0.97	0.91	0.97	0.91	245.4	228.6
11	0.93	0.90	0.95	0.94	0.97	0.95	264	247.2
12	1.00	1.00	1.00	1.00	1.00	1.00	12600	12168
13	1.00	1.00	1.00	1.00	1.00	1.00	18288	17100
14	0.87	0.99	1.00	1.00	1.00	1.00	12240	11880
15	1.00	1.00	1.00	1.00	1.00	1.00	174.6	156
16	0.77	0.77	0.63	0.63	0.63	0.63	193.2	189
17	1.00	1.00	1.00	1.00	1.00	1.00	2833.2	2635.8
18	0.84	0.82	0.73	0.71	0.73	0.71	2095.8	1951.8
19	0.97	0.96	0.97	0.95	0.97	0.95	897.6	864.6
20	0.67	0.61	0.56	0.46	0.57	0.47	2388	2125.8
21	0.90	0.90	1.00	1.00	1.00	1.00	71316	39276
22	0.99	0.99	0.98	0.98	0.98	0.98	41400	32940
23	0.93	0.86	0.92	0.86	0.92	0.86	119232	68292
24	1.00	1.00	1.00	1.00	1.00	1.00	20808	17964
Average	0.93	0.91	0.94	0.91	0.94	0.91	13499.55	9392
SD	0.083	0.096	0.119	0.135	0.118	0.13	27874	16426

In the cases where CRC did not outperform G-Rules-IQR, its scores were only marginally lower. For example, the differences in 5 cases (1, 2, 7, 18 and 23) were less than 4%. In terms of overall accuracy, as can be seen in Table 4, CRC achieves the highest results in most cases (21 out of the 24 datasets). Moreover, CRC achieves the highest tentative accuracies in 14 out of 24 datasets compared with G-Rules-IQR classifier. CRC was also very competitive with G-Rules-IQR, in 7 out of the remaining 8 datasets their results are very close. On only one dataset (# 20), CRC's tentative accuracy was much lower than the stand-alone G-Rules-IOR. However, this dataset also causes the highest abstaining rate for G-Rules-IQR in the current experiments, and therefore it had been classified using the majority class label method. As mentioned in Sect. 5.1 the abstained instances are not considered in the tentative accuracy.

Table 4. Comparison of the performance of CRC and G-Rules-IQR using F1 score, overall accuracy and tentative accuracy

#	F1 score		Accuracy		Tentative accuracy	
	G-Rules-IQR	CRC	G-Rules-IQR	CRC	G-Rules-IQR	CRC
1	**0.96**	0.93	0.91	**0.93**	**0.95**	0.93
2	**1.00**	0.97	**0.97**	0.97	**1.00**	0.97
3	0.98	**1.00**	0.94	**1.00**	0.98	**1.00**
4	0.98	**1.00**	0.97	**1.00**	0.97	**1.00**
5	**0.98**	0.87	**0.98**	0.84	**0.99**	0.84
6	**0.99**	0.91	**0.96**	0.92	**0.97**	0.92
7	**0.87**	0.83	0.93	**0.97**	0.96	**0.97**
8	**0.93**	0.82	**0.98**	0.98	**0.99**	0.98
9	**0.95**	0.87	0.72	**0.86**	**0.95**	0.87
10	0.77	**0.91**	0.66	**0.91**	0.81	**0.91**
11	0.86	**0.90**	0.86	**0.94**	**0.97**	0.95
12	0.99	**1.00**	1.00	**1.00**	1.00	**1.00**
13	**1.00**	1.00	1.00	**1.00**	1.00	**1.00**
14	0.96	**0.99**	0.97	**1.00**	0.99	**1.00**
15	**1.00**	1.00	1.00	**1.00**	1.00	**1.00**
16	0.49	**0.77**	**0.67**	0.63	**0.67**	0.63
17	**1.00**	1.00	0.99	**1.00**	1.00	**1.00**
18	**0.83**	0.82	**0.71**	0.71	**0.71**	0.71
19	0.95	**0.96**	0.87	**0.95**	0.94	**0.95**
20	**0.75**	0.61	0.39	**0.46**	**0.65**	0.47
21	**0.90**	0.90	1.00	**1.00**	1.00	**1.00**
22	**0.99**	0.99	**0.98**	0.98	0.98	**0.98**
23	**0.89**	0.86	0.85	**0.86**	**0.88**	0.86
24	0.99	**1.00**	1.00	**1.00**	1.00	**1.00**
Average	0.92	0.91	0.89	0.91	0.93	0.91
SD	0.12	0.10	0.15	0.14	0.11	0.13

6   Conclusion

The current work aims to increase the expressive power of rule-based ensemble learning models while maintaining the key advantage of the ensemble learners, which is the high predictive accuracy compared with the stand-alone classifiers. A new approach was presented in this paper to compress the ensemble ReG-Rules [3] learner into a single global classifier, which can be used directly in predictions without the need to combine multiple classifiers' votes on every classification attempt. The best ranked classifiers are consolidated in a single global rule set. The proposed ensemble learner is therefore called Consolidated Rules Construction (CRC). CRC was empirically evaluated and compared with the ensemble ReG-Rules classifier and the stand-alone G-Rules-IQR classifier. Compared with ReG-Rules, CRC achieved its overall aim and outperformed ReG-Rules in all cases and in terms of number of rules that have been constructed and used for predictions. In most cases the reduction of rules reached 90%. Abstaining of classification was almost non existent in both ensemble classifiers. CRC exhibited a similar F1 score, overall accuracy and tentative accuracy compared with ReG-Rules. CRC outperformed ReG-Rules in terms of learning time in all cases, which reaches up to 45% learning time reduction in some cases. CRC also achieved the highest results in most cases in terms of F1 score, overall accuracy and tentative accuracy. Ongoing work comprises incorporating further diversification techniques by initialising base classifiers with different learning parameters. CRC is also highly parallelisable, since its base classifiers are induced independently. Therefore, future work comprises the development of a parallel CRC ensemble classification framework to scale up CRC to large datasets.

Acknowledgements. The research in this paper is partly supported by the Ministry for Science and Culture, Lower Saxony, Germany, through funds from the Niedersächsische Vorab (ZN3480).

References

1. Almutairi, M., Stahl, F., Bramer, M.: Improving modular classification rule induction with g-prism using dynamic rule term boundaries. In: Bramer, M., Petridis, M. (eds.) SGAI 2017. LNCS (LNAI), vol. 10630, pp. 115–128. Springer, Cham (2017). https://doi.org/10.1007/978-3-319-71078-5_9
2. Almutairi, M., Stahl, F., Bramer, M.: A rule-based classifier with accurate and fast rule term induction for continuous attributes. In: 2018 17th IEEE International Conference on Machine Learning and Applications (ICMLA), pp. 413–420. IEEE (2018)
3. Almutairi, M., Stahl, F., Bramer, M.: Reg-rules: an explainable rule-based ensemble learner for classification. IEEE Access **9**, 52015–52035 (2021). https://doi.org/10.1109/ACCESS.2021.3062763
4. Almutairi, M., Stahl, F., Jennings, M., Le, T., Bramer, M.: Towards expressive modular rule induction for numerical attributes. In: Bramer, M., Petridis, M. (eds.) Research and Development in Intelligent Systems XXXIII, pp. 229–235. Springer, Cham (2016). https://doi.org/10.1007/978-3-319-47175-4_16

5. Almutairi, M.K.: ManalAlmutairi/PhD_Project_Codes: G-Rules-IQR. ReG-Rules and CRC, October 2021. https://doi.org/10.5281/zenodo.5557590

6. Bramer, M.: An information-theoretic approach to the pre-pruning of classification rules. In: Musen, M.A., Neumann, B., Studer, R. (eds.) IIP 2002. ITIFIP, vol. 93, pp. 201–212. Springer, Boston, MA (2002). https://doi.org/10.1007/978-0-387-35602-0_18

7. Bramer, M.: Principles of Data Mining, vol. 530. Springer, London (2016). https://doi.org/10.1007/978-1-4471-7307-6

8. Breiman, L.: Bagging predictors. Mach. Learn. **24**(2), 123–140 (1996)

9. Breiman, L.: Random forests. Mach. Learn. **45**(1), 5–32 (2001)

10. Cendrowska, J.: PRISM: an algorithm for inducing modular rules. Int. J. Man Mach. Stud. **27**(4), 349–370 (1987)

11. Freund, Y., Schapire, R.E.: A decision-theoretic generalization of on-line learning and an application to boosting. J. Comput. Syst. Sci. **55**(1), 119–139 (1997)

12. Fürnkranz, J., Gamberger, D., Lavrač, N.: Foundations of Rule Learning. Springer, Heidelberg (2012). https://doi.org/10.1007/978-3-540-75197-7

13. Han, J., Pei, J., Kamber, M.: Data Mining: Concepts and Techniques. Elsevier, Amsterdam (2011)

14. Ho, T.K.: Random decision forests. In: Proceedings of the Third International Conference on Document Analysis and Recognition, vol. 1, pp. 278–282. IEEE (1995)

15. Johnston, B., Mathur, I.: Applied Supervised Learning with Python: Use Scikit-Learn to Build Predictive Models from Real-World Datasets and Prepare Yourself for the Future of Machine Learning. Packt Publishing, Birmingham (2019). https://books.google.co.uk/books?id=LeVDwAAQBAJ

16. Lichman, M.: UCI machine learning repository (2013). https://archive.ics.uci.edu/ml

17. R Development Core Team: R: A Language and Environment for Statistical Computing. R Foundation for Statistical Computing, Vienna, Austria (2020). https://www.R-project.org, ISBN 3-900051-07-0

18. Rokach, L.: Ensemble-based classifiers. Artif. Intell. Rev. **33**(1–2), 1–39 (2010). https://doi.org/10.1007/s10462-009-9124-7

19. Rokach, L.: Ensemble Learning: Pattern Classification Using Ensemble Methods, vol. 85. World Scientific, Singapore (2019)

20. Sabzevari, M., Martínez-Muñoz, G., Suárez, A.: Vote-boosting ensembles. Pattern Recogn. **83**, 119–133 (2018)

21. Stahl, F., Bramer, M.: Random PRISM: a noise-tolerant alternative to random forests. Expert. Syst. **31**(5), 411–420 (2014)

22. Vong, C.M., Du, J.: Accurate and efficient sequential ensemble learning for highly imbalanced multi-class data. Neural Netw. (2020)

23. Witten, I.H., Frank, E., Hall, M.A., Pal, C.J.: Data Mining: Practical Machine Learning Tools and Techniques. Morgan Kaufmann, Burlington (2016)

24. Zhou, Z.H.: Ensemble Methods: Foundations and Algorithms. Chapman and Hall/CRC, Boca Raton (2012)

Competitive Learning with Spiking Nets and Spike Timing Dependent Plasticity

Christian Huyck$^{(\boxtimes)}$ and Orume Erekpaine

Middlesex University, London NW4 4BT, UK
c.huyck@mdx.ac.uk
http://www.cwa.mdx.ac.uk/chris/chrisroot.html

Abstract. This paper explores machine learning using biologically plausible neurons and learning rules. Two systems are developed. The first, for student performance categorisation, uses a two layer system and explores data encoding mechanisms. The second, for digit categorisation, explores competitive behaviour between categorisation neurons using a three layer system with an inhibitory layer. Both are successful. The competitive mechanism from the second system is more plausible biologically, and, by using one neuron per input feature, uses fewer neurons.

Keywords: Spiking neurons · Spike timing dependent plasticity · Categorisation · MNIST

1 Introduction

The authors have proposed, and still believe, that the best way to develop a full-fledged, Turing test passing, general AI is to follow the human model [14]. This means developing embodied agents that persist for a significant amount of time (e.g. years), are good cognitive models of most of the things that humans do, and are based on simulated neurons that are relatively close approximations to biology. Progress can be made by using commonly used spiking neurons, and commonly used Hebbian learning rules. These models have strong support from biological evidence, and many of their limitations are understood and are being actively explored [20].

While there is interest in passing the Turing test, there is appreciably more interest in machine learning. Deep nets, such as BERT [8] and Alpha Go [18], are widely used in modern industrial tasks. These make use of neuron like nodes, and synapse like connections; they take advantage of biologically implausible gradient descent methods, and vast data sets to learn the connection weights. These "neural nets" have impressive results and it is not surprising that they spark a great deal of interest.

They are not, however, particularly closely connected to biology. One way to bridge the gap is to use more biologically plausible systems to solve machine learning tasks. The systems described in this paper use simple spiking neurons,

© The Author(s), under exclusive license to Springer Nature Switzerland AG 2022
M. Bramer and F. Stahl (Eds.): SGAI-AI 2022, LNAI 13652, pp. 153–166, 2022.
https://doi.org/10.1007/978-3-031-21441-7_11

based on point models. They learn by spike timing dependent plasticity (STDP), a model with biological support (see Sect. 2.1). It uses the firing times of the pre and post-synaptic neurons to select the weight change with the weight increasing if the pre-synaptic neuron fires first, and decreasing if the post-synaptic neuron fires first.

This paper describes two machine learning systems, one for student performance categorisation (Sect. 4), and one for digit categorisation (Sect. 5). The student performance system is based on the authors' earlier work [15] and uses a two layer topology. The digit categorisation system makes use of a three layer topology inspired by Diehl and Cook [9] (see Sect. 2.2). Both make use of standard neural models, middleware and a neuron simulator (see Sect. 2.1), so that the systems can be readily used and modified[1] with an explanation of how to run the simulations to reproduce the data reported below.

2 Literature Review

The work reported in this paper is the third in a series of papers using biologically motivated simulated neurons and learning rules. The earlier papers [15,16] used a feed forward topology with input neurons connected to category neurons.

Like the systems introduced in the rest of the paper, these earlier papers used standard neural models, standard learning models, a widely used neural simulator, and commonly used middleware. These are described in Sect. 2.1.

Those earlier papers make use of a two layer architecture with an input layer connected to an output layer. The neurons in the output layer act as the categoriser, and the connections from input to output are plastic during training. During training, an input is presented by causing the appropriate input neurons to fire, followed by causing the appropriate categorisation neuron to fire. This leads to a mechanism where the synaptic weight reflects the co-occurrence value between the feature value neuron and the category neuron. The system from Sect. 4 also makes use of this mechanism.

Section 5 uses a different three layer topology that allows the categorisation neurons to compete with each other. This is a modification of the work of Diehl and Cook [9], described more fully in Sect. 2.2.

2.1 Standard Models and Commonly Used Systems

The simulations in the earlier papers [15,16] and those described below make use of commonly used computational neuroscience platforms. In particular, one commonly used mechanism is to use PyNN [7] as middleware to specify the neural topology, synaptic modification rules, neural stimulation, and recording. This acts as middleware between the developer and existing neural simulators; there are many simulators, and the simulations below use NEST [11].

---

[1] The code can be found on http://www.cwa.mdx.ac.uk/spikeLearn/spikeLearn.html.

In this paper, the leaky integrate and fire neural models with fixed threshold and exponentially decaying conductance are from Brette and Gerstner [4] (IF_cond_exp in PyNN). The model is based on Eqs. 1 and 2.

$$C\frac{dV}{dt} = f(V) - w + I \tag{1}$$

$$f(V) = -g_L(V - E_L) + g_L\Delta_T exp(\frac{V - V_T}{\Delta_T}) \tag{2}$$

V is the variable that represents the voltage of the neuron, and T is time. C is the membrane capacitance constant, and I is the input current. w is an adaptation variable that is 0 for these neurons. g_L is the leak conductance constant and E_L is the resting potential constant. Δ_T is the slope factor constant and V_T is the spike threshold constant.

In one set of simulations, neurons with adaptation are used. In this case, every time a neuron fires, its adaptation variable w is increased by a constant b. This then reverts to 0 depending on another constant a, and time as shown in Eq. 3. τ_w is the adaptation time constant. This in effect makes it more difficult for neurons to fire frequently.

$$\tau_w\frac{dw}{dt} = a(V - E_L) - w \tag{3}$$

Equations 1 and 2 determine the change in V (the voltage variable), and Eq. 3 manages the change in w (the adaptation variable). These variables are also changed when $V > V_T$ and the neuron spikes; V is reset to E_L, and w is increased by a constant b for spike triggered adaptation. The simulations described below in this paper use the default constants described by [4].

In the brain, most if not all learning is Hebbian [12]. If the pre-synaptic neuron tends to cause the post-synaptic neuron to fire, the weight will tend to increase. There are many variations of this rule, but a great deal of biological evidence supports STDP [3]. Bi and Poo [3] have perhaps the first published example that shows the performance of the changing efficiency of biological synapses. Song and colleagues [19] have developed an idealised curve that fits the biological data.

The simulations below use the standard spike pair STDP rule described by Eq. 4. The presynaptic neuron fires at t_r and the post-synaptic neuron fires at t_o. If the presynaptic neuron fires first, the weight is increased (modulated by a constant c_+) otherwise it decreases (modulated by the constant c_-).

$$\Delta_w = \begin{cases} c_+ * e^{t_r - t_o} & t_r <= t_o \\ c_- * e^{t_o - t_r} & t_o > t_r \end{cases} \tag{4}$$

2.2   Unsupervised Learning Using STDP

Perhaps the best working example of spiking nets learning using Hebbian rules is by Diehl and Cook [9]. This has several main differences from the authors' earlier work in this area [15,16]. The first is that there are not single neurons for each category but instead a group of neurons that are not explicitly associated with any category. Unlike Huyck and Samey [16], these category neurons are never explicitly fired during training, but are only activated from the input. Additionally, there is a set of inhibitory neurons that take input from the category neurons and in turn inhibits them. This enables the layer of category neurons to compete. The only plastic synapses are from the input to the category neurons. When the system is learning properly, the neurons compete for the synaptic strength, and each fires only when a particular type of input is presented.

This is unsupervised behaviour, and to this point the category labels have not been presented. Once this training is complete, the category neurons are assigned labels based on the categories of the inputs to which they respond.

This behaviour resembles that of a self organising map (SOM) [17]. The nodes of the SOM are like a category neuron. The SOM nodes move to a place that responds to particular inputs, and moves away from other nodes. When the category neurons are learning properly, they also respond to particular inputs and not others. If one wants to categorise with a SOM network, each of the nodes can be assigned a particular category. Novel input can then be categorised by the category of the node that responds.

The second difference is input. In Huyck and Samey [16], each value for each feature had its own neuron. In Diehl and Cook [9], each feature has a single neuron, and higher values lead to more activation, which leads to earlier firing or earlier firing along with more spikes. This allows fewer neurons to be used.

The third difference is an enforced balancing of firing for these categorisation neurons. Category neurons have to fire roughly the same amount over several data items. Diehl and Cook [9] enforce this by a dynamic firing threshold that responds to how often it has recently fired. This relates to adaptation. See Sects. 3.2 and 6 for more on balanced firing.

3   Methods

Biological neuron simulations run for a period of simulated time with the neuron behaving throughout the period. When a neuron fires, activation spreads from it to other neurons that have synapses from it.

The systems can learn via a Hebbian learning rule, and the simulations in this paper use one. Synaptic weights change via STDP, increasing when pre-synaptic neurons fire before post-synaptic neurons, and decreasing when pre-synaptic neurons fire after the post-synaptic neurons.

Both of the systems introduced in this paper work in a layered fashion, with input neurons in the first layer and category neurons in the second. There are no synaptic connections within layers, only between layers.

Neurons used in these simulations are leaky integrate and fire neurons. All use the default parameters. In both systems, training is performed by a system with plastic synapses. Data items are presented in sequence. In the Digit Categorisation task, one system variant uses leaky integrate and fire neurons with adaptation for the categorisation neurons. This uses all the default parameters except the adaptation increase rate b (see Eq. 3).

3.1 Student Performance Categorisation

The student performance system categorises based on data from the UCI machine Learning Repository [6]. The dataset includes performances for mathematics and Portuguese separately but only the performance for mathematics is used. The dataset contained 33 columns and 395 rows with 32 features and a numeric target. The data was originally intended for a regression task, but classification labels were derived from the initial target column for the categorisation task used in this paper.

Input to the student performance system is performed by a spike source array. A spike source is specified (based on the input data) and a particular time. The static synaptic weight from the source to the neuron is 0.1. This causes the neuron to spike exactly once. For testing there are no spike sources for the output layer.

Several input data encoding mechanisms are used. These and their translate to into input neuron spikes are explained in Sect. 4.

There are four output categories. The initial data has 21 categories, but these have been binned: 0–5 *Fail*; 6–10 *Pass*; 11–15 *Credit*; and 16–20 *Distinction*.

The input neurons are well connected to the category neurons. Each learns using the additive form of STDP.

3.2 Digit Categorisation

The digit categorisation experiments are based on a version of the widely used MNIST digit categorisation benchmark [1]. In this version, the digits are represented by a vector of 64 inputs (an 8×8 box) with values between 0 and 16, a transformation of the initial 28×28 bitmap of the digit.

The input layer consists of 64 neurons, one for each vector item. Input instances are given 100 ms of simulated time with neurons associated with non-zero items given clamped input (DC current or DCSource in PyNN) from 20 to 80 ms of that 100 ms. Simulations were run with a .1 ms time step. Higher value inputs are given a larger amount of current. The firing times of inputs are shown in Table 1.

Digit Topology. The basic topology of the digit recognition system shown in Fig. 1 is, like Diehl and Cook [9], three layers. All versions of the system have 64 inputs. The input layer is well connected to the categorisation layer (all to all); when plastic, the synapses are STDP synapses using the multiplicative form of the rule. During the STDP phases of training they are plastic, and during testing they are static.

Category neurons are well connected to the inhibitory neurons, and inhibitory neurons are also well connected back to the category neurons. These connections

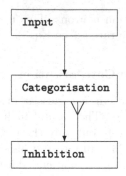

Fig. 1. The three layer topology has an input, a categorisation, and an inhibition layer.

Table 1. Table of input spike times in ms with DC clamp from 20 ms to 80 ms.

Input:	Spike 1	Spike 2	Spike 3	Spike 4	Spike 5	Spike 6	Spike 7
1:	75.5						
2:	55.9						
3:	47.8	75.7					
4:	43.0	66.1					
5:	39.7	59.5	79.3				
6:	37.3	54.7	72.1				
7:	35.4	50.9	66.4				
8:	33.9	47.9	61.9	75.9			
9:	32.7	45.5	58.3	71.1			
10:	31.7	43.5	55.3	67.1	78.9		
11:	30.8	41.7	52.6	63.5	74.4		
12:	30.1	40.3	50.5	60.7	70.9		
13:	29.5	39.1	48.7	58.3	67.9	77.5	
14:	28.9	37.9	46.9	55.9	64.9	73.9	
15:	28.4	36.9	45.4	53.9	62.4	70.9	79.4
16:	27.9	35.9	43.9	51.9	59.9	67.9	75.9

are static, throughout training and testing. The inhibitory layer is activated when neurons in the category layer fire, and if it receives sufficient activation, its neurons fire in turn reducing activation, and, perhaps, firing in the categorisation neurons.

Test Method. After training, the synaptic matrix from input to category neurons is stored; this weight matrix contains all of the parameters that have been learned from training. For testing, the trained synaptic weights are read back in to the now static synapses. Once trained, each category neuron is labelled with a category. The system, with the trained but now static synapses, is presented with some training data, and the firing behaviour of the category neurons recorded. For each instance of the data, a winning category neuron is selected; this is the neuron that fired first after the beginning of the instance input. (The neurons can be referenced by number, and in the event of a tie, the lowest numbered neuron won.)

At the end of this run, each neuron is labelled as the category it won most frequently. In the event of a tie between categories, the neuron was given the label of the first of which it won most. On the contrary, if the neuron never won, it was given (really quite arbitrarily) the category 8.

During testing, the static version of the input to category synapses is read in. An instance of the test data is presented, and the neuron that fired first (with lower numbered neuron used to resolve ties) is the winner. The category label associated with the winning neuron is used to predict the answer.

Balanced Firing. One of the problems with early experiments on this system was that particular category neurons would, in essence, win the overall competition. That is, each presentation would lead to a few neurons or even one neuron firing first on each instance. In the extreme event that only one category neuron always won, the resulting system would always predict the same category. When only a few neurons won, the results were also extremely poor, near chance, which is 10%.

What is needed is a mechanism to force all of the neurons to fire about the same amount of time. This enables them to compete for particular portions of the input space.

Diehl and Cook [9] used a dynamic threshold based on firing to force neurons to fire at about the same rate. Using their model would require a non-standard neural model for NEST. While it is possible to write user defined neural models for NEST, two other mechanisms are used. The first is a simple weight adjustment mechanism, and the second is to use standard neural models with adaptation.

The first balancing mechanism explicitly changes weights to balance firing. After an STDP run, the synaptic matrix is stored and then the system rerun with static synapses. The total number of spikes for each category neuron is recorded. A target upper and lower bound for the number of spikes is selected. If the category neuron is below the lower bound, all of its synapses from input are increased proportionally to how far the number of spikes are below the target. If the number of spikes is above the upper bound, the incoming synaptic weights are reduced proportionally to how far the number of spikes are above that bound. This change is all done in python code written in the PyNN script.

The second mechanism was to change the model of the categorisation neurons to one with adaptation [4] ($IF\_cond\_exp\_isfa\_ista$ in PyNN). The neural model is a leaky integrate and fire model, but when the neuron fires, an extra variable is increased. This slowly reverts to 0, but while it is above 0, increases the firing threshold.

Digit Training and Test Method. The training mechanism is to initiate the plastic synaptic matrix from input to category neurons using weights with some random variance. The system is then presented with data learning by STDP. The initial weights need to be sufficiently large to enable the input neurons to cause the category neurons to fire.

In the case of the first, compensatory mechanism, balancing is applied until the category neurons fire within the desired range on the particular training data.

The neurons are then labelled. The system is then presented with unseen test data. As the data set is divided into two, there is a two-fold cross validation.

4 The Student Performance Categorisation System

In this section, a system that categorizes student performance based on data from the UCI machine Learning Repository [6] is described. A spiking neural net learning via STDP is used. The main question to be answered in this implementation is how well a student grade categorizer could be learned by this type of network.

A secondary question is how the system performs with different input data to input neuron transformation techniques. Two preprocessing techniques (one hot encoding and integer encoding) are used for categorical inputs; up-sampling and down-sampling are used for target class balancing; and min-max scaling and no scaling are used for integer value features. This led to eight data encodings.

For one hot encoding, two neurons are allocated for each category, an on neuron and an off neuron. During presentation the on neuron for the feature value is turned on, and the off neurons for the other values. For integer encoding, there is just one neuron per feature value.

There are four categories, class 4 has 40 entries with the others having more including class 3, which has 169 entries. Down-sampling balances the number in each class by making them all have 40. Up-sampling generated new artificial data so that all classes have 169 items.

The integer encoding replaces them with the nearest integer. Min-Max scaling is described by Eq. 5. The actual input value, X_{SC}, was determined by using the feature value X, the smallest value of that feature in the dataset, X_{min}, and the largest value, X_{max}; the result was an input feature scaled between 0 and 1.

$$X_{SC} = \frac{X - X_{min}}{X_{max} - X_{min}} \tag{5}$$

The neurons allocated to each feature (neurons per feature) vary depending on the encoding mechanism used. There is also a feature breadth of 3 for integer values; each integer input value has its neuron and its adjoining neurons stimulated.

The data is split 70–30% training and test respectively in every case.

The system is a 2-layer feed-forward neural network consisting of conductance based leaky integrate and fire neurons with fixed thresholds. The code is written in the PyNN python package and is simulated in NEST [7,10]

4.1   Student Performance Spiking Net Model

The simulation time step is 1 ms. As are the minimum and maximum synaptic delay. The time between training data items is 30 ms. All training data items are presented four times (four epochs). Other intervals and epochs were explored but led to long training run times. So, these values are used for the all simulations described in the remainder of this section.

Training items are presented in time sequence 30 ms apart. At the beginning of training item presentation, a spike is sent to the input neurons, that is followed 3 ms later by a spike to the correct category neuron. The same approach is taken during testing, but there is no external input to the category neurons; the synaptic weights from the firing input neurons cause the category neurons to fire. The first to fire is the one that is used to predict the category.

The size of the input layer varied depending on the encoding mechanism; one hot encoding generated 9 extra columns in addition to the initial 32 and integer encoding did not. So, the total population of the input layer is neurons per feature multiplied by number of input data columns. For the output layer there were only 4 neurons, 1 neuron per output category.

The input and output layers are fully connected using plastic synapses that are governed by a biphasic STDP rule for long-term potentiation (LTP) and depression (LTD). This is a variant of the widely used Hebbian learning mechanism. The parameters that influenced the learning rule and their initial values are shown in Table 2.

Table 2. Parameter values for student classification system.

Parameter name:	Value	Description
τ_+	12.0 ms	Time constant required for LTP
τ_-	12.0 ms	Time constant required for LTD
A_+	0.003	Synaptic Weight increase applied when LTP occurs
A_-	0.014	Synaptic Weight reduction applied when LTD occurs
w_{min}	0.0	Minimum synaptic weight possible
w_{max}	0.03	Maximum synaptic weight possible
Weight	0.0	Initial synaptic weight at start of the simulation

When the output neuron has produced spikes, these spikes are counted and separated into different arrays by category. Then a maximum argument rule is used to pick the winning category from each row. So the category of any output layer neuron with the most responses for a row is the predicted category for that row. It is important to know that for this rule if there is a tie for most responses the first serially occurring neuron of the tied neurons is chosen as the winner.

4.2   Results

The encoding techniques used resulted in 8 datasets in total, which were up-sampled scaled and unscaled, down-sampled scaled and unscaled for integer encoding and one-hot encoding. During this phase of testing the initial values for the STDP parameters from Table 3 are used. $\tau_+ = \tau_- = 16.0$ are also shown. The best results are 72.4% for one hot encoded, up sampled, unscaled data.

Table 3. Results of data encoding experiments on the student performance data.

Data variation	$\tau_+ = \tau_- = 12.0$	$\tau_+ = \tau_- = 16.0$
Integer Encoded: Up-Sampled Unscaled	61.6%	70.9%
Integer Encoded: Up-Sampled Scaled	32.0%	23.6%
Integer Encoded: Down-Sampled Unscaled	50.0%	25.0%
Integer Encoded: Down-Sampled Scaled	29.2%	25.0%
One-Hot Encoded: Up-Sampled Unscaled	63.1%	**72.4%**
One-Hot Encoded: Up-Sampled Scaled	38.9%	23.6%
One-Hot Encoded: Down-Sampled Unscaled	62.5%	25.0%
One-Hot Encoded: Down-Sampled Scaled	22.9%	25.0%

The results of scaled data are low across the result set. The suspected reason for this is that in the implementation of input to neuron mapping, scaling resulted in floating point values for the values being scaled, which are rounded during the mapping, which resulted in a loss of information and caused the system to perform poorly.

For up-sampled data, the main concern is the use of 'fake' data, as new examples are generated to balance the classes. Down-sampling presented the issue of having far fewer examples to train and test the system.

Parameter exploration was performed on the learning window, τ_+ and τ_-, within ranges 10–17 ms in steps of 1 and both equal. The best overall results are reported in the final column of Table 3 with τ_+ and τ_- at 16.0 ms.

For performance comparison with other networks, a Multi-Layer Perceptron (MLP) with a 3-layer feed forward architecture, logistic activation function and a stochastic gradient solver for error correction learning was implemented using the Scikit learn MLPClassifier that was trained and tested on the same data. The network took 1000 epochs to reach an accuracy of 76.0% compared to the spiking net that took 4 epochs to reach 72.4% accuracy.

Cortez and Silva [6] evaluated systems on this data. A variety of models were implemented, but the one most relevant for comparison to the spiking net implemented in this paper is the 3-layer MLP. The results of that system are 49.8%. It is important to note that while the spiking net in this paper performs a four category classification task, the system in Cortez and Silva [6] performs a five category classification.

5   The Digit Categorisation System

The commonly used MNIST task involves 50000 training items, each with a 28×28 grid of inputs from 0 to 256. Each item is a digitised scan of hand written digit, with the associated correct category. This is the work that Diehl and Cook [9] used getting results of about 95%, on the 10000 item test set. The experiments described here work on a smaller, less widely used version of the task with 5620 items with an 8×8 grid of inputs from 0 to 16; this data set is from the University of California at Irvine [1]; and each 64D vector is derived from the original 28×28 picture by translating 4×4 squares depending on how many of them have any inputs on. So, if all the inputs are on (say, 12 at 256, and 4 at 18) then the number is 16. If only one is on (say the top left is 128) then it is 1. The authors have a great deal of experience with this data set having used it as the basis of a course work for several years for students in the final year of an undergraduate degree.

The data set is broken into two folds of 2810 items. A Euclidean distance categorisation metric gets 98.25%. Students have used a range of multi-layer perceptron learning with back propagation, and none have surpassed the Euclidean baseline, though one using a convolutional system recently was close. The standard mechanism that does better is a support vector machine, with some getting above 99%. The authors are unaware of any other spiking nets used to classify this data set.

5.1   Spiking Neuron Network Model

The two parts of the data were broken into 10 281 instance sets. The first 10 were used to train the first network for one pass. Each of the 10 STDP runs is followed by compensatory runs for the first balancing mechanism. The lower bound for neural firing is 100, and the upper bound is 281. The first of the ten training sets is used for labelling. Then the full test set is used. There are 100 category neurons and two inhibitory neurons. The second type of balancing uses adaptative neuron, and these runs have just one pass on the 10 parts of the training data.

5.2   Results

It is unclear how a variant of the Diehl and Cook [9] system would perform on this task. It is possible that the small training set size would limit its performance, but a result of 95%, like the result on the larger data set, seems reasonable. The result of the 100 category neuron test using the compensatory rule is 33.8%. Table 4

Table 4. Small MNIST categorisation results: Results from this paper are shown in the compensatory rule and adaptive neurons rows. The result for diehl and cook is a guess.

Algorithm:	Result
Euclidean Distance:	98.25%
SVM:	99.1%
Diehl and Cook:	~95.0%
Compensatory Rule:	32.1%
Adaptive Neurons:	25.5%

shows these results. The result using adaptive neurons with the adaptation rate $b = 0.1$ is 25.5%.

Clearly, the performance on the digit categorisation spiking nets described in this paper are poor, but they are also clearly above chance, 10%. Parameter exploration has been minimal, and a theory for competition has not been developed. While it is unlikely that improved versions of these systems will surpass even Euclidean distance, further parameter exploration should enable their categorisation performance to improve significantly.

6   Discussion

The brain is a poorly understood organ, but it is clear that its 65 billion neurons [5] are used to, for instance, classify digits. All of the neurons are not critical to the task, but as it involves the primary visual cortex, billions of neurons are. With less than 200 neurons, the digit categorisation system described above is clearly not a complete model of the human neural network for solving the task.

Both systems have a neural model that is a reasonable, if simple, approximation to biological neurons. They use only one or two types of neurons and they are relatively simple models, but their parameters are based on biological evidence. Similarly, the STDP learning rule is a reasonable approximation of some of the learning done in the brain.

However, the topologies are not reasonable. The layering and well connectedness between layers does not occur in biology. Moreover, the learning mechanism in the student performance system involves forcing the output neurons to fire at a particular time. This is clearly not biologically plausible and to some extent means that system is not using unsupervised learning. On the other hand, the digit system does not force the output neurons to fire, but uses their firing behaviour as part of the search, which is a truly unsupervised learning mechanism.

It is important that the category neurons fire at roughly the same rate over the training period because the synaptic weights only change when the pre and post-synaptic neurons both fire. If the post-synaptic neurons do not fire, the weights will remain unchanged. Diehl and Cook [9] call this homeostasis, and it is important for a system [13]. The method first used in this paper is to balance modify synaptic weights to force balanced firing. Diehl and Cook [9] use a dynamic threshold increasing the threshold when the category neuron fires and then allow it to decay back to base. It appears that this is a form of neural adaptation [2], which is similar to the second mechanism used in this paper.

Two basic learning mechanisms have been described in this paper; the two layer system learns co-occurrences. The three layer system is a competitive net providing another example of this mechanism for learning to categorise. The earlier paper [16] modifies the two layer system by using the multiplicative form of STDP, so that the synaptic weights are exact co-occurrence values, and by forcing the category neurons that are not the answer to fire after the input, causing a synaptic weight reduction. A reasonable extension to this work is to try all three mechanisms on the same data set.

The most important future work is to develop a theory of competition with spiking neurons and STDP. It seems plausible that this can be directly tied to SOMs [17]. Exploring the volume of input spiking, the inhibitory system, and the STDP parameters and mechanisms should support a well founded theory. Beyond this, more layers and reinforcement learning, may support improved categorisation performance. Full fledged recurrence and ongoing firing will make further advancements toward the actual biology.

7   Conclusion

These spiking systems can be used for categorisation. The digit system begins to explore how competition between the category neurons can be used to make each neuron "move" to recognise a particular part of the training states.

As machine learning systems, it is important that the mapping between input data and input neuron is understood. Several mechanisms for translating the input data are compared and contrasted in the student performance system. The digit categorisation system uses current to one neuron instead of a spike for the feature value. This means that the number of neurons needed as input is reduced, though the ramifications for learning are still unclear.

Following Diehl and Cook [9], the digit system does not force the output neurons to fire, but uses their firing behaviour as part of the search. The inhibitory layer, the input driven behaviour and the learning behaviour force the category neurons to compete, and move to recognise particular areas of the input space. This is more biologically realistic than forcing the output neurons to fire at particular times.

This two layer system and three layer competitive system extend understanding of neurobiologically realistic learning systems. The spiking neuron STDP based systems are flawed as biological models, but may help build understanding of the actual biological mechanisms. Moreover, they help build understanding of machine learning with these systems.

References

1. Bache, K., Lichman, M.: UCI machine learning repository (2013). http://archive. ics.uci.edu/ml
2. Benda, J.: Neural adaptation. Curr. Biol. **31**(3), R110–R116 (2021)
3. Bi, G., Poo, M.: Synaptic modifications in cultured hippocampal neurons: dependence on spike timing, synaptic strength, and postsynaptic cell type. J. Neurosci. **18**(24), 10464–10472 (1998)
4. Brette, R., Gerstner, W.: Adaptive exponential integrate-and-fire model as an effective description of neuronal activity. J. Neurophysiol. **94**, 3637–3642 (2005)
5. Churchland, P., Sejnowski, T.: The Computational Brain. MIT Press, Cambridge (1999)
6. Cortez, P., Silva, A.: UCI machine learning repository (2014). http://archive.ics. uci.edu/ml/datasets/student+performance
7. Davison, A., Yger, P., Kremkow, J., Perrinet, L., Muller, E.: PyNN: towards a universal neural simulator API in Python. BMC Neurosci. **8**(S2), P2 (2007)
8. Devlin, J., Chang, M., K.Lee, Toutanova, K.: BERT: pre-training of deep bidirectional transformers for language understanding. arXiv preprint arXiv:1810.04805 (2018)
9. Diehl, P., Cook, M.: Unsupervised learning of digit recognition using spike-timing-dependent plasticity. Front. Comput. Neurosci. **9**, 99 (2015)
10. Fardet, T., et al.: Nest 2.20.1. Comput. Syst. Neurosci. (2020)
11. Gewaltig, M., Diesmann, M.: NEST (NEural simulation tool). Scholarpedia **2**(4), 1430 (2007)
12. Hebb, D.: The Organization of Behavior: A Neuropsychological Theory. Wiley, New York (1949)
13. Hsu, D., Tan, A., Hsu, M., Beggs, J.: A simple spontaneously active Hebbian learning model: homeostasis of activity and connectivity, and consequences for learning and epileptogensis. Phys. Rev. E **76**, 041909 (2007)
14. Huyck, C.: The neural cognitive architecture. In: AAAI Fall Symposium on A A Standard Model of the Mind (2017)
15. Huyck, C.: Learning categories with spiking nets and spike timing dependent plasticity. In: International Conference on Innovative Techniques and Applications of Artificial Intelligence, pp. 139–144 (2020)
16. Huyck, C., Samey, C.: Extended category learning with spiking nets and spike timing dependent plasticity. In: International Conference on Innovative Techniques and Applications of Artificial Intelligence, pp. 33–43 (2021)
17. Kohonen, T.: Self-Organizing Maps. Springer, Heidelberg (1997). https://doi.org/10.1007/978-3-642-56927-2
18. Silver, D., Schrittwieser, J., Simonyan, K., Hassabis, D., et al.: Mastering the game of go without human knowledge. Nature **550**, 354–359 (2017)
19. Song, S., Miller, K., Abbott, L.: Competitive Hebbian learning through spike-timing-dependent synaptic plasticity. Nat. Neurosci. **3**(9), 919–926 (2000)
20. Taherkhani, A., Belatreche, A., Li, Y., Cosma, G., Maguire, L., McGinnity, T.: A review of learning in biologically plausible spiking neural networks. Neural Netw. **122**, 243–272 (2020)

An Evolutionary Game Theory Model of the Decision to Confront

Philippe Chassy[1]([✉]), Jon Cole[2], and Chloe Brennan[2]

[1] Mathematical Psychology Lab, University of Liverpool, Liverpool L69 7ZA, UK
philippe.chassy@liverpool.ac.uk
[2] Tactical Decision Making Research Group, University of Liverpool, Liverpool L69 7ZA, UK

Abstract. This article reports the use of evolutionary game theory to understand the role of various factors underpinning the decision to confront in the competition for resources. One factor was the intrinsic rate of confrontation an organism would display in absence of context sensitive factors. Two other factors were responsive to the environment and two others to the health status of the organism. Factors were implemented as genes that determine the rate at which confrontation or cooperation would be selected. Organisms were evolving in environments of different levels of reward and punishment. At each cycle they would be paired with another organism and decide whether to confront or cooperate. We used a genetic algorithm to simulate the evolution of the gene pool over 500 cycles. The main finding is that the baseline rate of confrontation is responsive to the conditions in the environment. Our results also indicate that the decision to confront or cooperate depends not only upon the immediate competitive conditions (reward and punishment) in which organisms evolve but is also sensitive to the state of the organisms.

Keywords: Evolutionary game theory · Evolutionary algorithm · Confrontation and cooperation

1 Evolution of Cooperation and Confrontation

1.1 A Competition for Resources

Natural selection is the force that shapes organisms and the variety of their traits [1]. Competition for resources sharpens these traits making them increasingly adaptive in stable environments. Often, however, competition is indirect. Trees for example try to outgrow each other to capture more sunlight than the neighboring trees. But for many species, including homo sapiens, competition is direct. The bulk of research indicates that cooperation has emerged to increase our chances of survival [2–4]. Along with it the necessary increase in cognition has been the main driver behind the brain's expansion [5], in particular the frontal cortices. Yet it is also clear that confrontation has not been eliminated. The passing on of successful genes to the next generation is often dependent upon the continuous confrontation with other members of the same species. There is ample evidence that confrontation has been part of human evolution as indicated by the numerous prehistoric sites documenting intentional (collective) violence [6–8]. Much of human history illustrates this principle at both the individual and group level. The classic example being Thucydides explaining the reasons of war between Sparta and Athens [9]. The rise of one power was challenging the domination by another and thus basically threatening to reduce its resources. In the 21st century the question of accessing resources has not changed and it is still the driver behind individual and group conflicts. Violence is often triggered when individuals estimate that the minimum number of resources necessary for survival will not be reached. As recently as 2018 the yellow vest movement in France was triggered by an increase in petrol taxes [10]. Suddenly a group formed from the collection of individual interests that was ready to confront the government. Throughout recorded history, and long before it, confrontations for resources have taken place. Investigating the factors that dictate the decision to confront or cooperate is thus essential to understanding violence between and within groups.

A question that the biological sciences faced in the 20th century was to explain how selfish organisms come to cooperate. A naïve interpretation of using confrontation as a means to acquire more resources would seem to suggest the conclusion that animals necessarily benefit from being aggressive. However, the gains from aggression are only valid as long as the competitor does not retaliate. Retaliation leads to a potential cost that might endanger the aggressor's life. The balance between benefit and cost is axiomatic for determining the conditions underpinning cooperation or confrontation. It is at this stage that the theory of games started to play a crucial role in the investigation of cooperation in animals and humans. The paradigm has been widely used to explore and formalize human decision making in several academic disciplines. In its most basic setting, the so-called game refers to two individuals, A and B, facing a situation that involves two options, for example cooperating or confronting. Each individual makes a decision independently but is aware of the potential outcomes and that the same options are available to the other individual. Traditionally the game is represented as a matrix of choices, see Table 1.

Table 1. Example of a theory of games.

		Individual B	
		Cooperate	Confront
Individual A	Cooperate	3, 3	0, 6
	Confront	6, 0	1, 1

The two-number vector in each cell represents the outcome for each of the two organisms. In the example showed in Table 1 we have the following outcomes. If both individuals decide to cooperate, they equally share the 6 points, each individual getting 3 points. If one individual decides to confront and the other one to cooperate, then the aggressor is rewarded with all the six points and the cooperative individual gains nothing. In cases where both decide to confront then a fight ensues, and they only get 1 point each. The objective of each individual is to maximize their gain. The choice or combination of choices that an individual will adopt to maximize gain is termed the strategy of that individual. Decisions, such as the one presented in Table 1, have largely been used to explore the conditions for cooperation [11]. One of the best-known thought experiments is the prisoner's dilemma where the outcomes are penalties rather than gains. The paradigm has been instrumental in demonstrating that selfishness can drive individuals to make suboptimal decisions [12]. It is later work by Robert Axelrod that made a significant progress in our understanding of cooperation [12, 13]. Axelrod noted that the prisoner's dilemma, like many other experiments within the paradigm, requires only one decision but in many real-life conditions individuals repeatedly interact with the same people, whether at home or at work, so it would be of interest to see how the strategy evolves when decisions are repeated. In such case, constant confrontation by both parties leads to penalties in the long run and thus systematically confronting is not a viable strategy. Axelrod and Hamilton have tested the efficiency of various strategies and demonstrated that the best one was a strategy consisting of offering cooperation in the first instance and then mirroring the behavior of the opponent. Since Axelrod's pioneering works, the evolutionary game theory paradigm has been immensely successful in answering questions in numerous disciplines interested in cooperation and/or confrontation [14–16]. The present paper aims to investigate the decision to confront or cooperate with the same approach but will introduce further refinements into the modelling of the evolutionary process.

In this paper we use evolutionary genetic algorithms to investigate how living conditions affect confrontational rates in a virtual population of agents. The main manipulation is the use of different genes to code for different factors playing a role in the decision to confront. This approach permits estimating the relative importance and responsiveness of each component that plays a role in the choice of a behavioral strategy. The first and main trait we implement as genes is the inclination to confront. Though confrontational reactions are often triggered by environmental stimuli, the literature also suggests that confrontation has a genetic component [17]. The choice to confront is a multidimensional decision with many of its underpinning factors such as aggression and impulsivity including a genetic component [18]. Some combination of psychological traits, such as psychopathy, involve behavioral strategies incorporating confrontation as an option within their behavioral repertoire, making confrontations an adaptive strategy for humans. In this context, although the inclination to confront possibly results from the Gene-Environment interaction we will be considering it in this study as an inherited trait. The second manipulation will be a set of genes coding for our reactivity to the environment. How humans react to different conditions of gain and loss has been largely studied in behavioral economics [19]. It has been demonstrated that individuals tend to be risk tolerant in the domain of losses. For example, they usually prefer a 50% chance of losing £120 rather than losing £60 for sure. Individuals are also risk avoidant in the domain of gain so they would prefer to gain £60 for sure rather than a 50% chance of winning £120. When individuals face a situation where the outcome could be either positive or negative (so-called 'mixed gambles') they tend to be more risk tolerant. These responses result from evolutionary processes that promote the conservation of one's own assets. Third, the last manipulation are genes that code for sensitivity to health status. Individuals that are weakened will tend to take less risk and avoid engaging in a confrontation as compared to those with a high health status who might be more inclined to confront.

In this context, the simulations carried out in this study aim to establish how the confrontation rate, defined as the number of confrontations per hundred decisions, varies as a function of the outcome. The second aim is to integrate the responsivity of moderating factors to our model of confrontation and cooperation. In the present paper we have implemented an evolutionary version of the experimental paradigm used in game theory to investigate how various factors underpinning the choice of confronting or cooperating are affected by different levels of reward and punishment.

2   Modelling the Evolution of Confrontation

2.1   Introduction

Our formal, simplified version of natural selection simulates an ecosystem of 1000 organisms. As the ecosystem is stable it systematically generates the same amount of food and thus can maintain the same number of organisms; thus, organisms that have disappeared get replaced before the next round of decisions. Each organism had initially 100 points of health. As the healthiest individuals (i.e., the top 10%) were selected for procreating, each organism was fighting in each cycle to potentially increase its health. Organisms that were paired had to decide whether to confront or cooperate. The combined decision of the two individuals in a pair created four potential outcomes that re-created the four conditions of game theory, see Table 2. The main difference between the original study by Axelrod and Hamiton [13] and the current implementation is that the decision is probabilistic, based upon the tendency of the individual to confront, rather than being stable over time and predictable. The probability to confront is δ and to cooperate is $(1-\delta)$.

Table 2. Outcome matrix as a function of the decision of each individual.

		Individual 2	
		Cooperate $(1-\delta_2)$	Confront (δ_2)
Individual 1	Cooperate $(1-\delta_1)$	Reward/2, Reward /2	0, Reward
	Confront (δ_1)	Reward, 0	(Reward-Punishment)/2

We manipulated two variables, reward and the punishment, to evaluate how the different genes determining the value of δ vary. Reward and punishment were varied at each integer value between 1 and 100; creating 10,000 conditions (100 × 100). For each condition the rate of confrontation was initially equally distributed over the population. After 500 cycles of decisions, we recoded the gene profiles, the number of survivors in the 500th generation and their average health. We expected the genetic profile of the 500th generation to differ drastically from the equiprobable distribution used to define populations at cycle 0. The model was implemented in Python 3.7.

2.2 The Organisms

Individuals were defined as instances of a class organism defined by 3 properties. The first property, health was a score that varied from 0 to 100. Organisms start with $\Gamma =$ 100, when the organism reaches a health of $\Gamma = 0$ it dies. The second property was age, noted τ, and was set as a counter of the number of cycles the organism has survived. Aging was implemented as a loss in health that is proportional to the number of cycles past the 25th cycle. For each cycle beyond 25, the organism would lose one more health point at that cycle. The third and most important property was genotype. Genotype was defined as 9 genes that coded five traits determining the probability of confrontation as reviewed above. The first trait was the natural propensity of organisms to use aggression to get resources. This tendency was coded by five genes that had an additive effect. Each of the genes had 5 alleles (A, B, C, D, & E) that coded for 5 different levels of confrontation (0%, 5%, 10%, 15%, & 20%), the genotype can thus vary from 0% (i.e., AAAAA) to 100% (i.e., EEEEE) and can take any value between that is a multiple of 5%, for example AABCA is 15% $(0 + 0 + 5 + 10 + 0)$. The five genes together were setting the probability that an organism would respond to a decision by choosing to confront. This trait defined by a combination of five genes, termed confrontational propensity (CP), implements the natural variance in the inclination to confront.

The other four genes implemented the context sensitive modulation of the natural tendency to undertake confrontation or cooperation. Each of the other four genes uses the same five-letter coding (A, B, C, D, & E) and thus can modulate the intrinsic level of risk by up to 20%. Two modulation genes were responsive to the type of situation organisms were facing. In line with the literature reviewed above, one gene (termed risk sensitive one (RS1) was coding for whether the decision was in the domain of gains. When the decision to confront led to a positive payoff the gene RS1 increased the rate of cooperation. In agreement with the literature showing an increase in risk taking in mixed gambles a gene termed risk sensitive two (RS2) was increasing confrontation rates when the decision to confront led to a negative payoff. The two other context-dependent genes were responsive to the health status of the organism. One gene, termed health sensitive one (HS1), was increasing confrontation rates when the potential gain would reach maximum health. The second health-sensitive gene (HS2) gene was activated when the potential loss would lead to the death of the organism. HS2 was thus increasing cooperation.

Three criteria were applied to select the parameters we used in our simulations. The first criterion is the exploratory nature of our study. We wanted to estimate the degree of fit between the theoretical predictions of evolution and the implementation of our paradigm. To this end we decided to cover as wide a range of environmental conditions as possible, even if these are not likely to happen in nature. The second criterion is the limit in computational power. Our choice for the rate of random mutations is much higher than the rate established for human genes. Implementing a rate that is similar to mutation rates in real genes would have the effect of increasing the demand in computational resources without changing the results in the long run. Even if our working hypothesis deserves empirical testing, we considered that setting a high random rate of mutation is a reasonable choice for an exploratory study. Third, in some cases the choice was arbitrary due to the lack of evidence of a well-established value. It is not possible to establish in the human population the proportion of individuals that contribute most to the gene pool of the next generation. Our choice of 10% of the population constituting the elite reflects the fact that, in most species close to humans, genes are passed by a restricted sample of the population at each generation. Hence, even if the exact proportion of what constitutes the elite is arbitrary to some degree it does implement a natural process. The same logic applies to the choice of five genes for implementing the individuals' propensity to use confrontation. It is clear that more than five genes enter the equation of determining the will to use aggression. It is also clear that an individual's propensity to use aggression is also largely determined by life experience. By using five genes we implemented the fact that multiple genes are involved and provided a ground to explore the influence of high variance on aggression while limiting the computational demand for resources.

At initialization the program generates the 1000 organisms and their genotypes. At this initial state the allele distribution of each gene would allow the population to have an equiprobable distribution in each trait.

2.3 The Survival Cycle

The survival cycle is constituted by all the events and processes that occur between two pairings of the population, including the changes in health and generation of new organisms. It was implemented in five steps.

In step 1 individuals were paired randomly thus creating 500 situations. The following three parameters were calculated as a function of the level of reward and punishment.

– The payoff of the decision to confront.
– The gain associated with the decision to cooperate.
– The cost associated with a fight.

In step 2 the decision was made individually by each organism as whether to confront or cooperate. First, the probability to confront of the organism was computed on the basis of the five genes CP, RS1, RS2, HS1, and HS2 with δ the probability of confronting, or confrontation rate, being determined as showed in Eq. 1.

$$\delta = CP - RS1 + RS2 + HS1 - HS2 \tag{1}$$

Each gene that is sensitive to a condition was activated if relevant and consequently modified the probability of being confrontational. That is,

• if payoff(confront) > 0 then RS1 was activated.
• if payoff(confront) < 0 then RS2 was activated.
• if health + gain > 100 then HS1 was activated.
• if health − cost < 0 then HS2 was activated.

For each individual, the decision was made by comparing the value of a random variable X [0,1] with equiprobable distribution, to their genetically determined value of δ. When X < δ, the individual cooperates; and when X > δ, the individual confronts the opponent.

The third step was the encounter, where the paired organisms confront or cooperate, and the reward and punishment are allocated to their health points.

The fourth step consisted of determining which individuals have survived the cycle. Any individual that would have a health Γ ≤ 0 was dead and any individual with Γ > 0 was alive for the next cycle. Individuals surviving one cycle were rewarded by one age point. The 10% of survivors with the highest health points were considered the elite who provide the genetic source for reproduction.

The fifth step consisted of generating organisms to bring the ecosystem back to its original capacity. As above, 90% of the new organisms were generated from the individuals with the highest health status. The genotype of the new individual was determined as follows: the genotype from one random individual of the elite was selected and copied. Each of the 9 genes of the parent would then be submitted to a 1% risk of being the target of a mutation. The genetic profile of the remaining 10% of the new individuals was random.

3 Results

This section reports the results of the 10,000 simulations. After evolving for 500 generations, the genes coding for confrontation rates expressed phenotypic effects that varied greatly as a function of the environmental conditions. The section is organized around each of the traits.

3.1 Genes Determining Confrontational Propensity (CP)

The mean confrontational propensity expressed by the five genes sensitive to reward and punishment is presented in Fig. 1. Visual inspection suggests that the genes were highly sensitive to the magnitude of punishment.

A linear regression accounts for the relationship between reward and punishment on the one hand and confrontational propensity on the other: The multiple regression provides the following Eq. 2:

$$CP = 0.367048 + \text{reward} \times 0.002721 + \text{punishment} \times -0.001801 \qquad (2)$$

The model is significant and accounts for 70% of variance in the gene phenotypic effect, $r = .87$, $F(2,9997) = 11736.908$, $p < .001$. Figure 2 shows the degree of fit between model CP and the mean value of CP.

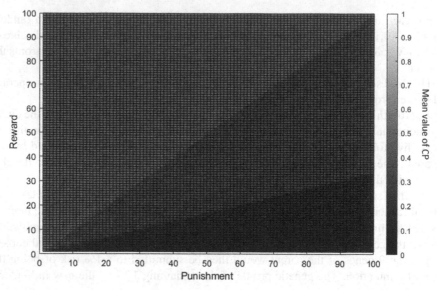

Fig. 1. Mean confrontational propensity per condition of reward and punishment.

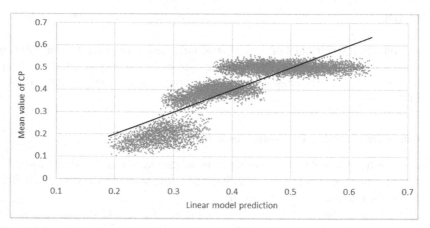

Fig. 2. Relationship between the values predicted by Model CP and mean values of the phenotypic effect of CP genes.

3.2 Gene Sensitive to Gain (RS1)

Gene RS1 was activated when the sum of the payoffs of the decision to confront is superior to zero. Figure 3 shows the phenotypic effects of gene RS1 as a function of the payoff.

A regression on the positive payoff shows that the evolution of the phenotypic effects of gene RS1 varies as a function of the payoff making the organisms less confrontational when a sure reward can be secured. The model, reported in Eq. 3, accounts for 31% of the variance, $r = .554$, $F(1,8348) = 3704.593$, $p < .001$.

$$\text{Model RS1} : \text{RS1} = 0.121617 + \text{payoff} \times -0.000204 \tag{3}$$

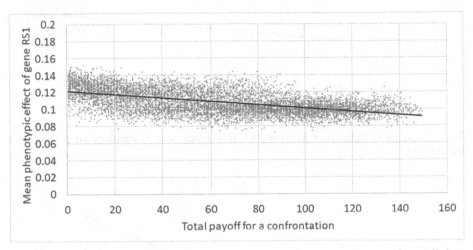

Fig. 3. Mean phenotypic effect of gene RS1 as a function of the anticipated payoff for a confrontation.

3.3 Gene Sensitive to Loss (RS2)

Gene RS2 could upregulate the confrontation rate by up to 20% in response to negative payoffs. Figure 4 shows the relationship between the payoff of deciding to confront and the mean phenotypic effect of gene RS2. The data have been fit with a linear model, see Eq. 4, yielding a significant relationship that accounts for 17% of the variance, $r = .419$, $F(1,1615) = 342.985$, $p < .001$.

$$\text{Model RS2} : \text{RS2} = 0.045159 + \text{payoff} \times 0.000427 \tag{4}$$

3.4 Gene Responsive to Health (HS1)

Gene HS1 was responsive to situations where the gain in health from a confrontation is less than what the organism has to gain to reach maximum health. As the 10000 simulations yielded different values on the two markers of health (i.e., number of survivors, and average health of the surviving population) we proceeded by binning the results per 10 percentile and calculated the regression model on the mean value per bin. The resulting model, reported in Eq. 5, is highly significant and explains 88% of variance, $r = .94$, $F(2,97) = 367.168$, $p < .001$ and is clearly indicative of a linear trend, see Fig. 5.

$$\text{HS1} = -1.459029 + 0.000912 \times \text{survivors} + 0.007162 \times \text{health} \tag{5}$$

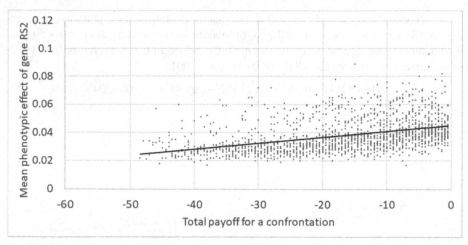

Fig. 4. Mean phenotypic effect of gene RS2 as a function of the anticipated payoff for a confrontation.

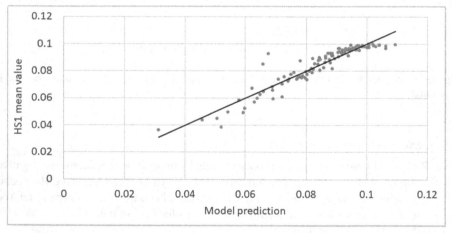

Fig. 5. Plot of the multilinear model linking the number of survivors at generation 500 and the health of the population to the mean phenotypic effect of gene HS1.

3.5 Gene Responsive to Death (HS2)

Gene HS2 was responsive to the opposite situation and downregulated confrontational levels when the organism was facing death. The model was calculated following the same procedure used for HS1 (see Eq. 6). It yielded a significant, but marginal, effect explaining 13% of variance, $r = .386$, $F(2,97) = 8.48$, $p < .001$, see Fig. 6.

Model HS2 : HS2 $= 0.082607 + -0.000020 \times$ survivors $+ 0.000374 \times$ health   (6)

Further investigation indicates that gene HS2 was highly sensitive to loss but could lead to either an increase or decrease in the confrontational rate.

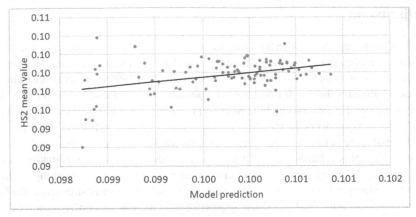

Fig. 6. Plot of the multilinear model linking the number of survivors and the health of the population to the mean phenotypic effect of gene HS2.

Ad hoc analysis indicates that the evolution of gene HS2 had high sensitivity to high penalty conditions, but the response of the gene (see Fig. 7) suggests a bifurcation in its evolution.

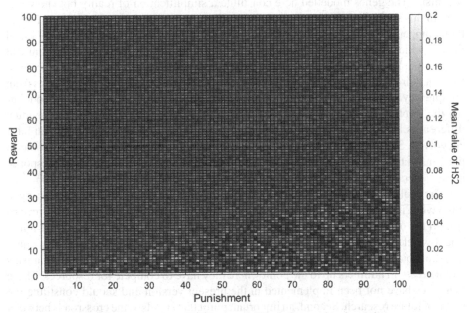

Fig. 7. Mean value of HS2 per condition of reward and penalty.

4 Discussion

The simulations reported above have yielded a number of important findings. First is the fact that a combination of genes sensitive to reward and punishment are determining the confrontation rate to adapt the organisms to different environments. Our results indicate a linear relationship between loss (reward - punishment) and confrontation rate. That the environmental conditions and the phenotypic effect of the CP genes are related by a linear relationship reflects the simplified environment that is used to run the simulations. Modelling of more genes and implementing the interaction between genes might bring to light more complex relationships. What our results nevertheless show is that organisms with no ability to project themselves into the future, such as with working memory, develop an adaptive level of confrontation. In doing so, our results strengthen the huge amount of research that indicates that aggression and the rate of confrontation (and by extension of cooperation) evolved well before humans appeared. The confrontation rate, like any other trait submitted to evolutionary pressures will mechanically be modified over generations if the conditions of reward and punishment change, and it can be an automated reaction that does not require conscious calculation.

Second our results corroborate the idea that confrontation derives from multiple factors that are acting at different levels. Some of the genes were directly responsive to the payoff associated with confronting but others were related to the health status of the organism. The genes modelled here constitute a simplification of reality but show that even in this simplified environment organisms develop a subtle response to variations in their competitive conditions. Our results argue against explanations based on solely social factors which have been put forth in social science and argue for a gene-environment interaction. It is the triggering of genes in specific conditions that might promote ancestrally acquired behaviors. Our results indicate that the willingness to confront stems from complex dynamics that involve the genetic background and the environment modulating the level of risk that people are willing to take. Our results suggest that individual differences in confrontation are likely to be determined by patterns of genes that have coevolved. Some of these genes are not directly involved in evaluating the outcome of the confrontation. Confrontation is thus not necessarily a primal (aggressive) response but is generated through complex dynamics.

The evolutionary simulations we conducted have two limits that are worth bearing in mind when interpreting the results. First, we note that in many instances where the reward is high the organisms did not depart significantly from the initial rate of confrontation. The low selection pressure would partly explain this result and calls for more research into the topic. In natural conditions if rewards are high and punishment is low organisms will increase in numbers up to the point where they have to compete for resources. These dynamics have not been implemented in the present version and should constitute the focus of future research. Second, an important point that stands at the crossroads between the limits of the work and its novelty is the fact that the organisms simulated were not conscious. There was no planning ahead (*e.g.*, avoiding potential confrontations) and the organisms were only reacting to situations. How consciousness influences decisions to confront was beyond the scope of this work but represent the next step in understanding the conditions that promote confrontation or cooperation. Future research should implement a rudimentary form of working memory and model the ability of organisms to make decisions based on an understanding of their future.

In conclusion, our study found that it is possible to simulate the impact of genes on the decision to confront or cooperate. Future iterations of this work may shed light on our understanding of how resource competition can lead to conflict and the potential dynamics of those conflicts.

References

1. Darwin, C.: On the origin of species. Penguin (1859)
2. Rand, D.G., Nowak, M.A.: Human cooperation. Trends Cogn. Sci. **17**, 413–425 (2013)
3. Trivers, R.L.: The evolution of reciprocal altruism. Q. Rev. Biol. **46**, 35–57 (1971)
4. Clutton-Brock, T.: Cooperation between non-kin in animal societies. Nature **462**, 51–57 (2009)
5. Dunbar, R.I.: The social brain hypothesis. Evolutionary Anthropology: Issues, News, and Reviews **6**, 178–190 (1998)
6. Armit, I., Knüsel, C., Robb, J., Schulting, R.: Warfare and violence in prehistoric Europe: an introduction. War and sacrifice, pp. 1–11. Brill (2007)
7. Churchill, S.E., Franciscus, R.G., McKean-Peraza, H.A., Daniel, J.A., Warren, B.R.: Shanidar 3 Neandertal rib puncture wound and paleolithic weaponry. J. Hum. Evol. **57**, 163–178 (2009)
8. Walker, P.L.: Cranial injuries as evidence of violence in prehistoric southern California. Am. J. Phys. Anthropol. **80**, 313–323 (1989)
9. Thucydides: History of the peloponesian war. (1972)
10. Jetten, J., Mols, F., Selvanathan, H.P.: How economic inequality fuels the rise and persistence of the Yellow Vest movement. International Review of Social Psychology **33**, 1–12 (2020)
11. Smith, J.M.: Evolution and the Theory of Games. Cambridge University Press (1982)
12. Axelrod, R.: Effective choice in the prisoner's dilemma. J. Conflict Resolut. **24**, 3–25 (1980)
13. Axelrod, R., Hamilton, W.D.: The evolution of cooperation. Science **211**, 1390–1396 (1981)
14. Nowak, M.A.: Five rules for the evolution of cooperation. Science **314**, 1560–1563 (2006)
15. Friedman, D.: Evolutionary games in economics. Econometrica: Journal of the Econometric Society 637–666 (1991)
16. Choi, J.-K., Bowles, S.: The coevolution of parochial altruism and war. Science **318**, 636–640 (2007)
17. Pavlov, K.A., Chistiakov, D.A., Chekhonin, V.P.: Genetic determinants of aggression and impulsivity in humans. J. Appl. Genet. **53**, 61–82 (2012)
18. Allen, J.J., Anderson, C.A., Bushman, B.J.: The general aggression model. Curr. Opin. Psychol. **19**, 75–80 (2018)
19. Kahneman, D., Tversky, A.: Prospect theory: An analysis of decision under risk. Handbook of the fundamentals of financial decision making: Part I, pp. 99–127. World Scientific (2013)

Hidden Markov Models for Surprising Pattern Detection in Discrete Symbol Sequence Data

Ken McGarry$^{(\boxtimes)}$ (iD)

School of Computer Science, Faculty of Technology, University of Sunderland, Sunderland, UK
ken.mcgarry@sunderland.ac.uk

Abstract. Detecting unusual or interesting patterns in discrete symbol sequences is of great importance. Many domains consist of discrete sequential time-series such as internet traffic, online transactions, cyberattacks, financial transactions, biological transcription, intensive care data and social sciences data such as career trajectories or residential history. The sequences usually consist of discrete symbols that may form regular patterns or motifs. We use regular expressions to construct the longest repeating sequences and sub-sequences that compose them, we then define these as motifs (which may or may not represent novel patterns). The sequences are now composed of simpler motifs which are used to build Hidden Markov Models which can capture complex relationships based on location, frequency of occurrence and position. New data that deviates from established motifs either in location of appearance, frequency of appearance, or motif composition may represent patterns that may be different in some way and hence interesting to the user.

Keywords: Motif · Regex · Sequence · Hidden Markov Model

1 Introduction

In this work we develop a novel anomaly detection method to uncover patterns or trends in discrete sequence data that differ from normal expectations. However, anomalies cannot always be expected to follow previously known patterns or trends. Anomalies are patterns in data that may be incorrect, noisy, novel or unusual in some respect. This can be with regard to magnitude of values, unusual timing of appearance, changing relationships with other patterns or some other factor that makes them different to the normal values encountered. The problem is that nearly every data mining problem is different and indeed patterns can change over time even within the same problem or area.

The ability to be surprised is fundamental to many human cognitive and intellectual endeavors, it is an essential trait for learning and discovering new knowledge [1,2]. Cognitive scientists generally agree that surprise is an emotion that

© The Author(s), under exclusive license to Springer Nature Switzerland AG 2022
M. Bramer and F. Stahl (Eds.): SGAI-AI 2022, LNAI 13652, pp. 180–194, 2022.
https://doi.org/10.1007/978-3-031-21441-7_13

arises when differences occur between our expectations and the actual results [6]. This mismatch can be accounted for in a principled way using Bayes theory, which is perfectly suited to update beliefs in the light of new information. We implement a modification of Bayesian surprise discussed by Itti which corresponds to subjective beliefs that are revised as new information appears [11]. Bayes theorem allows the conversion of our prior beliefs into posterior beliefs. Therefore, Bayesian surprise is a criterion to judge discrepancies between a systems prior and posterior beliefs on any given matter. The bigger the discrepancy then the more surprised we should be [12]. The use of surprise and novelty is also finding applications in goal directed learning when developing automated systems [8] and agent based systems [22]. Furthermore, product design has benefited from this approach whereby *surprise* is used as a creative metric to predict if customers will find new features and styles exciting and attractive [3]. In the past, the so-called interestingness measures were used to assess the novelty or unusualness of patterns in a data set, many such measures have been developed [19].

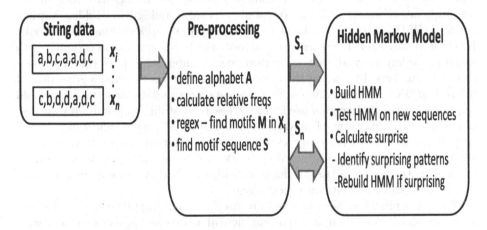

Fig. 1. Motif generation and analysis

In this work we develop novel methods to search for discrete sequences of symbols that may form motifs. Motifs are collections of discrete symbols (effectively a string) from an alphabet of variable but finite size. In Fig. 1 we show that motifs are repeated patterns found within discrete symbol sequences and time series data. The sequence of symbols are then pre-processed and will form recurring patterns or motifs that imply important changes or activities in the time-series [24].

2   Related Work

The SEQUITUR system of Nevill-Manning builds a structure from sequences of symbols by removing common phrases using a grammatical rule that models the phrase, this process continues until all sequences are read in. SEQUITUR operates by modelling repeated subsequences into if..then type rules. The whole process is recursive and the result is a hierarchical rule based system [20]. Previous work by Lin and Keogh in detecting motifs in time-series led to the development the Piecewise Aggregate Approximation (PAA) algorithm and the Symbolic Aggregate approXimation (SAX) algorithm [17]. PAA is a very popular algorithm used to convert the time series into discrete levels or symbols. The sequences/sub-sequences of symbols may form patterns or motifs that represent particular activity in the time series data [13]. Further improvements on PAA and SAX symbolic representation method for discretization includes preserving the information contained in the angle of the signals characteristics of the time series. Other Computer Science areas such as temporal association rules [27] have similar issues such as modelling the temporal aspects by integrating interval-based relationships to occurrences of items in the database.

Natural Language Processing and speech recognition provide many insights into modelling sequence information, especially when dealing with strings, letter and word occurrences [23, 26]. For example part-of-speech-tagging (POS) allows the sequence of words to be represented to resolve ambiguity. Hidden Markov Models (HMM) are able to label text data in POS applications, we describe HMM in detail later. DNA searching algorithms have elements in common with motif detection, they all search for recurring or interesting patterns in sequential, discrete data [14]. In fact the discovery of motifs has received a great deal of interest in DNA analysis, often suffix trees are common data structures used hold sequential data. Huang *et al* used suffix trees to contain temporal data for regularly occurring patterns of different sorts such as full, inner, and tail patterns [10]. Work by Cohen used segmentation by information theory to decompose strings [5]. Experiments conducted by Reick on the suitability of various hierarchical structures such as tries, suffix trees and sorted arrays for sequence analysis provided valuable insights into their usage [23].

Deep learning has been successfully used in many applications of discrete sequence data. For example, recurrent neural networks (RNN) can deal with variable-length sequences while maintaining sequence order and tracking long-term dependencies [25]. However, in order to model longer term dependencies than is currently possible with RNN, a variation called Long Short-Term Memory (LSTM) should be used. These LSTM networks have generally been applied to speech and handwriting recognition, machine translation, parsing, image captioning. This is made possible through LSTM models ability to keep information over many time steps by using a separate cell state from what of outputted and gates controlling data flow [15]. Other models useful for anomaly or unusual pattern detection in sequences include the range of auto-encoder networks.

Our contribution uses Hidden Markov Models which are simpler methods in comparison to the deep learning models and their architecture is more convenient to provide access to intermediate states using the (i) transition matrix , (ii) prior probability and (ii) emission probability matrices. It is variations in expected and actual emissions that are used by the Bayesian Surprise mechanism to determine the newness/surprisingness of a given pattern.

3   Hidden Markov Models

Hidden Markov Models (HMM) are often used to capture the dynamics of sequence data [21]. Furthermore, a Markov chain is a model we can employ to inform us about the probabilities of discrete variable sequences, states or events. These discrete variables normally take on predetermined values from an alphabet. The alphabet can be natural language words or symbols that represent changes or events occurring in the problem domain. A Markov chain makes a very strong assumption that if we want to predict the future in the sequence, all that matters is the current state [4]. All the states before the current state have no impact on the future except via the current state. The HMM is considered to be the model of choice for sequential problems, [16] and is used in sequence anomaly detection [7].

The main characteristic of Markov Chains is their *memory-less* property, that is to say each new state will only depend on the last or previous state. This enables the transition probabilities to be calculated for the next event or state, based on the current event or state:

$$P(x_i|x_{i-1}, ..., x_1) = P(x_i|x_{i-1})$$

where: A is the alphabet of symbols and S is the generative model (built on the alphabet) representing the probability A^ℓ. While $x \in A^\ell$ is the sequence presented to the HMM (S). These probabilities are used by the next stage to determine if a pattern or sequence is surprising or interesting.

Therefore, the columns of A^ℓ have to sum up to 1. Breaking down the given sequence, the probability for each symbol can be defined by:

$$P(x) = P(x_L, x_{L-1}, ..., x_1) = P(x_L|x_{L-1})P(x_{L-1}|x_{L-2})...P(x_2|x_1)P(x_1) \quad (1)$$

$P(x_1)$ is obtained from the transition probability matrix, multiplying the initial event probabilities at time $t = 0$ using the transition data, the probabilities of every event at time $t = 1$ can be determined and therefore we also have them for time $t = n$.

$$\forall \ell \in \{0, 1, 2, ...\} : \sum_{x \in A^\ell} P^S(x) = 1. \quad (2)$$

As shown in Fig. 2 we have a series of observed states and hidden states, by which the HMM will generate transition probabilities and emission probabilities for the hidden states, these are the model's main parameters. They can be setup prior to training or simply determined by the training algorithm. Observing the transition matrix the highest transition probabilities are generally found on the diagonal, this implies that particular state is unlikely to change. Interpreting the matrix we can say the probabilities of making a transition to another state depend on the data types and frequency of occurrence, e.g. a transition probability of 0.9 indicates that nine times out of ten, the hidden state remains the same [9]. The emission states indicate how long each *observed state* is likely to remain in a certain *hidden state*. Analysis of these two matrices allows us to estimate periods of stability and change in a dataset.

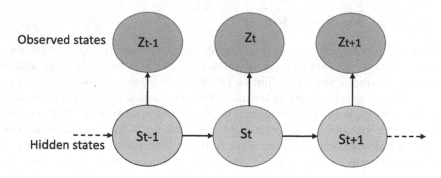

Fig. 2. Example HMM, hidden states and observed states.

4   Methods

We now define the notations for representing the data which comprise the alphabets, strings, letters and motifs. We consider strings and sequences to be similar and use the terms interchangeably. Consider the alphabet A comprised of elements or letters, $A = \{a, b, c, d\}$. The string x "abcdabcabcddda" consists of the letters "a", "b", "c" and "d" from A. Four unique letters in a string of length $|x|$ 14 giving the relative frequencies in Table 1. A motif M is defined as a recurring pattern or substring in the string x that appears at least twice. This cut-off point β is arbitrary and may be modified. The motifs can be of differing lengths, we use regular expressions to find the largest repeating substring that occurs at least twice in x. All occurrences of the newly discovered motif are removed from x and the subsequent largest motif is discovered, the process repeats until there are no further valid motifs to be found. The algorithm will return two lists; the first is a list of unique motif names M_n, the second is the ordered list of motif occurrences M_o from the original string x.

Table 1. Relative frequencies of letters in example string *abcdabcabcddda*

A	B	C	D
4	3	3	4
0.28	0.21	0.21	0.28

The relative frequency information is used to assist in the generation of motifs. The initial set of motifs is based on the assumption that the largest reoccurring sequences are important in the data mining domain i.e. they are typical patterns as shown in Algorithm 1. We set a minimum cut-off point β of at least two occurrences for a set of repeating substrings of length ψ of two letters to be considered as a viable motif. A single letter cannot be a motif since a motif should be a combination of symbols or events.

Algorithm 1. Motif generation

Input: set of strings: $x(alphabet), : A$
Output: Motif list of names $\mathbf{M_n}$; Motif ordered sequence $\mathbf{M_o}$
1: $\mathbf{M_o}; \mathbf{M_n} \leftarrow 0$
2: Initialize $\beta = 0$, $\psi = 0$.
3: **repeat**
4:     RegEx find largest substring in $x = \forall x$.
5:     Calculate length of ψ and β
6:     $M_n \leftarrow$ add substring to motif list if $\psi \geq 2$ and $\beta \geq 2$
7:     Remove M_n from x
8: **until** $M_n \notin x$
9: RegEx populate $\mathbf{M_o}$ with ordered occurrences of $M_n \in x$
10: **Return** $[\mathbf{M_o}; \mathbf{M_n}]$

When building the HMMs, the first stage is to identify best number of hidden states for the model. Examining the smallest AIC value for different hidden states.

We use the R, Hidden Markov Model (seqHMM) by Helske [9]. We make our source code (written in the statistical language R) and data available from: https://github.com/kenmcgarry/AI2022.

The Bayesian surprise measure provides a natural and useful method for defining and representing novel and surprising patterns [2]. Equation 3 calculates the distribution over all hypothesis $h \in \mathcal{H}$. The surprise is given as the two-fold difference between $P(h|D)$ and $P(h)$.

$$S(D, \mathcal{H}) = distance[P(h), P(h|D)]$$
$$= \sum_{\mathcal{H}} P(M|D) log \frac{P(M|D}{P|M} \tag{3}$$

However, without the ability to recognize previous interesting patterns, each presentation of data would result in similar outcomes of interesting scores being assigned. We use a decay function over time that will dampen surprise such as that proposed by Baldi [1]. This is used as post-processing stage.

$$\frac{1}{a_n} + log(1 - \frac{1}{a_N + b_N}) \approx \frac{1 - p}{p_N} \tag{4}$$

where: N is the number of data samples, a and b refer to the respectively to the prior and posterior probability values.

5   Data

We now define the notations for representing the data which comprise the alphabets, strings, letters and motifs. The data sets consist of a series of categorical data sequences of fixed length and also variable length vectors. The sequences represent a series of actions or situations that have occurred. The datasets also contain variables such as age, gender, biological measurements using a variety of data types. However, we do not use these and concentrate on the discrete event sequence data.

5.1 Sepsis Data Set

This data set consists of events of sepsis cases from a Swiss hospital. Sepsis is a life threatening condition usually caused by an infection. One case represents the pathway through the hospital from admission, drug treatments and finally discharge. The events were recorded by the ERP (Enterprise Resource Planning) system of the hospital. There are 1,000 individual patient records with a total 15,000 events that were recorded for 16 different activities. A further, 39 data attributes are recorded, such as the biological values from several tests conducted by the Doctors and the particular lab where the tests were made, along with any medication given. The main feature of interest of this dataset is the variable length of the discrete sequence records.

5.2 Self-rated Health Data Set

The self-rated health (SRH) data set contains sequences for 2,612 respondents of a survey conducted by the Swiss Household Panel (SHP). The individuals were aged between 20 and 80 years at the start of the survey. The data is organized into 11 variables of 2,612 records (one reading for each person over the 11 years of the survey 1999–2009). The survey has missing data. Respondents' self rated health is collected at each yearly wave of the SHP with the following question: "How do you feel right now?" Possible answers are: very well; well; so, so (average), not very well and not well at all.

– G1 (very well) ; G2 (well); M (so, so (average));
– B2 (not very well) ; B1 (not well at all) ; * (missing)

6 Results

For each data set motifs were derived using Eq. 1, as the motif detection algorithm analyses the data it will discover over several passes, decreasingly smaller motifs (repeating patterns of characters). For all data, the discovered motifs were split 75/25 for training and test data. In reality, the test data represents new sequences to be passed to the HMM. We wish to determine for all data sets the amount of *surprise* generated when new data becomes available. No cross-fold validation or other methods were used used to train the HMM. The test data was passed through the HMM and the output sequences were assessed by the Bayesian Surprise criteria to judge novelty and the "surprise" value for each sequence passed through the HMM.

6.1 Sepsis Data Analysis

Prior to motif discovery, the text descriptions of the discrete Sepsis sequences were converted into single letter characters, shown in Table 2 - this was to avoid computational issues with large strings. The motif finding results for the Sepsis data set are displayed in Table 3. Approximately, 67 motifs were discovered,

Table 2. Sepsis string to character conversion

String	Character
ERRegistration	A
Leucocytes	B
CRP	C
LacticAcid	D
ERTriage	E
ERSepsisTriage	F
IVLiquid	G
AdmissionNC	H
IVAntibiotics	I
AdmissionIC	X
ReleaseA	1
ReleaseB	2
ReleaseC	3
ReleaseD	4
ReleaseE	5
ReturnER	Z

Table 3. Sepsis motifs

ID	Motif
1	AEFBDCGIHCB
2	AEFCDBGIAEF
3	B1ZAEFGICDB
4	1AEFCDBGIH
5	AEFGIBCDHC
6	AEFBCDGIH
7	AEFDBCGIH
8	AEFGCDBIH
9	1ZAEFAEF
10	AECDBFGI

only the largest are shown. Prior to motif discovery, the text descriptions of the discrete sequences were converted into single letter symbols - this was to avoid computational issues.

The Sepsis HMM model was built using the motifs, the data divided into train and test sets. We used five hidden states, although empirically the most optimum number can be discovered by building several models and comparing the Bayesian Information Criteria (BIC) and the Akike Information Criteria (AIC), the highest value usually implies the best fit. These are shown in Fig. 3, the diagram on the left indicates the transition probabilities from one state to the next after training. The diagram on the right indicates the changes to the model as a result of the test data passed through the HMM and then refitting the model. The differences between the model's is used by the Bayes surprise algorithm to determine how interesting and unusual the data actually is. The decay function is then applied to reduce the effect of previously seen patterns and thus reduce *surprise*.

In Table 4 the statistically significant events from the Sepsis data subsequences that discriminate between interesting and not-interesting subsequences are presented, using the tagged sequences with the surprising label. The Surprising patterns have values for the key variables between 0.6 and 0.9, while the not-surprising sequences events have Pearson coefficients much lower between 0.05 and 0.5 - only the Lecoucyte $\rightarrow$ CRP sequence has a significantly higher value.

In Fig. 3 the HMM models are plotted, arbitrarily five hidden states were chosen to fit the data for both train and test conditions. Test data was passed

Table 4. Top sub-sequences discriminate between surprising and not-surprising sequences for sepsis data

ID	subseq	Sup	pvalue	statistic	surp	not-surp
1	(Leucocytes > CRP) - (CRP > Leucocytes)	0.39	0.00	75.48	0.61	0.06
2	(Leucocytes > CRP) - (Leucocytes > CRP)	0.35	0.00	67.87	0.56	0.05
3	(ERRegistration > ERTriage) - (Leucocytes > CRP) - (CRP > Leucocytes)	0.37	0.00	67.86	0.58	0.06
4	(ERRegistration) - (Leucocytes > CRP) - (CRP > Leucocytes)	0.36	0.00	66.39	0.57	0.06
5	(ERRegistration > ERTriage) - (Leucocytes > CRP) - (Leucocytes > CRP)	0.33	0.00	63.75	0.53	0.04
6	(ERRegistration) - (ERRegistration > ERTriage) - (Leucocytes > CRP)	0.35	0.00	62.11	0.55	0.06
7	(ERRegistration) - (Leucocytes > CRP) - (Leucocytes > CRP)	0.33	0.00	60.82	0.53	0.05
8	(ERRegistration) - (ERRegistration > ERTriage) - (Leucocytes > CRP)	0.32	0.00	59.67	0.51	0.04
9	(Leucocytes > CRP)	0.73	0.00	58.26	0.91	0.47
10	(CRP > Leucocytes) - (Leucocytes > CRP)	0.37	0.00	58.07	0.57	0.09

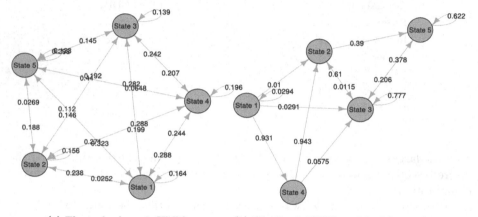

(a) The trained sepsis HMM   (b) The Sepsis HMM model with test data

Fig. 3. The sepsis HMM

through the trained model in Fig. 3a to produce a second model shown in Fig. 3b. The differences between the two models in terms of transition and emission probabilities are noted and used by the Bayesian Surprise algorithm.

Table 5 gives the transition probabilities for the trained model and how it changes from one state to the next. The initial starting probabilities are State 1 (1.0), State 2(0), State 3(0), State 4(0), State 5(0). Interpreting Table 5 we see that the sequences go from State 1 through to State 5. In Fig. 4 we break down the *surprising* sequences against the *not-surprising* sequences, the surprising patterns have Bayes values of 0.6 to 0.8, while the less interesting sequences have Bayes values of around 0.05.

The sepsis data set is rich in terms of the number of records and the large number of discrete symbols. The HMM was able to process these and to determine when new data was passed through it could identify sequences that were sufficiently different to what it had been trained on.

6.2   Self-reported Health (SRH) Data Analysis

The motifs for the SRH data are shown in Table 6, the motifs are composed of only six symbols and therefore more challenging to detect interesting patterns over time. However, it has found motifs that represent those individuals who have consistently good health over the 11 years.

Table 5. State transition probabilities for sepsis HMM

	State 1	State 2	State 3	State 4	State 5
State 1	0.03	0.00	0.00	0.01	0.96
State 2	0.00	0.83	0.15	0.01	0.01
State 3	0.00	0.00	1.00	0.00	0.00
State 4	0.00	1.00	0.00	0.00	0.00
State 5	0.00	0.00	0.00	1.00	0.00

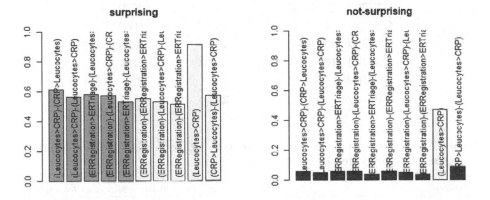

Fig. 4. The 10 most discriminating sub-sequences for Sepsis test data

The Self-reported Health data between surprising and not-surprising test data sub-sequences. In Fig. 6 the Swiss Health event sub-sequences are shown greater detail, we discover the most discriminating sequences between surprising and not-surprising sequences. The values of the event sequences are generally lower for the surprising patterns with the exception of the "well" event sequence. The not-surprising event sequences generally vary between 0.3 and 0.5 for the Pearson correlation coefficient. The reason for the not-surprising sequences having greater coefficients is probably because there is little difference between the two but the not-surprising patterns are more numerous. For the other Sepsis data the differences are more striking and noticeable, due to the larger number of symbols which provide more discrimination.

In Fig. 5 the HMM models are plotted, again arbitrarily five hidden states were chosen to fit the data for both train and test conditions. Test data was passed through the trained model in Fig. 5a to produce a second model shown in Fig. 5b. The differences between the two models in terms of transition and emission probabilities are noted and used by the Bayesian Surprise algorithm. The top 10 sub-sequences are displayed in Table 7, the surprising patterns generally do not have higher Bayesian Surprise scores.

The transition probabilities for the self-reported health is shown in Table 8. The initial starting conditions are State 1 (0.4), State 2 (0.04), State 3 (0.19), State 4 (0.3), State 5 (0.04), thus State 1 is the most probable.

Table 6. Motifs for self-reported health data

Id	Symbol sequence	Motif number	Motif
1	G2G2G2G2G2G2G2G2G2G2G2	11	MMG2G2G
2	G2G2G1G1G1G2G2G1G2G	12	2G2MG2
3	G1G1G2G1G2G2G	13	G1G1G1
4	G2G1G2G1G1G1G2G	14	2G1MG
5	G2G2G1G2G2G2G	15	2G2MM
6	G2G1MG1G2G2G	16	1G2M
7	G2G2G1G2G1G2	17	2MG2
8	G2G1G1G1G	18	21M
9	G2G1G2G1	19	22G
10	G1G2G2G	20	G2G

Table 7. Top sub-sequences discriminate between surprising and not-surprising sequences for Self-reported Health data

ID	Subseq	Sup	pvalue	Statistic	Surprising	Not-surprising
1	(very well > well) - (well > very well)	0.40	0.00	50.70	0.27	0.55
2	(very well > well) - (very well > well)	0.34	0.00	40.42	0.22	0.46
3	(very well > well) - (well > very well) - (very well > well)	0.33	0.00	38.79	0.22	0.46
4	(well)	0.54	0.00	37.12	0.65	0.41
5	(very well) - (well > very well)	0.22	0.00	31.96	0.13	0.32
6	(very well) - (very well > well) - (well > very well)	0.22	0.00	31.11	0.13	0.32
7	(so) - (so (average) > well, so) - (so (average))	0.16	0.00	28.54	0.08	0.24
8	(so) - (so (average) > well) - (so (average))	0.16	0.00	28.54	0.08	0.24
9	(very well) - (well > very well) - (very well > well)	0.20	0.00	28.52	0.12	0.29
10	(very well > well) - (very well > well) - (well > very well)	0.19	0.00	28.34	0.11	0.27

7   Discussion

This work only uses the sequences of discrete symbols to detect deviations and novel patterns. It does not use domain knowledge from experts, nor does it use the other variables provided with each data set. Data sets consisting of variable lengths have historically posed a problem for most probabilistic methods, however the Hidden Markov Model (HMM) and its variable length Markov chain property are ideal for this type of data. In fact variable length sequences such as the Sepsis data are the most interesting in terms of the results. They enable a richer variety of patterns to be encountered. In addition, having many different symbols in the data sets also enables a richer variety of patterns. We find that data sets with small variety of symbols and fixed length sequences such as the Self-reported health tend not to generate that many interesting patterns and their surprise measure rapidly falls away when the decay parameter is used.

Once trained, the HMM outputs a set of probability values for each new input (test) sequence. These new values (one for each symbol in the sequence) are then used as posteriors to be compared with the priors for each symbol based on the trained HMM estimates for those symbols. The Bayesian Surprise method will evaluate the differences and determine how anomalous or interesting these patterns are. The decay parameter is essential, otherwise there would be no "memory" of previously observed interesting patterns and the system would continuously view all patterns higher than the Bayesian Surprise cutoff point as interesting. This is in keeping with the cognitive reasoning of a human conducting the analysis.

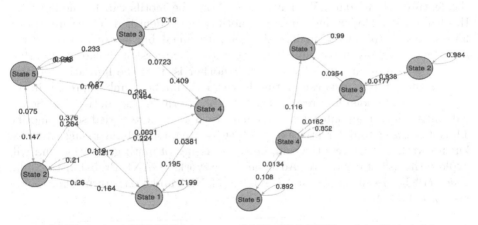

(a) The trained SRH HMM   (b) The HMM SRH model with test data

Fig. 5. The SRH HMM

Table 8. State transition probabilities for self-reported health HMM

	State 1	State 2	State 3	State 4	State 5
State 1	0.29	0.16	0.40	0.14	0.02
State 2	0.31	0.40	0.26	0.03	0.00
State 3	0.41	0.05	0.15	0.15	0.25
State 4	0.20	0.26	0.27	0.13	0.13
State 5	0.23	0.16	0.16	0.05	0.40

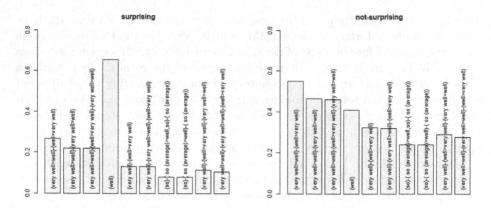

Fig. 6. The 10 most discriminating sub-sequences for Self-reported Health test data

8 Conclusions

In this work we have demonstrated that an unsupervised approach to seeking motifs in sequential, discrete data can provide a reasonable solution to capturing the features of the data. We have shown how the motifs can be modelled by Hidden Markov Models and surprising motifs can be identified. There are certain limitations of this work, mainly the computational burden of increasing the number of symbols in the alphabet. The regular expressions create motifs that currently require an exhaustive search. Another issue is the limitation of data such as the Self Reported Health that has a small number symbols present in the alphabet (6 symbols) and regularity of symbols forming the motifs. The Sepsis data has a larger alphabet (16 symbols) and has a more varied set of motifs. Thus it is easier to differentiate between surprising and not-surprising patterns. Future work will address the computational issues of motif generation and will explore the use of Generative Adversarial Networks (GAN), Probabilistic Suffix Trees (PST), Recurrent Neural Networks (RNN) and Long Term-Short Term memory (LSTM).

Acknowledgements. We would like to thank Satu Helske for useful advice on the seqHMM package and the two reviewers for their advice to improve the quality of the paper.

References

1. Baldi, P., Itti, L.: Of bits and wows: a Bayesian theory of surprise with applications to attention. Neural Netw. **23**, 649–666 (2010). https://doi.org/10.1016/j.neunet.2009.12.007
2. Barto, A., Mirolli, M., Baldassarre, G.: Novelty or surprise? Front. Psychol. **4**, 907 (2013). https://doi.org/10.3389/fpsyg.2013.00907

3. Becattini, N., Borgianni, Y., Cascini, G., Rotini, F.: Surprise and design creativity: investigating the drivers of unexpectedness. Int. J. Design Creativity Innov. **5**(1–2), 29–47 (2017). https://doi.org/10.1080/21650349.2015.1090913

4. Boldt, M., Borg, A., Ickin, S., Gustafsson, J.: Anomaly detection of event sequences using multiple temporal resolutions and Markov chains. Knowl. Inf. Syst. **62**, 669–686 (2019). https://doi.org/10.1007/s10115-019-01365-y

5. Cohen, P., Heeringa, B., Adams, N.: Unsupervised segmentation of categorical time series into episodes. In: 2002 IEEE International Conference on Data Mining, 2002. Proceedings, pp. 99–106 (2002). https://doi.org/10.1109/ICDM.2002.1183891

6. Ekman, P., Davidson, R.: The nature of emotion: fundamental questions. McGraw-Hill (1960)

7. Florez-Larrahondo, G., Bridges, S., Vaughn, R.: Efficient modeling of discrete events for anomaly detection using hidden Markov models. Inf. Secur. **3650**, 506–514 (2005)

8. Gottlieb, J., Oudeyer, P., Lopes, M., Baranes, A.: Information-seeking, curiosity, and attention: computational and neural mechanisms. Trends Cogn. Sci. **17**, 585–593 (2013). https://doi.org/10.1016/j.tics.2013.09.001

9. Helske, S., Helske, J.: Mixture hidden Markov models for sequence data: the seqHMM package in R. J. Statist. Softw. **88**(3), 1–32 (2019). https://doi.org/10.18637/jss.v088.i03

10. Huang, J., Jaysawal, B., Wang, C.: Mining full, inner and tail periodic patterns with perfect, imperfect and asynchronous periodicity simultaneously. Data Min. Knowl. Disc. **35**, 1225–1257 (2021)

11. Itti, L., Baldi, P.: A principled approach to detecting surprising events in video. In: 2005 IEEE Computer Society Conference on Computer Vision and Pattern Recognition (CVPR2005), vol. 1, pp. 631–637 vol. 1 (2005). https://doi.org/10.1109/CVPR.2005.40

12. Itti, L., Baldi, P.: Bayesian surprise attracts human attention. Vision. Res. **49**(10), 1295–1306 (2009). https://doi.org/10.1016/j.visres.2008.09.007

13. Keogh, E., Lonardi, S., Chiu, B.: Finding surprising patterns in a time series database in linear time and space. In: Proceedings of the Eighth ACM SIGKDD International Conference on Knowledge Discovery and Data Mining, pp. 550–556. Association for Computing Machinery, New York, NY, USA (2002)

14. Li, H., Homer, N.: A survey of sequence alignment algorithms for next-generation sequencing. Brief. Bioinform. **11**(5), 473–483 (2010)

15. Hochreiter, S., Schmidhuber, J.: Long Short-Term Memory. Neural Comput. **9**(8), 1735–1780 (1997)

16. Liao, T., Fasang, A.: Comparing groups of life-course sequences using the Bayesian information criterion and the likelihood-ratio test. Sociol. Methodol. **51**, 44–85 (2021)

17. Lin, J., Keogh, E., Wei, L., Lonardi, S.: Experiencing sax: a novel symbolic representation of time series. Data Min. Knowl. Discov. **15**(2), 107–144 (2007)

18. Maguire, P., Moser, P., Maguire, R., Keane, M.: Seeing patterns in randomness: a computational model of surprise. Top. Cogn. Sci. **11**(1), 103–118 (2019)

19. McGarry, K.: A survey of interestingness measures. Knowl. Eng. Rev. **20**(1), 39–61 (2005)

20. Nevill-Manning, C., Witten, I.: Identifying hierarchical structure in sequences: a linear-time algorithm. J. Artif. Int. Res. **7**(1), 67–82 (1997)

21. Rabiner, L., Juang, B.: An introduction to hidden Markov models. IEEE ASSP Mag. **3**(1), 4–16 (1986). https://doi.org/10.1109/MASSP.1986.1165342

22. Rhienberger, C., Hammitt, J.: Dinner with Bayes: on the revision of risk beliefs. J. Risk Uncertain. **57**(3), 253–280 (2018)
23. Rieck, K., Laskov, P.: Linear-time computation of similarity measures for sequential data. J. Mach. Learn. Res. **9**, 23–48 (2008). Jun
24. Ritschard, G.: Measuring the nature of individual sequences. Sociological Methods & Research (2021). https://doi.org/10.1177/00491241211036156
25. Shen, Z.: Bao, W., Huang, D.S.: Recurrent neural network for predicting transcription factor binding sites. Sci. Rep. **8**, 15270 (2018). https://doi.org/10.1038/s41598-018-33321-1
26. Wilson, W., Birkin, P., Aickelin, U.: The motif tracking algorithm. Int. J. Autom. Comput. **5**(1), 32–44 (2007). https://doi.org/10.1007/s10453-004-5872-7
27. Yang, P., Chen, K., Ching-Chi, H.: Subjective association rule mining: from point-based ranking sequence to interval-based temporal sequence. In: Proceedings of the 10th International Conference on Machine Learning and Computing (ICMLC 2018), pp. 167–171. Assoc Computing Machinery, 1515 Broadway, New York, NY 10036–9998 USA (2018)

AI for Industrial Applications

The ODeLIndA Dataset for Field-of-View Obstruction Detection Using Transfer Learning for Real-Time Industrial Applications

Abraham Anderson[1,2], Einar Julius Olafarson[1,2], Per-Arne Andersen[1(✉)] (iD), and Nadia Saad Noori[2] (iD)

[1] Centre for Artificial Intelligence Research (CAIR), University of Agder, Grimstad, Norway
per.andersen@uia.no

[2] Center for Integrated Emergency Management (CIEM), University of Agder, Kristiansand, Norway
nadiasn@uia.no

Abstract. Several challenges arise in industrial applications when using machine vision in safety-critical operations, such as field of view (FoV) obstruction, limited visibility of the equipment's operational perimeter, difficulty obtaining datasets, and high accuracy requirement. This research shows how machine learning methods such as convolutional neural networks (CNN) and transfer learning can tackle these challenges. Transfer learning works well when the source and target domain images are similar, which is the case for identifying the operational conditions and FoV status in a fixed industrial environment where heavy equipment is operating with the aid of a machine vision module.

In this work, eight categories describing FoV status and environmental conditions were selected as follows: clean lens/clear view, cracked lens, dirty lens, foggy, frost, dark view, flares, and rainy images. We used 21 616 images for the training set and 9450 for the test and validation. We benchmark the performance of several transfer learning models and networks (i.e., MobileNet, VGG16, VGG19, DenseNet, Inceptionv3, ResNet50, and Xception) against a CNN model/network trained from scratch. The experiments show that MobileNet combined with transfer learning performs best, with 98% accuracy compared to 93% for the traditional CNN model. Furthermore, the model can detect obstructions in real-time using commodity hardware when tested with a video stream. Finally, we provide a novel dataset for multi-class obstruction detection, which can be found here.

Keywords: Obstruction detection · Object detection · Deep learning · Transfer learning · Machine vision

M. Bramer and F. Stahl (Eds.): SGAI-AI 2022, LNAI 13652, pp. 197–210, 2022.
https://doi.org/10.1007/978-3-031-21441-7_14

1   Introduction

In the fourth industrial revolution age, industries are moving towards automation in different ways [28]. Machine vision is one of the key technological enablers of self-automation in many industrial processes. Machine vision algorithms utilize inputs from various sensors (e.g., cameras, LiDAR, and radar) to perform different operations such as pattern recognition, object detection, and tracking [8]. Machine vision is integral to quality control in product lines, self-driving vehicles, pattern matching, and automated surveillance. Earlier image and data processing algorithms for machine vision were designed for specific use-cases with a hand-crafted design. However, it is often assumed that the camera's field of view (FoV) is clear and the lens is clean. Obscuring field-of-view is a common problem in machine vision applications. Some examples include weather conditions, lens cleanness, object obstruction, or other unexpected factors that lead to obscured data input.

Consequently, when deploying applications to outdoor environments, there is less control over the FoV translucency that might cause a control process failure or trigger safety procedures. In industrial applications, safety is critical. Therefore, process automation must consider various safety measures when developed and deployed. Applications that utilize machine vision for quality control or operating machines must ensure high accuracy. These machines depend on the quality of the input from the camera sensors. Therefore, having a safety module to assess the lens conditions and FoV obstruction is vital for operating in safety-critical industrial environments.

Fig. 1. Obscure view examples

In this paper, we develop an AI-based framework that can identify different environmental factors that could impair a camera's field of view. The proposed method uses transfer learning to speed up the training and achieve remarkable accuracy across several categories of obstruction. Previous work has primarily addressed the detection of just a single obstruction category. However, this work proceeds to detect several categories, such as **close-to-camera** (dirt, cracked lens, and dark view), **environmental obstructions** (fog, lens flares, rain), **full camera obstructions** (snow, tagging), and **object obstacles** (chair, animals (Fig. 1).

This work aims to develop a solution to significantly improve the applicability of machine vision for tasks in society. We limit ourselves to evaluating the proposed framework in a maritime environment where typical obstructions include: fog, dirt on the lens, raindrops, lens damage, lens flares, dark view, and objects in the camera FOV. Hence, we focus on achieving a system that can identify and report a set of obstructions with high accuracy that meets industrial requirements.

We propose a two-step transfer learning framework using convolution-based neural network estimators to learn features in the data. We evaluate the proposed training framework with state-of-the-art machine vision models, including MobileNet, VGG16, VGG19, DenseNet, InceptionV3, ResNet50, and Xception. We provide a novel dataset for learning obstructed FOV, published at https:// github.com/uiaikt/ODeLIndA, along with the source code for the experiments. The evaluation compares our proposed transfer learning approach to traditional FOV classification and demonstrates its effectiveness.

This paper is organized as follows: Sect. 2 presents relevant computer vision, transfer learning, and deep learning background. Section 3 outlines current approaches and their limitations in view obstruction, transfer learning in machine vision, and deep learning models. Section 4 presents the ODeLIndA dataset for training computer vision models in obstruction detection tasks. Section 5 demonstrates how transfer learning is used to significantly reduce training and inference time with fewer parameters and less model complexity. Section 6 reports our initial results comparing state-of-the-art models with transfer learning and traditional convolutional neural networks. Finally, Sect. 7 concludes and outlines a path forward for continued research.

2   Background

Efficient classification and identification of operational conditions in many industrial applications related to manufacturing, transport, and surveillance are critical to the system's performance and safety. Machine vision applications in industrial contexts range from quality control, inspection, supporting autonomous units, and surveillance. The key components in the process are the data quality and how it is affected by the conditions of the camera sensors acquiring the data. Thus, challenges exist concerning the field of view obstruction stemming from lens defects (like cracks), lens cleanness, or objects covering the lens, such as environmental conditions like fog, rain, snow, and dust. Several studies exist to tackle these challenges by applying computer vision methods to traditional image processing or machine learning. However, most previous literature focuses on only one or two of the mentioned conditions [5,9,11,16,31].

Deep neural networks are used to detect several conditions, such as fog [5], lens flares [32], rain [25,31], and dirt on the lens [16]. Furthermore, others have used different methods for identifying general obstructions in the field of view of a camera from a single image [19] or image stream. In video streams with a static camera view or a controlled degree of rotation, PCA can be employed for image segmentation to remove the foreground from background environments [3]. Haresse et al. (2004) focused on the edges of the camera view instead of details in the view to detect camera dysfunction and obstruction. They calculate the gradient of each edge and get each edge by employing adaptive thresholding. Thus, to detect an obstructed view in the camera, they use the information from the calculated stable edges in the camera stream to determine whether the missing part of these edges is present. However, this solution makes sense only if there are sufficiently stable edges in the camera view. When the camera view changes frequently, it is challenging to find stable edges and decide whether there is an obstruction before the camera [11].

Palvanov and Cho (2019) created a model, VisNet, that can make visibility estimations under foggy weather conditions. This model consists of deep integrated and parallel connected convolutional neural networks, which are trained with three datasets in different visibility ranges from around three million outdoor images that belong to different classes. Although this model performs with high accuracy in the three different scenarios, the training process is time-consuming and valid for only daytime images. Furthermore, the model's scope is limited to a foggy camera view [21]. Chen and Ou created an algorithm to detect foggy vision problems due to foggy weather by calculating the normalized differences between the residual energy ratios of different wavelengths of RGB channels. This model is also limited to detecting foggy camera views [6].

In this paper, we develop a CNN-based classification model for FoV obstruction classification for operational environmental conditions in two phases: data preprocessing and classification. In the preprocessing data phase, we prepare all the input images for the classifier to ensure that the classifier learns different features related to the eight identified operational conditions categories to prevent bias in the network models. In this phase, we also perform data augmentation by adding slightly modified copies of our dataset. These modifications include image rotation, image width, and height shift, adding zoom range, making horizontal flips, distorting images along an axis so that models can see details from different angles, minimizing the overfitting problem, and increasing the variety of data.

In the classification phase, we develop an integrated CNN architecture with various transfer learning models so that our CNN architecture can utilize a model trained on a large dataset and transfer its knowledge to a smaller dataset. The idea is that our model can use a previously trained model in a massive dataset, namely ImageNet, and apply it to our problem in that common and low-level features are shared between images. Hence, we can also utilize many features in our smaller dataset. Our first hypothesis is that a model with transfer learning will provide better accuracy than a model with a limited and primarily artificial dataset. Our second hypothesis is that MobileNet will provide better accuracy because the model has more complexity and embedded convolutional layers than other models. We also create our own CNN without adding any transfer learning model as a benchmark for comparison.

3   Related Work

3.1   View Obstructions for Moving Cameras

With the exponential increase in digitization and automation of industrial processes and the adoption of autonomous unit operations, efficient machine vision
sensory systems need to support the safety and stability of these operations.
Identifying obstacles in a moving scene or detecting an object inside a safety
operation perimeter is critical in an industrial context. Hence, many studies
have been conducted to solve specific obstacles or generic obstructions. In studies that only consider a single imaging source, the scope is generally limited to
controlled environments or only accounts for a handful of elements that match
the paper's criteria for an obstruction [10].

Other research into dynamic environments with a moving video source
includes works that incorporate diverse additions to the singular camera detection
system that has been previously mentioned. These include using multiple camera
sources to find obstacles via view comparisons and feature extraction [9,22].

3.2   Transfer Learning and Machine Vision

The quantity and quality of data is a core challenge of artificial intelligence,
including machine learning and deep learning techniques. While ideal AI scenarios highlight the technology's immense processing capacity and overly optimistic
outcomes, real implementations begin with unprocessed, often imbalanced data
classes. There are several techniques to produce extra data samples artificially
(oversampling), but simple picture alterations might result in photos with little differences. Modern neural networks are trained on millions of images even
though there are only a few hundred practical problems.

Moreover, data generated artificially inherits some characteristics from its
source. Consequently, a trained model may not adequately reflect the whole
variety of a class. Even if we have access to a huge dataset, training a network
with millions of data points demands substantial computational resources and
time. Using models that were previously trained on similar data might therefore
provide a strategy for extending the knowledge of the pre-trained model by
exposing it to new data to construct a new model, a process known as transfer
learning [4].

CNNs have demonstrated excellent performance in classification, segmentation, visual comprehension, content recognition, and perception. A phenomeno-
logical method for predicting aspects of complex systems, such as obstruction view detection, can be represented using CNN-based models. An extensive labeled dataset that supports the learning process and innovative network
designs with hundreds of millions of parameters are also crucial for the success
of machine vision applications. [21]

Typically, transfer learning is used in computer vision, signal processing, and
natural language analysis. CNNs are useful in various computer vision issues
due to their robust feature representation. In several of our studies, complete

algorithms require modest data preprocessing and enhancement. The last layers of an existing model are then re-trained using transfer learning.

3.3 Deep Learning Models for Computer Vision

VGG-16 and VGG-19. In 2012, K. Simonyan and A. Zisserman proposed novel architectures for large-scale image recognition [26]. Their work won first and second place in the localization and classification tracks, respectively, with two comparable network architectures: VGG-16 and VGG-19. The novelty of the VGG models is that they only require small convolution filters (3×3), which, combined with the power of the GPUs, allows substantially deeper networks, consisting of 16 and 19 layers, respectively. The VGG model has a simple architecture and has demonstrated good generalization capabilities. As a result, the VGG model is considered one of the best models for transfer learning in image recognition tasks. The VGG-16 model comprises around 134 million parameters and 16 trainable layers. These layers include convolutional, fully connected, max pooling, and dropout layers. VGG-19 has 144 million parameters and 19 trainable layers.

Inception. Szegedy et al. propose the Inception architecture with GoogLeNet [29]. It outperforms VGG-19 substantially while having 12 times fewer parameters. In particular, the authors argued that perhaps the simplest solution to increase performance is to increase the model complexity with additional network width and depth. However, such an approach has a significantly higher risk of overfitting and requires substantially more computational resources for training. The solution for InceptionNet is to change from a fully connected to a sparsely connected layer architecture. As a result, the Inception model connects several layers parallelly in reduction blocks instead of horizontal layer stacking.

ResNet. A residual learning framework in deep learning networks facilitates the preservation of good results through very deep neural networks. The main contribution of residual learning is to conserve input information throughout the model. A Residual network (ResNet) comprises residual blocks or layers stacked on top of one another. This architecture is characterized by a skip connection at each layer that connects the input to the output [12]. The ResNet architecture aims to learn the identity function or the data, which allows it to pass the input through the block without passing through the other weight layers!

Xception. Chollet et al. began exploring several forms of Inception-based models, and the proposed architecture was dubbed extreme Inception - Xception for short [7]. Introducing depth-wise separable convolution layers to the underlying Inception model was novel to this method. Separable convolution in deep learning frameworks is a depthwise convolution, which is a spatial convolution conducted individually over each input channel. The Xception architecture consists of 36 convolutional layers organized into 14 modules, while data flow is composed of three steps: entry flow, middle flow (repeated eight times), and exit flow.

DenseNet. Huang et al. have advanced this notion by proposing the Dense Convolutional Network, or DenseNet for short [14]. Each layer connects to every other layer in a feed-forward manner. It's been shown that the DenseNet model offers numerous advantages. For example, DenseNet with 20 million parameters can achieve comparable results to ResNet with 40 million parameters. Second, the better flow of information and gradients in DenseNet improves training, the propagation of robust features, and the avoidance of the vanishing gradient problem.

MobileNet. MobileNetV1 is a useful model for mobile and embedded devices. MobileNets, based on streamlined architecture, employ depthwise separable convolutions to build smaller deep neural networks [13]. Depthwise separable convolutions are made up of depthwise and pointwise convolutions. The separable convolution module in MobileNet reduces both parameters and processing complexity. It enables modern mobile devices to fully utilize the computing capabilities of the CPU and GPU, speeding up image recognition without compromising performance. [20]

4   The ODeLIndA Dataset for FOV Obstruction Detection

The literature lacks datasets for training deep learning models to detect camera obstructions. Consequently, state-of-the-art models mainly focus on single-class prediction, e.g., only dirt or rain [2,16,27]. As a result, the lack of data makes it hard to create a computer vision model that works in environments with various challenges. A camera in marine environments is prone to environmental obstructions such as fog, rain, and salt-water residues. In contrast, cameras in urban areas are more prone to vandalism, leading to lens cracks. To address this major constraint in camera obstruction detection, we propose a novel dataset consisting of 8 classes of camera obstruction.

The collected data originates from several sources. The first part of the dataset consists of images from a marine environment in the southern part of Norway. The manually collected images are primarily images without obstruction (clean class). However, we apply postprocessing techniques to add obstacles to the data collected. More specifically, we create synthetic variations for the remaining 7 classes using collected data from the *clean* class.

The second data source is selected images and classes from WoodScape: Fisheye Dataset for Autonomous Driving [33] that contain soiling of the camera lens. Although the data is from fish-eye cameras, it is nonetheless relevant as it could prove that computer vision models could learn the patterns of how dirt obstructs the view. Furthermore, we used images that contained rain, clean, and fog from the WoodScape dataset.

Finally, we collect data from the internet where the license adheres to the creative commons requirements (CC-BY) requirements. More specifically, we collect images from Pixabay [23,24], Kaggle [1], and various sources on the internet [15,17,18], which provide real-world images in various classes in the contributed dataset.

Table 1. The dataset is split into three parts: the training, testing, and validation sets. There are a total of 8 classes in the dataset.

Class	Name	Train samples	Test samples	Validation samples
0	clean	3744	949	454
1	crack	737	184	572
2	dark	456	111	489
3	dirty	2032	507	510
4	flare	3653	910	473
5	fog	967	277	453
6	frost	5321	1331	582
7	rain	5134	482	482

Table 1 shows the data sample distribution over the training, testing, and validation sets. The training set comprises 21 616 images, a test set of 5441, and a validation set of 4009 images. These image samples are distributed over all classes to achieve the best possible data balance. The dataset is found freely available at https://github.com/uiaikt/ODeLIndA.

5   Transfer Learning for Efficient Obstruction Detection

The transfer learning research problem aims to accumulate knowledge about one problem and transfer this knowledge to another problem. In the event that a perfect transfer learning model exists, it should enable models to infer a broken camera lens from data that depicts a broken window. Figure 2 depicts the overall training scheme used in this work. First, we train a CNN-based model on a large and generic dataset, such as ImageNet. After training, the model weights are frozen except for an arbitrary number of layers at the network tail, which is reinitialized with random weights. Finally, the model is trained for tenfold epochs using the ODeLIndA dataset, which is domain-specific for camera obstruction detection.

A considerable benefit of this approach is that many state-of-the-art models come pre-trained on ImageNet and save substantial computation resources, ranging from a 90–99% reduction. Furthermore, it is empirically proven that transfer learning improves the model's generalization when introducing the domain-based dataset instead of training a model solely on the target domain [9].

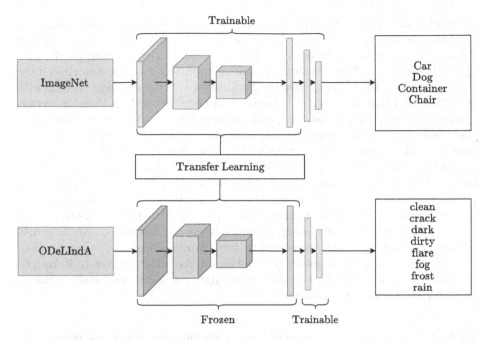

Fig. 2. The transfer learning concept in a two-step process. First, the model trains on a large dataset, following a smaller target dataset. Note that a majority of the weights are frozen when training on the target problem.

6   Results

In order to develop the framework based on the dataset created for the different use-cases within the scope of this research work, we tested different types of transfer learning methods using the ODeLIndA dataset, namely MobileNet [13], VGG16 [26], VGG19 [26], DenseNet [14], InceptionV3 [30], and ResNet50 [12], and Xception [7]. The aim was to generate a final model capable of detecting the conditions of the operational premier from visual data (i.e., images) and based on the FoV environment visibility and obstruction levels. The different transfer learning models were compared to a classic CNN model trained from scratch using the same dataset. For all the models, the artificial neural network had the same numbers of neurons in hidden layers and output layers and the same images for both the test and training dataset. All the models are trained with the same epoch size (10 epochs due to computational limitations or, in some cases, training stopped as accuracy decreased), with the same activation function (ReLU) and optimizer (adam optimizer). We compare the transfer learning framework to the traditional training of CNNs, where all parameters are learned.

All models are evaluated on the novel dataset, which consists of eight categories: (0)clean camera view, (1)cracked camera lens, (2)dark camera view, (3)dirty camera view, (4)flare in camera view, (5)foggy camera view, (6)frost on the lens, and (7)rainy drops. Figure 3 shows a confusion matrix for all categories on the tested models.[1] Table 2 compares the performance of the different models with a CNN model that was used as a baseline to benchmark deep learning performance in general and transfer learning applicability to the use-case subject of this research work. In general, all the models performed highly with an accuracy rate (precision) ranging between 93% and 98%, except for ResNet, where the model the precision score was 65%-70%. From Fig. 2, we observe that the resulting models vary in the complexity of the network architecture, i.e., the total parameter number - Tot. P. Among the different tested transfer learning models, the MobileNet model scored the highest precision with 98%. The advantage of MobileNet, its moderate size and complexity of the model, i.e., Tot.P is 6.44 million parameters, which translates to less training time and computational resources. Such attributes make the MobileNet model attractive to industrial applications, where real-time performance, high precision, and deployment on edge devices are key requirements.

Table 2. Results from the investigated transfer learning models were compared to the classic CNN model, which was trained from scratch. ODeLIndA dataset was used in training and validating all models.

Model	Train.P	Tot.P	Precision	Recall	F1
CNN (Baseline)	19.03 m	19.03 m	0.96 ± 0.03	0.96 ± 0.02	0.96 ± 0.03
VGG-16-TL	524 807	14.71 m	0.96 ± 0.03	0.95 ± 0.02	0.95 ± 0.03
VGG-19-TL	524 807	20.5 m	0.95 ± 0.03	0.95 ± 0.03	0.95 ± 0.03
InceptionNetv3-TL	3 277 319	26.86 m	0.94 ± 0.01	0.94 ± 0.05	0.93 ± 0.03
ResNet-50-TL	3 277 319	25.80 m	0.65 ± 0.25	0.70 ± 0.31	0.64 ± 0.27
Xception-TL	3 277 319	24.13 m	0.93 ± 0.04	0.92 ± 0.05	0.92 ± 0.04
DenseNet-TL	1 966 599	20.28 m	0.95 ± 0.02	0.95 ± 0.02	0.95 ± 0.02
MobileNetV3-TL	3 211 783	**6.44 m**	**0.98 ± 0.01**	**0.98 ± 0.01**	**0.98 ± 0.00**

---

[1] Additional results, along with detailed model architectures, are found at https:// github.com/uiaikt/ODeLIndA.

	0	1	2	3	4	5	6
0	92	8	0	0	0	0	1
1	0	61	0	0	0	0	3
2	0	2	100	6	0	0	1
3	4	0	0	740	0	8	0
4	1	0	0	0	80	0	1
5	10	0	0	2	0	210	0
6	3	4	0	1	0	1	66

3(a) CNN without TL

	0	1	2	3	4	5	6
0	100	0	0	0	0	0	0
1	0	64	0	0	0	0	0
2	0	0	110	6	0	0	0
3	0	0	0	740	0	11	0
4	0	0	0	0	81	0	1
5	8	0	0	0	0	220	0
6	0	0	2	1	1	0	71

3(b) MobileNetV3-TL

	0	1	2	3	4	5	6
0	94	1	0	3	1	1	1
1	1	62	0	0	1	0	0
2	1	0	100	6	1	2	1
3	4	0	0	740	0	10	0
4	0	1	0	0	80	1	0
5	14	0	0	0	0	210	0
6	1	1	2	1	10	1	59

3(c) VGG-16-TL

	0	1	2	3	4	5	6
0	93	2	0	2	0	2	2
1	0	63	0	0	0	0	1
2	0	0	110	6	1	1	0
3	4	0	0	740	0	11	0
4	0	3	2	0	75	1	1
5	8	0	1	3	0	210	0
6	1	9	2	3	3	1	56

3(d) VGG-19-TL

	0	1	2	3	4	5	6
0	92	1	0	3	0	5	0
1	1	61	0	0	0	2	0
2	0	0	110	6	0	2	0
3	1	0	0	740	0	11	0
4	0	1	0	1	77	3	0
5	8	0	0	12	0	200	0
6	2	5	5	6	5	9	43

3(e) InceptionNetv3-TL

	0	1	2	3	4	5	6
0	0	44	0	43	0	10	4
1	0	31	1	3	0	9	20
2	0	5	19	13	0	74	3
3	0	0	0	710	0	43	0
4	0	27	0	10	0	38	7
5	0	0	0	27	0	200	0
6	0	21	1	10	0	14	29

3(f) ResNet-50-TL

	0	1	2	3	4	5	6
0	81	0	0	1	0	12	7
1	1	60	0	0	0	0	3
2	0	1	100	6	0	4	0
3	2	0	0	730	0	23	0
4	1	2	0	0	66	7	6
5	8	0	0	1	0	220	0
6	2	4	2	2	4	8	53

3(g) XceptionNet-TL

	0	1	2	3	4	5	6
0	95	2	0	0	0	1	3
1	0	64	0	0	0	0	0
2	0	0	110	6	0	1	0
3	2	0	0	740	0	13	0
4	0	3	0	2	70	0	7
5	8	1	0	3	0	210	0
6	0	2	6	3	2	0	62

3(h) DenseNet-TL

Fig. 3. Confusion matrices for tested models. The labels are described in Sect. 4.

7   Conclusion and Future Work

The work presented in this paper provides a novel framework for predicting operational environmental conditions based on FoV obstruction-detection with the aid of a small dataset and transfer learning methods $ODeLIndA$. The dataset created in the process of developing this research work provides examples for eight operational environment conditions for FoV obstruction: clean (0), crack (1), dark (2), dirty (3), flare (4), fog (5), frost (6), and rain (7), with an approximate total of 10,000 images. The developed dataset comprises smaller datasets and new data points (images) from maritime/port operational environments. The dataset is freely available, and we hope it can provide a good benchmark platform for future work in FoV obstruction classification.

Furthermore, the proposed framework extends existing methods for detecting or classifying FoV obstruction and weather/environmental conditions by introducing a single system capable of classifying eight classes of FoV obstruction in a single training and inference pipeline with high accuracy and throughput. While previous work addresses object detection as a binary classification problem, the developed framework can detect dirt, cracks, raindrops, lens flare, dark view, foggy view, frost, and object obstruction. The proposed framework achieves high detection accuracy with 98% accuracy using MobileNet. Due to the fact that the MobileNet model has approx. 6.44 million parameters in contrast to traditional CNN with 19.03 million parameters, our approach achieves real-time inference throughput to meet industry standards.

The framework can be validated further by replicating the process for other operational contexts or extending the model by acquiring more data representing other conditions to be detected. In either case, the process will expose the models to new requirements and learning patterns. Expanding the models to cover operational context or more operational conditions might impact the system's performance, thus, the framework scalability.

Therefore, in the future, we aim to extend the dataset with different weather phenomena and make more replications of lens obstructions that are non-synthetic in order to validate the framework's scalability and ability to cover more categories. Another aim is to develop a system that can be deployed on edge devices such as Raspberry Pi or NVIDIA Jetson to process live data feeds from cameras deployed in the field.

References

1. Bhathena,   J.:   Weather   image   recognition.   https://www.kaggle.com/jehanbhathena/weather-dataset
2. Bijelic, M., et al.: Seeing through fog without seeing fog: deep multimodal sensor fusion in unseen adverse weather. In: The IEEE Conference on Computer Vision and Pattern Recognition (CVPR) June 2020
3. Bouwmans, T., et al.: On the applications of robust PCA in image and video processing. Proceed. IEEE **106**(8), 1427–1457 (2018)

4. Brodzicki, A., et al.: Transfer learning methods as a new approach in computer vision tasks with small datasets. In: Found. Comput. Decis. Sci. **45**(3), 179–193 (2020)
5. Bronte, S., Bergasa, L., Alcantarilla, P.F.: Fog detection system based on computer vision techniques. In: 12th International IEEE Conference on Intelligent Transportation Systems, pp. 1–6 (2009)
6. Chen, Z., Ou, B.: Visibility detection algorithm of single fog image based on the ratio of wavelength residual energy. Math. Prob. Eng. **2021**, 5531706 (2021)
7. Chollet, F.: Xception: deep learning with depthwise separable convolutions. In: Proceedings of the IEEE Conference on Computer Vision and Pattern Recognition, pp. 1251–1258 (2017)
8. Cognex: Industry 4.0 and machine vision. https://www.cognex.com/what-is/industry-4-0-machine-vision
9. Garnett, N., et al.: Real-time category-based and general obstacle detection for autonomous driving. In: IEEE International Conference on Computer Vision Workshops (ICCVW), pp. 198–205 (2017). https://doi.org/10.1109/ICCVW.2017.32
10. Guo, Y., Kumazawa, I., Kaku, C.: Blind spot obstacle detection from monocular camera images with depth cues extracted by CNN. Automot. Innov. **1**(4), 362–373 (2018) https://doi.org/10.1007/s42154-018-0036-6
11. Harasse, S., et al.: Automated camera dysfunctions detection. In: 6th IEEE Southwest Symposium on Image Analysis and Interpretation, pp. 36–40 (2004)
12. He, K., et al.: Deep residual learning for image recognition. In: Proceedings of the IEEE conference on computer vision and pattern recognition, pp. 770–778 (2016)
13. Howard, A.G., et al.: MobileNets: efficient convolutional neural networks for mobile vision applications. arXiv preprint arXiv:1704.04861 (2017)
14. Huang, G., et al.: Densely connected convolutional networks. In: Proceedings of the IEEE Conference on Computer Vision and Pattern Recognition, pp. 4700–4708 (2017)
15. Curie, K.A.J.: Nighttime vehicle detection dataset. https://github.com/ntnu-arl/vehicles-nighttime (2018)
16. Belhumeur, P., Gu, J., Ramamoorthi, R., Nayar, S.: Removing image artifacts due to dirty camera lenses and thin occluders. In: ACM Trans. Graph. **28**(5), 1–10 (2009). New York, NY, USA (2009)
17. Computer Vision Lab: Dark Zurich Dataset
18. Liao, K., et al.: Unsupervised deep image stitching: reconstructing stitched features to images. https://github.com/nie-lang/UnsupervisedDeepImageStitching
19. Liu, J., Raghavan, A., Price, R.R.: Detection of near-field camera obstruction (2015)
20. Liu, X., et al.: Real-time marine animal images classification by embedded system based on mobilenet and transfer learning. In: OCEANS 2019-Marseille, pp. 1–5. IEEE (2019)
21. Palvanov, A., Cho, Y.I.: VisNet: deep convolutional neural networks for forecasting atmospheric visibility. Sensors **19**(6), 1424–8220 (2019)
22. Pinggera, P., Franke, U., Mester, R.: High-performance long range obstacle detection using stereo vision. In: IEEE/RSJ International Conference on Intelligent Robots and Systems (IROS), pp. 1308–1313 (2015)
23. Pixabay: Free images of fog. https://pixabay.com/images/search/fog/
24. Pixabay: Free images of rain. https://pixabay.com/images/search/rain/
25. Porav, H., Bruls, T., Newman, P.: I can see clearly now : image restoration via de-raining. arXiv preprint arXiv: 1901.00893 (2019)

26. Simonyan, K., Zisserman, A.: Very deep convolutional networks for large-scale image recognition. arXiv preprint arXiv:1409.1556 (2014)
27. Soboleva, V., Shipitko, O.: Raindrops on windshield: dataset and lightweight gradient-based detection algorithm (2021). arXiv preprint arXiv: 2104.05078
28. Son, H., et al.: Trend analysis of research and development on automation and robotics technology in the construction industry. KSCE J. Civ. Eng. **14**, 131–139 (2010). Mar
29. Szegedy, C., et al.: Going deeper with convolutions. In: Proceedings of the IEEE Conference on Computer Vision and Pattern Recognition, pp. 1–9 (2015)
30. Szegedy, C., et al.: Rethinking the inception architecture for computer vision. In: IEEE Conference on Computer Vision and Pattern Recognition (CVPR), pp. 2818–2826 (2016)
31. Wei, W., et al.: Semi-supervised transfer learning for image rain removal. In: The IEEE Conference on Computer Vision and Pattern Recognition (2019)
32. Wu, Y., et al.: How to train neural networks for flare removal. In: Proceedings of the IEEE/CVF International Conference on Computer Vision (ICCV), pp. 2239–2247 (2021)
33. Yogamani, S., et al.: WoodScape: a multi-task, multi-camera fisheye dataset for autonomous driving. In: Proceedings of the IEEE/CVF International Conference on Computer Vision (ICCV) (2019)

Automated Quality Inspection of High Voltage Equipment Supported by Machine Learning and Computer Vision

Piotr Misiak$^{(\boxtimes)}$ and Daniel Szempruch

IT Innovation Acceleration, Hitachi Energy, Ul. Pawia 7, 31-154 Krakow, Poland
{piotr.misiak,daniel.szempruch}@hitachienergy.com

Abstract. Computer vision is an emerging subfield of machine learning, where the computer can discover patterns and learn from the provided set of pictures and additional information. Because technology is becoming increasingly reliable, companies tend to leverage it for quality inspection in their manufacturing processes. Such systems offer increased accuracy of quality control and reduction of operational costs due to full process automation. Also, cloud services providers are continuously releasing out-of-the-box or easily adaptable solutions supporting visual inspection. This paper presents how we used image classification, object detection, and semantic segmentation to automate the defects detection process during the assembly of high voltage equipment produced in our company. We described the production process and risks associated with improper product quality, as well as discussed developed prototypes, failures, and the components of the final application. We also presented the advantages of our on-prem application compared to general cloud-based solutions.

Keywords: Machine learning · Computer vision · Automated quality inspection · Defects detection · High voltage equipment

1 Introduction

Artificial Intelligence (AI) and Machine Learning (ML) have been used in industry for years and have been becoming more mature. One of the fields of ML is computer vision which allows the machine to receive image data and return necessary information.

AI algorithms are often developed using Convolutional Neural Networks (CNN). CNNs are successfully used in various domain, including medicine (dermoscopy analysis for skin cancer detection) [1, 2], structural engineering (classification of linear bifurcation buckling eigenmodes in cylindrical shells) [3], chemistry (water position on protein structures) [4] and energy (ultracapacitor life prediction) [5]. CNNs are an important building block of ML-based computer vision algorithms.

Computer vision found a great field of application in visual inspection since it lets the manufacturers control product quality during every production stage [6]. That is why multiple cloud service providers develop solutions designed particularly for visual quality inspection. For example, IBM described IBM Maximo Visual Inspection [6], Google released the Google Visual Inspection AI [7], and Mariner together with Microsoft presented Spyglass Visual Inspection powered by Azure services [8]. Also, manufacturing companies set up out-of-the-box or custom, cloud-powered AI solutions for visual inspection, of which the examples are defects detection in FIH Mobile powered by Google Cloud Platform [9] and glass defects detection in Vitro [8]. However, we have not found a solution that would match our needs in the context of fulfilling different requirements related to our Bi-mode Insulated Gate Transistor (BIGT) devices and gluing validation process. The major problem was that the BIGT and the assembly process have been defined in our company, so no general off-the-shelf solution exists that would match our production process. Also, both are considered strictly internal and are custom solutions, so it was preferred to avoid involving external parties in looking for a suitable solution. What is more, the solution needed to let the employees work without disruption or obstacles. In this sense, the Hacarus [10] online tool was tested for glue detection in one part of the BIGT – however, good results were achieved only when the camera was positioned very close to the examined element (which made the manual assembly steps extremely difficult) and the position had to be kept fixed. Add to that, on-prem solution was highly preferred.

2 Problem Statement

The context of the application for assembly process verification relates to power converters enabling effective, long-distance, transmission of direct current. One of the most promising solutions in this area are multilevel converters proposed in the late 1990s [11, 12]. They evolved to modular multilevel converters defined in early 2000s [13] and proved to be efficient solution in a variety of power conversion systems like high-voltage direct current transmission [14], systems for renewable energy [15] and others.

2.1 Bi-mode Insulated Gate Transistor

One of the components of power converters is electronic switch used in switching power supplies. In high power applications insulated-gate bipolar transistor (IGBT) [16] is used, which is a three-terminal semiconductor device. Finally, to solve technical limits and to respond to demand for increased power densities, Bi-mode Insulated Gate Transistor (BIGT) [17] was created as the extension of reverse conducting IGBT (RC-IGBT) by enabling bi-directional operation using a single chip [18].

2.2 BIGT Assembly Process Verification

In our architecture, we need to ensure high BIGT quality by validating the equipment condition during the assembly process. This will let us deliver high-quality products and avoid failure costs being as high as 100 000 euros per day. The crucial problem is how not to jeopardize air insulation at destructive short circuit events, and this is the issue a lot of producers struggle with.

To automate this validation and avoid costly issues, we developed an application for gluing quality check according to defined requirements, among which there was on-prem verification performed in 2 steps and archiving the results in secure storage.

3   Solution Overview and Development Process

To implement the solution, we proposed a set of hardware together with a software application using three machine learning models. During the prototyping phase, various image processing techniques were tested, and eventually, the application of ML models helped us to create the most reliable and universal solution. All models are on-prem, so the application can work without access to the Internet, avoiding issues related to data latency and data privacy.

3.1   Hardware Architecture

To ensure good image quality and constant imaging and lighting conditions in the factory, where the conditions are restricted by health and safety regulations for instance, the complete hardware architecture needed to be defined, including vision devices, isolation from external factors and mounting equipment.

We observed that automatic exposure and focus settings used by the cameras were not reliable – it happened that the lens focused on the foreground, thus making the most crucial elements of the equipment blurred; also, brightness and exposure measurement could not deal with a high-contrast image. Due to that, some pictures suffered from overexposure, and it was not possible to distinguish between glued and not glued parts of the BIGT. As a result, the following set of equipment was proposed:

- Three Full HD web cameras connected to the computer with the application: two cameras used to capture pictures from different angles, the third camera used to scan QR codes necessary to identify the verified element.
- Wrapping metal box with black background, containing LED lighting and cameras mounting points to ensure constant lighting condition, separate captured elements from external factors, and fix the cameras position (see Fig. 1).
- Plastic BIGT fixture and position limiters help the factory employees to keep the BIGT in the cameras' field of view.

The exposure-related issues were making it impossible to perform image analysis. The effect of overexposure is presented in Fig. 2. It is extremely hard for humans to decide if a glue layer is put in the opening, so it was impossible to train a reliable semantic segmentation model for glue detection.

Fig. 1. The wrapping box with the fixture placed inside

Fig. 2. Effect of overexposure – it is impossible to decide if the glue is present in the opening

3.2 Machine Learning Layer

The ML component of the application consists of three on-prem models implemented in Python language and trained with Azure Machine Learning service. They aimed to localize essential elements of the device, determine the state of gluing in detected corners, detect the amount of glue in the main slot, and verify if the protective sticker was placed. We used standard Full HD pictures as it ensured both high details level and low solution cost. These pictures are used in ML algorithms, which can adapt and rescale the pictures according to their needs. The implemented models are described in the following subsections.

Object Detection

To localize essential elements of the assembled device like main glue slot, device corners, and protective sticker, YOLO (You Only Look Once) model was used [19]. We implemented the solution using the 5th version of the framework, released in May 2020. Unlike other object detection methods like sliding window or region proposal, YOLO is a single-shot algorithm, which means that the whole input picture is processed at once. Thanks to that, YOLO can be leveraged to detect objects in real-time – the authors say their base YOLO model can process 45 frames per second. What is more, various extended versions of YOLO are developed parallelly, e.g., YOLO-Z increases detection accuracy for YOLOv5 on small objects [20]. We observed that standard YOLOv5 dealt with the detection of small device corners, where the object size was about 40-by-40 pixels.

In total, our dataset consisted of 276 pictures and 4 classes distributed among the pictures with the following constraints:

- Each picture representing the first stage of gluing contained slot (1 annotation) and corner (2 annotations) classes.
- Each picture representing the second stage of gluing contained slot (1 annotation) and either protective_sticker_pres or protective_sticker_abs (1 annotation) classes.

The pictures were annotated using open-sourced, Python-based *labelImg* tool licensed under the MIT License [21]. The application window is presented in Fig. 3. In the next step, the dataset was split into training and test sets using a 75/25 proportion, so 219 images were used for training and 57 images were used for testing. The model was trained for 160 epochs – this value was chosen as the maximal one where model accuracy may have increased. Basic hyperparameters selection was performed, and finally 640 and 16 were established as the best set for input image resolution and batch size, respectively.

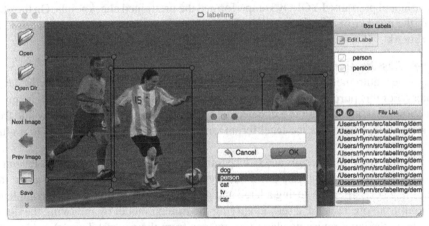

Fig. 3. Screenshot of the *labelImg* application with annotated sample picture (Source: [21]).

The following Table 1 presents the test metrices returned by the YOLO training code: number of labels for each class, precision, recall and two variants of mean average precision for two different ranges of intersection over union (IoU) – these are metrices typically used for object detection [22]. As can be observed, most values are above 90% except values for mAP calculated for IoU in a range from 0.5 to 0.95. The low value for a corner class is a result of the small size of these objects – in this case, a small shift (in pixels) between ground truth and prediction causes a significant decrease of IoU.

However, we observed that detections for all classes are accurate, detection confidence is high (above 80%), and no false positives are returned.

Table 1. Test metrices returned after training the YOLO model.

Class	Labels	Precision	Recall	mAP@.5	mAP@.5:.95
All	127	0.976	0.978	0.971	0.749
Corner	29	0.933	0.965	0.925	0.461
Slot	57	0.982	0.948	0.968	0.854
Prot_stick_abs	13	0.993	1	0.995	0.798
Prot_stick_pres	27	0.995	1	0.996	0.882

To put it into context, the authors of YOLOv5 published a table with benchmark results for tests performed on COCO val2017 dataset [23, 24]. Their results present that in case of 640-by-640 input pictures (as we applied in our application) mAP@.5 metric value raises from 0.457 to 0.689 depending on YOLOv5 subvariant (from Nano to Extra-large, respectively) and mAP@.5:.95 metric value raises from 0.28 to 0.507 depending on YOLOv5 subvariant (from Nano to Extra-large, respectively). Other metrices mentioned in Table 1 were not included in their report. As it is visible, our model trained using Small subvariant of pretrained YOLOv5 outperformed the pretrained checkpoints. On the other hand, the number of classes in our problem is much smaller than in the dataset used for benchmark.

Image Classification

One of the requirements was to determine whether the glue is present or not on the device corners. For this purpose, an image classification algorithm was used. It takes an image of a corner extracted by the object detection component and returns a single value from the range 0–1, where 0 is the label for an empty corner, and 1 corresponds to a glued corner.

To improve training results and reduce training time, transfer learning was leveraged [25, 26]. Shortly speaking, this technique consists on training a model for a given task (e.g., image classification) using a large and general dataset (which may be completely different from our target dataset), modifying the trained model by removing the output layer (e.g., the layer returning classes for images from the general dataset), replacing it with the custom layer designed for the custom task (in our case, it was a layer with a single neuron determining whether the image present an empty or a glued corner), and fine-tuning (i.e., training) the model using the custom dataset. For our project, we used the pre-trained convolutional neural network model trained on the ImageNet dataset and available via TensorFlow Hub [27, 28].

The dataset consisted of 242 pictures of corners extracted by the object detection model. The pictures containing empty and glued corners (evenly distributed) were then divided manually into two groups named empty and glued.

To enlarge the dataset effectively, it was augmented by applying a horizontal flip, and it was finally split into training and test sets using a 75/25 proportion. Horizontal flip corresponds to designed hardware setup, where pictures are taken by two cameras placed on both sides of the BIGT (but not perfectly symmetrically), so as a result we get more data items reflecting real world usage. The model was trained for 160 epochs – typically, after this number of epochs the training process was stopped because of detected plateau in model accuracy (so called early stopping). As previously, hyperparameters selection was performed, and the final set was 96 for input image size (to get the right balance between keeping information on pictures and size of the trained model) and 32 as batch size. The final training accuracy was about 97% and test accuracy was about 95%.

Semantic Segmentation

For glue detection in the main slot, it was required to determine the amount of glue, that is why semantic segmentation was used. The semantic segmentation [29] consists on assigning the detected class to individual pixels rather than to rectangular areas like in object detection. For our purpose, we trained a semantic segmentation model that takes the extracted slot as input and labels each pixel with a value of 0 (background) or 1 (glue).

Manual preparation of dataset for semantic segmentation is time-consuming, so here we also used transfer learning to be able to achieve better results with a smaller dataset. We applied the U-Net convolutional neural network model [30] being the state-of-the-art architecture for semantic segmentation, trained it on the CARLA dataset [31] to get the pre-trained model, and finally, we fine-tuned it using our dataset.

The dataset consisted of 385 pictures of extracted slots, and 385 corresponding pictures defining the labels for each pixel. We used the Hasty.ai web platform [32] to annotate images. Again, we augmented the dataset by applying a horizontal flip and it was finally split into training and test sets using a 70/30 proportion. Here, we increased test percentage because of larger dataset and more complex task (to ensure good generalizability of the model). As for other models, some hyperparameters were tested and the best results were achieved for 384-by-288 (width and height of input pictures) and batch size of 32. We trained the model for 200 epochs – again, after this number of epochs the training process was interrupted because of early stopping. The final training accuracy was about 95% and test accuracy was about 90%.

3.3 Software Architecture

To ensure a good user experience for non-technical users, the application with a graphical user interface was developed using the.NET framework and C# language and is a middleware between the user and ML layer. The application is responsible for managing input cameras, controlling the quality verification process for each verified device, capturing images, calling the ML layer, and presenting results. Figure 4 presents information flow starting from input pictures received by.NET application and ending with final verification results returned to the application by the computer vision module.

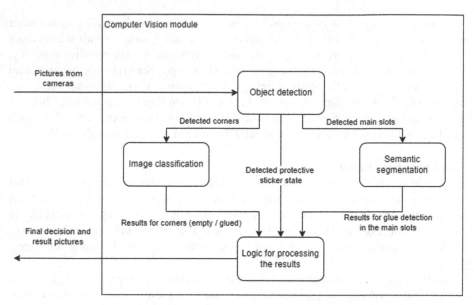

Fig. 4. Diagram with information flow.

Figure 5 presents the application window after one validation step with a negative result. Required and detected elements (glue in the slot, protective sticker) are marked with a green label, while missing elements (missing glue in the slot) are marked with a red label. To make it clearer on the paper, green and red colors were replaced by white and black, respectively.

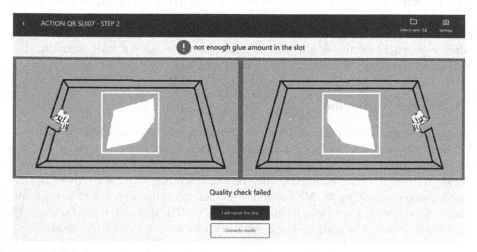

Fig. 5. Application window with validation result presented on a schematic drawing.

Apart from displaying immediate results, the application archives both input pictures and results, thus making it possible to perform an assembly audit after a batch of devices is assembled. Thanks to the on-premise models, the application does not require a constant connection with the Internet.

3.4   Issues Related to Moving to Production

The ML components started to be developed at the initial stage of the project, so to go forward with our research and to analyze the project feasibility, we started to build models using Python language and commonly used Python libraries like TensorFlow and PyTorch. Later, when the wrapping application and its development framework (.NET) were chosen, we needed to solve the problem of integrating the ML components (Python) with the main application (C#). Initially, we considered three options:

- Building Python web application exposing the REST API with ML services, called by the.NET application
- Converting ML models files to the general ONNX format and using them directly in C# code
- Embedding Python environment into main application, preparing Python scripts performing inference and executing them inside C# application via command line interface.

Finally, to avoid the risk connected to converting models and to deal with limited infrastructure at the factory, we decided to embed the Python environment and attach Python scripts to the application. The main drawback of this approach is that ML models are loaded every time the script is executed, so we observe about 5 s of additional time effort, however, the application is not time-critical, and it will be easier for end-users to perform application updates when only one piece of software exists.

Another issue we faced while developing ML models for business cases is the limited amount of data to use. The use case we worked on was new, so when we discussed it, no data samples were available. Also, this use case is specific and there is no publicly available dataset answering our needs. To overcome these obstacles, we decided to develop a simple application capable of capturing pictures and saving them on the cloud server, from which we could download them. Thanks to that and thanks to cooperation with factory employees, we were able to receive necessary data in batches.

Also, when you need to label data manually and you are not an expert in the domain, you will need support from domain experts to determine unsure data items. In our case, we struggled to clearly see which pictures of slots and corners represent "good" gluing and which do not. In addition, we observed rare cases, where a very thin glue layer was put on the main slot – in these cases, we were not sure how to label these areas. For these unclear cases we consulted our domain experts to clarify the cases – that helped us keep the dataset more consistent, however a few data items were so vague that deciding required longer consulting and more domain experts needed to be involved.

Another important lesson is the time we spent preparing different datasets. While the image classification dataset is simple (it is enough to move pictures to a correct group), labeling pictures for the semantic segmentation model is the hardest part. In these moments, it is immensely helpful to use labeling tools offering any kind of automation. For instance, the tool we used can learn after a new batch of pictures is labeled, and later it can generate labels automatically – it makes the process faster, although one needs to verify the label and improve if necessary.

4 Summary

In this article we described the concept of visual inspection using computer vision and presented our custom solution leveraging ML models for quality checks. We also presented the benefits and issues which occurred during the development process.

The described solution can be generalized and adapted to other production processes by defining a new product verification process, combining used computer vision techniques (object detection, image classification, semantic segmentation) according to the verification process, and providing new datasets. For instance, if it is required that a produced item contains specific elements, one needs to create a dataset for object detection algorithm with labeled required elements and labeled item. If these elements need to be placed in a specific position (like protective sticker placed in our case), the conditions can be defined based on elements position. If a state of a given element needs to be detected (like empty or glued corners of the BIGT device), the dataset with split pictures needs to be provided. The implementation of image classification model training automatically assigns classes when pictures are located among different directories corresponding to the classes. The semantic segmentation algorithm can be used to infer non-binary or space-aware state of a component (like distribution of glue in the main slot) or to detect damages or defects – a good example is corrosion or dirt detection.

Currently, we are in the process of monitoring the accuracy of the application to maintain the high reliability of ML components and to retrain the models if errors tend to occur.

References

1. Cheng, X., Kadry, S., Meqdad, M.N., Crespo, R.G.: CNN supported framework for automatic extraction and evaluation of dermoscopy images. In: The Journal of Supercomputing, pp. 1–18 (2022)
2. Reis, H.C., Turk, V., Khoshelham, K., Kaya, S.: InSiNet: a deep convolutional approach to skin cancer detection and segmentation. In: Medical & Biological Engineering Computing **60**(3), pp. 643–662 (2022)
3. Sadowski, A.J.: Automated classification of linear bifurcation buckling eigenmodes in thin-walled cylindrical shell structures. Advances in Engineering Software, p. 173 (2022)
4. Park, S., Seok, C.: GalaxyWater-CNN: prediction of water positions on the protein structure by a 3D-convolutional neural network. J. Chem. Inf. Model. **62**(13), 3157–3168 (2022)
5. Wang, C., Xiong, R., Tian, J., Lu, J., Zhang, C.: Rapid ultracapacitor life prediction with a convolutional neural network. Applied Energy, p. 305 (2022)
6. Visual inspection for improved quality in manufacturing: Monitor smarter with IBM Maximo Visual Inspection, https://www.ibm.com/blogs/internet-of-things/quality-manufacturing-visual-inspection. Last accessed 10 June 2022

7. Visual Inspection AI: https://cloud.google.com/solutions/visual-inspection-ai. Last accessed 10 June 2022
8. A Deep Learning AI Solution that Improves Defect Detection and Eliminates Pseudo-Defects, https://www.mariner-usa.com/solutions/spyglass-visual-inspection. Last accessed 10 June 2022
9. FIH Mobile automates smartphone manufacturing with Visual Inspection AI, https://cloud.google.com/blog/products/ai-machine-learning/fih-mobile-automates-mobile-handset-def ect-detection-with-ai. Last accessed 23 May 2022
10. HACARUS – Sparse Modeling based AI, Edge AI with learning and inference capability, White box AI. https://hacarus.com/. Last accessed 31 August 2022
11. Lai, J.J., Peng, F.Z.: Multilevel converters-a new breed of power converters. In: IAS '95. Conference Record of the 1995 IEEE Industry Applications Conference Thirtieth IAS Annual Meeting, 3, 2348–2356 vol.3
12. Tolbert, L.M., Peng, F.Z., Habetler, T.G.: Multilevel converters for large electric drives. IEEE Transactions on Industry Applications **35**, 36–44
13. Lesnicar, A., Marquardt, R.: An innovative modular multilevel converter topology suitable for a wide power range. In: 2003 IEEE Bologna Power Tech Conference Proceedings, vol. 3, p. 6 vol. 3
14. Alyami, H., Mohamed, Y.A.: Review and development of MMC employed in VSC-HVDC systems. In: 2017 IEEE 30th Canadian Conference on Electrical and Computer Engineering (CCECE), pp. 1–6
15. Verdugo, C., Candela, J.I., Blaabjerg, F., Rodríguez, P.: Three-phase isolated multimodular converter in renewable energy distribution systems. In: IEEE Journal of Emerging and Selected Topics in Power Electronics, vol. 8, pp. 854–865
16. Takahashi, H., Yamamoto, A., Aono, S., Minato, T.: 1200V reverse conducting IGBT. In: 2004 Proceedings of the 16th International Symposium on Power Semiconductor Devices and ICs, pp. 133–136
17. Rahimo, M.T., Schlapbach, U., Schnell, R., Kopta, A., Vobecký, J., Baschnagel, A.: Realization of higher output power capability with the Bi-mode insulated gate transistor (BIGT). In: 2009 13th European Conference on Power Electronics and Applications, pp. 1–10
18. Rahimo, M.T., Kopta, A., Schlapbach, U., Vobecký, J., Schnell, R., Klaka, S.: The Bi-mode insulated gate transistor (BIGT) a potential technology for higher power applications. 2009. In: 21st International Symposium on Power Semiconductor Devices & IC's, pp. 283–286
19. Redmon, J., Divvala, S., Girshick, R., Farhadi, A.: You only look once: Unified, real-time object detection. In: Proceedings of the IEEE conference on computer vision and pattern recognition, pp. 779–788
20. Benjumea, A., Teeti, I., Cuzzolin, F., Bradley, A.: YOLO-Z: Improving small object detection in YOLOv5 for autonomous vehicles (2021)
21. Tzutalin: LabelImg. Git code (2015). https://github.com/tzutalin/labelImg. Last accessed 06 June 2022
22. Padilla, R., Netto, S.L., da Silva, E.A.: A survey on performance metrics for object-detection algorithms. In: 2020 International Conference on Systems, Signals and Image Processing (IWSSIP), pp. 237–242
23. YOLOv5 in PyTorch > ONNX > CoreML > TFLite – GitHub. https://github.com/ultralytics/yolov5. Last accessed 31 August 2022
24. COCO - Common Objects in Context. https://cocodataset.org/. Last accessed 31 August 2022
25. Bozinovski, S.: Reminder of the First Paper on Transfer Learning in Neural Networks, 1976. Informatica (Slovenia) 44 (2020)
26. Pratt, L.Y., Mostow, J., Kamm, C.A.: Direct Transfer of Learned Information Among Neural Networks. AAAI

27. Deng, J., Dong, W., Socher, R., Li, L., Li, K., Fei-Fei, L.: ImageNet: A large-scale hierarchical image database. CVPR (2009)
28. Transfer learning with TensorFlow Hub: https://www.tensorflow.org/tutorials/images/transfer_learning_with_hub. Last accessed 09 June 2022
29. Shelhamer, E., Long, J., Darrell, T.: Fully convolutional networks for semantic segmentation. In: IEEE Transactions on Pattern Analysis and Machine Intelligence, vol. 39, pp. 640–651 (2017)
30. Ronneberger, O., Fischer, P., Brox, T.: U-Net: Convolutional Networks for Biomedical Image Segmentation. In: Navab, N., Hornegger, J., Wells, W.M., Frangi, A.F. (eds.) MICCAI 2015. LNCS, vol. 9351, pp. 234–241. Springer, Cham (2015). https://doi.org/10.1007/978-3-319-24574-4_28
31. Dosovitskiy, A., Ros, G., Codevilla, F., López, A.M., Koltun, V.: CARLA: an open urban driving simulator. In: ArXiv, vol. abs/1711.03938 (2017)
32. Hasty's data-centric ML platform: https://hasty.ai/. Last accessed 09 June 2022

On Predicting the Work Load for Service Contractors

Himadri Sikhar Khargharia[1]([✉]), Siddhartha Shakya[1], Sara Sharif[2], Russell Ainslie[3], and Gilbert Owusu[3]

[1] EBTIC, Khalifa University, Abu Dhabi, UAE
{himadri.khargharia,sid.shakya}@ku.ac.ae
[2] Department of IoT and AI, Etisalat, Abu Dhabi, UAE
sarahmad@etisalat.ae
[3] BT Research, British Telecom, London, UK
{russell.ainslie,gilbert.owusu}@bt.com

Abstract. Service Industries rely on resource planning and service optimisation to improve operational efficiency. Forecasting the demand for the service with high accuracy plays a significant role in proactively planning the resources to support the expected demand. With the evolution of the Internet Of Things (IoT), the service contractors use different types of devices connected to the internet to capture the demand and monitor the historical pattern. In this work, we analyse the arrival pattern tracked using different IoT devices of personnel employed by a contractor at different zones for providing service. This arrival pattern at a specific zone is considered the service demand. We document this analysis and forecast the future arrival pattern of personnel at different zones. We compare different regression models based on their accuracy to select the best fit model and report the results. The best fit model is used for forecasting the arrival pattern by a real-life application.

Keywords: Forecasting · Work load prediction · ElasticNet · SVR · KNN regressor · Neural network · Random forest regressor · Decision tree regressor · Gradient boosting regressor

1 Introduction

Extensive outsourcing of service operations means that the operational performance of contractors has an immense impact on the service industry [14]. Knowing the future demand of the service required would aid the contractors in optimising their operational efficiency. These contractors could provide services across the various domain of the service industry like telecom, banking, utilities etc. With the advancement and affordability of the Internet of Things (IoT), these service contractors use it to improve their processes, minimise waste, maximise savings, and capture demand data [2]. Analysis of the historical demand assists in the estimation of the direction of future trends. The estimated and projected demand for goods and services could help determine the budget and plan for anticipated expenses and required human, and machine resources [20].

© The Author(s), under exclusive license to Springer Nature Switzerland AG 2022
M. Bramer and F. Stahl (Eds.): SGAI-AI 2022, LNAI 13652, pp. 223–237, 2022.
https://doi.org/10.1007/978-3-031-21441-7_16

As IoT evolves, billions of devices connect to the internet, creating a data-centric ecosystem [22]. IoT bridges the gap between the digital and the physical world, allowing applications and services built using IoT platforms to be widely accepted across the world [30]. The IoT devices can be complex machines with the amalgamation of software, hardware, actuator and sensors or just a simple sensor (e.g. Thermostat, camera, smart bulb, etc.). These devices can be ambient sensing and push the sensed data to infrastructures, accumulating the information [12]. For service contractors, these IoT devices would help accumulate and monitor the data required for analysing the pattern of historical service demand. Usually, some view of future demand is available with an existing contract of a certain set of services for a certain period. But in the majority of cases, it is forecasted, with historical demand and other correlated factors affecting the expected volumes [5, 18, 19, 23].

Figure 1 illustrates our use-case. Here, the service personnel (referred to as technicians henceforth) could be Heating, Ventilation and AirConditioning (HVAC) Technicians, Chiller Technicians, Electricians, Plumbers, Compressor technicians or even be Drivers carrying other technicians to designated zones. Zones are locations with pre-defined geo boundaries and where services need to be offered. These technicians employed by the contractor carry two types of tracking devices, (i) a GPS-enabled industrial phone or (ii) a GPS-enabled watch. These devices are connected to the internet and could push the sensed geo location data to the cloud. The data sensed and generated by the devices are used for various purposes, such as real-time monitoring, jeopardy management, Heath and safety, and trend and patterns analytic with historical data. We consider the arrival pattern of the technician as a measure of demand, as the demand for facilitating the tools and facilities essential for the technician to provide the services at designated zones are proportional to the volume of the technician arrival.

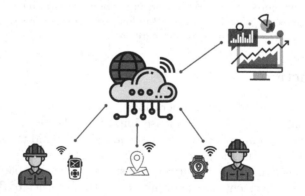

Fig. 1. Overview of tracking technician's effort

In this paper, we focus on the analysis of the zone visit data of the technicians. The data was provided by our partner telecom, which aimed to build a system to monitor and forecast the expected zone visits constantly. For this paper, we choose four different zones representing a diverse set of zone configurations in the operational area. We then use the regression technique to forecast the zone arrival pattern of the technicians to understand the future demand for work in different zones. This arrival pattern at a specific zone is considered the service demand or work demand at that zone. We also compare these regression models to select the best fit model for the forecasting tool. In a service zone, we consider a technician's entry within the zone's geo boundary as a demand data point. The devices carried by the technician keep track of them entering or leaving the premises and thus generating a huge volume of historical data. These data can be used to forecast future demand by analysing the pattern of past demand [18,19]. We also use an ad-hoc approach of tuning the hyper-parameters of the algorithms to improve the accuracy of forecasting the arrival pattern at different zones. The regression techniques implemented for forecasting were ElasticNet [36], SVR [3], KNN regressor [33], Neural Network [25], Random Forest Regressor [6], Gradient Boosting Regressor [9], Decision Tree Regressor [26] etc.

The paper is divided into five sections. Section 2 presents a background study of the investigated forecasting techniques and reviews previous approaches for tuning their parameters. Section 3 provides a formulation of the regression techniques used while identifying the parameters for tuning and the approach for calculating model accuracy. Section 4 describes experiments comparing different regression models and presents an analysis of the results. Section 5 concludes the paper.

2   Background

A variety of establishments incentivized outsourcing of different levels of work in different domains such as utilities, telecom, construction, banking etc., to service contractors. For these service contractors, visibility and understanding of the future trend of work demand help in planning their available resources. Forecasting is a process of predicting future demand trends by analyzing historical and current trends and using any other correlated inputs. Multiple mechanisms exist for forecasting these demand trends. Non-linear regression techniques like KNN regressor, ElasticNet, SVR, neural network, random forest regressor, decision tree regressor and gradient boosting regressor are widely used in the forecasting problem space. The success of each of these techniques depends on many factors, including the effectiveness of the input data, the noise, correctly selected features, and chosen model parameters for topology building and training.

KNN regressor [28,33] uses the mean of the label of its nearest neighbour to compute the labels assigned to a query point. Maltamo et al. [24] used K-nearest neighbour regression for basel area diameter distribution of trees prediction. Forecasting of solar power using gradient boosting and K-nearest neighbour regressor is done by Huang, and others [13]. A *Decision Tree Regressor* builds a regression or classification model in the form of a tree structure. It breaks down a dataset into smaller and smaller subsets while, at the same time, an associated decision tree is incrementally developed. The final result is a tree with decision nodes, and leaf nodes [32]. In [11], authors use Decision Tree Regressor for solar energy prediction, while in [15], airline price analysis and prediction are made using decision tree regressor. A *Random Forest Regressor* is a meta estimator that fits many classifying decision trees on various sub-samples of the dataset and uses averaging to improve the predictive accuracy and control over-fitting [6]. In [10], global marine sediment density is predicted using a random forest regressor. The authors in [8] use a random forest regressor for detecting fault location and duration in power systems. *Gradient Boosting Regressor* is one of the ensemble methods variants where multiple weak models are created and combined to get better performance as a whole [9]. Gradient Boosting Regressor is used in [17] to predict the stress intensity factor of a crack propagating in small bore piping.

SVR is a support vector machine [3] that supports both linear and non-linear regression. In [27,34], Support Vector Regression was used for financial time series forecasting and travel-time prediction. *ElasticNet* is a regularized regression method used when there are multiple features that are correlated with one another and both of them are being picked. In [4,29], Elastic Net is used to forecast economic time series and the US real house price index respectively. *Neural networks (NN)* [25] are popular models in machine learning and deep learning literature. Neural networks are used in various real-world applications like future trading volume forecasting [16], work demand prediction for service providers along with optimal resource planning allocation [1], building energy prediction models [7] etc. In [21] a neural network is used for stock market price prediction.

3 Methodology

In this section, we provide a formulation for the regression techniques we have used to understand their input parameters and tune them for improved accuracy. We conclude the section with how the result is validated.

ElasticNet. Elastic Net [28,36] is a regressor which is useful when there are multiple features which are correlated with one another, elastic net will pick both of them. The objective is a minimization function

$$\min_{w} \frac{1}{2n_{samples}}||Xw - y||_2^2 + \alpha\rho||w||_1 + \frac{\alpha(1 - \rho)}{2}||w||_2^2 \tag{1}$$

The accuracy of a elasticNet model is dependent of the parameters

- α : It is the constant that multiplies the penalty terms. Defaults to 1.0 has no upper bound.

– l1-ratio : It is the elasticNet mixing parameter with

$$0 \le l1 - ratio \le 1 \tag{2}$$

– intercept : is an independent term in decision function.
– max-iteration : is the maximum number of iteration for minimizing the objective function.

SVR. Support Vector Regressor (SVR) [3,28] states that given training vector $x_i \in R^p, i = 1, ..., n$ and a vector $y \in R^n$. The ϵ-SVR solves the following problem

$$\min_{w,b,\zeta,\zeta^*} \frac{1}{2}w^T w + C \sum_{i=1}^{n} (\zeta_i + \zeta_i^*) \tag{3}$$

subject to
$$y_i - w^T \phi(x_i) - b \le \epsilon + \zeta_i \text{ and}$$
$$w^T \phi(x_i) + b - y_i \le \epsilon + \zeta_i^* \text{ and}$$
$$\zeta_i, \zeta_i^* \ge 0, i = 1, .., n.$$
Its dual is

$$\min_{\alpha,\alpha^*} \frac{1}{2}(\alpha - \alpha^*)^T Q(\alpha - \alpha^*) + \epsilon e^T(\alpha + \alpha^*) - y^T(\alpha - \alpha^*) \tag{4}$$

subject to
$$e^T(\alpha - \alpha^*) = 0 \tag{5}$$

$$0 \le \alpha_i, \alpha_i^* \le C, i = 1, ..., n \tag{6}$$

where e is the vector of all ones, $C > 0$ is the upper bound Q is an n by n positive semidefinite matrix, $Q_{i,j} \equiv K(x_i, x_j) = \phi(x_i)^T \phi(x_j)$ is the kernel. Here training vectors are implicitly mapped into a higher (may be infinite) dimensional space by the function ϕ. The decision function is: $\sum_{i=1}^{n}(\alpha_i - \alpha_i^*)K(x_i, x) + \rho$.

In our work, accuracy of the ϵ-SVR model is improved by tuning the ϵ parameter and the kernel. The selected kernels are linear, polynomial, rbf and sigmoid.

Neural Network. An artificial neural network is a supervised learning algorithm that learns the function

$$f(.) : R^m \to R^o \tag{7}$$

where m and o are the input and the output dimensions. Given a set of inputs $X = x_1, x_2, ..., x_m$ and target y it can learn non-linear function approximation and regression. A neural network consists of nodes, an input layer, hidden layer and output layer. Each node in the hidden layer converts the value from the previous layer with a weighted linear summation $w_1x_1 + w_2x_2 + w_3x_3 + ... + w_mx_m$ followed by a non-linear activation function $f(.) : R \to R'$. The output layer receives the values from the last hidden layer and transforms them into output values.

In this paper, we use a feed forward neural network model with the resilient back propagation algorithm [31]. Early stopping strategy is used to avoid overfitting [35]. It subdivides the data from the training set into training and validation set. This validation set is used to evaluate the accuracy of the model. Once the accuracy of the model stops improving and starts to decrease this indicates overfitting and the training process is stopped. The activation function of the nodes are of sigmoid form [25]. We restrict the neural network model to support a maximum of 3 hidden layers and 12 nodes for each layer, which are tuned to improve the model's accuracy.

KNN Regressor. KNN regressor [33] is based on learning by comparing given test instances with the training set. Let $T = (x_1, y_1), (x_2, y_2), ..., (x_N, y_N)$ be the training set with distance metric d, where, $x_i = (x_{i1}, x_{i2}, ..., x_{im})$ is the ith instance denoted by m attributes with its output y_i, and N is the number of instances. When given a test instance x, it needs to compute the distance d_i between x and each instance x_i in T, and sorts the distance d_i by its value. If d_i ranks in the ith place, then the distance d_i corresponding instance is called the i_{th} nearest neighbor $NN_i(x)$, and its output is noted as $y_i(x)$. Finally the prediction output $\hat{y}$ of x is the mean of the outputs of its k nearest neighbors in regression, i.e.

$$\hat{y} = 1/k \sum_{i=1}^{k} y_i(x) \tag{8}$$

Accuracy of a KNN regressor is dependent on the number of neighbors K and the algorithm a for calculating the nearest neighbor e.g. KD-Tree, Ball-Tree, Brute-Force.

Decision Tree Regressor. Given training vectors $x_i \in R^n$, i=1,..., l and a label vector $y \in R^l$, a decision tree [28] recursively partitions the feature space such that the samples with the same labels or similar target values are grouped together.

Let the data at node m be represented by Q_m with N_m samples. For each candidate split $\theta = (j, t_m)$ consisting of a feature j and threshold t_m, partition the data into $Q_m^{left}(\theta)$ and $Q_m^{right}(\theta)$ subsets.

$$Q_m^{left}(\theta) = \{(x, y) | x_j <= t_m\}$$
$$Q_m^{right}(\theta) = Q_m \setminus Q_m^{left}(\theta) \tag{9}$$

The quality of a candidate split of node m is then computed using an impurity function or loss function $H()$, the choice of which depends on the task being solved (classification or regression).

$$G(Q_m, \theta) = \frac{N_m^{left}}{N_m} H(Q_m^{left}(\theta)) + \frac{N_m^{right}}{N_m} H(Q_m^{right}(\theta)) \tag{10}$$

Select the parameters that minimises the impurity

$$\theta^* = \text{argmin}_\theta \, G(Q_m, \theta) \tag{11}$$

Recurse for subsets $Q_m^{left}(\theta^*)$ and $Q_m^{right}(\theta^*)$ until the maximum allowable depth is reached, $N_m < \text{min}_{samples}$ or $N_m = 1$.

In our work, the parameters considered for tuning in order to improve the accuracy of decision tree regressor are (i) maximum depth max_depth, which is the maximum depth of the tree.

Random Forest Regressor. Random forests for regression [6] are formed by growing trees depending on a random vector such that the tree predictor $h(x, \Theta)$ takes on numerical values as opposed to class labels. The output values are numerical and we assume that the training set is independently drawn from the distribution of the random vector Y, X. The mean-squared generalization error for any numerical predictor $h(x)$ is

$$E_{X,Y}(Y - h(X))^2 \tag{12}$$

The random forest predictor is formed by taking the average over k of the trees $h(x, \Theta_k)$. Then the following holds

$$E_{X,Y}(Y - av_k h(X, \Theta_k))^2 \rightarrow E_{X,Y}(Y - E_\Theta h(X, \Theta))^2 \tag{13}$$

In our work, accuracy of the random forest regressor is improved by tuning the parameters (i) maximum depth max_depth, which is the maximum depth of a tree and (ii) number of estimators $n\_estimators$, which is the number of trees in the forest.

Gradient Boosting Regressor. Gradient Boosting regression tree (GBRT) [28] technique are additive models whose prediction y_i for a given input x_i is of the following form:

$$\hat{y}_i = F_M(x_i) = \sum_{m=1}^{M} h_m(x_i) \tag{14}$$

where the h_m are estimators called weak learners in the context of boosting. Gradient Tree Boosting uses decision tree regressors of fixed size as weak learners. The constant M corresponds to the $n\_estimators$ parameter, where the newly added tree h_m is fitted in order to minimize a sum of losses.

In our work, accuracy of the Gradient Boosting regressor is improved by tuning (i) maximum depth max_depth, which is the maximum depth of a tree and (ii) number of estimators $n\_estimators$, which is the number of trees considered.

3.1   Tuning Hyper Parameters

The ad-hoc approach is an experimental design method where a range was specified for each parameter of a regression technique, and a relatively higher step value was used to get the test sequence within the range. Each combination of sequences for each parameter was tested, and the best-performing settings were recorded. It is noted that not all parameters were tested to all possible ranges, and some were kept to a smaller range to limit the possible increase in the number of configurations to be tested. Table 1 shows each technique's range, upper and lower bound range. For SVR, each kernel is labelled numerically such that the kernel of type linear is given number 1, the polynomial is given number 2, rbf is given number 3, and sigmoid is given number 4.

Table 1. Regressor with parameter range for tuning

Algorithm	Parameter description	Lower bound	Upper bound	Step count
Elastic Net	$CV(cv)$	1	5	1
	$random\text{-}state\ (rs)$	1	8	1
KNN	$Neighbours\ (K)$	1	8	1
SVR	kernel	1	4	1
	epsilon	0	1	0.1
Neural Net	Hidden Layer (h)	1	3	1
	Layer 1 - node	1	13	4
	Layer (2 & 3) - node	0	13	4
Decision Tree	Max Depth	5	20	5
Random Forest	Max Depth	5	15	1
	No of Estimators	10	150	10
GBRT	Max Depth	5	20	5
	No of Estimators	20	100	10

3.2   Validation

The model, which provides the lowest mean absolute percentage error (MAPE) represented by Eq. 15 and thus the highest accuracy is being selected as the best fit model for forecasting arrival pattern of technicians in the service zones. The accuracy can be calculated as $(1 - MAPE) * 100$.

$$MAPE(M) = \frac{1}{n} \sum_{t=1}^{n} \frac{|A_t - F_t|}{|A_t|} \tag{15}$$

4   Experiment Setup and Analysis of Results

In this section, we analyze the data of the five different service zones. We discuss the experiment setup and then analyze and report the results of the regression techniques applied for forecasting the technician arrival pattern.

4.1 Data-Set

Figure 2 shows the captured five months of data for four services zones, viz. zone 1, zone 2, zone 3 and 4. The dataset contains daily arrival data of different technicians aggregated together for each of the five service zones. We use this dataset to forecast future arrival patterns. The arrival data of the technicians employed by the contractor in different zones act as the estimated work demand for the contractor in those zones. The figure captures the diverseness of zones. It can be seen that zone 2 has the highest number of arrivals captured, while zone 1 has the lowest. Also, zone 4 and zone 3 have the average number of arrivals. The pie chart in Fig. 3 shows the busiest zone by technician visits. It can be seen that zone 2 is the busiest, with 73% of the visits happening to zone 2. The distant second busiest zone is zone 1, with 11% of the visits happening to it. While zone 3 is the least busy with only 6% of the visit happening to it.

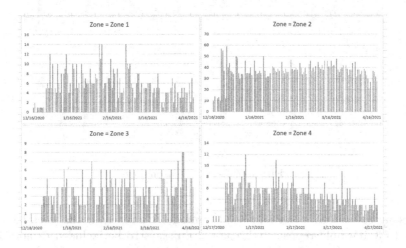

Fig. 2. Zone data

4.2 Experiment Setup

Apart from the hyper parameters owned by the regression models as mentioned in Sect. 3.1 there are hyper parameters related to lag value. The lag value represents how many past periods will be used to predict the future. For example, a day-lag value represents how many immediate days from the past should be used as an input to predict the next day, whereas a week-lag represents how many data points from past weeks should be used. To explain the day-lag and the week-lag a bit further, if the day-lag is set to 3 and the next period to be predicted is a Sunday, the value of the last three days, i.e., Saturday, Friday and

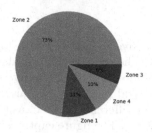

Fig. 3. Busiest zone analysis

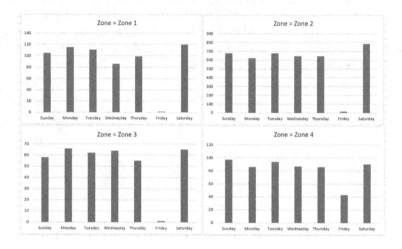

Fig. 4. Zone data seasonality

Thursday to be used as an input to the model. Similarly, if the week-lag value is set to 3, it would represent the past 3 Sundays to be included as additional input features. We have done experiments with multiple setups for the lags and picked up the best setting that gave the highest accuracy, where the day lag was set to 6, and the week lag was set to 2.

Apart from these, we can also notice from Fig. 4 that there is a seasonality pattern in the data, with weekdays having higher values than weekends. Hence, we use the day of the week as an additional categorical feature for the model.

4.3 Evaluation and Results

We experiment with different regression models and multiple sets of model parameters for each zone data set and record the MAPE. The total number of models together with different parameter settings tested for each zone were for Elastic Net 5 combination of CV with eight combinations of random state totalling (5 × 8) 40 models, eight models of KNN regressor because of 8 combinations of neighbours considered, (4 kernel combinations × 10 epsilon combinations), i.e. 40 models of SVR, (3 combinations of hidden layers x 3 combinations of nodes for layer 1 × 3 combinations of nodes for layer 2 × 3 combinations of nodes for layer 3), i.e. 81 models of Neural Network, three models of Decision Tree because of 3 combinations of max_depth allowed, (10 combinations of max_depth x 15 combinations of the number of estimators), i.e. 150 models of Random Forest, (3 combinations of max_depth x 8 combinations of the number of estimators), i.e. 24 models of GBRT. All of these amounted to a total of 346 models. These number of models are quantified from Table 1.

Table 2 shows the top five best-performing regression models with the tuned hyper-parameters for each of the four service zones sorted by the accuracy value. Also, Fig. 5 shows the actual vs predicted arrival pattern for all the four zones when predicted by the best fit model. The solid line is the actual plotted against the dashed line representing predicted values. The dashed line further continues to the future to show the future prediction made by the model.

It can be seen that the accuracy for zone 2 is the highest with around 90% accurate forecast by each of the top 5 models, and Random Forest Regressor with max_depth as 5 and n_estimators of 20 is selected as the best fit model in zone 2. Zone 4 has the next highest accuracy, with the best accuracy being 76.5%; this is using the K nearest neighbour regression technique with the nearest neighbour parameter being selected as 8. Next is Zone 3, with the best accuracy being 74.6%. This is infact being produced by an SVR with a polynomial kernel, for value 2 as mentioned in Sect. 3.1 and ϵ value as 1.0. Zone 1 has the least accuracy, with the best fit model only able to forecast with an accuracy of 72.9%. The best fit model is a Random Forest regressor with a 'max_depth' as nine and 'n_estimators' as 10.

The results suggest that no single algorithm performs best in all the cases and that different algorithms may provide better results for different data sets. This approach contrast with traditional approaches where a single machine learning algorithm tend to be implemented for a specific domain.

The described methodology is built into a forecasting tool that implements all of the regression models, tests different versions of them for each zone, and automatically saves the best model, which is then used for daily prediction. The tool is periodically retrained to adapt to the recent change in the visit pattern. Our partner telecom is testing the tool to produce daily forecasts to aid in the critical decision-making process of analysing resource shortage/surplus and to decide on contractor hiring.

Table 2. Regressors with accuracy

Zone	Model with tuned parameter	Accuracy(%)
1	Random Forest: max_depth = 9, n_estimators = 10	72.9
	Random Forest:max_depth = 13, n_estimators = 70	71.6
	Random Forest:max_depth = 11, n_estimators = 50	71.2
	Random Forest:max_depth = 5, n_estimators = 20	71.2
	Random Forest:max_depth = 9, n_estimators = 150	70.3
2	Random Forest:max_depth = 5,n_estimators = 20	90.9
	Random Forest:max_depth = 7,n_estimators = 100	90.3
	Random Forest:max_depth = 7,n_estimators = 120	90.2
	Random Forest:max_depth = 7,n_estimators = 80	90.0
	GBRT:n_estimators = 100, max_depth = 11	90.0
3	SVR:kernel = 2, epsilon = 1.0	74.6
	GBRT:n_estimators = 40, max_depth = 5	74.1
	Neural Net:hidden_layer = 1,h1-node = 3	74.0
	GBRT:n_estimators = 50, max_depth = 11	73.6
	GBRT:n_estimators = 50, max_depth = 3	73.6
4	KNN:n_neighbors = 8	76.5
	KNN:n_neighbors = 5	75.1
	GBRT:n_estimators = 50, max_depth = 5	74.5
	GBRT:n_estimators = 30, max_depth = 5	74.0
	Decision Tree:max_depth = 5	73.9

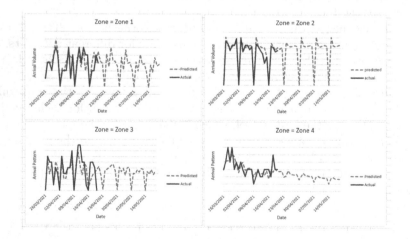

Fig. 5. Actual vs Predicted

5   Conclusion

In this paper, our goal was to find the best model to predict the arrival pattern of the technicians at different zones. The forecast act as the demand of work for the fixed and contractor resources for each of the zone. The data was provided by one of our partner telecoms.

We implemented an end-to-end process to automatically test multiple forecasting techniques with different hyper parameters on the historical arrival data of the technicians at different zone. We performed a detailed experimental analysis of proposed regression models and compared their performance. We found that a single algorithm is not always the best approach and that a different algorithm with a different hyper parameter set was better for a different zone. The model is incorporated into a prediction framework with an analytical dashboard to provide additional insights from a large amount of data collected from the IoT infrastructure that will help the partner telecom with resource decision-making. The number of hyper parameters to test can be increasingly large. While our experimental setup approach to tuning hyper parameters gave us a good result, we understand that implementing intelligent tuning such as heuristic search and optimisation-based approaches could improve results. This forms part of our future work.

References

1. Ainslie, R., McCall, J., Shakya, S., Owusu, G.: Predictive planning with neural networks. In: 2016 International Joint Conference on Neural Networks (IJCNN), pp. 2110–2117. IEEE (2016)
2. Al-Amleh, K.: A study into the adoption of internet of things-IoT technologies within contractors in Dubai, United Arab Emirates, Ph. D. thesis, The British University in Dubai (BUiD) (2020)
3. Awad, M., Khanna, R.: Support vector regression. In: Efficient Learning Machines, pp. 67–80. Apress, Berkeley, CA (2015). https://doi.org/10.1007/978-1-4302-5990-9_4
4. Bai, J., Ng, S.: Forecasting economic time series using targeted predictors. J. Econometr. **146**(2), 304–317 (2008)
5. Balwani, S.S.V.: Operational efficiency through resource planning optimization and work process improvement, Ph. D. thesis, Massachusetts Institute of Technology (2012)
6. Breiman, L.: Random forests. Mach. Learn. **45**(1), 5–32 (2001)
7. Ekici, B.B., Aksoy, U.T.: Prediction of building energy consumption by using artificial neural networks. Adv. Eng. Softw. **40**(5), 356–362 (2009)
8. El Mrabet, Z., Sugunaraj, N., Ranganathan, P., Abhyankar, S.: Random forest regressor-based approach for detecting fault location and duration in power systems. Sensors **22**(2), 458 (2022)
9. Friedman, J.H.: Stochastic gradient boosting. Comput. Stat. Data Anal. **38**(4), 367–378 (2002)
10. Graw, J., Wood, W., Phrampus, B.: Predicting global marine sediment density using the random forest regressor machine learning algorithm. J. Geophys. Res. Solid Earth **126**(1), e2020JB020135 (2021)

11. Gupta, A., et al.: Solar energy prediction using decision tree regressor. In: 2021 5th International Conference on Intelligent Computing and Control Systems (ICICCS), pp. 489–495. IEEE (2021)

12. Gupta, B.B., Quamara, M.: An overview of internet of things (iot): architectural aspects, challenges, and protocols. Concurrency Comput. Pract. Exp. **32**(21), e4946 (2020)

13. Huang, J., Perry, M.: A semi-empirical approach using gradient boosting and k-nearest neighbors regression for gefcom2014 probabilistic solar power forecasting. Int. J. Forecast. **32**(3), 1081–1086 (2016)

14. Johansson, M., Erlandsson, E., Kronholm, T., Lindroos, O.: Key drivers and obstacles for performance among forest harvesting service contractors-a qualitative case study from sweden. Scand. J. For. Res. **36**(7–8), 598–613 (2021)

15. Joshi, N., Singh, G., Kumar, S., Jain, R., Nagrath, P.: Airline prices analysis and prediction using decision tree regressor. In: Batra, U., Roy, N.R., Panda, B. (eds.) REDSET 2019. CCIS, vol. 1229, pp. 170–186. Springer, Singapore (2020). https://doi.org/10.1007/978-981-15-5827-6_15

16. Kaastra, I., Boyd, M.S.: Forecasting futures trading volume using neural networks. J. Futures Markets (1986–1998) **15**(18), 953 (1995)

17. Keprate, A., Ratnayake, R.C.: Using gradient boosting regressor to predict stress intensity factor of a crack propagating in small bore piping. In: 2017 IEEE International Conference on Industrial Engineering and Engineering Management (IEEM), pp. 1331–1336. IEEE (2017)

18. Khargharia, H.S., Shakya, S., Ainslie, R., AlShizawi, S., Owusu, G.: Predicting demand in iot enabled service stations. In: 2019 IEEE Conference on Cognitive and Computational Aspects of Situation Management (CogSIMA), pp. 81–87. IEEE (2019)

19. Khargharia, H.S., Shakya, S., Ainslie, R., Owusu, G.: Evolving prediction models with genetic algorithm to forecast vehicle volume in a service station (best application paper). In: Bramer, M., Petridis, M. (eds.) SGAI 2019. LNCS (LNAI), vol. 11927, pp. 167–179. Springer, Cham (2019). https://doi.org/10.1007/978-3-030-34885-4_14

20. Khargharia, H.S., Shakya, S., Ainslie, R., Owusu, G.: Evolving large scale prediction models for vehicle volume forecasting in service stations. In: Bramer, M., Ellis, R. (eds.) SGAI-AI 2021. LNCS (LNAI), vol. 13101, pp. 224–238. Springer, Cham (2021). https://doi.org/10.1007/978-3-030-91100-3_19

21. Lawrence, R.: Using neural networks to forecast stock market prices. Univ. Manitoba **333**, 2006–2013 (1997)

22. Liu, Y., Hassan, K.A., Karlsson, M., Pang, Z., Gong, S.: A data-centric internet of things framework based on azure cloud. IEEE Access **7**, 53839–53858 (2019)

23. Madanhire, I., Mbohwa, C.: Enterprise resource planning (erp) in improving operational efficiency: case study. Procedia CIRP **40**, 225–229 (2016)

24. Maltamo, M., Kangas, A.: Methods based on k-nearest neighbor regression in the prediction of basal area diameter distribution. Can. J. For. Res. **28**(8), 1107–1115 (1998)

25. Mitchell, T.: Machine learning (1997)

26. Myles, A.J., Feudale, R.N., Liu, Y., Woody, N.A., Brown, S.D.: An introduction to decision tree modeling. J. Chemometr. J. Chemometr. Soc. **18**(6), 275–285 (2004)

27. Nava, N., Di Matteo, T., Aste, T.: Financial time series forecasting using empirical mode decomposition and support vector regression. Risks **6**(1), 7 (2018)

28. Pedregosa, F., et al.: Scikit-learn: machine learning in python. J. Mach. Learn. Res. **12**, 2825–2830 (2011)

29. Plakandaras, V., Gupta, R., Gogas, P., Papadimitriou, T.: Forecasting the us real house price index. Econ. Model. **45**, 259–267 (2015)
30. Ray, P.P.: A survey on internet of things architectures. J. King Saud Univ.-Comput. Inf. Sci. **30**(3), 291–319 (2018)
31. Riedmiller, M., Braun, H.: RPROP-a fast adaptive learning algorithm. In: proceedings of ISCIS VII (1992)
32. saedsayad: decision tree - regression. https://www.saedsayad.com/decision_tree_reg.htm
33. Song, Y., Liang, J., Lu, J., Zhao, X.: An efficient instance selection algorithm for k nearest neighbor regression. Neurocomputing **251**, 26–34 (2017)
34. Wu, C.H., Ho, J.M., Lee, D.T.: Travel-time prediction with support vector regression. IEEE Trans. Intell. Transp. Syst. **5**(4), 276–281 (2004)
35. Yao, Y., Rosasco, L., Caponnetto, A.: On early stopping in gradient descent learning. Constr. Approx. **26**(2), 289–315 (2007)
36. Zou, H., Hastie, T.: Regularization and variable selection via the elastic net. J. Royal Stat. Soc. Ser. B (statis. Methodol.) **67**(2), 301–320 (2005)

OAK4XAI: Model Towards Out-of-Box eXplainable Artificial Intelligence for Digital Agriculture

Quoc Hung Ngo[✉], Tahar Kechadi, and Nhien-An Le-Khac

School of Computer Science, College of Science, University College Dublin, Belfield, Dublin 4, Ireland

hung.ngo@ucdconnect.ie, {tahar.kechadi,an.lekhac}@ucd.ie

Abstract. Recent machine learning approaches have been effective in Artificial Intelligence (AI) applications. They produce robust results with a high level of accuracy. However, most of these techniques do not provide human-understandable explanations for supporting their results and decisions. They usually act as black boxes, and it is not easy to understand how decisions have been made. Explainable Artificial Intelligence (XAI), which has received much interest recently, tries to provide human-understandable explanations for decision-making and trained AI models. For instance, in digital agriculture, related domains often present peculiar or input features with no link to background knowledge. The application of the data mining process on agricultural data leads to results (knowledge), which are difficult to explain. In this paper, we propose a knowledge map model and an ontology design as an XAI framework (OAK4XAI) to deal with this issue. The framework does not only consider the data analysis part of the process, but it takes into account the semantics aspect of the domain knowledge via an ontology and a knowledge map model, provided as modules of the framework. Many ongoing XAI studies aim to provide accurate and verbalizable accounts for how given feature values contribute to model decisions. The proposed approach, however, focuses on providing consistent information and definitions of concepts, algorithms, and values involved in the data mining models. We built an Agriculture Computing Ontology (AgriComO) to explain the knowledge mined in agriculture. AgriComO has a well-designed structure and includes a wide range of concepts and transformations suitable for agriculture and computing domains.

Keywords: Explainable AI · Knowledge map · Agriculture computing ontology · Knowledge management · Digital agriculture

1 Introduction

Artificial Intelligence (AI) applications are present in many domains nowadays. These applications have a direct impact on human lives, such as healthcare, self-driving vehicles, smart homes, the military, etc. The advances in AI and big data have led to the rise of explainable AI (XAI) and have gained much attention in recent years. Several studies have provided the main concepts, motivations, and implications of enabling explainability in intelligent systems [1,3,5]. Other studies have provided an overview of the existing XAI approaches and future XAI research opportunities. The concept of explainability is closely related to interpretability. XAI systems are interpretable if they can make human-understandable operations and decisions. Some previous studies considered the XAI goals as the need for interpretable AI models, such as trustworthiness, causality, transferability, informativeness, fairness, accessibility, confidence, interactivity, and privacy awareness [1,3,5]. Some others synthesized the definitions for the XAI goals and provided a set of WH-questions to classify explainability approaches, including what, who, why, what for, and how [2,3].

XAI approaches can be used to explain one of the three stages: pre-model, in-model, and post-model [1,7]. Pre-modelling targets a better understanding of the datasets, while post-model aims at model approximation and reporting of the results. Explainable modelling focuses on understanding how an AI model makes decisions. Many recent studies have focused on explainable modelling; however, it is not enough to understand the decision-making process in AI applications.

In agriculture, AI applications are constantly growing at a very high rate during the last decade. These include soil studies, weather forecasting, crop yield prediction, disease predictions, etc. For instance, there are several soil studies, building soil profiles [12], monitoring soil characteristics under the effects of other factors and crop yield [4], or using soil characteristics to predict other soil characteristics [14]. Although the number of XAI studies in digital agriculture is not too high, XAI for digital agriculture is necessary because agronomists and farmers do not have a strong background in machine learning and AI. [13] proposed an explainable AI decision support system based on fuzzy rules to automate field irrigation. Moreover, even though the number of knowledge models is small, the input and output attributes of forecasting models are different, and the number of agricultural features is large and diversified. The majority of these results (knowledge) are stored as pre-trained models, computer software, or scientific papers/reports. They also lack explanations to assist different users in accessing and understanding them.

In this paper, we propose an ontology-based knowledge map [6,9] for representing and explaining the mined knowledge, which has been produced previously by the data mining process, including classification, regression, clustering, association rules, and other forms of mining. The main contribution of the model as an out-of-box approach for DM models is to support data scientists and agronomists in managing, understanding, and using mined results/knowledge for decision-making.

The next section overviews the OAK model as a foundational theory for the proposed approach and details the core of the ontology used in this study. Section 3 presents the proposed ontology-based knowledge map model for explainable AI, including its architecture and XAI transparency. We describe the implementation process for validating the proposed model based on the knowledge repository in digital agriculture in Sect. 4. Finally, we conclude the paper and give some future research directions in Sect. 5.

2 OAK - Ontology-Based Knowledge Map Model

2.1 Knowledge Definitions

We introduced the ontology-based Knowledge Map Model (OAK) to handle the knowledge extracted from a DM process [8,9]. Before going into the details of the proposed approach, we give some key definitions of the OAK model. The model includes *knowledge representation, ontology, knowledge map, concept, attribute, transformation, instance, state,* and *relation.*

Knowledge represents the result of an experience or a data mining process, which uses some learning algorithms to predict a target based on the input dataset. Knowledge is of two types: processed knowledge and factual knowledge. The *Processed Knowledge* represents the result of a data mining process. This knowledge has some attributes that characterise it; input and output attributes and learning algorithms. *Factual Knowledge* is information validated by experts in the domain. It is characterised by some attributes, such as the transformation of input to output, its states/values, etc.

In the OAK model, the processed knowledge can be of four types: classification, regression, clustering, and association rule [8,9]. *Regression* is a ML function that predicts a continuous outcome variable based on the values of the condition variables. This means that the *Regression* model (k_{Reg}) uses regression type algorithms (t, $t \in \mathbb{T}_{DM}$, and t to predict the value of the attribute (*target* of the model) based on its input attributes (*conditions* of the model) [9]. These are defined as follows:

$$k_{Reg} = (\{i\}, \{r\}, \{t\}, \{s\})$$

$$\{i\} = i_{regressor} \cup \{i_{condition}\} \cup \{i_{target}\} \cup \{i_{dataset}\} \cup \{i_{evaluation}\}$$

$$\{r\} = \{(i_{regression}, hasAlgorithm, t_{DM})\} \cup$$

$$\{(i_{regressor}, hasRegressor, i_{regressor})\} \cup$$

$$\{(i_{regressor}, hasCondition, i_{condition})\} \cup$$

$$\{(i_{regressor}, predicts, i_{target})\} \cup$$

$$\{(i_{condition}, hasTransformation, t_D)\} \cup$$

$$\{(i_{target}, hasTransformation, t_D)\} \cup$$

$$\{t\} = \{t_{DM} = algorithm(c) \in \mathbb{T}_{DM}; c = Regression)\} \cup$$

$$\{t_D = f(i) : \Re_x \rightarrow \Re_y \ ; \ i \in \{i_{condition}\}\} \cup$$

$$\{t_D = f(i) : \Re_x \rightarrow \Re_y \ ; \ i \in \{i_{target}\}\}$$

$$\{s\} = \{\forall s \in \mathbb{S}, \exists i \in \{i_{condition}\} : i \xrightarrow{hasState} s\} \cup$$

$$\{\forall s \in \mathbb{S}, \exists i \in \{i_{target}\} : i \xrightarrow{hasState} s\}$$

The regressor k_{Reg} is characterised by its main components, which are datasets, prediction targets, conditions, and evaluation information. In addition, the processed knowledge can have other attributes related to locations, research context, etc.

In summary, the proposed model includes all the information necessary to characterise a given knowledge (result) at any time within a data mining application. The model has an efficient knowledge representation that facilitates its storage and retrieval from the knowledge repository. However, it still needs an explainable mechanism to interpret the concepts as well as its processing steps. Therefore, an explainable knowledge base or a suitable ontology can be used in interpreting the mined knowledge within a given DM application.

2.2   Ontology: Role and Design

While the OAK model is designed to handle any domain knowledge, its ontology is specific to a given domain for efficient exploitation. One of the main objectives of ontology is to assist in the explanation and interpretation of the mined results. In the proposed approach, the ontology covers three main functions: 1) agriculture common concepts definition and representation, 2) concept transformations handling, and 3) Representation of the main types of relationships between concepts.

In this study, we developed and implemented an Agriculture Computing Ontology (AgriComO) that contains the most common classes (concepts), instances, attributes, and relations in crop farming. The AgriComO's architecture is derived from the knowledge map (KMap) model and contains the following components:

- **Concepts:** Concepts in the agriculture *field, farmer, crop, organization, location*, and *product*. The DM concepts include *clustering, classification, regression*, and *association rule*.
- **Transformations:** are predefined transformation functions of agriculture and DM (see Fig. 1).
- **Relations:** They represent relationships between concepts/instances, and they also represent the analysis process to create the knowledge.

The AgriComO ontology describes agricultural concepts, their relationships, and lifecycles between seeds, plants, harvesting, transportation, and consumption. The concept relationships concern weather, soil conditions, fertilizers, and farms description. Moreover, AgriComO includes DM concepts, such as classification, clustering, regression, and association rules. The combination of agricultural and DM concepts represents mined knowledge efficiently. For instance, in the current implementation, AgriComO has 450 classes and over 3,381 axioms related to agriculture based on [10]. Finally, it provides an overview of the agricultural domain with its most general concepts.

AgriComO is the core ontology for building knowledge maps (KMaps) for digital agriculture and adopts an XAI-oriented design at the levels of the concepts and relationships. Therefore, every concept, transformation, and relation

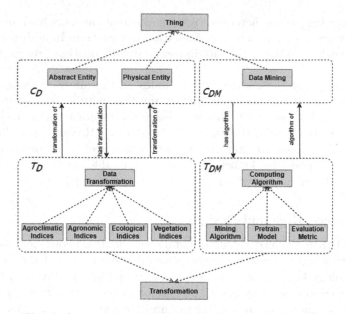

Fig. 1. An overview of Agriculture Computing Ontology

in the ontology has at least two attributes; one for the title (*rdfs:label*) and the other for the description (*rdfs:comment*). Moreover, we provided extra attributes; *rdfs:isDefinedBy* and *rdfs:seeAlso* to provide external references for further information for each concept. These attributes are considered basic information for each entity in the ontology. The definitions, descriptions, and comments on concepts, transformations, and relations in the ontology provide transparency and explainability for AgriComO and the overall model.

- *URI* - Universal Resource Identifier.
- *rdfs:label* - name of concepts or instances.
- *rdfs:comment* - description of concepts, instances, relations, or transformations for explanation purposes.
- *dc:identifier* - formula, expression, or function to calculate and transform data if it has.
- *rdfs:isDefinedBy* - sources or creators of the concepts.
- *rdfs:seeAlso* - external references for further information for each concept.

In summary, a well-defined ontology design provides explainability to each concept in the DM applications and each instance value in the knowledge representation and its processing. It supports the OAK4XAI model (described in the next section) in interpreting the accurate meaning of concepts and values in knowledge items and in helping users understand their decision-making.

3   OAK4XAI Model and Architecture

3.1   OAK4XAI Architecture

The overall OAK4XAI architecture is developed around OAK [8]. It organises knowledge into two separate classes: knowledge and its explanation. The knowledge class manages a DM application result (item) based on its relationships with other concepts and entities and is defined in the KMap module. The knowledge explanations are stored in a pre-defined ontology (aee Fig. 2). This architecture handles both factual and mined knowledge [8]. We use a multi-layer approach where knowledge items are in the KMap, and their explanations are located in the ontology.

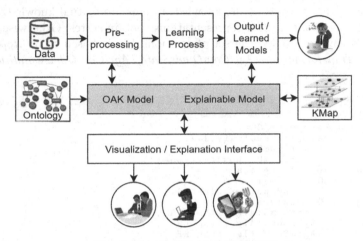

Fig. 2. Architecture of OAK4XAI

As mentioned in Sect. 2.2, AgriComO includes agriculture concepts and the DM domain. Each concept contains necessary descriptions and attributes to identify the concept and its data processing methods. They are defined under the prefix for AgriComO[1] ontology. All knowledge representations (DM prediction models) in the agriculture knowledge maps repository (AgriKMaps) are represented and stored as KMaps with a prefix for the AgriKMaps[2] knowledge repository.

3.2   Using OAK4XAI for Modeling and Explaining

The proposed approach converts the mined knowledge into its corresponding representation. This procedure is defined in the module *Knowledge Wrapper*.

---

[1] URI prefix for concepts of *AgriComO*: http://www.ucd.ie/consus/AgriComO#.
[2] URI prefix for instances of *AgriKMaps*: http://www.ucd.ie/consus/AgriKMaps#.

More precisely, it creates a representation for the mined knowledge using the model $k = (\{i\}, \{t\}, \{s\}, \{r\})$ (see Sect. 2) before converting it into RDF turtles and importing them into the RDF Triple storage. This consists of six steps: 1) identify the model; 2) identify concepts; 3) generate instances; 4) identify transformations; 5) generate states; and 6) generate scripts. The Knowledge Wrapper implementation depends on the type of knowledge items, such as *Factual Knowledge* items published in scientific papers or *Processed Knowledge* items extracted directly from DM modules.

A representation k includes a set of instances, transformations, states, and relations. The set of instances $\{i\}$ is created in Step 1 and Step 3, while the set of transformations $\{t\}$ is created in Step 1 and Step 4. These transformations are linked to instances to represent the way data is processed in the prediction model. The set of states $\{s\}$ is generated in Step 5. Note that not all knowledge representations have sets of states. If the knowledge items are factual knowledge items, they include values, and their representations contain states. Otherwise, the set of states is empty. Finally, the set of relations $\{r\}$ is based on *rdf:type, AgriComO:hasTransformation, AgriComO:hasState, AgriComO:hasCondition,* and *AgriComO:predicts*, etc.

Listing 1.1. Triples of Regressor_004

```
AgriKMaps:Regressor_004
    rdf:type owl:NamedIndividual ,
            AgriComO:Regressor ,
            AgriComO:KnowledgeModel;
    rdfs:label ''Regressor 004" .
    AgriComO:definedIn
            AgriKMaps:Article_004 ;
    AgriComO:hasAlgorithm
            AgriComO:Algorithm_DTR ,
            AgriComO:Algorithm_LR  ,
            AgriComO:Algorithm_RF ,
            AgriComO:Algorithm_GBRT;
    AgriComO:hasCondition
            AgriKMaps:SoilPH_004 ;
    AgriComO:predicts
            AgriKMaps:SoilPH_004x ;
    AgriComO:hasDataset
            AgriKMaps:Dataset_CONSUS_001 ;
AgriKMaps:SoilPH_004
    rdf:type owl:NamedIndividual ,
            AgriComO:SoilPH ,
    AgriComO:hasTransformation
            AgriComO:Transformation_SoilPH_Max ,
            AgriComO:Transformation_SoilPH_Min ,
            AgriComO:Transformation_SoilPH_Avg ,
```

For example, when applying this modelling process, the knowledge item *Regressor_004*, published in article *Article_004* [11], can be converted into a set of triples. The brief triple example of *Regressor_004* (shown in Listing 1.1) shows that *Regressor_004* is used to predict soil pH and this attribute uses the soil pH transformation *Transformation_SoilPH_Max, Transformation_SoilPH_Min,* and *Transformation_SoilPH_Avg.*

The semantic interpretation of concepts, transformations, and values (such as *Transformation_SoilPH_Max*) in this knowledge item is done through the one-way retrieval process; from AgriKMaps to AgriComO and from AgriComO to AgriComO. This means that using predefined information in the AgriComO ontology to interpret instances and processing in the AgriKMaps. The explanation process starts with an instance in *AgriKMap*. It browses the knowledge item to identify the concept class (prefix *AgriComO*) and its attributes.

3.3 XAI Transparency with OAK4XAI

In this section, we discuss the proposed model's XAI functions by answering a set of WH-questions (What, What for, Who, When, Where and How) along with a summary as shown in Fig. 3.

Fig. 3. OAK4XAI Model for explainable AI

What? The OAK4XAI model focuses on representing and explaining the results of the DM analysis process. It supports four types of analyses: *Classification, Clustering, Regression*, and *Association Rule*.

What for? OAK4XAI can assist in describing the meaning of data, provide ways to transform raw data into input data for learning models and explain the results of the learning models. Therefore, this model helps to increase transparency, usability, trust, and confidence in mined knowledge, which are the XAI's main goals.

Who? The model can explain the results of the ML algorithms to different types of users. More precisely. The implemented version of this model supports the following user groups:

- *Managers and executive boards* understand an overview of knowledge items, including inputs, outputs, algorithms, training datasets, and results evaluation.
- *Data scientists and developers* understand attributes, values, and labels used in the knowledge items (DM models).
- *Agronomists and experts* understand states and processing steps of knowledge items, select then apply them in farming.

How? Recall that OAK4XAI contains a predefined ontology, which helps to explain the attributes in the knowledge representation. A representation is an entry of KMap with nodes for concepts, instances, transformations, states, and edges for relationships between them. All KMap entries are stored using the linked data technique. Finally, explainable interfaces provide different explanations to different user groups. Moreover, the explanations need to be written in suitable language (and with a description strategy) for the intended audience. These include:

- *Formal language* can be structured or syntax explanation, and it is based on structured and unique linked data in the knowledge repository layer. The linked data are sets of triples *(subject, predictive, object)*. These triples can be transformed and interpreted in a certain format language.
- *Natural language:* written texts can be generated from the description of concepts and instances in the ontology. Each concept in the ontology has some attributes (*rdfs:label* and *rdfs:comment*), which support the model in a human-friendly explanation.
- *Graphic language:* visualizations can be supported by the explanation interface layers based on the knowledge repository layer.

Where? It is worth noting that OAK4XAI can explain data outside the mining steps, including the *pre-model* and *post-model* stages of the DM applications.

- *Pre-model:* With this model, the users can pre-process and transform the data and input it into learning models. Moreover, they have more options for improving the pre-processing and transformation steps by using predefined *Transformation* instances of the AgriComO ontology.
- *Post-model:* Trained models and final decisions contain data values, which need extra information and semantics. At this stage, different users may have different concerns (for example, why this decision was taken). This can be solved by exploring detailed information about each concept and extra information.

When? This model can be used to develop AI processes and XAI in three stages:

- *Designing:* planning pre-processing algorithms can help understanding data better by accessing predefined knowledge from the core ontology in the OAK4XAI model.

- *Implementation:* allowing scientists to have a deep understanding can contribute to the process of developing and improving machine learning models.
- *Knowledge Use:* explaining knowledge results can assist in understanding the model better.

4 Validation

4.1 Implementation

OAK4XAI is implemented using the linked data technique, the graph database server, and the web-based explanation application. The graph database server supports RDF triple storage and SPARQL protocol for query, while web-based explanation application (including *Knowledge Wrapper* module and *Knowledge Browser* module for visualization). The search engine searches for knowledge items from the AgriKMaps domain, while the explainable engine retrieves the domain knowledge from the predefined ontology, the AgriComO domain. All instances and concepts from AgriKMaps and AgriComO have a URI and they link together based on their URI. The graph database uses Apache Jena[3] (for the native knowledge graph storage), SPARQL[4] 1.1 (for SPARQL Engine), and Fuseki[5] (for SPARQL Endpoint), while the Knowledge Browser is a web-based application for exploring knowledge and providing explanations.

4.2 Explanation

Knowledge Browser functions are twofold: it assists users in locating mined knowledge items based on their input queries or keywords and validates the explainability of the DM analysis process results.

Moreover, Knowledge Browser is a knowledge search engine, which looks for knowledge items (knowledge maps) in the RDF storage and queried input concepts and their roles. The retrieved results are represented and explained in many levels of detail, from general to details. Knowledge Browser is very efficient in finding knowledge items in the knowledge repository based on input queries, such as "predict soilPH" (with the result shown in Fig. 4). The process includes:

- Finding knowledge items by search queries from *AgriKMaps*;
- Segmenting concepts into parts AI models;
- Generating SPARQL queries;
- Generating summaries of knowledge items from return triples.

The explanation content depends on users concerns when exploring given items. The explanation process with the OAK4XAI approach consists of the following steps:

---

[3] https://jena.apache.org/index.html.
[4] https://www.w3.org/TR/sparql11-query/.
[5] https://jena.apache.org/documentation/fuseki2/.

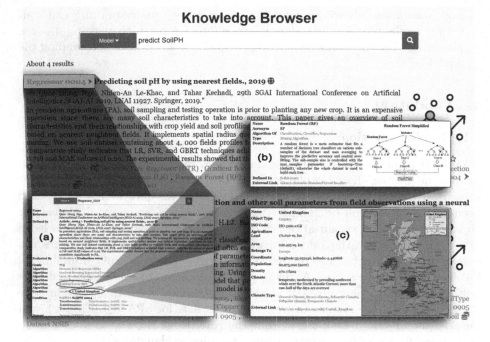

Fig. 4. Explanation in knowledge browser

- Determine the concept in the knowledge item;
- Retrieve related attributes and descriptions from *AgriComO* ontology;
- Generate explanations interface (from return triples).

For example, to locate the knowledge item shown in Listing 1.1, the results of the query "predict SoilPH" are represented as summaries of knowledge items (AgriKMaps) (Fig. 4a), and the details of their concepts and states are interpreted based on knowledge from the ontology (AgriComO) (Fig. 4b/c). Details of the data processing stage (formulas and values) in the knowledge items are described in the predefined ontology, so their information can be represented and explained. Based on different user questions, the system has different levels of interpretations of the post-model stage of the knowledge items.

Moreover, the system also supports searching for concepts and related details in the ontology. This explainability can assist users in the pre-model stage of building the knowledge items. For example, Listing 1.2 provides the information of transformation *Transformation_SoilPH_Max* using in *Regressor0004* (Listing 1.1) and other transformations (such as, *Transformation_SoilPH_Tier11*[6] (defined by US. Department of Agriculture, Natural Resources Conservation Service) as a category of 11 types) for the *soil pH* attribute.

---

[6] https://en.wikipedia.org/wiki/Soil_pH.

Listing 1.2. Information of Transformations for Soil pH attribute

```
[Transformation_SoilPH_Max]
    Definition:
            This transformation returns the maximum value of
            Soil pH values in the sampling area, for example in
            the radius of 100m.
    Values:
            0.0-14.0 ;
[Transformation_SoilPH_Tier11]
    Definition:
            This transformation returns a state of soil pH,
            defined by the United States Department of
            Agriculture Natural Resources Conservation Service,
            classified soil pH ranges as 11 types.
    States:
            Ultra acidic              <3.5
            Extremely acidic          3.5-4.4
            Very strongly acidic      4.5-5.0
            Strongly acidic           5.1-5.5
            Moderately acidic         5.6-6.0
            Slightly acidic           6.1-6.5
            Neutral                   6.6-7.3
            Slightly alkaline         7.4-7.8
            Moderately alkaline       7.9-8.4
            Strongly alkaline         8.5-9.0
            Very strongly alkaline    >9.0
    [...]
```

In summary, with a predefined AgriComO ontology, OAK4XAI provides consistent information and definitions of concepts, algorithms, and values involved in a knowledge item. The explainability information enables researchers to communicate and compare the results of various classifiers and support stakeholders in making informed decisions for the implementation and usage of machine learning models.

4.3   Statistics

Numerous algorithms and transformation techniques have been extracted from several resources to support the outside-of-box explanation of DM applications in agriculture. They are collected manually from programming libraries, scientific articles, etc. A list of algorithms is collected from programming libraries, such as Scikit-learn[7], NLTK[8], Huggingface[9], etc. Then, each algorithm requires necessary information, such as authors, definitions, reference information, and programming libraries. The algorithm structure of basic information or transformation is provided in Sect. 2.2. Moreover, well-known algorithms were defined in the AgriComO ontology. Similarly, all evaluation metrics for data mining processes and common pre-trained models were collected and put into the ontology. In the current implementation, AgriComO contains 176 algorithms, 110 pre-trained models, and 51 evaluation metrics, as shown in Table 1.

---

[7] https://scikit-learn.org/stable/.

[8] https://www.nltk.org/.

[9] https://huggingface.co/docs/transformers/index.

Table 1. Statistics of Main Indices and Transformations in AgriComO

Indices	Examples	Count
Agronomic Indices	Soil, weeds, nutrient, water indices	310
Agroclimatic Indices	GDD, AFD, CDD, FX	172
Vegetation Indices	LAI, NDVI, GDVI, RVI, SAVI, SAVO	322
Ecological Indices	Water Index: WZI, WFI	15
Pretrain Models	GoogLeNet, AlexNet	110
Mining Algorithms	Linear, DT, ANN, RF, LSTM, LASSO	176
Evaluation Metrics	Accuracy, CCR, Jscore, F1, R2, RSME	51
Data Transformations	RGB or BW for Colour, SoilPH Types	326
Total		**1,310**

5   Conclusion and Future Work

We proposed the OAK4XAI model that consists of an ontology-based knowledge map and a knowledge management system. The OAK4XAI architecture has the potential to be expanded to other knowledge domains. The knowledge items can easily be imported into the knowledge management system. The knowledge management system implements a knowledge browser to access and explore knowledge of any kind and with different levels of interpretations depending on the DM applications.

We defined an agriculture ontology, AgriComO, and populated it with the most well-known algorithm for mining agricultural data. AgriComO provides definitions and information for concepts, algorithms, and states in crop farming. We believe that the proposed model and its ontology can provide consistent information and explanation not only for DM applications in agriculture but also for other domains by pre-defining their corresponding ontology.

In future work, we will focus on two areas: a) implement the explanation interface as a service, to interact with several user groups. It will take user questions as input and retrieve the corresponding knowledge, and b) extend the proposed model to include several ML algorithms for prediction based on explainable approaches.

Moreover, we plan to represent the result of several predictive algorithms in agriculture, such as decision trees, Bayesian analysis, or support vector machines with rule-based extraction. Representations will be compatible with different explanation interfaces, and then develop a reasoning module to decide the most appropriate explanation.

Acknowledgment. This work is part of CONSUS and is supported by the SFI Strategic Partnerships Programme (16/SPP/3296) and is co-funded by Origin Enterprises Plc.

References

1. Adadi, A., Berrada, M.: Peeking inside the black-box: a survey on explainable artificial intelligence (XAI). IEEE Access **6**, 52138–52160 (2018)
2. Akula, A.R., Todorovic, S., Chai, J.Y., Zhu, S.-C.: Natural language interaction with explainable AI models. In: CVPR Workshops, pp. 87–90 (2019)
3. Arrieta, A.B., et al.: Explainable artificial intelligence (XAI): concepts, taxonomies, opportunities and challenges toward responsible AI. Inf. Fusion, **58**, 82–115 (2020)
4. Bishop, T., McBratney, A.: A comparison of prediction methods for the creation of field-extent soil property maps. Geoderma **103**(1–2), 149–160 (2001)
5. Gunning, D.: Explainable artificial intelligence (XAI). Defense advanced research projects agency (DARPA). ND Web **2**(2) (2017)
6. Le-Khac, N.-A.: M-Tahar Kechadi, Joe Carthy. Distributed data mining on data grid platforms, Admire framework (2017)
7. bibitemch17molnar2020interpretable Molnar, C.: Interpretable Machine Learning. Lulu. com (2020)
8. Ngo, Q.H., Kechadi, T., Le-Khac, N.-A.: OAK: ontology-based knowledge map model for digital agriculture. In: Dang, T.K., Küng, J., Takizawa, M., Chung, T.M. (eds.) FDSE 2020. LNCS, vol. 12466, pp. 245–259. Springer, Cham (2020). https://doi.org/10.1007/978-3-030-63924-2_14
9. Ngo, Q.H., Kechadi, T., Le-Khac, N.: Knowledge representation in digital agriculture: a step towards standardised model. Comput. Electr. Agric. **199**, 107127 (2022)
10. Ngo, Q.H., Le-Khac, N.-A., Kechadi, T.: Ontology Based approach for precision agriculture. In: Kaenampornpan, M., Malaka, R., Nguyen, D.D., Schwind, N. (eds.) MIWAI 2018. LNCS (LNAI), vol. 11248, pp. 175–186. Springer, Cham (2018). https://doi.org/10.1007/978-3-030-03014-8_15
11. Ngo, Q.H., Le-Khac, N.-A., Kechadi, T.: Predicting Soil ph by using nearest fields. In: Bramer, M., Petridis, M. (eds.) SGAI 2019. LNCS (LNAI), vol. 11927, pp. 480–486. Springer, Cham (2019). https://doi.org/10.1007/978-3-030-34885-4_40
12. Shangguan, W., et al.: A China data set of soil properties for land surface modeling. J. Adv. Model. Earth Syst. 5(2), 212–224 (2013)
13. Tsakiridis, M., et al.: Versatile internet of things for agriculture: an explainable ai approach. In: Maglogiannis, I., Iliadis, L., Pimenidis, E. (eds.) AIAI 2020. IAICT, vol. 584, pp. 180–191. Springer, Cham (2020). https://doi.org/10.1007/978-3-030-49186-4_16
14. Wang, F., Yang, S., Yang, W., Yang, X., Jianli, D.: Comparison of machine learning algorithms for soil salinity predictions in three dryland oases located in Xinjiang Uyghur Autonomous Region (XJUAR) of China. Euro. J. Remote Sens. **52**(1), 256–276 (2019)

Feasibility Studies of Applied AI

Deep Learning for Detecting Tilt Angle and Orientation of Photovoltaic Panels on Satellite Imagery

Ammar Memari[1]([✉])[iD], Van Cuong Dam[1], and Lars Nolle[1,2]

[1] Jade University of Applied Sciences, Friedrich-Paffrath-Straße 101,
26389 Wilhelmshaven, Germany
ammar.memari@jade-hs.de, lars.nolle@dfki.de
[2] German Research Center for Artificial Intellingece, Marie-Curie-Straße 1,
26129 Oldenburg, Germany
https://www.jade-hs.de/ , https://www.dfki.de/

Abstract. The goal of this research is to accomplish two tasks that increase the accuracy of the process of estimating solar power generation in real time for different regions around the world. Specifically, we explain a method for detecting the tilt angle and installation orientation of photovoltaic panels on rooftops using satellite imagery only. The method for detecting tilt angles is based on their dependence on the roof shapes. As for the architectures used in this research, we chose MobileNetV2 and Yolov4 since both require only medium hardware resources, without the need for graphics processing units (GPUs). Since it was difficult to find a suitable data set, we had to create our own, which, although not large, was proven to be sufficient to confirm the capabilities of our method. As for the final results, our approach provides good predictions for the tilt angle and the orientation of photovoltaic panels based on a data set of images from six different locations in Europe collected via Google Maps.

Keywords: Solar energy · Object detection · Object classification · YOLOv4 · MobilenetV2

1 Introduction

In this day and age, renewable energy is constituted as the best solution when it comes to providing energy to mankind for living and manufacturing. The major rationale for this is that producing energy from solar or wind power is an environmentally friendly process. Furthermore, utilizing these power sources is also deemed as an excellent approach owing to their unlimited availability. The intermittency of solar energy is its main obstacle for widespread integration into the mix of energies in current electricity networks. Solar energy is produced only when the sun is shining, and even then, its output can vary depending on cloud cover. This makes it difficult to rely on solar energy as a primary source of power, since there must always be a backup source of energy available to fill in

© The Author(s), under exclusive license to Springer Nature Switzerland AG 2022
M. Bramer and F. Stahl (Eds.): SGAI-AI 2022, LNAI 13652, pp. 255–266, 2022.
https://doi.org/10.1007/978-3-031-21441-7_18

the gaps. To overcome this obstacle, efforts have been made for predicting the solar power output for the next few hours or days, so that network operators can adjust the schedule of backup sources of energy accordingly.

Fundamentally, our project supports the prediction of power outputs from photovoltaic panels in specific areas. In terms of the prediction, the installation orientation of the panels and the weather in the area in addition to the installed capacity of the panels are the main factors that could impact on the final results. Regarding local climate predictions, modern forecast methods are capable of predicting the regional weather conditions for the next days quite precisely. Hence, local weather prediction are no problem when it comes to power output prediction. Nevertheless, when it comes to the direction of the solar panels, there are numerous factors that affect the power output. The two most influential parameters are the orientation of the installed panels and the tilt angles on the roofs. Our research solves this problem of predicting the installation orientation as well as the tilt angle from satellite imagery. If satellite images are not available or are outdated, drone images can be used instead, considering the low cost of high-end camera drones today.

Since the last decade, computer vision has improved remarkably. The applications of computer vision could be witnessed in various aspects of real-life, such as in transportation, health-care, manufacturing or even retail. This has been achieved thanks to the advancement of artificial intelligence and machine learning technologies. The most well-known sub-discipline of machine learning is deep learning, which prevalent applications are in natural language processing and computer vision. For this reason, we chose to apply deep learning algorithms as the initial approach to solve our problem.

The paper starts with a discussion of related work in Sect. 2. The next section depicts the methodology used, including building and utilizing the data set. Section 4 presents the results for testing the models developed on random images from different locations in different countries. The last section concludes this paper and points out relevant directions for further work on the topic.

2   Related Work

DeepSolar [13] is researched by Stanford University in 2018 with a view of developing an accurate deep learning framework to automatically localize photovoltaic panels from satellite imagery for the contiguous United States and to estimate their sizes.

Fundamentally, the research aims at tasks different from ours. Nonetheless, the idea of applying Transfer Learning [15] to detect the panels from satellite imagery gave us an initial direction to find the solution for our own tasks.

Position Detection And Direction Prediction for Arbitrary-Oriented Ships by Yang et al. [12] proposed a new detection model based on a multi-task rotational region convolutional neural network with a view to detect positions and to predict directions of arbitrary-oriented ships.

At first sight, the proposed method seems to be able to solve one of our tasks, namely the detection of rooftop directions. Nonetheless, the method could not distinguish the orientation of two roofs with the same angle. In Fig. 1, it can be observed that the two rooftops have the similar angle θ in the rotational bounding box regression [12]. Nevertheless, the two rooftops demonstrate entirely different directions (southeast and southwest). Therefore, the result is incorrect. In addition, it also seems to be possible to improve results by applying prow direction prediction, like in the research. However, it is only feasible with rectangular rooftops that have long and short edges. This does not apply to the majority of rooftops, as there are various types that make the model impossible to work.

Fig. 1. Despite the similar angle θ, the two rooftops have different directions

Maji and Bose [5] proposed a method to detect the orientation angle of a captured image. Namely, a post-processing step captured in any camera (both older and newer camera models) with any tilted angle (between $0°$ and $359°$).

Zhou et al. [14] proposed a kernel mapping CNN which can recognize the rotated images without altering the network's basic structure and requiring extra training samples for the rotated data. Shima et al. [10] proposed a novel orientation detection method for face images that relies on image category classification by deep learning. Rotated images are classified in four classes, namely $0°$, $90°$ clockwise, $90°$ counter-clockwise, or $180°$. Unfortunately, the three methods mentioned above only predict the direction of image frames, not the direction of objects in the images. Nevertheless, they still gave us several thoughts for dealing with the problem of detecting object directions.

3   Methodology

There are four fundamental challenges, which commonly arise when solving problems in the field of computer vision.

1. Object classification
2. Object localization
3. Object detection
4. Object segmentation

Based on the attributes of each task, we try to combine them to come up with a solution for our problem. We rely on the dependence of the panels' arrangements on the roof shape; They are mostly installed parallel to one of the roof sides. From this rationale, we eventually build the solution depicted in Fig. 2.

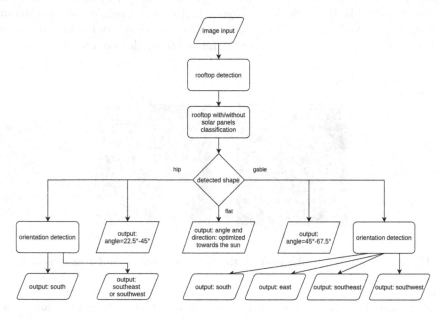

Fig. 2. Schematic of solution

1. Input satellite images are obtained from Google Maps
2. A trained model is applied to detect rooftops in the input images. Afterwards, the rooftop images are cropped out from the original ones.
3. Subsequently, the rooftop images are classified based on whether they are equipped with photovoltaic panels or not. Only the ones with photovoltaic panels proceed to be examined.
4. Then the rooftop shape of each image is classified with the aim to categorize them into the respective tilt angles.
5. Eventually, another trained model is used to detect, in which orientation the photovoltaic panels are installed.

3.1   Rooftop Detection

First and foremost, there are various algorithms for detecting objects in images, which could be applied to locate photovoltaic panels, such as R-CNN (Region-Based Convolutional Neural Networks) or YOLO (You Only Look Once). As far as we are concerned, the R-CNN algorithm is extremely slow. Even though its updated versions Fast R-CNN [3] and Faster R-CNN [9] present an improvement, they still are no match for the YOLO algorithm in terms of computational costs. Out of five YOLO versions [1, 6–8], we chose "YOLOv4" [1], which has the best accuracy in comparison to the others.

Secondly, a proper data set containing images and annotations is a prerequisite to be able to apply "YOLOv4" for object detection. Unfortunately, in computer vision, image data sets are always the most challenging ones to acquire. After a lot of effort to find an appropriate data set, we have only found one, which lead to very poor results. That is why we decided to create our own data set instead of looking further for an existing one. Basically, our data set consists of 430 images generated through Google Maps from 6 different cites in 5 countries in Europe: Oldenburg (Germany), Wilhelmshaven (Germany), Liverpool (England), Bordeaux (France), Milan (Italy), and Vigo (Spain). These images are captured from a height of around 10 m above ground level (an example is depicted in Fig. 3). We also used the free open-source tool "LabelImg" [11] to accelerate the labeling of images as seen in Fig. 4. Subsequently, the recommendations from the authors of Yolov4 [1] were followed for training a detection model using our data set.

Fig. 3. Image input

Owing to the restriction of using GPU in standard "Google Collab" accounts, it took for each data set about 2 days to gain the weights files. Actually, it could have been better had we trained for longer, but the test results already satisfy our expectation. Moreover, we have also modified the source code of YOLOv4 in order to gain the required outputs as a collection of roof images, which are cropped out from the image input. Table 1 shows the accuracy achieved for the rooftop detection model.

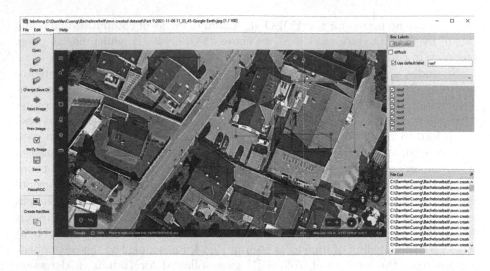

Fig. 4. LabelImg

Table 1. Accuracy metrics of rooftop detection model

	Precision	Recall	F1-score	mAp@0.50
conf_thresh = 0.25	0.61	0.89	0.72	80.71%

3.2   Rooftop Classification

The next step is the classification of roofs, whether they are equipped with photovoltaic panels or not. Based on the old data set for YOLOv4, we have generated a new data set by cropping out all single roof images from the big ones and dividing them into two classes, "roof with photovoltaic panels" and "roof without photovoltaic panels". The new data set contains 340 images of rooftops with or without photo voltaic panels. For the training, 80% of the images in our data set were used for training and the remaining 20% of the images were used for testing. To build a model for this step, we have used "Transfer learning" [15], which facilitates building our model by applying pre-trained models. In our case, we chose "MobileNetV2" [4] because of its lightweight deep neural networks. In addition, we have also used the data augmentation technique to expand the amount of training images. Table 2 shows the accuracy achieved for the rooftop classification task.

Since only the roofs with photovoltaic panels are examined, all the others without such panels were deleted from the output folder.

3.3   Tilt Angle Estimation

The tilt angle estimation of installed photovoltaic panels can be achieved by classifying roof shapes, since the tilt angles of the panels and their roof are

Table 2. Accuracy metrics of rooftop classification model

	Precision	Recall	F1-score	Support
Roof with pv	0.85	0.94	0.89	31
Roof without pv	0.94	0.86	0.90	37
Accuracy			0.90	68
Macro avg	0.90	0.90	0.90	68
Weighted avg	0.90	0.90	0.90	68

usually the same. Hence, the prediction of the tilt angle of the panels boils down to the task of detecting roof shapes. The three most ubiquitous roof shapes are flat, hip and gable (Fig. 5. It is well-known that gable roofs typically have an angle from 22.5 to 45 °C, while hip roofs have an angle between 45 and 67.5 °C. Additionally, the angle of flat roofs is always 0 °C. Thus, if a roof is classified as gable, hip or flat, the tilt angle of the panels on this roof will be 22.5 − 45.5°, 45 − 67.5°, or a manually optimized tilt angle in the case of flat roofs.

Hip   Gable   Flat

Fig. 5. Three most common roof shapes [2]

To build a model for classifying rooftop shapes, we have repeated the same process that we have conducted in the previous step. This time, the data set consists of 819 images that are divided equally in three classes "gable", "flat", and "hip". The ratio remains unchanged, with 80% for the training set and 20% for the testing set. Data augmentation technique is still applied during the training process. The resulting model, which was built based on the pre-trained model "MobileNetV2" to predict whether the roof shape is flat, gable or hip, provides quite a good precision (Table 3).

3.4   Orientation Detection

The final step is detecting the orientation of the panels. According to the conventional construction, the panels in the Northern Hemisphere are intentionally installed on the roof side facing south as much as possible. Thus, the directions of the panels on the gable roof are normally south, east, southeast or southwest. Furthermore, in light of the special shape with 4 similar edges, the collectors on hip roofs are installed on either the south or the southwest+southeast orientation. Furthermore, it is understandable that based on the house's latitude and longitude, the collectors on flat roofs are installed straight towards the sun in

Table 3. Accuracy metrics of rooftop shape classification model

	Precision	Recall	F1-score	Support
Flat	0.84	0.91	0.87	57
Gable	0.88	0.75	0.81	51
Hip	0.90	0.95	0.92	55
Accuracy			0.87	163
Macro avg	0.87	0.87	0.87	163
Weighted avg	0.87	0.87	0.87	163

order to optimize the power produced. There are two models, which need to be built for this task.

The first model is used to detect the orientation of gable roofs. As mentioned, the data set needs to be divided into 4 classes "south", "east", "southeast" and "southwest". This data set consists of 3728 images for 4 classes with the percentage of 80% and 20% for the training and the testing set respectively. The unusual feature during the training process of this model is that the data augmentation technique could not be applied to avoid rotating the images, since the orientation of the roofs is not preserved in the rotated images. For this reason, we had to rotate the images and then label them manually. Once again, we used "MobileNetV2" as the pre-trained model in the training process. Table 4 presents the accuracy achieved for the orientation detection for gable roofs.

Table 4. Accuracy metrics of orientation detection model for gable roofs

	Precision	Recall	F1-score	Support
east	0.99	1.00	1.00	169
south	0.99	1.00	1.00	198
southeast	0.89	0.97	0.93	162
southwest	0.98	0.91	0.94	216
accuracy			0.97	745
macro avg	0.97	0.97	0.97	745
weighted avg	0.97	0.97	0.97	745

Another model is built for estimating the orientation of hip roofs. Like the idea mentioned above, there are two classes for the model "south" and "southwest+southeast". Due to the minority of houses built with a hip roof in general, we could only collect a smaller data set with 760 images in comparison with the data set of gable roofs. The images are also divided with 80% for training and 20% for testing. Similar to the first model, the data augmentation technique is not applied and "MobileNetV2" is used as basis for the training. Table 5 shows the accuracy achieved by the orientation detection model for hip roofs.

Table 5. Accuracy metrics of orientation detection model for hip roofs

	Precision	Recall	F1-score	Support
east or south	0.99	0.99	0.99	73
southeast or southwest	0.99	0.99	0.99	79
accuracy			0.99	152
macro avg	0.99	0.99	0.99	152
weighted avg	0.99	0.99	0.99	152

4   Results

Performances of the individual models are described in the aforementioned tables. Moreover, we are confident that a trained model would also be able to correctly detect and classify objects that were not included in the data set. This is because the features extracted by the model are abstract enough to be applicable for a variety of different situations.

In order to test the validity of this claim, we included a simple "out-of-sample"-test. We had tested the whole pipeline on random images from five different European cities. Sample results are depicted in Figs. 6, 7, and 8.

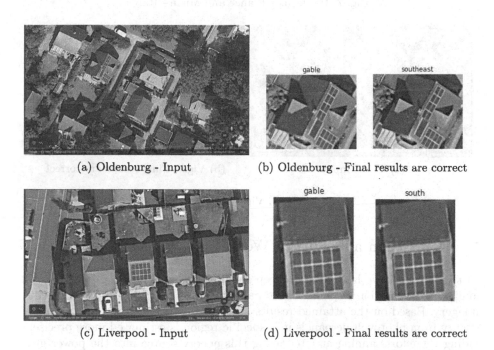

(a) Oldenburg - Input

(b) Oldenburg - Final results are correct

(c) Liverpool - Input

(d) Liverpool - Final results are correct

Fig. 6. Oldenburg - Germany and Liverpool - England

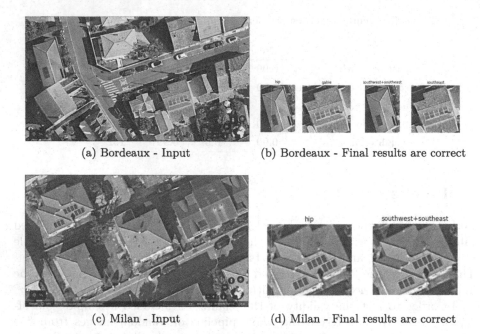

(a) Bordeaux - Input   (b) Bordeaux - Final results are correct

(c) Milan - Input   (d) Milan - Final results are correct

Fig. 7. Bordeaux - France and Milan - Italy

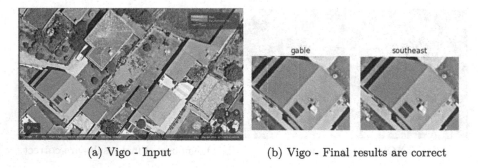

(a) Vigo - Input   (b) Vigo - Final results are correct

Fig. 8. Vigo - Spain

5   Conclusion and Future Work

In this research, we have applied deep learning technologies to predict the tilt angle and orientation of photovoltaic panels installed on rooftops from satellite imagery. Based on the attained results and the weather forecast, the produced energy from photovoltaic panels in a specific region is estimated more precisely, aiding the efforts aiming at integrating this energy source into the power grid, and maintaining the stability of grids that rely on solar power.

The trained model have performed fairly well and produced usable results, even though only relatively few resources and little time were devoted for the training thereof. We are confident, that having a larger and more diverse data set and dedicating more time on more power full computer hardware for the training would improve the overall performance even more.

Merging results from [13] and building upon them, we were able to build a model that can reliably scan a region of the world and provide us with all data necessary for describing its photovoltaic capacity, including the installed power, directions, and tilt angles of the panels. Applying weather forecast to such data provides a high-resolution forecast of expected produced power. For areas without proper resolution satellite images, drone footage can be used for extracting still frames for the training and recognition purposes.

It is acknowledged that nowadays, despite the considerable technological advancement, results of deep learning still cannot overcome human performance, especially when it comes to computer vision tasks, such as object detection or localization. However, it is worth mentioning that even the human eyes could not tell the exact angle of roofs when looking at satellite imagery. Shortcomings of our approach are unfortunately related to such limitations.

In years to come, we would like to apply the same principle used in this work to solve the problem of detecting tilt angle and orientation of objects from images. This remains a problem that has not been solved yet.

References

1. Bochkovskiy, A., Wang, C.Y., Liao, H.Y.M.: YOLOV4: optimal speed and accuracy of object detection. arXiv preprint arXiv:2004.10934 (2020)
2. Chrinco.com: Roof shapes matter with home insurance! https://chrinco.com/roof-shapes-matter-with-home-insurance/ (2019). Accessed 25 Sep 2021
3. Girshick, R.: Fast R-CNN. In: Proceedings of the IEEE International Conference on Computer Vision, pp. 1440–1448 (2015)
4. Howard, A.G., et al.: MobileNets: efficient convolutional neural networks for mobile vision applications. arXiv preprint arXiv:1704.04861 (2017)
5. Maji, S., Bose, S.: Deep image orientation angle detection. arXiv preprint arXiv:2007.06709 (2020)
6. Redmon, J., Divvala, S., Girshick, R., Farhadi, A.: You only look once: unified, real-time object detection. In: Proceedings of the IEEE Conference On Computer Vision and Pattern Recognition, pp. 779–788 (2016)
7. Redmon, J., Farhadi, A.: YOLO9000: better, faster, stronger. In: Proceedings of the IEEE Conference on Computer Vision and Pattern Recognition (CVPR), July 2017
8. Redmon, J., Farhadi, A.: Yolov3: An incremental improvement. arXiv preprint arXiv:1804.02767 (2018)
9. Ren, S., He, K., Girshick, R., Sun, J.: Faster R-CNN: towards real-time object detection with region proposal networks. In: 28th Proceedings of the Conference on Advances in Neural Information Processing Systems (2015)
10. Shima, Y., Nakashima, Y., Yasuda, M.: Detecting orientation of in-plain rotated face images based on category classification by deep learning. In: TENCON 2017–2017 IEEE Region 10 Conference, pp. 127–132. IEEE (2017)
11. Tzutalin: Labelimg. https://github.com/tzutalin/labelImg (2015). Accessed 30 Sep 2021

12. Yang, X., Sun, H., Sun, X., Yan, M., Guo, Z., Fu, K.: Position detection and direction prediction for arbitrary-oriented ships via multitask rotation region convolutional neural network. IEEE Access **6**, 50839–50849 (2018)
13. Yu, J., Wang, Z., Majumdar, A., Rajagopal, R.: DeepSolar: a machine learning framework to efficiently construct a solar deployment database in the United States. Joule **2**(12), 2605–2617 (2018)
14. Zhou, Y., Shi, J., Yang, X., Wang, C., Wei, S., Zhang, X.: Rotational objects recognition and angle estimation via kernel-mapping CNN. IEEE Access **7**, 116505–116518 (2019)
15. Zhuang, F., et al.: A comprehensive survey on transfer learning. Proc. IEEE **109**(1), 43–76 (2020)

Recurrent Neural Networks for Music Genre Classification

Chaitanya Kakarla, Vidyashree Eshwarappa, Lakshmi Babu Saheer[✉],
and Mahdi Maktabdar Oghaz

Anglia Ruskin University, Cambridge, UK
{ck606,vh288}@student.aru.ac.uk,
{lakshmi.babu-saheer,mahdi.maktabdar}@aru.ac.uk

Abstract. Music genre classification refers to identifying bits of music
that belong to a certain tradition by assigning labels called genres.
Recommendation systems automatically use classification techniques to
group songs into their respective genres or to cluster music with similar
genres. Studies show deep Recurrent Neural Networks (RNN) are capable
of resolving complex temporal features of the audio signal and identifying music genres with good accuracy. This research experiments with
different variants of RNN including LSTM, and IndRNN on the GTZAN
dataset to predict the music genres. Scattering transforms along with
Mel-Frequency Cepstral Coefficients (MFCCs) are used to construct the
input feature vector. This study investigates various LSTM and simple
RNN network architectures. Experiment results show a 5-layered stacked
independent RNN was able to achieve 84% accuracy based on the aforementioned input feature vector.

Keywords: Music genre classification · Mel-frequency cepstral
coefficients (MFCCS) · Spectrograms · Scattering transforms · Feature
extraction · Independent RNN

1 Introduction

In the current generation, music has transformed into one of the main recre-
ational interests among individuals. Based on occasions and moods, a particular
genre is preferred over the other. The genre can be simply defined as the style or
type of music. The role of genre is very important in a music recommendation
task and machine learning has shown good performance in genre classification.
The machine learning algorithms closely rely on the features extracted from the
raw audio signal to identify the music genre. The Music Information Retrieval
(MIR) technique is widely used to extract discriminative information from audio
files which can be used to classify music genres. Many music streaming services
like Tidal, Amazon music, Wynk, Spotify, etc. have developed music recommendation systems to enhance users' experience and ease browsing. The primary
step in achieving a decent music recommendation system is to create an accurate

© The Author(s), under exclusive license to Springer Nature Switzerland AG 2022
M. Bramer and F. Stahl (Eds.): SGAI-AI 2022, LNAI 13652, pp. 267–279, 2022.
https://doi.org/10.1007/978-3-031-21441-7_19

music genre classification model by analyzing the tempo, acoustics, and energy of the song and correctly organizing it under the right genre. The main phases in music genre classification include pre-processing of the raw music data, extracting the features, and classification of the genre. Among these pre-processing of the raw music and extracting features are considered as crucial steps.

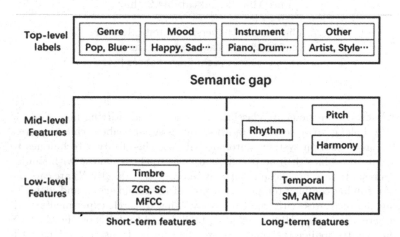

Fig. 1. Hierarchical taxonomy of music features

Fu *et al.* [1] proposed a taxonomy that divided music features and levels hierarchically as shown in Fig. 1. The top-level segment depicts how individuals understand or perceive music. The mid and low-level segments represent features of music. All top, mid, and low-level features could be used by machine learning or deep learning algorithms to resolve music semantics. Music is essentially a sequential audio signal, and RNNs are tailored to work with such data. Having said that, this research proposes the usage of RNN aided with Long Short Term Memory (LSTM) and Independent RNN (IndRNN) concepts to address the music genre classification problem. In genre classification, the representation of larger time scales is vital. These time scales can range up to or more than 500ms. The usage of Mel-Spectrogram can enlarge the time scale but leads to information loss. Hence, the Scattering transform which is invariant on larger time scales is used for feature extraction along with MFCCs. The next section investigates the literature on music genre classification.

2   Literature Review

To build an effective music genre classification system, two most important aspects are to be considered: feature extraction and model classification. Fu *et al.* [1] divided features as high-level and low-level where low-level features include MFCC and Scattering Transforms (SC). A study by Tzanetakis *et al.*

[2] investigates how music can be automatically labeled and how special characteristics of music related to instruments, and rhythms can be used to categorize
and classify it. Several studies offer unique feature engineering methods such as
octave frequency cepstral coefficients [3], stereo planning spectral feature, fluc-
tuation pattern, and rhythmic coefficient [1], Gabor filterbank coefficients [4],
and Daubechies wavelet coefficients histogram [5]. Ahmet *et al.* [6] used Short
Time Fourier Transform (STFT) for genre classification which made a notable
contribution to analyzing time-related frequencies.

Despite all the above features, MFCCs proved to be one of the best feature
extraction method for audio data. A study by Fu *et al.* [1] used low and high-
level features along side classifiers including Support Vector Machines (SVM)
[7], and K-Nearest Neighbours [8] over GTZAN dataset and achieved reasonable
genre classification results. Rajanna *et al.* [9] has proposed a case study for
classification of music genres where Logistic Regression achieves an accuracy of
38.84%. Kaur *et al.* [10] has made various feature dependent study with the use
of Mel-Frequency Cepstral Coefficients (MFCCs), Time Domain Zero Crossing,
Flux and Spectral Rolloff functions along with Gaussian mixture model (GMM)
as classifier and obtained accuracy of 70%.

With great success of deep neural networks in field of speech and sound
recognition [11], these techniques have now become industry standard in this
domain. Deep learning incorporates feature extraction and classification and
offers an end-to-end solution. Dieleman *et al.* [12] in their initial work proposed
a unsupervised feature extraction method using stacked Restricted Boltzmann
Machine (RBM) along with a convolution layer to a multi-layer perceptron model
and attained an accuracy of 29.52% in music genre classification. Feng *et al.*
[13] worked with the parallel CNN and RNN and has obtained accuracy of 51%.
Another CNN based model also attained a fairly low accuracy of 30% [14]. Using
raw spectrograms of audio data to spectrogram images, a CNN-based model was
able to achieve a surprisingly decent accuracy of 73.1% [15]. They used only 5
genres in this study which include classical, electric, jazz, pop, and rock.

3   Methodology

3.1   Dataset

This study uses GTZAN dataset. It consists of 1000 audio clips equally scattered
across 10 genres of music. Each audio clip is 30 s in duration. Correspondingly,
Our proposed model would be capable of classifying music into 10 genres. The
training and test set split is set to 90:10 ratio. The size of this dataset is considerably small for the training of a neural network in its current shape. To address
this issue, each audio file is divided into 10–3 s long segments which results in
a total of 1000 audio files per genre (10k total). Also, in the exploratory data
analysis, it has been identified that there are some corrupted files under the Jazz
genre which have been compensated by oversampling other music clips from the
same genre.

3.2   Feature Extraction

Mel Frequency Cepstral Coefficients (MFCC) are widely used frequency domain features representing the frequencies perceived by the human ear. First, the music file is split into frames with the help of hamming window. Then to calculate the power spectrum, the Fast Fourier transform is used for each frame. In order to smoothen the periodogram a stack of triangular shaped filters is utilized. Lastly, by taking the distinct cosine transform (DCT) of logarithmic of triangular filter stack we can obtain MFCC. Figure 2 shows the steps involved in MFCC extraction.

Fig. 2. Process of MFCC extraction

Figure 3 shows a sample audio file and its corresponding Mel-Spectrogram representation in which the frequencies are represented in Mel scale. The values or features extracted as Mel spectrogram are the visual representation of MFCC features for the audio file. In the majority of music classification tasks, long-time scales that could range more than 500ms need to be represented. MFCCs and Mel-spectrograms are limited to window lengths of 25ms. Scattering Transforms have been successfully used in Music Genre classification tasks [20, 21]. The Scattering Transform is capable of recovering the lost information from the usage of Mel-frequency with a cascade of modulus operators and decomposed wavelets. For a music sample, Scattering Transforms can be calculated using the wavelet transforms, ψ_{λ_t} as shown in the equation below.

$$|x * \psi_{\lambda_t}| * \phi(t) \tag{1}$$

The set of modulus of wavelet redeems the high frequencies that are lost by the low pass filter, $\phi(t)$. For signal x, the scattering coefficient can be given by S_{nx}, where the value of n is the order. A time-average operation on X is to obtain a local translation invariant descriptor which removes high frequencies.

$$S_0 X(t) = X * \phi(t) \tag{2}$$

These high frequencies can be recovered by wavelet modulus transform $|W_1|$ which is given by the following equation.

$$|W_1|x = (x^* \phi(t), |x * \psi_{\lambda_t}(t)|) \tag{3}$$

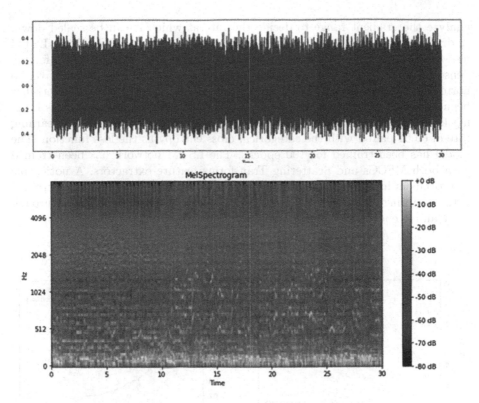

Fig. 3. Representation of audio file and corresponding Mel-Spectrogram

For audio signals, wavelets with a frequency similar to that of Mel frequency filters are considered. To make the coefficient of wavelet modulus invariant to translation, the average time unit is used in this transform. By taking the average of coefficients of wavelet modulus approximate values for Mel-spectrum spectral coefficients are obtained. Thus the nth order scattering coefficients is defined as:

$$S_n x(t, \lambda_1, \lambda_2, ..., \lambda_n) = |x * \psi_{\lambda_1}| * ...| * \psi_{\lambda_n}| * \phi(t) \tag{4}$$

3.3 Model Training

Long short-term memory (LSTM) networks [16] are well known for remembering long-term dependent data and predicting time series or sequences. An empirical experimental methodology is followed here to tune the model parameters (including the number of hidden layers and neurons), and hyperparameters (including learning rate and optimizers). Our empirical studies show a simple 4-layered LSTM network with two hidden layers worked better than a deep multi-layered LSTM network with too many hidden layers. This can be attributed to the fact that LSTM with too many layers will tend to face gradient decay problems. Before deciding on the optimization setup, a gradient norm was plotted to analyze the gradient range to decide the rate at which it can be scaled down. A dropout layer with a value of 20% succeeds the input layers of the LSTM network to avoid the over-fitting issue. Relu activation function is used for the dense layer while SoftMax activation function is used for the output layer to normalize the output for the 10 classes used in the network. The network has been compiled with different optimizers and with different learning rates ranging from 0.0 to 0.1. Results show the minimum loss achieved with the learning rate of 0.001 paired with the categorical cross entropy as the loss function. The model has been trained for 100 epochs. The LSTM network has been trained with both MFCCs and Scattering Transforms feature extractors. A noticeable Improvement in the performance has been observed when the model was trained with scattering transform features. The accuracy and loss parameters through the training epochs are shown in Fig. 4.

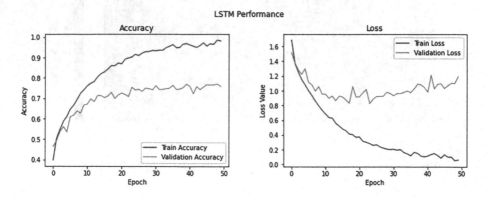

Fig. 4. LSTM training

Vogler and Othman [17] developed two separate neural networks for MFCCs and octave-based spectral contrast with a composite CNN-RNN model and combined them to create a deep and long neural network which achieved an accuracy of 83%. So, with the motivation of creating a longer and deeper neural network with RNN to predict the genres using GTZAN dataset, a variant of RNN called Independent Recurrent Neural Network has been used in this work. The Keras implementation of IndRNN cells has been used to build the model. Due to the use of tangent hyperbolic and sigmoid layers in LSTM, the model tends to face gradient decay [18]. Hence, building a deeper network even with LSTM is challenging. Whereas IndRNNs are not entangled with each other on the same layer. They are connected across the layers and hence, so Independent RNNs can regulate gradient vanishing and decaying problems better than the LSTM. At the same time IndRNNs will allow the network to learn and remember the long-term information from the previous cells. The neuron's hidden state is represented as below:

$$h_{n,t} = \sigma(w_n x_t + u_n h_{n,t-1} + b_n) \tag{5}$$

where w and u are weights of input and recurrent layer respectively and $h_{n,t}$ and $h_{n,t-1}$ are cell states that are independent of each other. The main purpose of W is to obtain the spatial that is frequency data from the music file and U represents the temporal data. The recent experiments show that the length of sequence IndRNN can process is >5000 compared to LSTM which is <1000. The time-based weights U have adjusted accordingly in the backpropagation to resolve the gradient vanishing problem. Multiple IndRNN layers stacking up on each other will create a dense and robust network using the Relu activation function.

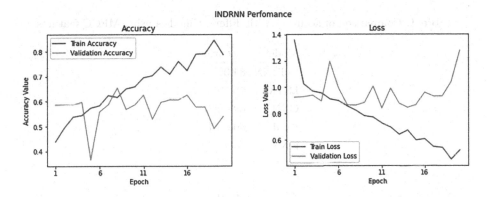

Fig. 5. IndRNN training

The Keras implementation of the Independent Recurrent Neural Network was based on the work by Li *et al.* [18]. The two different classes created for this implementation are IndRNNCell and RNN. IndRNNCell is constructed based on the architecture of the Keras SimpleRNNCell. The recurrent kernel for this IndRNNCell is a single-row matrix. The kernel will use the previous output generated by the model at each time step to multiply element-wise. This will create a robust stacked model to be trained by sequential data. The other class created is RNN and this uses a single IndRNNCell. The stacked IndRNN cells with 128 neurons have been used for the proposed model. By default IndRNN model uses Relu activation function as the recurrent kernel of the IndRNNCell is constrained by the random values between -1 and 1. The accuracy and loss value through the training are depicted in Fig. 5.

4   Evaluation Results

The results are generated for genre classification using 5 different models - KNN (K-mearest neighbours), SVM (Support Vector Machines), CNN (Convolutional Neural Networks), LSTM (Long Short Term Memory) network, and IndRNN (Independent RNN) model. While KNN and SVM are traditional machine learning models, LSTM, IndRNN and CNNs are state-of-the-art deep learning models. As mentioned earlier, data segmentation was used in all models as it was observed that the accuracy attained by the same LSTM model before segmenting the data was just 62% and improved to 78.7 after the segmentation using MFCC features. Table 1 shows the performance of the five models using the MFCC features. IndRNN model was the best performing model and was able to achieve 84% accuracy. The simple ML models (KNN/SVM) was not able to achieve the performance of LSTM or IndRNN.

Table 1. Comparison of accuracy with different models using MFCC features

Model	Accuracy
IndRNN	84.32%
LSTM	78.7%
CNN	64.60%
SVM	69.30%
KNN	64%

Further experiments are performed to find the best performing features. Only deep learning models are considered in these experiments as their performance was considerably higher. Results of deep learning models with both MFCCs and Scattering Transforms are represented in the Table 2. Scattering transforms are observed to performing better than MFCCs with all models. It can be observed that IndRNN performance the best with both MFCCs and Scattering transforms with marginal differences between the two. CNN results are much lower even though it was attributed as the best performing model in the literature. LSTM results are not as good as the IndRNN models. The results are split per genre as shown in Table 3 and it is observed that IndRNN consistently performs better for almost all genres. The biggest improvement in performance was observed for Country style with over 16% relative improvement in accuracy. But overall, all genres have better performance.

Other classification metrics are reported in Table 4 and Table 5. It is noted that the Country style is the genre that has highest performance improvement with the IndRNN model and the results are consistent across all performance

Table 2. Comparison of features in different models

Features	IndRNN	LSTM	CNN
MFCC	84.32%	78.70%	64.60%
Scattering transform	**84.70%**	79.40%	66.20%

metrics including precision, recall, and F1-score. There is a consistent improvement in the precision metric similar to accuracy with the IndRNN. The recall does not show as much consistency in improvement with IndRNN as the other metrics, especially for the genres like Blues and Reggae. From the above observations it can be concluded that the IndRNN model is able to better distinguish between the genres, especially, was able to recognize the difficult genres like Country, Pop, metal, and Rock very well. The corresponding confusion matrices are shown in Fig. 6 and Fig. 7. Confusions between genres like: Reggae and Hiphop; or Rock and Country; or Jazz and Country was resolved by IndRNN model.

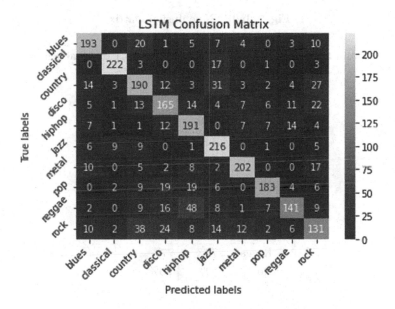

Fig. 6. LSTM confusion matrix

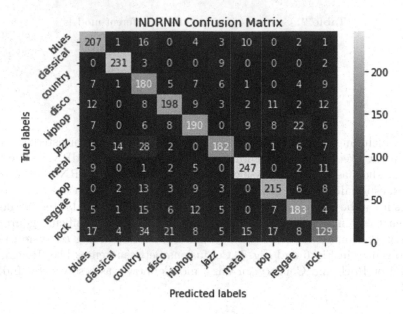

Fig. 7. IndRNN confusion matrix

Table 3. Accuracy of LSTM and IndRNN on individual genres

Genre	LSTM	IndRNN
Blues	81%	**89%**
Classical	92%	**98%**
Country	70%	**83%**
Disco	79%	**81%**
Hip-hop	76%	**84%**
Jazz	79%	77%
Metal	88%	**95%**
Pop	83%	**92%**
Reggae	77%	77%
Rock	59%	**70%**

Table 4. Classification report for LSTM

Genre	Accuracy	Precision	Recall	F1-Score	Support
Blues	81%	0.77	0.85	0.81	244
Classical	92%	0.91	0.94	0.93	245
Country	70%	0.59	0.82	0.69	220
Disco	79%	0.81	0.77	0.79	257
Hip-hop	76%	0.78	0.74	0.76	256
Jazz	79%	0.84	0.74	0.79	245
Metal	88%	0.87	0.89	0.88	277
Pop	83%	0.83	0.83	0.83	259
Reggae	77%	0.78	0.77	0.77	238
Rock	59%	0.68	0.50	0.58	258
Accuracy				0.79	2499
Macro Avg		0.79	0.79	0.79	2499
Weighted Avg		0.79	0.79	0.79	2499

Table 5. Classification report for IndRNN

Genre	Accuracy	Precision	Recall	F1-Score	Support
Blues	89%	0.89	0.85	0.87	243
Classical	98%	0.98	0.97	0.95	246
Country	83%	0.83	0.75	0.77	289
Disco	81%	0.81	0.82	0.80	248
Hip-hop	84%	0.84	0.81	0.81	244
Jazz	77%	0.77	0.77	0.77	247
Metal	95%	0.95	0.91	0.93	246
Pop	92%	0.92	0.90	0.91	248
Reggae	77%	0.77	0.75	0.75	241
Rock	70%	0.70	0.69	0.69	247
Accuracy				0.84	2499
Macro Avg		0.84	0.84	0.84	2499
Weighted Avg		0.84	0.84	0.84	2499

5   Conclusion and Future Work

Several models of genre classification were tried in conjunction with multiple feature extraction techniques for music genre classification. The research results shows that deep learning models like IndRNN or LSTMs can give good performance for genre classification. Experiments are performed on a standard dataset GTZAN and show the best performance achieved using the Scattering Transform features paired with the IndRNN model. The model performance could be measured using other popular datasets such as FMA to identify the adaptability of the proposed model and research findings. More sophisticated feature extractors including temporal features could also be investigated in the future to find the best performing system.

References

1. Fu, Z., Lu, G., Ting, K., Zhang, D.: A survey of audio-based music classification and annotation. IEEE Trans. Multimedia **13**, 303–319 (2010)
2. Tzanetakis, G., Cook, P.: Musical genre classification of audio signals. IEEE Trans. Speech Audio Process. **10**, 293–302 (2002)
3. Sridhar, R., Geetha, T.: Music information retrieval of Carnatic songs based on Carnatic music singer identification. In: 2008 International Conference on Computer and Electrical Engineering, pp. 407–411 (2008)
4. Zlatintsi, A., Maragos, P.: Comparison of different representations based on nonlinear features for music genre classification. In: 2014 22nd European Signal Processing Conference (EUSIPCO), pp. 1547–1551 (2014)
5. Li, T., Ogihara, M., Li, Q.: A comparative study on content-based music genre classification. In: Proceedings of the 26th Annual International ACM SIGIR Conference on Research and Development in Information Retrieval, pp. 282–289 (2003)
6. Elbir, A., İlhan, H., Serbes, G., Aydın, N. Short time Fourier transform based music genre classification. In: 2018 Electric Electronics, Computer Science, Biomedical Engineerings' Meeting (EBBT), pp. 1–4 (2018)
7. Boser, B., Guyon, I., Vapnik, V:. A training algorithm for optimal margin classifiers. In: Proceedings of the Fifth Annual Workshop on Computational Learning Theory, pp. 144–152 (1992)
8. Cover, T., Hart, P.: Nearest neighbor pattern classification. IEEE Trans. Inf. Theory **13**, 21–27 (1967)
9. Rajanna, A., Aryafar, K., Shokoufandeh, A., Ptucha, R. Deep neural networks: a case study for music genre classification. In: 2015 IEEE 14th International Conference On Machine Learning And Applications (ICMLA), pp. 655–660 (2015)
10. Kaur, C.,Kumar, R.: Study and analysis of feature based automatic music genre classification using Gaussian mixture model. In: 2017 International Conference on Inventive Computing and Informatics (ICICI), pp. 465–468 (2017)
11. Nakashika, T., Takiguchi, T., Ariki, Y.: Voice conversion based on speaker-dependent restricted boltzmann machines. IEICE Trans. Inf. Syst. **97**, 1403–1410 (2014)
12. Dieleman, S., Brakel, P., Schrauwen, B.: Audio-based music classification with a pretrained convolutional network. In: 12th International Society For Music Information Retrieval Conference (ISMIR-2011), pp. 669–674 (2011)
13. Feng, L., Liu, S., Yao, J.: Music genre classification with paralleling recurrent convolutional neural network. ArXiv Preprint ArXiv:1712.08370. (2017)
14. Li, T., Chan, A., Chun, A:. Automatic musical pattern feature extraction using convolutional neural network. Genre. **10**, 1x1 (2010)
15. Lee, H., Pham, P., Largman, Y., Ng, A.: Unsupervised feature learning for audio classification using convolutional deep belief networks. In: 22nd Proceedings of Conference Advances In Neural Information Processing Systems (2009)

16. Hochreiter, S., Schmidhuber, J.: long short-term memory. Neural Comput. **9**, 1735–1780 (1997)
17. Vogler, B., Othman, A.: Music genre recognition. Benediktsvogler, Com (2016)
18. Li, S., Li, W., Cook, C., Zhu, C., Gao, Y.: Independently recurrent neural network (INDRNN): Building a longer and deeper RNN. In: Proceedings of the IEEE Conference on Computer Vision and Pattern Recognition, pp. 5457–5466 (2018)
19. Song, G., Wang, Z., Han, F., Ding, S., Iqbal, M.: Music auto-tagging using deep recurrent neural networks. Neurocomputing **292**, 104–110 (2018)
20. Andén, J., Mallat, S.: Multiscale scattering for audio classification. In: SMIR, pp. 657–662 (2011)
21. Andén, J., Mallat, S.: Deep scattering spectrum. IEEE Trans. Signal Process. **62**, 4114–4128 (2014)

Explainable Boosting Machines for Network Intrusion Detection with Features Reduction

Tarek A. El-Mihoub[1]([⊠]), Lars Nolle[1,2], and Frederic Stahl[1]

[1] German Research Center for Artificial Intelligence (DFKI), Marine Perception, Oldenburg, Germany
{tarek.elmihoub,lars.nolle,frederic_theodor.stahl}@dfki.de
[2] Department of Engineering Science, Jade University of Applied Sciences, Wilhelmshaven, Germany

Abstract. Explainable Artificial Intelligence (XAI) can help in building trust in Artificial Intelligence (AI) models. XAI also helps in the development process of these models. Furthermore, they enable getting insight into problems with fundamental incomplete specifications. Trust in AI models is crucial, especially when used in high-stakes domains. Network security is one of these domains, where AI models have established themself. Network intrusion attacks are amongst the most dangerous threats in the field of information security. Detection of these attacks can be viewed as a problem with incomplete specifications. Using AI models with XAI facilities, such as glass-box models, in tacking network intrusion attacks can help in acquiring more knowledge about the problem and help to develop better models. In this paper, the use of Explainable Boosting Machine (EBM) as a glass-box classifier for detecting network intrusions is investigated. The performance of EBM is compared with other AI classifiers. The conducted experiments show that EBM outperforms its competitors in this domain. The work also demonstrates that the explainability of EBMs can help reducing the number of features needed for detecting attacks without degrading the performance.

Keywords: Explainable AI (XAI) · Explainable boosting machines · Network intrusion detection · Features reduction

1 Introduction

AI models have been widely used in different aspects of human life to solve real-world problems. These models are applied in high-stakes disciplines, such as medicine, criminal justice, financial markets and automation [1]. They outperform humans on some tasks [2, 3] and can support the human decision-making process [4]. The complexity of AI models combined with the simplicity of utilising them are the main reasons for dealing with them as black-box systems. However, data can influence the AI model's behavior, which can introduce modifications into the abstraction and the boundaries of a given problem [5]. Furthermore, the wide spread of their applications and their extensive use in mission-critical and business-critical systems necessitates the need for high confidence in their performance. Transparent models instead of black-box models are

M. Bramer and F. Stahl (Eds.): SGAI-AI 2022, LNAI 13652, pp. 280–294, 2022.
https://doi.org/10.1007/978-3-031-21441-7_20

required for better trust in AI methods. Such transparent models, when used to solve problems with fundamental incomplete specifications, can help get insight into these problems [6]. They can help in developing new solutions and acquiring new knowledge. There is a need to optimise AI models, not only for the expected task performance. They should also be optimised for safety [7], nondiscrimination [8], avoiding technical hidden costs for model maintenance and improvement [5] and explanation [6].

This paper investigates the use of Explainable Boosting Machines (EBMs) as glass-box models for building several network intrusion detection classifiers. To evaluate the performance of the proposed classifiers, the reported results of five different machine classifiers in [9] are used. The work undertaken in [9] is selected as a benchmark for two reasons. The first reason is that it reports the results of evaluating five different machine learning classifiers for network intrusion detection. The second reason is that the dataset used for evaluating these classifiers is also available. Thus, the proposed EBMs classifiers can be benchmarked against these classifiers based on the reported results in [9]. The work presented in this paper also studies the possibilities of using the explanation facility of EBM to extract new knowledge to improve the performance of the classifier. Several non-payload intrusion detection classifiers are built using EBMs aiming to address the following questions:

1. Can EBM classifiers outperform the classifiers used in [9]?
2. Can EBMs be used to help in deciding on the classifier's features, which contain information about obfuscated attacks?
3. Can EBMs be used to further reduce the number of features without degrading the classifier performance?

Table 1 lists the acronyms, which are used in this paper.

Table 1. List of acronyms.

Acronyms	Names	Acronyms	Names
AD	Anomaly-based Detection	GAM	Generalised Additive Model
CF	CounterFactual	LIME	Local Interpretable Model-agnostic Explanations
EBM	Explainable Boosting Machine	SD	Signature-based Detection
DARPA	Defense Advanced Research Projects Agency	SHAP	SHapley Additive exPlanations
DiCE	Diverse Counterfactual Explanations	SPI	Shallow Packet Inspection
DL	Direct + Legitimate	SVM	Support Vector Machine
DNN	Deep Neural Network	TCP	Transmission Control Protocol
DOL	Direct + Obfuscated + Legitimate	TPR	True Positive Rate

(continued)

Table 1. (*continued*)

Acronyms	Names	Acronyms	Names
DPI	Deep Packet Inspection		
FFS	Forward Feature Selection	XAI	Explainable Artificial Intelligence
FPR	False Positive Rate		

The remainder of the paper is structured as follows: Section two introduces eXplainable Artificial Intelligence (XAI). Section three focuses on EBMs and shows their main concepts. The problem of network intrusion attacks is briefly explained in section four. It also introduces the different detection mechanisms and the classifiers used in [9]. In section five, the experimental setup is described. It defines several classifiers that were used to address the paper's questions. The evaluation of these classifiers is discussed in this section. The paper ends with conclusions and future work.

2   Explainable Artificial Intelligence (XAI)

The concept of explaining the behaviour of an AI model for its stakeholders is referred to as Interpretable AI, Explainable AI or XAI. The root of XAI goes back to the development of expert systems [10]. In spite of being used interchangeably, explainability has a wider meaning than interpretability [11]. Interpretability is often associated to answering the question of *why*, related to a specific phenomenon and based on a specific opinion. Meanwhile, explainability is the ability to provide a set of related inference rules to answer the questions of *how* and *why*. An explanation relies on facts, which can be described by words or formulas. Explanations can reveal the facts and the rules that are governing the behaviour of a phenomenon. Furthermore, explanations can help to uncover new knowledge and to relate different aspects of a phenomenon. The emergence of complex learning models raises the need for explaining the model's behaviour to the stakeholders. The behaviour should be explained using suitable, understandable terms to serve the aims of the model's stakeholders.

The stakeholders for explainable AI can be divided into three main groups. These include the developers, the consumers and the regulators. For each of these groups, explainability can have a slightly different meaning. For developers, it means a better understanding to increase the chances of improving the performance and developing better models; for consumers, explainability is associated with transparency, fairness and trust; for regulators; unbiased models mean compliance with regulations.

XAI systems aim to provide AI models with the ability to justify their outcomes, describe their strengths and weakness, and reveal a clear view of their behaviour in the future [12]. XAI aims to improve explainability without degrading the performance of AI models [12].

Explainability can be incorporated within the workflow of AI models in different ways. According to DARPA, three strategies can be followed to enable expandability [12]. These strategies are deep explanation, model induction and interpretable models.

Deep explanation aims to make use of the success of deep learning in solving complex problems to solve the explanation problem. Deep explanations combine deep learning models with other models to produce richer representations of the features utilised during learning to enable extraction of underlying semantic information [13]. Generating accurate and suitable explanations of the model's behaviour to a user is the main challenge of deep explanation models [12].

The other two strategies try to ease the tension between the performance and the expandability of the AI models. Usually, AI models with a complex internal behaviour surpasses the models with a simple and a clear internal behaviour in terms of performance. The high performance of black-box models when combined with ease of use opens the doors widely for them to enter different applications domains. Induction strategy can be used to explain the behaviour of black-box models and to decouple the link between the performance and the explainability. Induction techniques conclude explainable models from black-box models. Local Interpretable Model-agnostic Explanations (LIME) [14], SHapley Additive exPlanations (SHAP) [15] and Diverse Counterfactual Explanations (DiCE) [16] are examples of induction techniques. They are also known as post-hoc explanation models [17].

LIME [14], which is also classified as a local agnostic-model, focuses on the local space of the features of a sample, to build a linear classifier of the sample's features to extract the relation between the prediction and the features. SHAP [15] is another local agnostic-model. However, it estimates the importance of different features, by comparing the prediction of the model with the feature value of the sample and with a random value of it. It also uses the same way to estimate the combined effect of different features. DiCE [16] is a post-hoc explanation tool that uses a set of diverse counterfactual examples to inspect the behaviour of AI models. A counterfactual (CF) example is used to show how an input parameter of a model can be modified to change the model's outcome.

The interpretable models' strategy aims to decouple the explanation and performance relation by combining the clarity of the internal behaviour of AI models with high quality performance. Linear regression, logistic regression and decision tree are examples of interpretable models [18] with the least accuracy compared to black box models [12, 17]. The simple internal behaviour of these models enables explaining and predicting their behaviour. Explainable Boosting Machine (EBM) [19] is a highly explainable model with an accuracy comparable to state-of-the-art AI models [19, 20]. Due to the clarity in the internal behaviour of these models, they are classified as glass-box [19] or transparent [18] models. In addition to the explainability of EBM, it can produce comparable performance to black-box models.

Utilising such an explainable model can produce a model with a high accuracy. Furthermore, when applied to problems with incomplete specifications, it can provide new knowledge usable for building a better AI model.

3 Explainable Boosting Machine

Explainable Boosting Machines (EBMs) [19] can be viewed as a generalised and more efficient version of the Generalised Additive Model (GAM) [21]. GAMs are extension versions of multiple linear regression models [17].

In multiple linear regression, a linear relation is assumed between the output of the model and its inputs [17] as shown in Eq. 1.

$$y = \beta_0 + \sum_{i=1}^{n} \beta_i x_i \tag{1}$$

where y is the output of the model, β_0 is the intercept and β_i is the linear coefficient that relates each input x_i to the output of the model. The output of a model is predicted through learning the values of the intercept and the β_i coefficients. The output is assumed to follow a Gaussian distribution with a mean of y. In GAMs [21], the output can follow any distribution and the β_i coefficients of a multiple linear regression are replaced with the relations $f_i(x_i)$, which can be nonlinear. The relations between the output of the model, which is the expected mean of the assumed distribution, and its inputs are represented using GAMs as shown in Eq. 2.

$$E(y) = \beta_0 + \sum_{i=1}^{n} f_i(x_i) \tag{2}$$

where $E(y)$ is the expected mean of the output's distribution, β_0 is the intercept and $f_i(x_i)$ is the relation of input x_i and the output of the model. GAMs assume nonlinear relations between each input and the output of the model. They use smoothing techniques, such as splines, to model these relations. The output of the model is predicted though learning the value of the intercept and the functions that describes the $f_i(x_i)$. Using this model, a separated function is learned for each input independently. This enables determining the impact of each individual input on the model output.

Explainable Boosting Machines (EBMs) build upon GAMs to combine interpretability with improved predictive performance [19]. EBMs can be represented as shown in Eq. 3.

$$g(E[y]) = \beta_0 + \sum_{i=1}^{n} f_i(x_i) \tag{3}$$

where g is a function that adjusts GAMs to an appropriate setting of regression or classification. EBMs learn each relation, $f_i(x_i)$, using modern machine learning techniques such as gradient boosting. In order to eliminate the order of selecting a specific input for learning during the learning process, only one function, $f_i(x_i)$, is learned in round-robin fashion using the boosting procedure with a very low learning rate. It uses round-robin cycles through different inputs while learning the best function for each input to alleviate the effects of co-linearity. Easing the impact of co-linearity helps to determine the contribution of each input on the model output. To increase the accuracy, EBMs can also automatically detect pairwise interactions between inputs [22]. EBMs can be represented as a generalised sum GAMs and as pairwise interaction terms, as shown in Eq. 4.

$$g(E[y]) = \beta_0 + \sum_{i=1}^{n} f_i(x_i) + \sum_{i=1, j=1, j \neq i}^{n,n} f_{ij}(x_i, x_j) \tag{4}$$

EBM is an efficient implementation of the GA^2M algorithm [19, 22]. In addition to enabling building AI models with high accuracy, the built-in explanation facility can be utilised to debug the model, retrain it and improve its accuracy. It can also help the developer to acquire new knowledge of the problem to be solved.

To shed light into the benefits of utilising XAI in solving real-world problems, network intrusion detection was selected as a test problem. In addition to the importance of finding effective AI models to deal with this problem, this problem can be viewed as a problem with incomplete specifications. Using XAI models such as EBMs can help in acquiring new knowledge for better understating of the problem.

4   Network Intrusion Detection

Network intrusion detection is essential for protecting information technology infrastructure from external attacks [23]. Traditional intrusion detection methods can identify previously known network attacks. However, for tackling new unknown attacks, AI models are better candidates to deal with such kind of attacks due to their dynamic prediction capabilities [24]. Detecting network attacks or intrusion detection is one of the most important applications of AI models.

Different methodologies can be used for network intrusion detection [23]. These methodologies include Signature-based Detection (SD) and Anomaly-based Detection (AD). In SD, also known as misuse detection [25], patterns are compared against captured events for recognizing possible attacks. SDs are based on the knowledge of known attacks. They are simple and effective. They can provide a detailed analysis of these attacks for a better understanding of the nature of the attacks. Nevertheless, they are ineffective in detecting unknown attacks or variants of a known attack. On the other hand, in AD [26], patterns are compared against normal profiles with observed events to detect attacks. ADs can detect new and unforeseen vulnerabilities in many cases. However, the main difficulty in developing ADs is to define accurate profiles of normal [23]. This methodology might be slow in attacks detection. It also may misclassify normal traffic as intrusion, or in other words, may generate many false positives [9]. Classifications based on machine learning combine both AD and SD models to get the best out of them. It uses samples of intrusions and legitimate traffic instances to build a model that can detect some unknown intrusions. However, they may be vulnerable to evasion by obfuscation techniques [9].

For network traffic classification in general, packet-based, flow-based and port-based methods are commonly used [24]. However, this section focuses on packet-based and flow-based detection as two methodologies for network intrusion classification. Payload-based methods [27] investigate the content of the packets, especially the application layer-related information, in order to classify it. These methods usually compare the content of the packet with predefined signatures or patterns. Shallow Packet Inspection (SPI) and Deep Packet Inspection (DPI) can be used to investigate a packet's contents [24]. Payload-based intrusion detection classification techniques may not be suitable for dealing with encrypted data. Furthermore, privacy policies may limit access to the contents of the packets. These techniques can impose heavy computational overhead on the network. To eliminate the need for inspecting the contents of a packet and alleviate its associated problems, flow-based intrusion [9] detection has been proposed. The underlying concept behind this technique is that traffic associated with network attacks has almost different characteristics compared with normal network traffic. Therefore, it is possible for a flow-based classifier to handle both encrypted and non-encrypted traffic. AI models, such as decision tree, logistic regression, Support Vector Machine (SVM) and Deep Neural Network (DNN), have been used successfully for flow-based intrusion detection [25]. Artificial intelligence intrusion detection classifiers are able to perform with a remarkable accuracy. However, a massive amount of fully labelled data is required for modeling purposes [25].

Five non-payload intrusion detection classifiers were evaluated in [9]. These include Gaussian Naïve Bayes, Gaussian Naïve Bayes with kernel density estimation, Logistic Regression, Decision Tree, and Support Vector Machine. A dataset that consists of legitimate, direct-attack and obfuscation-attack samples was collected and used to train these classifiers. These features are Transmission Control Protocol (TCP) connection-level features. Each sample of this dataset consists of more than 900 features. The dataset is described in [9] and is available from:

http://www.fit.vutbr.cz/~ihomoliak/asnm/ASNM-NPBO.html.

The Forward Feature Selection (FFS) process has been used to select a number of features, which have the highest impact on differentiating between legitimate and attacks samples. The FFS is described in table A.1 in [9]. Table 2 shows these features with the same names and descriptions as in table A.1. These FFS features were divided further into two sets. These sets are DOL (Direct + Obfuscated + Legitimate) and FFS DL (Direct + Legitimate). In [9], DL features are assumed as less informed than FFS DOL features. It is also assumed using only the DL features means training a model without any knowledge about obfuscated attacks. On the other hand, DOL features are assumed to contain information about obfuscated attacks. These sets are shown in Table 3. This table also shows the exact names of the features as they appear in ASNM-NPBO v2 dataset.

5   Experiments and Evaluations

To address the research questions, several EBM network intrusion classifiers were developed using the dataset mentioned above. The performances of these classifiers are compared with the reported results of the five classifiers in [9].

The InterpretML [19] platform was used to implement the proposed EBMs classifiers. InterpretML is an open-source Python platform. It contains different interpretability and explanation tools. Glass-box and black-box explanation facility types are available with this platform. The glass-box models of InterpretML, such as EMBs, provide global and local explanation facilities. InterpretML also has visualisation tools, which allows for easy comparison of the different methods.

5.1   Can EBMs Classifiers Outperform Other Classifiers?

To answer the first question, three EBMs were developed. The first classifier was built using all FFS features and is referred to as the FFS classifier. The second classifier was trained using DL features; hence it is referred to as the DL classifier. The third one was

Table 2. TCP connection-level features selected by FFS [9].

Feature ID	Description
SigPktLenOut	Std. Deviation of outbound (client to server) packet sizes
MeanPktLenIn	Mean of packet sizes in inbound traffic of a connection
CntOfOldFlows	The number of mutual connections between client and server, which started up to 5 min before start of an analysed connection
CntOfNewFlows	The number of mutual connections between client and server, which started up to 5 min after the end of an analysed connection
ModTCPHdrLen	Modus of TCP header lengths in all traffic
UrgCntIn	The number of TCP URG flags occurred in inbound traffic
FinCntIn	The number of TCP FIN flags occurred in inbound traffic
PshCntIn	The number of TCP PUSH flags occurred in inbound traffic
FourGonModulIn [1]	Fast Fourier Transformation (FFT) of inbound packet sizes. The feature represents the module of the 2nd coefficient of the FFT in goniometric representation
FourGonModulOut [1]	The same as the previous one, but it represents the module of the 2nd coefficient of the FFT for outbound traffic
FourGonAngleOut [1]	The same as the previous one, but it represents the angle of the 2nd coefficient of the FFT
FourGonAngleN [9]	Fast Fourier Transformation (FFT) of all packet sizes, where inbound and outbound packets are represented by negative and positive values, respectively. The feature represents the angle of the 10th coefficient of the FFT in goniometric representation
FourGonAngleN [1]	The same as the previous one, but it represents the angle of the 2nd coefficient of the FFT
FourGonModulN[0]	The same as the previous one, but it represents the module of the 1st coefficient of the FFT
PolyInd13ordOut [13]	Approximation of outbound communication by polynomial of 13th order in the index domain of packet occurrences. The feature represents the 14th coefficient of the approximation
PolyInd3ordOut [3]	The same as the previous one, but it represents the 4th coefficient of the approximation
GaussProds8All [1]	Normalized products of all packet sizes with 8 Gaussian curves. The feature represents a product of the 2nd slice of packets with a Gaussian function that fits to the interval of the packets' slice
GaussProds8Out [7]	The same as the previous one, but computed above outbound packets and represents a product of the 8th slice of packets with a Gaussian function that fits to the interval of the packets' slice
InPktLen1s10i [5]	Lengths of inbound packets occurred in the first second of a connection, which are distributed into 10 intervals. The feature represents totalled outbound packet lengths of the 6th interval
OutPktLen32s10i [3]	The same as the previous one, but computed above the first 32 s of a connection. The feature represents totalled outbound packet lengths of the 4th interval

(continued)

Table 2. (*continued*)

Feature ID	Description
OutPktLen4s10i [2]	The same as the previous one, but computed above the first 4 s of a connection. The feature represents totalled outbound packet lengths of the 3rd interval

Table 3. Different sets of FFS features.

Feature ID	Feature ID as ASNM-NPBO v2 dataset	DOL	DL	FFS-13	DOL-10	FFS-10	FFS-7
SigPktLenOut	SigPktLenSrc	X	X	X	X	X	X
MeanPktLenIn	MeanPktLenDst	X	X	X	X	X	X
CntOfOldFlows	cntOfOldFlows	X	X	X	X	X	X
CntOfNewFlows	cntOfNewFlows	X	X	X	X	X	X
ModTCPHdrLen	modTCPHdrLen	X		X	X		
UrgCntIn	urgCnt <In>	X					
FinCntIn	finCnt <In>		X	X		X	
PshCntIn	pshCnt < In >		X	X		X	
FourGonModulIn [1]	fourCoefsGonModulIn [1]	X	X	X	X	X	X
FourGonModulOut [1]	fourCoefsGonModulOut [1]		X	X		X	
FourGonAngleOut [1]	fourCoefsGonAngleOut [1]	X			X		
FourGonAngleN [9]	fourCoefsGonAngleIn [9]	X	X				
FourGonAngleN [1]	fourCoefsGonAngleIn [1]	X		X	X	X	X
FourGonModulN[0]	fourCoefsGonModulIn[0]		X				
PolyInd13ordOut [13]	polynomIndexes13ordOut [13]	X		X	X	X	X
PolyInd3ordOut [3]	polynomIndexes3ordOut [3]		X				
GaussProds8All [1]	gaussProds8All [1]	X			X		
GaussProds8Out [7]	gaussProds8Out [7]		X	X			
InPktLen1s10i [5]	InPktLen1s10i [5]	X					
OutPktLen32s10i [3]	OutPktLen32s10i [3]		X				
OutPktLen4s10i [2]	OutPktLen4s10i [2]		X	X			

trained using DOL features and is referred to as the DOL classifier. Table 4 compares the performance of these classifiers with the reported performance of the best SVM in [9]. The SVM classifier was trained using the DOL FFS features with cross-validation. This classifier produced the best performance among the different classifiers evaluated in [9].

Table 4. The performances of different classifiers.

Classifier	TPR	FPR	F1	Avg. recall
SVM	99.53%	0.13%	98.68%	99.70%
FFS	99.24%	0.08%	99.55%	99.62%
DL	63.70%	0.59%	80.97%	62.96%
DOL	99.42%	0.10%	99.39%	99.43%

The results show that the DL classifier produced the worst performance compared to the other classifiers in Table 4. However, its results are better than those reported for the Gaussian Naïve Bayes classifier using DL features with cross-validation [9]. The poor performance of the DL classifier is in accordance with the assumption that DL features contain no useful information about obfuscated attacks. Meanwhile, the results demonstrate that the FFS and the DOL EBMs classifiers outperform the SVM classifier in terms of FPR. They also show a comparable performance with SVM in terms of the F1 score, average recall and TPR. The FFS and the DOL classifiers outperform all other classifiers evaluated in [9].

5.2 Deciding on Features with Obfuscation Information

To answer this question, the global explanation facility of the FFS classifier was used to select the features with the highest impact on the output. Since the DOL classifier uses 13 features, only 13 features were selected. Figure 1 shows the FFS features with the highest mean absolute importance score.

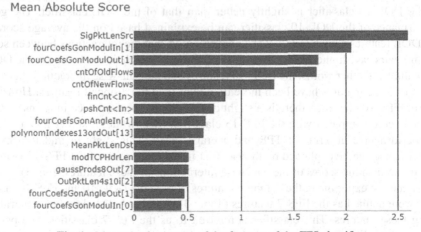

Fig. 1. Mean absolute score of the features of the FFS classifier.

Another EBM classifier was trained using these 13 features that have the highest impact score in Fig. 1. This classifier is referred to as the FFS-13 classifier. The selected features were not identical to the DOL features (Table 3). This set has only eight common features with the DOL features. The classifier was trained using the same dataset. The performance of this classifier is shown in Table 5. The FFS-13 classifier shows a similar performance to that of the DOL classifier. The two classifiers show similar performance despite using different features for classifications. However, the results show that the explanation facility of EBMs can help in deciding on selected features that can produce performance comparable to that based on expert knowledge.

Table 5. Comparing the DOL and the FFS-13 classifiers.

Classifier	TPR	FPR	F1	Avg. recall
DOL	99.42%	0.10%	99.39%	99.43%
FFS-13	99.43%	0.16%	99.15%	99.43%

5.3   Reducing the Number of Features Without Degrading the Performance

To answer the third question, the global explanation tools of EBMs were utilised. The features' scores of both the DOL and the FFS-13 classifiers are shown in Figs. 2 and 3. Ten features, which had the highest score impact on the output of each classifier, were used to train two EBMs classifiers, namely the FFS-10 and the DOL-10 (Table 3). In Fig. 3, there is a change in the rank of scores of some features compared with that of Fig. 1. The change can be a result of the interactions, which are higher than pair-wise interactions. EBMs only consider individual and pair-wise interactions.

The performances of these two classifiers are shown in Table 6. The performance of the DOL-10 classifier is slightly better than that of the DOL classifier. The good performance of the DOL-10 classifier can be explained based on the average score of the DOL features shown in Fig. 2. The figure shows that the interactions between some feature pairs have higher scores than those of features, which do not belong to the DOL-10 features. In other words, the DOL-10 features and the pair-wise interactions between some of these features have been more dominant than the dropped features. However, for the FFS-10 classifier, there is a slight degrade in the performance in terms of FPR and F1 score compared with the FFS-13 classifier. Meanwhile, it shows no change in the performance in terms of TPR and average recall. This slight degradation in the performance can be explained by the fact that individual scores of the FFS-13 features are higher than the scores of the pair-wise interactions of these features (Fig. 3).

In the last experiment, the common features of both the DOL-10 and FFS-10 classifiers were defined as the FFS-7 features (Table 3). Another EBM classifier was trained using these features. This classifier is referred to as the FFS-7 classifier. The performance of the FFS-7 is shown in Table 6. The classifier shows similar performance to the classifiers with 10 features, with a slight decline in FPR. The degradation can be explained based on the assumption that by training the classifier with knowledge about some obfuscated attacks, it is able to detect these attacks and other similar obfuscated attacks.

Table 6. Comparing the DOL-10, FFS-10 and FFS-7 classifiers.

Classifier	TPR	FPR	F1	Avg. recall
DOL-10	99.42%	0.07%	99.54%	99.43%
FFS-10	99.43%	0.12%	98.90%	99.43%
FFS-7	99.43%	0.22%	98.80%	99.43%

Through the conducted experiments, the research questions mentioned in Sect. 1 was addressed. For the first question, the experiments show that it is possible for EBMs, as explainable classifiers, to produce a comparable performance to state-of-the-art machine learning classifiers. Regarding the second question, the experiments demonstrated that the explanation capabilities of the EBMs can be utilised as features selection to determine the features with information about obfuscated attacks. With respect to the last question, this work shows that EBMs can be used for features reduction without a considerable decrease in the performance.

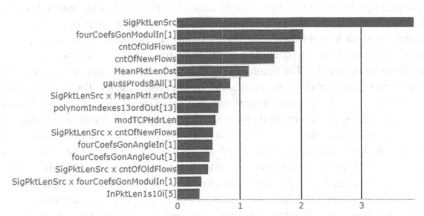

Fig. 2. Mean absolute score of the features of DOL classifier.

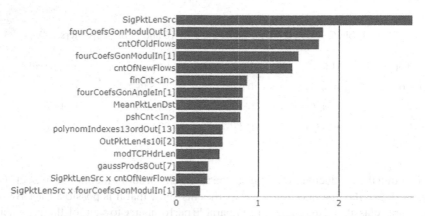

Overall Importance:
Mean Absolute Score

Fig. 3. Mean absolute score of the features of FFS-13 classifier.

6   Conclusion and Future Work

The conducted experiments show that it is possible to build an explainable classifier for network intrusion detection using EBMs. The proposed classifiers, when used with features that contain information about obfuscated attacks and direct attacks, can produce a comparable accuracy to state-of-the-art classifiers. Furthermore, these EBM classifiers can provide new knowledge, which might be used to improve the classifier's design. The EBM classifiers help in reducing the number of the features that are used to train network intrusion classifier without degrading the classifier performance. First, the explanation tools of EBMs were used to decide on the FFS features that contain more information about obfuscation attacks. The features selected based on the results of the explanation tools proved to have good information about obfuscation attacks. The classifier trained using these features shows a similar performance compared with the classifier trained on features selected by an expert. Furthermore, another step in the direction of reducing the classifier features was taken. The reduction is done relying on the explanation facilities of EBMs. Both classifiers with a reduced number of features were able to produce a comparable performance to the classifier, which use the whole set of FFS features.

The reported results of the proposed classifiers are based on a single dataset. A possible future step is to evaluate the performance of the proposed classifiers on other datasets to help in generalising the research's findings. Meanwhile, the experiments shed light into the possible benefits of incorporating explainability within the framework of developing AI models. The features' scores facility of EBMs, for example, can be used for features reduction. The possibility of boosting the performance of state-of-the-art machine learning classifiers through combining them with EBMs as a feature selection tool needs to be investigated. Another possible future step for this research is to build a tool for automatic reduction of classifiers' features using the capabilities of EBMs models and their explanation tools.

Acknowledgements. The research in this paper is partly supported by the Ministry for Science and Culture, Lower Saxony, Germany, through funds from the Niedersächsische Vorab (ZN3480).

References

1. Davinder, K., Suleyman, U.K.J.R., Arjan, D.: Trustworthy Artificial Intelligence: A Review. Association for Computing Machinery (2022)
2. Silver, D., Huang, A., Maddison, C.J., Guez, A., Sifre, L.: Mastering the game of Go with deep neural networks and tree search. Nature **529**, 484–489 (2016)
3. Mnih, V., Kavukcuoglu, K., Silver, D., Graves, A., Antonoglou, I.: Playing Atari with Deep Reinforcement Learning. arXiv preprint arXiv:1312.5602 (2013)
4. Nauman, M., Akhtar, N., Alhudhaif, A., Alothaim, A.: Guaranteeing correctness of machine learning based decision making at higher educational institutions. IEEE access **9**, 92864–92880 (2012)
5. Sculley, D., et al.: Hidden technical debt in machine learning systems. In: Advances in Neural Information Processing Systems 28 (NIPS 2015), 2015
6. Doshi-Velez, F., Kim, B.: Towards a rigorous science of interpretable machine learning. Machine learning (2017)
7. Mock, M., et al.: An Integrated Approach to a Safety Argumentation for AI-Based Perception Functions in Automated Driving. In: Habli, I., Sujan, M., Gerasimou, S., Schoitsch, E., Bitsch, F. (eds.) SAFECOMP 2021. LNCS, vol. 12853, pp. 265–271. Springer, Cham (2021). https://doi.org/10.1007/978-3-030-83906-2_21
8. Oneto, L., Chiappa, S.: Fairness in Machine Learning. In: Oneto, L., Navarin, N., Sperduti, A., Anguita, D. (eds.) Recent Trends in Learning From Data. SCI, vol. 896, pp. 155–196. Springer, Cham (2020). https://doi.org/10.1007/978-3-030-43883-8_7
9. Homoliak, I., Teknös, M., Ochoa, M., Breitenbacher, D., Hosseini, S., Hanacek, P.: Improving network intrusion detection classifiers by non-payload-based exploit-independent obfuscations: an adversarial approach. EAI Endorsed Transactions on Security and Safety (2018)
10. Hopgood, A.A.: Intelligent Systems for Engineers and Scientists. CRC Press, A Practical Guide to Artificial Intelligence (2022)
11. Buhrmester, V., Arens, M.: Analysis of explainers of black box deep neural networks for computer vision: a survey. Machine learning & knowledge extraction **3**, 966–989 (2021)
12. Gunning, D., Aha, D.: DARPA's Explainable Artificial Intelligence (XAI) Program. AI Magazine **40**(2), 44–58 (2019)
13. Park, D.H., et al.: Multimodal explanations: justifying decisions and pointing to the evidence. In: 2018 IEEE/CVF Conference on Computer Vision and Pattern Recognition (2018)
14. Ribeiro, M.T., Singh, S., Guestrin, C.: Why should i trust you?: explaining the predictions of any classifier. In: the 22nd ACM SIGKDD international conference on knowledge discovery and data mining. San Francisco, California, USA (2016)
15. Lundberg, S.M., Lee, S.-I.: A unified approach to interpreting model predictions. In: the 31st International Conference on Neural Information Processing Systems. Long Beach, California, USA (2017)
16. Mothilal, R.K., Sharma, A., Tan, C.: Explaining machine learning classifiers through diverse counterfactual explanations. In: FAT* '20. Barcelona, Spain (2020)
17. Molnar, C.: Interpretable Machine Learning: A Guide for Making Black Box Models Explainable, Leanpub (2022)
18. Guidotti, R., Monreale, A., Ruggieri, S., Turini, F., Giannotti, F., Pedreschi, D.: A survey of methods for explaining black box models. ACM Comput. Surv. **51**(5) (2018)

19. Nori, H., Jenkins, S., Koch, P., Caruana, R.: InterpretML: A Unified Framework for Machine Learning Interpretability. arXiv (2019)
20. Maxwell, A.E., Sharma, M., Donaldson, K.A.: Explainable boosting machines for slope failure spatial. Remote Sens. **13**(4991) (2021)
21. Hastie, T.T.R.: Generalized additive models: some applications. J. Am. Stat. Assoc. **82**(398), 371–386 (1987)
22. Yin, L., Caruana, R., Gehrke, J., Hooker, G.: Accurate intelligible models with pairwise interactions. In: the 19th ACM SIGKDD International Conference on Knowledge Discovery and Data Mining, Chicago, Illinois, USA (2013)
23. Liao, H.-J., Lin, C.-H.R., Lin, Y.-C., Tung, K.-Y.: Intrusion detection system: a comprehensive review. J. Netw. Comput. Appl. **36**(1), 16–24 (2013)
24. Abbasi, M., Shahraki, A., Taherkordi, A.: Deep learning for network traffic monitoring and analysis (NTMA): a survey. Comput. Commun. **170**(15), 19–41 (2021)
25. Dimitrios, P., Gómez, M.F., Georgios, K.: Introducing deep learning self-adaptive misuse network intrusion detection systems. IEEE Access **7**, 13546–13560 (2019)
26. Lane, T., Brodley, C.E.: An application of machine learning to anomaly detection. In: the 20th National Information Systems Security Conference, Baltimore, USA (1997)
27. Wang, K., Stolfo, S.J.: Anomalous Payload-Based Network Intrusion Detection. In: Jonsson, E., Valdes, A., Almgren, M. (eds.) Recent Advances in Intrusion Detection. RAID 2004. LNCS, vol. 3224. Springer, Berlin, Heidelberg (2004). https://doi.org/10.1007/978-3-540-30143-1_11

Short Papers

Short Papers

Accelerating Cyber-Breach Investigations Through Novel Use of Artificial Immune System Algorithms

Benjamin Donnachie[1]([⊠]) [iD], Jason Verrall[1] [iD], Adrian Hopgood[1,2],
Patrick Wong[1], and Ian Kennedy[1]

[1] The Open University, Walton Hall, Milton Keynes, UK
{benjamin.donnachie,jason.verrall,adrian.hopgood,patrick.wong,
ian.m.kennedy}@open.ac.uk
[2] University of Portsmouth, Winston Churchill Avenue, Portsmouth, UK

Abstract. The use of artificial immune systems for investigation of cyber-security breaches is presented. Manual reviews of disk images are impractical because of the size of the dataset. Machine-learning algorithms for detection of misuse require labelled training data, which are generally unavailable. They are also necessarily retrospective, so they are unlikely to detect new forms of intrusion. For those reasons, this article proposes the use of artificial immune systems for unsupervised anomaly detection. Specifically, a deterministic dendritic cell algorithm (dDCA) has been implemented that has successfully detected automated SQL injection attacks from sample disk images. For comparison, it outperformed an unsupervised k-means clustering algorithm. However, many significant anomalies were not detected, so further work is required to refine the algorithm using more extensive datasets, and to encode complementary expert knowledge.

Keywords: Anomaly detection · Artificial Immune Systems · Cybersecurity · Dendritic cell algorithm · Unsupervised learning

1 Introduction

The hostile penetration of computer systems is an increasing security concern for organisations globally. Unauthorised access to a computer system ("cyber-breach") can either prevent it from doing something it should and/or cause it to do something it should not [12].

Following a cyber-breach, investigators are often under extreme pressure to deliver results quickly to meet regulatory or business timelines or to identify enhancements to bring systems back online. These investigations require the analysis of significant volumes of log information, in a process that is often manually intensive, inefficient, and liable to confirmation bias.

While more traditional log sources, such as firewall logs, intrusion detection system logs, and audit logs offer a partial view of any intrusion, a more detailed

M. Bramer and F. Stahl (Eds.): SGAI-AI 2022, LNAI 13652, pp. 297–302, 2022.
https://doi.org/10.1007/978-3-031-21441-7_21

view can be obtained by examining the filesystems of affected computer systems. One common method is assembly of a "super-timeline" of filesystem events with a specialist tool, such as Plaso [8], that typically includes metadata from:

1. Filesystem including file birth (created) times, access & change times
2. Extracted from known filetypes; e.g. system logs, office documents etc.
3. Additional plugins to detect potential or known malicious software.

Such output can be overwhelming with a simplified disk image for training human examiners [9] generating over 1.3 m entries, consisting of all recognised log metadata over the lifetime of the system, compounding the analysis workload.

This paper presents a novel unsupervised anomaly detection method to prioritise cyber-breach investigations, using these complex super-timelines. Section 2 reviews selected previous work in this area; Sect. 3 describes the proposed approach; Sect. 4 details preliminary experimental results; and Sect. 5 concludes the paper with suggestions for future work.

2   Related Work

Existing investigation methods involving event reconstruction from log files, have disadvantages such as prior training requirements, or are significantly time-consuming [3]. Techniques also exist for identifying potentially malicious file content, such as fraudulent documents, but these do not identify anomalous behaviour [6]. Within the field of intrusion detection, two principal approaches to detecting potentially malicious behaviour from real-time log information are reported: misuse detection vs anomaly detection [4].

In addition to expert systems, Machine Learning and Artificial Intelligence (ML/AI) methods have been used to explore both detection approaches. However, similar to detecting malicious file content, misuse detection requires previous training; with models suffering from class imbalance with training data biased towards the non-attack activities [13]. Anomaly detection can demonstrate more flexibility by not requiring prior training for an application.

3   Proposed Approach

3.1   Artificial Immune Systems

Artificial Immune Systems (AIS) are a branch of ML/AI modelling inspired by the human immune system. AIS algorithms can encompass Danger Theory, whereby the immune system responds preferentially to signals (antigens) from tissue undergoing uncontrolled cell death (necrosis), typically arising from injury or infection; leading to development of a Deterministic Dendritic Cell Algorithm (dDCA), based on immunological antigen-presenting Dendritic Cells (DCs) [7].

dDCA requires two input signals:

Safe: Within the physiological analogue, an indicator of benign apoptosis. Digitally, an indicator of normal system behaviour, e.g. a (reasonably) constant rate of computer system activity.

Danger: Physiologically, an indicator of necrosis. Digitally a measure of potential abnormality, e.g. anti-virus alerts or known malicious activity.

While there is no need to define, or train, a normal pattern of activity, dDCA requires domain expert knowledge about the application to define these signals.

3.2   Deterministic Dendritic Cell Algorithm

As illustrated in Fig. 1, digital DCs begin in an immature, or initialised, state. Each super-timeline time window is presented as a separate antigen, acting as the vector of calculated safe and danger signals to locate any relevant activity. dDCA then fuses the input data across multiple time windows, individual DCs become either 'semi-mature' under the influence of safe signals and hence not provoking an immune response (normal behaviour); or 'mature' under the influence of danger signals and invoking a response (abnormal/malicious behaviour).

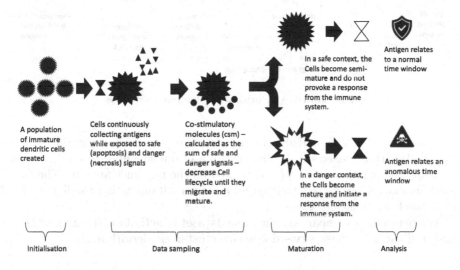

Fig. 1. Illustration of dDCA showing phases and data fusion (based on [5]).

3.3   Methodology

Inspired by work using k-means clustering algorithm with minimal features for incident response triage [11], this feasibility study calculates the safe and danger signals derived from the super-timeline data sampled into fixed-time windows. Log activity levels are used as a proxy for system activity, and thus rate of change, to calculate the safe signal as shown in equation (1). A yara rule repository [1] used by cybersecurity researchers to share malicious software patterns was used as an indicator of potential malicious activity, and derive the danger signal (2).

For each time window i:

$$Safe_i = 100 - \left[\frac{100 \log\left(|activityCount_{i+1} - activityCount_i|\right)}{\log\left(\max activityCount\right)} \right] \quad (1)$$

$$Danger_i = \frac{100 \log\left(yaraCount_i\right)}{\log\left(\max yaraCount\right)} \quad (2)$$

Plaso [8] was used to extract all recognised metadata from the training image discussed above, and derive safe and danger signals as outlined in Fig. 2.

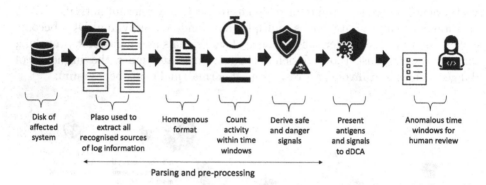

Fig. 2. dDCA algorithm implementation steps

The calculated safe and danger signals were presented sequentially to the dDCA algorithm (based on Dr Greensmith's C implementation - with thanks) with the time window pointer (i) presented as the reference antigen. The calculated anomaly score k_a was collated with values >0 indicating the likelihood of an anomaly or malicious event [7].

For benchmark comparison, the same dataset of activity and yara counts was clustered using the unsupervised k-means clustering algorithm.

4   Experiment Results and Application

Significant events which human examiners are expected to uncover were collated [14] and manually confirmed, as detailed in Table 1. Times indicate when malicious activity began; detections may be lagged to reach a threshold. Table 2 shows an extract of all anomalous detections from running dDCA, as detailed above, together with the results from the k-means algorithm.

Comparison between the tables show this experiment successfully detected the automated SQL injection attacks that began at 11.15 on 2015/09/02 in the 11:19 time window. However, many significant items were not detected; this is likely to be due to the lack of necessary expert knowledge encoded into this experiment. This implementation also out-performed the k-means algorithm, which only detected software installs and did not cluster any malicious activity.

Table 1. Start of significant events contained within the training image.

Date	Time	Event Description	Comments
2015-09-02	07:10	Webserver reconnaissance activity begins	**Correctly** not detected
2015-09-02	09:04	Begin command injection attacks; create	Not detected
		Users and add to remote desktop group	
2015-09-02	09:31	Local files exploited through webserver	Not detected
2015-09-02	10:49	SQLi attacks begin	Not detected
2015-09-02	11:15	Begin SQLmap to automate SQLi attacks	**dDCA detection**
			During activity
2015-09-02	11:25	Malicious webshells created and executed	Not detected
2015-09-03	07:14	Further malicious webshells dropped	Not detected
2015-09-03	07:21	Use of webshell to execute commands	Not detected

Table 2. Filtered potentially anomalous time windows identified by dDCA and k-means.

Time window (i)	Summary values		Input		Output		Comments
	Activity Count	Yara Count	Danger	Safe	dDCA ($k_a>0$)	k-means Cluster	
2015-07-20 12:55	3404	1731	64	29	7	–	Software install
2015-08-23 21:25	8191	7043	77	21	35	–	Software install
2015-08-23 21:26	3688	2859	69	26	51	–	Software install
2015-08-23 21:41	39920	32802	90	7	76	**Abnormal**	Software install
2015-08-23 21:42	75072	61673	95	8	155	**Abnormal**	Software install
2015-08-23 21:43	90163	69738	96	16	65	**Abnormal**	Software install
2015-08-23 21:44	1098	852	58	0	16	–	Software install
2015-08-24 06:52	8577	7537	77	22	34	–	Software install
2015-08-24 06:57	3172	2650	68	29	9	–	Software install
2015-08-24 07:43	66032	64979	96	3	91	**Abnormal**	Software install
2015-08-24 07:44	38167	34035	90	10	160	**Abnormal**	Software install
2015-08-24 07:45	16248	15855	84	12	59	–	Software install
2015-08-24 07:46	28446	27138	88	17	112	–	Software install
2015-08-24 07:47	41360	36091	91	17	57	**Abnormal**	Software install
2015-08-24 07:48	113678	105019	100	2	96	**Abnormal**	Software install
2015-08-24 07:49	38707	37593	91	2	88	**Abnormal**	Software install
2015-08-24 07:50	1113	897	59	8	132	–	Software install
2015-09-02 11:19	13481	9530	79	29	22	–	**Malicious SQLmap**

5   Conclusions and Further Work

This study demonstrates the potential of dDCA to triage vast volumes of log data for human review, identifying 18 potential anomalies from a dataset of 1,381,976 log entries with non-malicious anomalous detections potentially discounted using expert domain knowledge; and performing better than unsupervised k-means clustering algorithm.

The anomalous indications correlate with peaks in activity across the disk images; due partly to the derivation of safe and danger signals from overall activity, and also because the images are intended to train human breach investigators rather than accurately simulate malicious activity.

To address the limitations of deriving the input signals, further research is needed to determine a more effective way to encode domain expertise, potentially combining other types of ML within hybrid AI systems [10]. Training sets exist for network traffic, albeit with limitations [2], whilst datasets from real-world intrusions are difficult to obtain. Consequently, generating datasets which reflect real-world cyber-attack patterns are essential for the evaluation of future work.

References

1. Repository of Yara rules (March 2022). https://github.com/Yara-Rules/rules
2. Al-Daweri, M.S., Zainol Ariffin, K.A., Abdullah, S., Md. Senan, M.F.E.: An analysis of the KDD99 and UNSW-NB15 datasets for the intrusion detection system. Symmetry **12**(10), 1666 (2020)
3. Bhandari, S.: Research and implementation of timeline analysis method for digital forensics evidence. Ph.D. thesis, Kaunas University of Technology (2022)
4. Çavuşoğlu, Ü.: A new hybrid approach for intrusion detection using machine learning methods. Appl. Intell. **49**(7), 2735–2761 (2019)
5. Costa Silva, G., Palhares, R.M., Caminhas, W.M.: A transitional view of immune inspired techniques for anomaly detection. In: Yin, H., Costa, J.A.F., Barreto, G. (eds.) IDEAL 2012. LNCS, vol. 7435, pp. 568–577. Springer, Heidelberg (2012). https://doi.org/10.1007/978-3-642-32639-4_69
6. Du, X., Le, Q., Scanlon, M.: Automated artefact relevancy determination from artefact metadata and associated timeline events. In: International Conference on Cyber Security and Protection of Digital Services, Cyber Security 2020 (2020)
7. Gu, F., Greensmith, J., Aicklein, U.: The dendritic cell algorithm for intrusion detection. In: Lio, P., Verma, D. (eds.) Biologically Inspired Networking and Sensing. IGI Global , Hershey (2012)
8. Guðjónsson, K.: Mastering the Super Timeline (2010). https://bit.ly/3DjJpSf
9. Hadi, A.: Web server case (September 2015). https://bit.ly/3LbYR4z
10. Hopgood, A.A.: Intelligent Systems for Engineers and Scientists, 4th edn. CRC Press, Oxon (2022)
11. Nila, C., Patriciu, V.: Taking advantage of unsupervised learning in incident response. In: 12th International Conference on Electronics, Computers and Artificial Intelligence. IEEE, Bucharest, Romania (2020)
12. Price, B., Tuer, J.: Digital forensics. In: White, P. (ed.) Crime Scene to Court: The Essentials of Forensic Science, 4th edn,. Chap. 12. The Royal Society of Chemistry, London (2016)
13. Singhal, A., Maan, A., Chaudhary, D., Vishwakarma, D.: A hybrid machine learning and data mining based approach to network intrusion detection. In: 2021 International Conference on Artificial Intelligence and Smart Systems, pp. 312–318. IEEE, Coimbatore, India, March 2021
14. Swartwood, A.: Web server case write-up (March 2017). https://bit.ly/3eLWY2g

Comparing ML Models for Food Production Forecasting

Nouf Alkaabi[1](✉) and Siddhartha Shakya[2](✉)

[1] Electrical and Computer Engineering, Khalifa University, Abu Dhabi, UAE
`100041573@ku.ac.ae`
[2] EBTIC, Khalifa University, Abu Dhabi, UAE
`sid.shakya@ku.ac.ae`

Abstract. Food production forecasting is a challenge to decision-makers at agriculture authorities. In this study, we compare the performance of three different Machine Learning (ML) approaches for predicting the production of food items. Particularly, we compare Long Short-Term Memory (LSTM) that can handle sequence-based data, such as time-series data, against classical machine learning time-series analysis models, such as Auto Regression (AR) and Auto-Regressive Integrated Moving Average (ARIMA). The algorithms are incorporated into a forecasting tool to perform a periodic prediction of food production. The results show that different algorithms can work better in different datasets, with the LSTM approach being more flexible that can be further improved.

Keywords: Time-series forecasting · LSTM · ARIMA

1 Introduction

Managing food production is the kernel of a stable food supply chain. It is one of the critical resource management problems that many agricultural authorities face regularly. A proper periodic supply chain optimization is required to satisfy the food demand. Optimal planning will help to prevent both under and over-supply. Data analysis, Artificial Intelligence (AI), and Machine Learning (ML) play an essential role in generating more reliable forecast. AI-driven demand forecasting techniques use historical data and other available parameters to predict behaviors and trends accurately. In this paper, we focus on the production forecast using ML techniques. The aim is to build models to accurately forecast food items' expected production to facilitate the decision on import, export, and expected wastage. A controlled set of data was provided by one of our partner organizations with the aim to build a tool that can assist with periodical production assessment. We compare the performance of a deep ML approach known as Long Short-Term Memory (LSTM) [18] which is a class of Recurrent Neural Networks (RNN) [14], with classical machine learning time-series analysis models, such as Auto Regression (AR) [17] and Auto-Regressive Integrated Moving Average (ARIMA) [15].

M. Bramer and F. Stahl (Eds.): SGAI-AI 2022, LNAI 13652, pp. 303–308, 2022.
https://doi.org/10.1007/978-3-031-21441-7_22

The rest of the paper is organized as follows. Section 2 reviews time series forecasting literature. Section 3 describes the methodology. Section 4 presents the experimental result and the performance comparison. Finally, Sect. 5 presents the conclusion and recommends future work.

2 Background

Deep learning approaches are powerful tools in dealing with complex time-series forecasting problems [3]. The authors of [11] conduct a survey that lists many different deep learning approaches for time-series forecasting. AR, ARIMA, and LSTM models were reviewed, among many other approaches, along with their applications. For example, an application of forecasting financial data was reported with two tested models: LSTM and ARIMA, with the results showing that LSTM was a better predictor than ARIMA. LSTM was the best approach for another reported application by Fischer and Krauss [6] for stock prediction. LSTM was compared to memory-free algorithms such as Random Forest [9], Logistic Regression Classifier [13], and deep neural network [16]. Similarly, some approaches have been proposed in literature targeting food production forecasting. One example can be found in [1], where the authors predict soybean production in Brazil using Artificial Neural networks (ANN) [16]. The results were compared with the classical methods of time-series analysis. They found that the ANN model was the best approach that provided reliability and accuracy. ANN was also used in [2] to predict wheat production in India. The authors used different methods with an ANN model and found that the best training models are Bayesian Regularization [4] and Levenberg-Marquardt [12]. Moreover, In [8], the authors used deep neural networks for predicting fruit production in Pakistan. They adopted Levenberg-Marquardt optimization, and Bayesian regularization backpropagation.

3 Methodology

In this section, we provide a brief definition of the used prediction models and the accuracy metrics used.

AR model is one of the early models for describing and modeling time-series data. Equation (1) shows the formulation of AR, where y_t is the predicted value, p is the past timesteps to be used, $\alpha_1, ..., \alpha_p$ are the parameters of the model, c is a constant, and η_t is white noise.

$$y_t = c + \alpha_1 \cdot y_{t-1} + \alpha_2 \cdot y_{t-2} + ... + \alpha_p \cdot y_{t-p} + \eta_t \tag{1}$$

ARIMA is a mixture of AR model and Moving Average (MA) model, frequently used in timeseries analysis. ARIMA is defined by ARIMA (p, d, q), where p is the number of AR terms, d is the number of first differences, and q is the number of MA terms.

LSTM is a class of RNNs, which intern is ANNs with recurrent connections that can represent sequential data for sequence recognition and prediction. LSTM is more advanced than simple RNN and can deal with the vanishing gradient problem [18] that RNN has. We do not go into details of these models, interested readers are reffered to [18].

We separated the data into training and testing sets with the testing set being the dataset's most recent 12 months production. The model's accuracy is then determined by comparing predicted production to actual production in the testing set. We choose three error matrices as the measures of accuracy. They are Root Mean Square Error (RMSE) [5], Weighted Average Percentage Error (WAPE) [10], and Symmetric mean absolute percentage error (SMAPE) [7]. Due to limited space, we do not provide a formulation of RMSE, WAPE, and SMAPE, they can be found in respective literature.

4 Experimental Results

4.1 Dataset and Model Setting

We were provided with a multiyear dataset from our partner organization to perform this study. The dataset includes hundreds of food items together with their monthly production. For this paper, we choose four sample products representing typical products in the dataset with different distributions. The model parameters were tuned empirically, where we performed multiple experiments with many settings for the hyperparameters and chose the settings that resulted in the best accuracy. The lags parameter was set to 12, which means that the predicted value is based on the previous 12 values in the series. To validate the models, the last batch of the training set (12 months) was used to predict the testing set. For ARIMA, after insuring that the data is stationary, the order of the ARIMA model that best minimizes the AIC score was (12, 1,4). For LSTM, the data were normalized and a model with a single LSTM layer (nine neurons) and one dense layer was created. Relu activation function was used with Adam optimizer [14]. The model is fitted on the training set over 100 epochs.

4.2 Results

Each model was trained against the dataset for each of the four products, and the test accuracy was recorded. Table 1 shows the results for each algorithm on four products using different accuracy measures and also shows the average accuracy. Note that for WAPE and SMAPE, the error value was converted to accuracy % by subtracting it by one and multiplying it by 100.

We can see that the performance of LSTM and AR is comparable, with one outperforming another on different products, and also on different accuracy metrics. The result for ARIMA is the least favorable one with it not being able to outperform the other two algorithms in all but one case. This suggests that, for our dataset, the addition of the Moving Average parameter q in ARIMA, which differentiates it from AR model, is not adding extra benefit. Overall, the average RMSE was better for AR but was closely followed by LSTM. At the same time, for WAPE and SMAPE, LSTM was better, again closely followed by AR. This shows that both AR and LSTM are good models to apply for this problem.

Table 1. RMSE results (in million kg), WAPE results, and SMAPE results

	RMSE			WAPE			SMAPE		
	AR	ARIMA	LSTM	AR	ARIMA	LSTM	AR	ARIMA	LSTM
Product #1	2.30	3.17	**2.23**	92.49%	81.06%	**96.12%**	94.15%	92.57%	**94.93%**
Product #2	**1.78**	3.13	2.49	**92.62%**	88.57%	90.20%	**98.14%**	96.63%	97.18%
Product #3	**1.80**	1.88	1.80	73.13%	75.78%	**75.93%**	92.24%	**93.43%**	93.24%
Product #4	1.09	**0.78**	1.15	83.66%	**89.40%**	83.29%	95.56%	**97.24%**	95.44%
Average	**1.74**	2.24	1.92	85.48%	83.70%	**86.39%**	95.02%	94.97%	**95.20%**

4.3   Detail Timeseries Comparison

It is interesting to see the time series of actual against prediction and visually analyze the results. For this, we use product #1 as an example and plot the actual against prediction data for all three tested models.

Figure 1 shows the AR forecasting results together with the past data points. We can notice that the values are close, but in most cases, the predicted value was greater than the actual one. The future prediction, however, looks convincing with the upward production trend being followed. The model's accuracy is 92.49% using WAPE, 94.15% using SMAPE, and RMSE is 2.30.

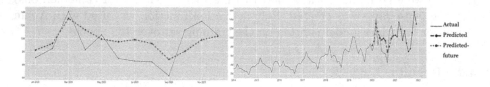

Fig. 1. Actual vs. prediction, and corresponding future forecasting using AR model

Similarly, Fig. 2 shows ARIMA results. We can notice that the prediction values follow an average trend rather than closely following the actual values. This is also evident in the future prediction graph, where the prediction does not seem to follow an upward trend. The model's accuracy is 81.06% using WAPE, 92.57% using SMAPE, and RMSE is 3.17.

Figure 3 shows the LSTM results. We can notice that the prediction values closely follow actuals and have a smoother pattern of going upward or downward

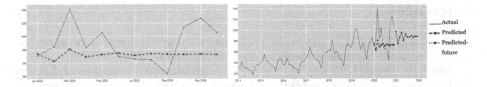

Fig. 2. Actual vs. prediction, and corresponding future forecasting using ARIMA model

compared to AR. The future prediction also looks convincing, with the upward trend being followed but not as aggressively as the AR prediction. The model's accuracy is 96.12% using WAPE, 94.93% using SMAPE, and RMSE is 2.23.

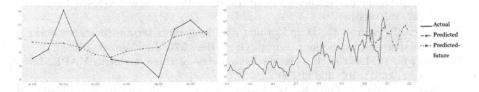

Fig. 3. Actual vs. prediction, and corresponding future forecasting using LSTM model

In general, we can notice that both AR and LSTM performed well for our problem, with one outperforming another in different products and matrices. However, the LSTM approach seems to produce the most balanced forecast, with the accuracy plots showing a less aggressive forecast than AR, while making a better fitting curve than ARIMA. This pattern was consistent across the other three products. LSTM also has more hyperparameters in comparison to the other two approaches, which gives it more degree of freedom to better fit against the data.

5   Conclusion

In this work, we tested three different ML approaches to forecasting food production based on historical data provided by our partner organization. We performed a detailed experimental analysis showing that different models can perform better in the different datasets. However, in general, the LSTM approach seems to be the most flexible approach with more degree of freedom that can be further tuned to improve accuracy. The tested models were incorporated into a prediction framework, which is being tested by our partner organization. The feedback is encouraging and is helping with proactive planning of food import and export. Further work can be done to improve the accuracy of the LSTM model, where the intelligent tuning of LSTM hyperparameters with heuristic-based search and optimization techniques and the addition of external factors such as weather and seasonality could improve the results.

References

1. Abraham, E., et al.: Time series prediction with artificial neural networks: an analysis using Brazilian soybean production. Agriculture **10**, 475 (2020)
2. Bindu, G., Neha, K., Suraj, M., Tanya, S.: A performance comparison of different back propagation neural networks methods for forecasting wheat production. CSI Trans. ICT **4**, 305–311 (2016)
3. Bontempi, G., Ben Taieb, S., Le Borgne, Y.-A.: Machine Learning strategies for time series forecasting. In: Aufaure, M.-A., Zimányi, E. (eds.) eBISS 2012. LNBIP, vol. 138, pp. 62–77. Springer, Heidelberg (2013). https://doi.org/10.1007/978-3-642-36318-4_3
4. Burden, F., Winkler, D.: Bayesian Regularization of Neural Networks, pp. 23–42. Humana Press, Totowa (2009)
5. Chai, T., Draxler, R.: Root mean square error (RMSE) or mean absolute error (MAE)?-Arguments against avoiding RMSE in the literature. Geosci. Model Dev. **7**, 1247–1250 (2014)
6. Fischer, T., Krauss, C.: Deep learning with long short-term memory networks for financial market predictions. Eur. J. Oper. Res. **270**(2), 654–669 (2018)
7. Goodwin, P., Lawton, R.: On the asymmetry of the symmetric MAPE. Int. J. Forecast. **15**(4), 405–408 (1999)
8. Khan, T., Qiu, J., Qureshi, M., Shahid Iqbal, M., Mehmood, R., Hussain, M.: Agricultural fruit prediction using deep neural networks. Procedia Comput. Sci. **174**, 72–78 (2020)
9. Liu, Y., Wang, Y., Zhang, J.: New machine learning algorithm: random forest. In: Liu, B., Ma, M., Chang, J. (eds.) Information Computing and Applications, pp. 246–252. Springer, Berlin (2012)
10. Louhichi, K., Jacquet, F., Butault, J.P.: Estimating input allocation from heterogeneous data sources: a comparison of alternative estimation approaches. Agric. Econ. Rev. **13** (2012)
11. Mahmoud, A., Mohammed, A.: A survey on deep learning for time-series forecasting. In: Hassanien, A.E., Darwish, A. (eds.) Machine Learning and Big Data Analytics Paradigms: Analysis, Applications and Challenges. SBD, vol. 77, pp. 365–392. Springer, Cham (2021). https://doi.org/10.1007/978-3-030-59338-4_19
12. Moré, J.J.: The levenberg-marquardt algorithm: implementation and theory. In: Watson, G.A. (ed.) Num. Anal., pp. 105–116. Springer, Berlin Heidelberg, Berlin, Heidelberg (1978)
13. Peng, J., Lee, K., Ingersoll, G.: An introduction to logistic regression analysis and reporting. J. Educ. Res. **96**, 3–14 (2002)
14. Salehinejad, H., Sankar, S., Barfett, J., Colak, E., Valaee, S.: Recent advances in recurrent neural networks. Int. J. Mach. Learn. Cyber. **11**, 747–750 (2017)
15. Shumway, R., Stoffer, D.: Time Series and Its Applications, Springer Cham (2017). https://doi.org/10.1007/978-3-319-52452-8
16. Suk, H.I.: An Introduction to neural networks and deep learning. Deep Learn. Med. Image Anal. **2017**, 3–24 (2017)
17. Ullrich, T.: On the autoregressive time series model using real and complex analysis. Forecasting **3**(4), 716–728 (2021)
18. Van Houdt, G., Mosquera, C., Nápoles, G.: A review on the long short-term memory model. Artif. Intell. Rev. **53** (2020)

Comparing Peircean Algorithm with Various Bio-inspired Techniques for Multi-dimensional Function Optimization

Quratulain Quraishi, Hammad Rizwan, and Mian Muhammad Awais[✉]

Lahore University of Management Sciences, Lahore 54792, Pakistan
{quratulain.quraishi,hammad.rizwan,awais}@lums.edu.pk

Abstract. Peirce's theory of evolution gives a highly efficient optimization algorithm in the domain of evolutionary computation (EC). Peircean Evolutionary Algorithm (P-EA) has the potential to solve the existing drawbacks of classical Evolutionary Algorithms such as loss of diversity, stagnation, or premature convergence. In this work, we compare P-EA with other state- of-the-art algorithms on a set of benchmark mathematical functions that are widely used to gauge their performance. These algorithms are already tested on several mathematical functions, but never have been compared with P-EA. The experimental results show that P-EA outperforms on complex functions like Michalewicz and Rastrigin with higher number of dimensions. These results help to improve the viability of P-EA for EC community.

Keywords: Functional optimization · Evolutionary algorithms · Unimodal and multimodal functions

1 Introduction

The bio-inspired evolutionary algorithms (EAs) are widely used by researchers for solving optimization problems [6]. Several adaptations of evolutionary algorithms have been proposed to solve unimodal, multi-model, and multi-objective optimization problems [8]. Some popular EAs are genetic algorithms (GAs), particle swarm optimization (PSO), biogeography-based optimization (BBO), differential evolution (DE), Firefly Algorithm (FA) and cultural evolution (CA).

There is another evolutionary algorithm called Peircean Evolutionary Algorithm (P-EA) that is least explored in the EC Community but has great potential for solving complex problems. P-EA is the interpretation of Charles Sanders Peirce's evolutionary theory that ensures diversity through the evolutionary process. He believed that contemporary evolutionary theories cater two elements "chance" and "competition" responsible for evolutionary process, while neglecting the contribution of habit and cooperation. He introduced this as a third evolutionary agent and proposed a triadic theory of evolution. Peirce identified that there are three elements simultaneously working in the evolutionary

M. Bramer and F. Stahl (Eds.): SGAI-AI 2022, LNAI 13652, pp. 309–314, 2022.
https://doi.org/10.1007/978-3-031-21441-7_23

growth process, he named them: "firstness", "secondness", and "thirdness". The firstness represents chance or possibility, the secondness represents mechanical necessity or competition, while the thirdness represents cooperation or generalizing tendency. This concept makes his theory different from classical evolutionary approaches.

Literature shows the effectiveness of PEA over Classical EA tested on a set of benchmark problems. P-EA has potential to overcome issues faced by other EAs like loss of diversity, stagnation, and premature convergence. Unfortunately, P-EA has not tested or compared with other bio-inspired approaches to shed further light on the authors' claims [1,2].

Through this paper we try to explore the potential of P-EA and find out where it stands among other bio-inspired evolutionary approaches. For this P-EA along with six other evolutionary approaches are tested on ten different benchmark mathematical functions. This attempt highlights the significance of Peirce's approach that has been overlooked so long and to attract the attention of EC Community.

Section 2 gives a brief overview of the relevant work. Sections 3 describes the problem setup. Section 4 gives insight into the results and performance comparison of selected approaches. Section 5 concludes the paper.

2   Related Work

Optimization problems have been a focus of significant attention in the EC community for many years, particularly focusing on global optimization of numerical or real-valued problems where analytical solutions don't work. Recently, dedicated efforts have been made to compare new algorithms with older ones that are known to work well, these comparisons are based on numerical benchmark problems to identify which algorithm outperforms others on a given set of problems [10].

GA is the most commonly used evolutionary approach, it has been widely used in diverse areas of global optimization problems, VLSI design, combinatorial problems, constraints optimization, and machine learning [6,8]. GA's ability to deal with complex problems and explore search space simultaneously in all directions makes it more applicable than traditional approaches. Several variants of GA have offered to solve mathematical optimization functions [12], and tested its performance on a set of benchmark test functions conducted in comparison with different evolutionary techniques [6,8]. DE used twenty-one benchmark functions to test the performance of the selected algorithms with 100 dimensions and 30 dimensions [10]. In a comparative report on variants of DE algorithms, authors used thirteen benchmark test functions to identify the best variant of DE [7]. FA has recently developed, and is a very promising metaheuristics algorithm [11]. Yang uses various mathematical test functions to validate the performance of FA in comparison with other evolutionary algorithm. FA is introduced to solve the optimization problem of mixed variable structure [5]. BBO has been used in several mathematical benchmarks and practical optimization problems. BBO and its variant algorithm have applied to the test function suite of twelve functions in comparison with five diffrent state of the art approaches [4]. A hybrid approach of Tabu Search and CA has proposed to solve the optimization problem of engineering design. Authors used basic CA, Tabu, and variants of PSO to compare the results for analysis [3]. A set of high dimensional and complex mathematical functions has used to compare the performance of P-EA with Classical EA [2]. The P-EA has showed promising results, but so far it has not been compared with other bio-inspired approaches.

3   Problem Setup

The objective is to compare the results of P-EA with GA, PSO, CA, FA, BBO, and DE on the set of mathematical functions shown in Table 1. Each function is tested on these selected bio-inspired algorithms with different number of dimensions (d) i.e. 10, 20, 30, and 40. Function 1–4 are unimodal functions while 5–10 are multimodal functions. The global minima is 0 for all functions except function 8 it is -9.6601517, -19.6370136, -29.6308839, and -39.6267489 for dimensions 10, 20, 30, 40 respectively [9]. The population size, maximum number of generations for all algorithms are fixed at 100 and 10000. Crossover rate, number of crossover points, mutation rate are 0.7, 4 and 0.02 along with tournament selection for GA and P-EA [2]. Each algorithm is executed for 30 independent runs to obtain the data for analysis. All algorithms are programmed in Matlab.

Table 1. Mathematical test functions used to evaluate algorithms

	Name	Formulation	Search domain
Unimodal	Sphere	$f_1(x) = \sum_{i=1}^{d} x_i^2$	$[-5.12, 5.12]^d$
	Rosenbrock	$f_2(x) = \sum_{i=1}^{d-1} [100(x_{i+1} - x_i^2)^2 + (x_i - 1)^2]$	$[-1.5, 1.5]^d$
	Quartic	$f_3(x) = \sum_{i=1}^{d} i x_i^4 + random[0, 1]$	$[-1.28, 1.28]^d$
	Rotated Hyper-Ellipsoid	$f_4(x) = \sum_{i=1}^{d} \sum_{j=1}^{i} x_j^2$	$[-65.536, 65.536]^d$
Multimodal	Griewank	$f_5(x) = \sum_{i=1}^{d} \frac{x_i^2}{4000} - \prod_{i=1}^{d} \cos(\frac{x_i}{\sqrt{i}}) + 1$	$[-600, 600]^d$
	Ackley	$f_6(x) = -a \exp(-b\sqrt{\frac{1}{d} \sum_{i=1}^{d} x_i^2} - \exp(\frac{1}{d} \sum_{i=1}^{d} \cos(cx_i)) + a + \exp(1)$	$[-32.768, 32.768]^d$
	Rastrigin	$f_7(x) = 10d + \sum_{i=1}^{d} [x_i^2 - 10\cos(2\pi x_i)]$	$[-5.12, 5.12]^d$
	Michalewicz	$f_8(x) = -\sum_{i=1}^{d} \sin(x_i)\sin^{2m}(\frac{i x_i^2}{\pi})$	$[0, \pi]^d$
	Schwefel	$f_9(x) = 418.9892d - \sum_{i=1}^{d} x_i \sin(\sqrt{|x_i|})$	$[-500, 500]^d$
	Salomon	$f_{10}(x) = -\cos(2\pi\sqrt{\sum_{i=1}^{d} x_i^2}) + 0.1\sqrt{\sum_{i=1}^{d} x_i^2} + 1$	$[-100, 100]^d$

4   Results and Discussion

The results for our experiments are shown in Table 2. Table 2 shows the best minimum values, the bold font represent the best result among all the algorithms. Other metrics like average minimum value, worst minimum values and standard deviation have been recorded for result's discussion and analysis. We have removed the fitness curves and table for Sphere, Ackley, Quartic and Rotated Hyper-Ellipsoid function but we do include them in the discussion. Convergence curves and result metrics are available at Metrics-Graphs.

Table 2. Best minimum value achieved for test functions

Rosenbrock				
Models	Dimension-10	Dimension-20	Dimension-30	Dimension-40
PSO	7.99e-09	0.06638	9.2273	18.95
CA	0.00086053	0.0025044	0.0046061	0.028479
FA	**2.98e-28**	**1.56e-28**	**1.93e-28**	**3.75e-28**
BBO	0.037893	10.229	24.522	33.776
DE	0.036907	7.2151	17.821	28.436
GA	8.775	18.998	29.131	39.546
P-EA	5.9148	16.721	26.762	36.135
Rastrigin				
PSO	1.9899	10.945	23.879	29.849
CA	2.9849	90.025	208.26	363.38
FA	0.99496	6.9647	21.889	41.788
BBO	6.91e-08	4.9748	9.9497	21.944
DE	0	0	0	**4.29e-09**
GA	0.02062	1.7334	1.2495	15.552
P-EA	0	0	0.0001892	0.0005676
Griewank				
PSO	0.01723	0	0	0
CA	0.11082	0	0	0
FA	0.00739	0	0	0
BBO	-3.00e-16	4.79e-09	0.000234	0.037
DE	0	0	0	0
GA	0.08867	0.07382	0.02802	0.035501
P-EA	7.34e-07	3.06e-07	4.01e-07	4.6e-07
Michalewicz				
PSO	−9.4721	−18.994	−28.065	−37.35
CA	−6.1475	−8.4372	−9.1387	−11.808
FA	−9.6184	−18.979	−27.933	−36.593
BBO	−9.6552	−19.217	−28.834	−36.921
DE	−9.6602	**−19.637**	**−29.631**	−35.729
GA	−9.253	−17.242	−22.955	−30.767
P-EA	**−9.7329**	−19.507	−29.276	**−38.103**
Salomon				
PSO	**0.099873**	0.19987	0.29987	0.49987
CA	0.19988	0.60986	1.7933	3.3407
FA	0.099873	**0.099873x**	**0.099873**	**0.099873**
BBO	0.099873	0.19987	0.29987	0.39987
DE	0.099873	0.099873	0.19987	0.19987
GA	0.95488	1	0.47452	0.55258
P-EA	0.099873	0.19987	0.39987	0.49987
Schwefel				
PSO	572.45	2526.8	4263.9	6139.3
CA	−1979.5	−6443.2	−11613	-9677
FA	0.00012728	712.15	1284.6	2057.5
BBO	0.00012728	690.89	2131.9	3375.7
DE	0.00012728	**0.00025455**	**0.00038183**	**0.0005091**
GA	4157	8235.3	12464	16622
P-EA	**0.00010326**	0.0013646	139.23	504.27

PSO performs best on Sphere and Rotated Hyper-Ellipsoid. P-EA generates satisfactory results with the increase in dimensions. FA performs best on Rosenbrock and Quartic. The performance of P-EA is also good on Quartic, it improves with increase in the number of dimensions. P-EA and DE performs equally well on Michalewicz with 10, 20, and 30 dimensions, while P-EA continues to outperform with 40 dimensions as well. The graph shows that FA, GA, CA and PSO get stuck in local minima, while BBO and DE continue to converge, but P-EA successfully converge to minima. DE performs best on Schwefel while P-EA performs second-best through all the given dimensions. The convergence graph shows that GA, PSO, BBO, CA, and FA get stuck in global minima, P-EA continues to converge while DE successfully converge to minima. On Rastrigin DE performs best, P-EA second-best in initial dimensions, but P-EA surpasses the performance of other algorithms in the highest dimensions. The graph shows that PSO, FA, BBO, and GA get stuck in local minima while DE and CA continue to converge but P-EA successfully converges to minima. DE performs best on Griewank in all dimensions, while BBO performs second-best with initial dimensions, but it gets worse with the increase in dimensions. DE performs best on Ackley in all dimensions, while P-EA performance increases with the increase in number of dimensions. PSO performs second-best with dimension 10, but it drops its performance on dimension 40. P-EA improves its performance on third best average fitness values with same dimensions. FA and DE both perform best on Salomon with dimension 10. FA performs best and DE second best over the increases in dimensions. PSO and P-EA perform satisfactory throughout all dimensions.

In Schwefel, Rastrigin, Michalewicz functions where majority of efficient algorithms like FA, PSO, GA get trapped in local minima, the P-EA not only overcomes this trap but successfully converges or thrives to evolve to optimum solution. This behaviour adds credit to the authors' claim i.e. P-EA has ability to overcome the issues like stagnation, loss of diversity, and premature convergence.

5   Conclusion

In this paper, we highlight the potential of Peirce's theory by using the P-EA for mathematical optimization test functions. The comparison shows that PSO and FA generate excellent results for unimodal problems while DE, FA, and P-EA outperforms for multimodal test functions. P-EA performance is commendable on the complex multimodal functions i.e. Rastrigin and Michalewicz especially when the number of dimensions are 40. P-EA also generates competitive results on other multimodal functions. The graphs of Rastrigin and Michalewicz show that P-EA converge very quickly toward global minima as compared to other algorithms. P-EA convergence pattern portrays that it has the ability to avoid local minima trap and thrives to evolve for global minima. The experimental results depict that P-EA has the potential to solve complex problems, therefore, it should need to be explored further.

Acknowledgments. We would like to acknowledge the support of National Agriculture Robotics Lab (NARL) towards this research project.

References

1. Akhtar, J., Awais, M.M., Koshul, B.B.: Putting peirce's theory to the test: Peircean evolutionary algorithms. Trans. Charles S. Peirce Soc. Q. J. Am. Philos. **49**(2), 203–237 (2013)
2. Akhtar, J., Koshul, B.B., Awais, M.M.: A framework for evolutionary algorithms based on Charles sanders Peirce's evolutionary semiotics. Inf. Sci. **236**, 93–108 (2013)
3. Ali, M.Z., Reynolds, R.G.: Cultural algorithms: a Tabu search approach for the optimization of engineering design problems. Soft Comput. **18**(8), 1631–1644 (2014)
4. Boussaïd, I., Chatterjee, A., Siarry, P., Ahmed-Nacer, M.: Biogeography-based optimization for constrained optimization problems. Comput. Oper. Res. **39**(12), 3293–3304 (2012)
5. Gandomi, A.H., Yang, X.S., Alavi, A.H.: Mixed variable structural optimization using firefly algorithm. Comput. Struct. **89**(23–24), 2325–2336 (2011)
6. Mahmoodabadi, M., Nemati, A.: A novel adaptive genetic algorithm for global optimization of mathematical test functions and real-world problems. Eng. Sci. Technol. Int. J. **19**(4), 2002–2021 (2016)
7. Mezura-Montes, E., Velázquez-Reyes, J., Coello Coello, C.A.: A comparative study of differential evolution variants for global optimization. In: Proceedings of the 8th Annual Conference on Genetic and Evolutionary Computation, pp. 485–492 (2006)
8. Salomon, R.: Re-evaluating genetic algorithm performance under coordinate rotation of benchmark functions. a survey of some theoretical and practical aspects of genetic algorithms. BioSystems **39**(3), 263–278 (1996)
9. Vanaret, C., Gotteland, J.B., Durand, N., Alliot, J.M.: Certified global minima for a benchmark of difficult optimization problems. arXiv preprint arXiv:2003.09867 (2020)
10. Vesterstrom, J., Thomsen, R.: A comparative study of differential evolution, particle swarm optimization, and evolutionary algorithms on numerical benchmark problems. In: Proceedings of the 2004 Congress on Evolutionary Computation (IEEE Cat. No. 04TH8753), vol. 2, pp. 1980–1987. IEEE (2004)
11. Yang, X.-S.: Firefly algorithms for multimodal optimization. In: Watanabe, O., Zeugmann, T. (eds.) SAGA 2009. LNCS, vol. 5792, pp. 169–178. Springer, Heidelberg (2009). https://doi.org/10.1007/978-3-642-04944-6_14
12. Yang, X.S.: Nature-inspired optimization algorithms. Academic Press, Cambridge (2020)

Medical Recommendation System Based on Daily Clinical Reports: A Proposed NLP Approach for Emergency Departments

Regina Sousa[ID], Daniela Oliveira[ID], Dalila Durães[✉][ID], Cristiana Neto[ID], and José Machado[ID]

ALGORITMI Centre, University of Minho, Braga, Portugal
{regina.sousa,daniela.oliveira,dalila.duraes,
cristiana.neto}@algoritmi.uminho.pt, jmac@di.uminho.pt

Abstract. The operational management of an emergency department (ED) requires more attention from hospital administration since it can have a global impact on the institution's management, increasing the probability of adverse events and worsening hospital expenses. Effective management of an ED potentially results in fewer hospitalisations after an ED admission. The purpose of the present study is to perform a multi-class prediction based on: a) structured data and unstructured data in an ED episode; and b) unstructured data generated during the inpatient event, just after the ED episode. The designed prediction model will lay the foundation for an ED Decision Support System based on symptoms and principal diagnoses.

Keywords: Emergency health department · Text mining · Natural language processing · Recommendation systems

1 Introduction

The number of people who access the ED daily has become a substantial global health problem [9]. Despite debates on the causes of this phenomenon, there are still significant problems in conceiving successful and targeted solutions [11]. The accumulation of people in the ED can occur due to three factors: 1) volume of patients waiting to be seen; 2) delays in the evaluation or treatment of patients who are already in the emergency room; and 3) impediments for patients to leave the emergency room after finishing the treatment [9]. Thus, the causes of excess people in ED differ depending on the three factors. However, it is necessary to foresee these causes and maintain the trustworthiness of the system response.

The use of information systems in the health field started a few decades ago. However, there are still many issues that have not yet been addressed. Also, platforms for health service increased her great importance because of the Health Information Systems. Health Recommendation Systems (HRS) are a promising

M. Bramer and F. Stahl (Eds.): SGAI-AI 2022, LNAI 13652, pp. 315–320, 2022.
https://doi.org/10.1007/978-3-031-21441-7_24

alternative to providing tools to assist physicians in diagnosing diseases. For the ED services, the HRS are proposed as complementary instruments in the decision-making procedures. Furthermore, HRS improve the usability of technologies and relieve information overabundance and process duplication [10].

The diagnostic coding system is the International Classification of Diseases of the World Health Organisation. The last two revisions, the 9th revision, Clinical Modification (ICD-9-CM) and the 10th revision, Clinical Modification (ICD-10-CM), were the most significant transformation in health care coding. In each ICD-10 code, the space available is seven characters, an increase of two characters compared to the five available in the ICD-9. The nearly 70,000 diagnostic codes available in the ICD-10 provide much greater detail than the 14,500 codes available in the ICD-9 [2].

The present study aims to conduct a multi-class prediction based on structured data and unstructured data in an ED episode and on the unstructured data generated during the inpatient event just after the ED episode. Examples of structured data are biometric, demographic and Complementary Diagnostic and Therapeutic Procedures (CDTP) requests information. Examples of unstructured data are diaries and medical notes [17].

The paper is organised into four sections. Section 2 has related work related studies discussed HRS, Natural Language Processing (NLP), Text Mining, and classification. Section 3 presents materials and methods, and Sect. 4 shows the discussion and conclusion about the proposed architecture. Thuis section, summarizes all preceding themes, presenting the key findings and suggesting future research prospects.

2 Related Work

Over the last few years, research involving recommendation systems in the healthcare field has attracted increasing attention. Thus, some works have been developed in this scope, with different focuses, in different contexts and using different machine learning techniques.

Focusing on the CDTP topic, there are few studies specifically oriented to this area, showing that there is still room for further research. In [14], the authors describe the development of a personalized clinical order decision recommender. The authors concluded that the study shows how an automated system may be able to infer what clinical orders and order sets a physician will need by determining the patient's context in the EHR through an algorithm. Regarding the data used in this study, it includes patient history, lab results, diagnoses and orders, but the study does not mention the use of unstructured data.

Furthermore, there are many studies in the literature that refer to the use of natural language processing in the healthcare field, as we can see in [5,6,12,13]. Its use in the context of HRS arises mainly to deal with unstructured data that are relevant to the classification process.

In [4], the authors describe the implementation of a natural language processing algorithm to detect recommendations for additional imaging, including discharged ED patients in the study. This research demonstrates the great challenges inherent in natural language processing algorithms.

Further studies reveal that deep learning-based NLP is becoming more widely accepted, including in the medical sector. Clinical NLP is beginning to see the effects of Deep Learning (DL), which is expanding quickly [16].

The studies found in this literature research also show the importance of using text mining in hospital information systems, as can be analyzed in [3, 7]. Concretely, the authors in [8] used text mining methods to process data from early ED patient records using the SOAP framework, and predict future hospitalizations and discharges. They concluded that the Nu-Support Vector Machine was the text mining method with the best overall performance.

Nowadays some more modern techniques are beginning to be implemented in HRS. Thus, neural networks [1] or DL [15] provide high-quality customized suggestions.

3   Materials and Methods

The input data for the artefact to be developed refers to a Portuguese University Hospital Center with a high dimension and importance in the region where it is located. In the context of the ED, the Internal Medicine (IM) specialty has a key role in the management of hospitalisations compared to other clinical areas. The focus of this study will be the episodes of ED in IM that led to consequent inpatient admissions and their requested CDTP, as well as clinical annotations and diaries.

3.1   Materials: Data Sources and Data Collection

The time horizon of the data collection will be for the last 20 years, from the year 2002 to the year 2022. Two datasets inserted in this time frame were crossed, where one of them contains all ED admissions and the other dataset only contains inpatient episodes. After joining these two datasets, two other restrictions were applied, in which only adult patients (over 18 years of age) and urgent admissions (admissions that were not planned) were considered. At the end of this processing and cross-referencing, the original dataset will have a sample of 62,101 records about inpatient episodes from ED episodes. Based on the original dataset, CDTP, clinical diaries, and annotations datasets were also collected. Note that the CDTP data was divided into exams and clinical analyses over the last 20 years. To arrive at reliable datasets, outliers were removed, and this required the calculation of the median over the aggregation of exams and analyses. Figure 1 illustrate the data collection workflow to arrive at the datasets that will be the target of the following process phases.

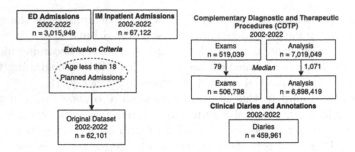

Fig. 1. Data collection approach from multiple Portuguese HIS.

3.2   Methods: Proposed Architecture

The proposed architecture consists mostly of 3 main phases, illustrated in Fig. 2. The first is the data preprocessing, then the classification model and finally the recommendation system. The following paragraphs will briefly describe the phases above enunciated.

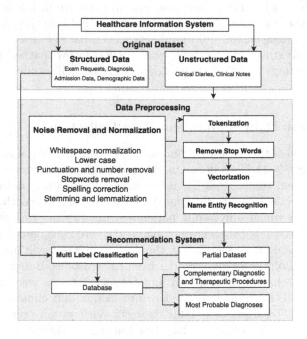

Fig. 2. Complete architecture proposal.

Data Preprocessing: After obtaining the data, and given the fact that they are unstructured (free text) and are in Portuguese they need to go through an exhaustive preprocessing phase. In short, we intend to use NLP techniques in order to obtain a vectorized, structured and classified dataset (through Named Entity Recognition (NER)). For example, from words or sets of words, classify if it is a symptom: "dor de cabeça (headache) - symptom".

Recommendation System: The intention is to use a pre-trained model for biomedical data, such as the Bidirectional Encoder Representations from Transformers for Biomedical Text Mining (BioBERT) and the Biomedical Entity Recognition and Normalisation (BERN) pre-trained language models. As illustrated in the Fig. 2, the main goal is to obtain a recommendation system that, given a set of symptoms and demographic data (age, sex, diseases, ...), suggests CDTP and a list of the most likely diagnoses for the particular patient.

4   Discussion and Conclusions

This study's related work revealed a scarcity of hybrid prediction systems in hospital environments. Unstructured clinical text, which can be a valuable source of information for a variety of healthcare reasons, continues to receive insufficient awareness at the present day. The improvement of pre-trained models for the Portuguese language is another aim of this research. Future work will include the development of a Python algorithm capable of classifying models and processing unstructured data using a multi-label approach. The best results will be used to develop an Emergency Department recommendation system for both predicting Complementary Diagnostic and Therapeutic Procedures requests and the most likely diagnosis.

Acknowledgements. This work has been supported by FCT-Fundação para a Ciência e Tecnologia within the R&D Units Project Scope: UIDB/00319/2020.

References

1. Christakopoulou, K., Beutel, A., Li, R., Jain, S., Chi, E.H.: Q&r: a two-stage approach toward interactive recommendation. In: Proceedings of the 24th ACM SIGKDD International Conference on Knowledge Discovery & Data Mining, pp. 139–148 (2018)
2. Columbo, J.A., et al.: Validating publicly available crosswalks for translating ICD-9 to ICD-10 diagnosis codes for cardiovascular outcomes research. Cir. Cardiovasc. Qual. Outcomes **11**(10), e004782 (2018)
3. van Dijk, W.B.: Text-mining in electronic healthcare records can be used as efficient tool for screening and data collection in cardiovascular trials: a multicenter validation study. J. Clin. Epidemiol. **132**, 97–105 (2021)
4. Dutta, S., Long, W.J., Brown, D.F., Reisner, A.T.: Automated detection using natural language processing of radiologists recommendations for additional imaging of incidental findings. Ann. Emergency Med. **62**(2), 162–169 (2013)
5. Fernandes, M., et al.: Predicting intensive care unit admission among patients presenting to the emergency department using machine learning and natural language processing. PloS ONE **15**(3), e0229331 (2020)

6. Khurshid, S., et al.: Cohort design and natural language processing to reduce bias in electronic health records research. NPJ Digit. Med. **5**(1), 1–14 (2022)
7. Kim, J.C., Chung, K.: Associative feature information extraction using text mining from health big data. Wireless Pers. Commun. **105**(2), 691–707 (2019)
8. Lucini, F.R., et al.: Text mining approach to predict hospital admissions using early medical records from the emergency department. Int. J. Med. Inf. **100**, 1–8 (2017)
9. Morley, C., Unwin, M., Peterson, G.M., Stankovich, J., Kinsman, L.: Emergency department crowding: a systematic review of causes, consequences and solutions. PLoS ONE **13**(8), e0203316 (2018)
10. Pincay, J., Terán, L., Portmann, E.: Health recommender systems: a state-of-the-art review. In: 2019 Sixth International Conference on eDemocracy & eGovernment (ICEDEG), pp. 47–55. IEEE (2019)
11. Sezgin, E., Özkan, S.: A systematic literature review on health recommender systems. In: 2013 E-Health and Bioengineering Conference (EHB), pp. 1–4. IEEE (2013)
12. Sheikhalishahi, S., Miotto, R., Dudley, J.T., Lavelli, A., Rinaldi, F., Osmani, V., et al.: Natural language processing of clinical notes on chronic diseases: systematic review. JMIR Med. Inf. **7**(2), e12239 (2019)
13. Turchioe, M.R., Volodarskiy, A., Pathak, J., Wright, D.N., Tcheng, J.E., Slotwiner, D.: Systematic review of current natural language processing methods and applications in cardiology. Heart **108**(12), 909–916 (2022)
14. Wang, J.X., Sullivan, D.K., Wells, A.C., Chen, J.H.: Clinicnet: machine learning for personalized clinical order set recommendations. JAMIA Open **3**(2), 216–224 (2020)
15. Wu, G., Luo, K., Sanner, S., Soh, H.: Deep language-based critiquing for recommender systems. In: Proceedings of the 13th ACM Conference on Recommender Systems, pp. 137–145 (2019)
16. Wu, S., et al.: Deep learning in clinical natural language processing: a methodical review. J. Am. Med. Inf. Assoc. **27**(3), 457–470 (2020)
17. Zhang, D., Yin, C., Zeng, J., Yuan, X., Zhang, P.: Combining structured and unstructured data for predictive models: a deep learning approach. BMC Med. Inf. Decis. Making **20**(1), 1–11 (2020)

MentaLex: A Mental Processes Lexicon Based on the Essay Dataset

Francisco S. Marcondes[1], Maria Aráujo Barbosa[1], Ricardo Queiroz[2], Luis Brito[2], Adelino Gala[3], and Dalila Durães[1(✉)]

[1] Algoritmi Centre, University of Minho, Braga, Portugal
{francisco.marcondes,dalila.duraes}@algoritmi.uminho.pt,
pg42844@alunos.uminho.pt
[2] Portucalense University, Porto, Portugal
{44830,44881}@alunos.upt.pt
[3] Digimedia, University of Aveiro, Aveiro, Portugal
adelino@ua.pt

Abstract. Considering that the performance of personality predictors are not consistently increasing throughout the years, as an alternative, the idea was to provide big5 personality traits lexicon based on the Essay dataset. The weight of relevance for every trait of each word is calculated by tf/idf on the words in the Essay dataset. However, it was eventually realized that three personalities wordset were overlapped requiring a change of course. The research changed the underlying model from big5 to Vann Joines' mental processes as it appear to suit better with the empirical findings. The resulting lexicon dataset is composed with 3432 commonly used words and 3639 avoided prone words for each mental process. The commonly used words are capable of covering 81% of the Twitter Personality dataset.

Keywords: Mental processes · Lexicon · Personality · NLP

1 Introduction

Personality is an important aspect of life and plays a decisive role in how people behave in different scenarios, determining patterns of thinking, acting, personal and social individuality. These aspects can be seen in the writing or speaking style, and in other aspects of an individual social life [1]. Like language, writing is also something unique in every person. In another perspective, an analysis of the frequency of words can identify letters written by soldiers, the speeches of politicians and also identify the authors of literary works [2].

The patterns that identify an individual are a qualitative metric to define personality such as Allport's theory of traits, the 16-factor Cattell's model [3], Vann Joines' mental traits [4], the Myers-Briggs Type Indicator (MBTI) [5] and the Big Five (big5) [6]. This paper is centered in big5 and Joines' mental processes.

© The Author(s), under exclusive license to Springer Nature Switzerland AG 2022
M. Bramer and F. Stahl (Eds.): SGAI-AI 2022, LNAI 13652, pp. 321–326, 2022.
https://doi.org/10.1007/978-3-031-21441-7_25

2   Related Work

The current state of the art in big5 personality trait detection can be illustrated by Table 1. Similar numbers are presented in other surveys [7–9] and papers [10–12]. In short, the average scores ranges on 60% except for Ren *et al.* [13] that appears as an outlier with an strategy based on BERT with SenticNet on CNN (it was not possible to easily find the code for reproduction).

Table 1. The state of the art in personality detection. For full references about the mentioned studies see [9]

Authors	Opn	Con	Ext	Agr	Neu	AVG	Proposals
Xue *et al.*	63.16	57.49	58.91	57.49	59.51	59.312	GLOVE and BiGRU model
Ren *et al.*	**80.35**	**80.23**	**79.94**	**80.30**	**80.14**	**80.192**	BERT with SenticNet on CNN
Ramezani *et al.*	56.30	59.18	64.25	60.31	61.14	60.24	HAN based on: term frequency vector, ontology, enriched ontology, LSA and BiLSTM.
Wang *et al.*	64.80	59.10	60	57.70	63	60.92	Personality GCN
Jiang *et al.*	65.86	58.55	60.62	59.72	61.04	61.158	Five models developed: ABCNN, ABLSTM, HAN , BERT, RoBERTa and BERT + RoBERTa
Mehta *et al.*	64.6	59.2	60	58.8	60.5	60.62	SVN + MLP
Kazameini *et al.*	62.09	57.84	59.30	56.52	59.39	59.028	SVM
Majumder *et al.*	62.68	57.30	58.09	56.71	59.38	58.832	Word2Vec and CNN
Tighe *et al.*	61.95	56.04	55.75	57.54	58.31	57.918	PCA

The Essays dataset [2] is being studied for 20 years and the prediction values have not yet increased consistently [8]. This paper approach is then a step back and, instead of trying to develop a new predictor, to build a lexicon. This is inspired by the EmoLex [14,15] that can be considered a gold standard for emotion detection and has been used for around 10 years with more than 1000 citations on each paper. It is expected that a lexicon as such may provide, at least, useful insights for advancing the state of the art.

In 2010, Tal Yarkoni [16] conducted a thorough examination of the personalities and words used in 694 blogs posts. He performs a big5 questionnaire to the authors in order to categorise their personalities. The outcomes included a summary of the relationships between the big5 and the 20 words that more represent each trait. However, there is no information regarding a potential lexicon developed from the study results. Since then, no significant research on the creation of personality lexicons has been found.

3   Methodology

The Essays dataset [2] is composed of 2468 open topic essays written by people whose personality was already assessed. Therefore, together with each essay there are five personality traits (also called big5 as proposed by [6]) binary flagged.

A big5 assessment is made through a form from which the subject chooses a set of words that are considered most related to himself or herself [6]. Analogously, the hypothesis explored in this paper is that, the personality trait of a person would be revealed by the words chosen for creating a text. For testing this hypothesis, the tf/idf *cf.* [17] value is computed for each lemmatized word on each personality trait, excluding those whose tf/idf value is 0.0. This value presents a numerical statistic that reflect how important a word is to each personality trait in Essay dataset. That procedure, shown in Algorithm 1, results in a lexicon with the words commonly chosen and not used words by each personality.

Algorithm 1. Meaningful Words per Trait.

Require: Essay_Dataset ← **pipe**([lemmatize | remove stop words | standardize in lowercase | extract
    adjectives, verbs and nouns]).
  procedure GETWORDSFOR(trait)
    trait_texts ← **retrieveTextFor**(trait, Essay_Dataset)
    TF/IDF ← **computeTF/IDF**(trait_texts)
    for word, tf/idf **in** TF/IDF **do**
      if tf/idf > 0 **then**
        Words ←+ word
      end if
    end for
    return Words
  end procedure
  for trait **in** big5 **do**
    Used_Lexicon ←+ **getWordsFor**(trait)
    Avoided_Lexicon ←+ **getWordsFor**(big5 - trait)
  end for

The deducing hypothesis is that a set of words is meaningful enough to provide at least a personality insight. For that claim to be true, the identified words shall be "insistently" used on different texts as a sort of "trail". For testing that deduced hypothesis, the Twitter Personality dataset [18] with 9879 tweets is used to verify how in-depth the resulting lexicon is. That dataset was chosen because in little texts the probability of a word happening is reduced compared to larger texts. The use of the lexicon for classification lies outside the scope for this paper.

4 Results and Discussion

By the assessment made upon the Essays dataset it was not possible to find all the 5 personality traits. It was possible to distinguish agreeableness and neuroticism with almost disjoint word sets. However, the word-set for extroversion, openness and conscientiousness are overlapping (despite being almost disjoint with the other two). That experimental result may suggest that these three traits may be considered one when personality is abducted from open topic essays. An alternative cognition theory that suits better with these findings is the one proposed by [4] called "Personality Adaptations" (the relation between big5 and Personality Adaptations is presented in [6]).

Personality Adaptations theory suggests the existence of six mental processes, three of them primary and the other three secondary. Each person has at least one primary process and may or may not have a secondary one [4]. What is suggested is that the primary processes that are being revealed when someone writes a text. Accepting that suggestion, adapting from the Personality Adaptations theory, the primary processes would be: paranoid, schizoid and neuroticism. For a reference, the terms associated with the respective mental process and the unrelated words are presented as word-clouds in Figure 1, constructed directly by calculating the tf-idf value described in Algorithm 1.

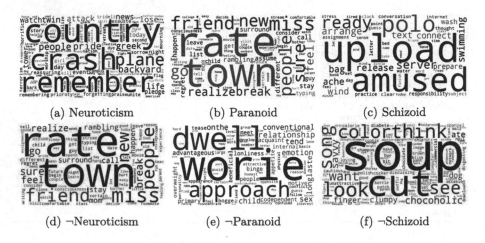

| (a) Neuroticism | (b) Paranoid | (c) Schizoid |
| (d) ¬Neuroticism | (e) ¬Paranoid | (f) ¬Schizoid |

Fig. 1. Word-cloud that includes both the words connected to each mental process and the words that are not.

As can be noticed the number of words related to each mental process is actually small. To evaluate its suitability of the lexicon, the Twitter Personality dataset is used to verify how many tweets are composed by words that are in the lexicon (coverage analysis). The generated lexicon named MentaLex, composed by 276 words, presented a coverage of 69% in that dataset. The frequency of the words of the lexicon in the Twitter dataset was within an suitable distribution. As an attempt to increase the coverage the wordset, synonyms were retrieved resulting in a dataset with 3432 words covering 81% of the dataset. That coverage is considered sufficient due to the tweets' peculiarities; *i.e.* very short unstructured texts with misspelled words and slangs, eventually, with only a link or emoji. As an analogous procedure, upon the 316 words found to be avoided, their synonyms was gathered resulting into a lexicon of 3639 words.

The MentaLex lexicon and related source-code files are available in the GitHub at https://github.com/maria85290/MentaLex_. For a summary, the lexicon characteristics are presented in Tables 2a and 2b.

Table 2. Summary of MentaLex Characteristics

(a) Summary of commonly used words Lexicon

	words	synonym	words & synonym	%	nouns	verbs	adj.
Paranoid	87	1003	1090	32%	523	443	124
Schizoid	53	762	815	24%	407	335	75
Neuroticism	136	1391	1527	44%	793	560	174
Total	276	3156	3432	100%	1723	1338	373
Coverage	69%	–	81%	–	–	–	–

(b) Summary of commonly used words Lexicon

	words	synonym	words & synonym	%	nouns	verbs	adj.
¬Paranoid	85	766	851	23%	399	125	327
¬Schizoid	144	1554	1698	47%	827	235	636
¬Neuroticism	87	1003	1090	30%	523	126	449
Total	316	3323	3639	100%	1749	482	1408

5 Conclusion

The current study examines how individual personality traits connect to writing style and present an alternative to the commonly approach of personality detection using predictors. The big5 and Personality Adaptations theories served as the study's scientific guidance in this aspect. The results allowed to identify three different traits. Based on the Personality Adaptations theory, the authors identified the primary processes: paranoid, schizoid and neuroticism. The final generated lexicon contained 3432 commonly used words and 3639 avoiding prone words for each mental process (both including noun, verb, and adjectives).

For future works, it occurred to the authors that the verb tenses may embed additional personality information, therefore a reassessment but without lemmatization may be worthful. In addition, there was a glimpse that there could also be information in the stop-words, therefore, perhaps, an assessment using n-grams, therefore preserving some syntactic information, may also help in improving the lexicon. Also, another future work is a statistical validation of the data.

Acknowledgments. This work is supported by: FCT - Fundação para a Ciência e Tecnologia within the RD Units Project Scope: UIDB/00319/2020.

References

1. Feizi Derakhshi, A.R., et al.: The state-of-the-art in text-based automatic personality prediction, vol. 10 (2021)
2. Pennebaker, J., King, L.: Linguistic styles: Language use as an individual difference. J. Personality Soc. Psychol. **77**(6), 1296-312 (2000)

3. Preoţiuc-Pietro, D., Carpenter, J., Ungar, L.: Personality driven differences in paraphrase preference. In: Proceedings of the Second Workshop on NLP and Computational Social Science, (Vancouver, Canada), pp. 17–26, Association for Computational Linguistics (2017)
4. Joines, V., Stewart, I.: Personality Adaptations: A New Guide to Human Understanding in Psychotherapy and Counselling. Lifespace (2002)
5. Briggs, K.C.: Myers-Briggs Type Indicator. Press, Consulting Psychologists (1987)
6. McCrae, R.R., John, O.P.: An introduction to the five-factor model and its applications. J. Pers. **60**, 175–215 (1992)
7. Kerz, E., Qiao, Y., Zanwar, S., Wiechmann, D.: Pushing on personality detection from verbal behavior: A transformer meets text contours of psycholinguistic features. arXiv preprint arXiv:2204.04629 (2022)
8. Mehta, Y., Majumder, N., Gelbukh, A., Cambria, E.: Recent trends in deep learning based personality detection. Artif. Intell. Rev. **53**(4), 2313–2339 (2019). https://doi.org/10.1007/s10462-019-09770-z
9. Feizi-Derakhshi, A.-R., et al.: Text-based automatic personality prediction: A bibliographic review. (2021)
10. Sun, X., Liu, B., Cao, J., Luo, J., Shen, X.: Who am i? personality detection based on deep learning for texts, In: 2018 IEEE International Conference on Communications (ICC), pp. 1–6, IEEE (2018)
11. Arambašic, L.., Bicanic, M., Rajic, F.: Essays are a fickle thing. Text Analysis and Retrieval Course Project Reports, p. 1 (2021)
12. Ramezani, M., Feizi-Derakhshi, M.-R., Balafar, M.-A.: Text-based automatic personality prediction using kgrat-net; a knowledge graph attention network classifier. arXiv preprint arXiv:2205.13780 (2022)
13. Ren, Z., Shen, Q., Diao, X., Xu, H.: A sentiment-aware deep learning approach for personality detection from text. Inform. Process. Manage. **58**(3), 102532 (2021)
14. Mohammad, S.M., Turney, P.D.: Crowdsourcing a word-emotion association lexicon. Comput. Intell. **29**(3), 436–465 (2013)
15. Mohammad, S., Turney, P.: Emotions evoked by common words and phrases: Using mechanical turk to create an emotion lexicon. In: Proceedings of the NAACL HLT 2010 Workshop on Computational Approaches to Analysis and Generation of Emotion in Text, pp. 26–34 (2010)
16. Yarkoni, T.: Personality in 100,000 words: A large-scale analysis of personality and word use among bloggers. J. Res. Personality **44**(3), 363–373 (2010)
17. Jurafsky, D., Martin, J.: Speech and Language Processing: An Introduction to Natural Language Processing, Computational Linguistics, and Speech Recognition. Prentice Hall series in artificial intelligence, Pearson Prentice Hall (2009)
18. Ahmad, N., Siddique, J.: Personality assessment using twitter tweets. Proc. Comput. Sci. **112**, 1964–1973 (2017)

Credit Card Fraud Using Adversarial Attacks

Hafya Ullah, Aysha Thahsin Zahir Ismail, Lakshmi Babu Saheer$^{(\boxtimes)}$, and Mahdi Maktabdar Oghaz

Anglia Ruskin University, Cambridge, UK
{az303,hu142}@student.aru.ac.uk,
{lakshmi.babu-saheer,mahdi.maktabdar}@aru.ac.uk

Abstract. Banks lose billions to fraudulent activities every year, affecting their revenue and customers. The most common type of financial fraud is Credit Card Fraud. The key challenge in designing a model for credit card fraud detection is its maintenance. It is pivotal to note that fraudsters are constantly improving their tactics to bypass fraud detection checks. Several fraud detection methods for identifying fraudulent credit card transactions have been developed. However, in order to further improve on the existing strategies, this paper investigates the domain of adversarial attacks for credit card fraud. The goal of this work is to show that adversarial attacks can be implemented on tabular data and investigate if machine learning approaches can get affected by such attacks. We evaluate the performance of adversarial samples generated by the LowProfool algorithm in deceiving the classifier.

Keywords: Adversarial attacks on tabular data · Financial fraud detection · Machine learning · Lowprofool algorithm

1 Introduction

The 2021 Nilson report[1] stated that financial industries will experience fraud loss amounting to 408.50 billion dollars over the next decade. In most situations, credit card data is leaked due to phishing of financial websites where the user is unaware of the data leak. Machine learning classification algorithms are considered to be state-of-the-art techniques to identify legitimate and fraudulent transactions with greater precision and accuracy. The user spending pattern is obtained from the available transaction data that can be analyzed by machine learning classification algorithms to identify actual transactions made by the customer [1]. It is also critical to consider that the fraudsters are persistent and consistently upgrade their techniques and sophisticated activities with the aim of bypassing the fraud detection systems. This is widely referred to as concept drift [2]. This study aims to raise awareness of fraud detection in the

---

[1] https://nilsonreport.com/mention/1515/1link/.

© The Author(s), under exclusive license to Springer Nature Switzerland AG 2022
M. Bramer and F. Stahl (Eds.): SGAI-AI 2022, LNAI 13652, pp. 327–332, 2022.
https://doi.org/10.1007/978-3-031-21441-7_26

financial sector by testing the robustness of machine learning algorithms against unforeseen adversarial attacks. The effectiveness of machine learning algorithms is studied on an imbalanced credit card transaction dataset by applying a novel Synthetic Minority Oversampling Technique (SMOTE) with majority undersampling. Furthermore, this paper evaluates the success rate of adversarial examples in deceiving the classifier from making the right prediction.

2 Related Work

Khatri et al. [5] analyzed performance metrics outside the accuracy of the algorithm when dealing with imbalanced datasets and adopting sampling approaches for obtaining satisfactory results. Wang et al. [6] suggests outlier detection techniques can be a good workaround to address imbalanced datasets issues in fraud detection studies. A recent study by Tanouz et al. [1] implements different machine learning algorithms including decision tree, Naive Bayes, Random Forest, and Logistic Regression for fraud detection in credit cards. Undersampling and oversampling techniques were used in preprocessing stage to improve the performance of their algorithm. Many recent studies [7–9] suggest numerous possibilities of machine learning approaches in developing fraud detection mechanisms. Since adversarial attacks came into light [3], it has become a subject of major importance in the machine learning domain. While it has been used mostly for image recognition tasks using Deep Neural Networks(DNN), a recent paper by Carlini and Wagner [10] discussed the use of adversarial machine learning in audio recognition. Ballet et al. [12] coined the idea of implementing adversarial attacks on a tabular domain during the time when adversarial approaches were popular in testing the robustness of image classifiers. This study initiated the research on the impact of unobservable adversarial attacks on organized tabular data.

Ghamizi et al. [15] studied failures (false negative) of the state-of-the-art techniques fraud detection techniques to generate unobservable adversarial samples. This research addressed the usefulness of "Random Forest Attack" and "Gradient-Based attack" and concluded that these state-of-the-art approaches were ineffective to generate relevant adversarial samples for any chosen domain. The main differentiating factor of this research from the existing literature is generating adversarial samples on a highly imbalanced financial transaction dataset by incorporating suitable data preprocessing strategies. The novelty of this study also includes the use of Synthetic Minority Oversampling Technique (SMOTE) with majority undersampling to overcome data imbalance issues. It is important to look at the imbalanced dataset as most of the real-world datasets in this domain are highly imbalanced with very few real samples of positive fraudulent cases of credit card usage. The adversaries are generated using the LowProfool algorithm instead of conventional adversarial generation techniques. LowProfool is implemented using the Adversarial Robustness Toolbox(ART), thereby generating adversaries constrained to the chosen domain.

3   Methodology

3.1   Dataset

This project utilizes publicly available transactional credit card data sourced from several European card companies [15]. The data set contains online credit transactions within a 48-h time frame. The dataset is extremely imbalanced where the total number of fraudulent transactions constitutes approximately 0.17% of total transactions. The actual features in the dataset are hidden to ensure the confidentiality of individual card owners. The dataset represents features V1, V2, ...V27, V28 obtained via Principal Component Analysis (PCA) transformation. The known features in the dataset include time and amount of transactions. The class feature represents the category of each transaction; 0 represents a legit transaction and 1 denotes a fraudulent transaction. The initial data analysis shows that the dataset contains 284807 transactions with no null values however there were 1081 duplicate rows that were removed resulting in 283726 unique transactions. The dataset is extremely unbalanced with only 473 fraudulent transactions in the entire dataset. The correlation among the variables is represented using a heat map shown in Fig. 1. The features which are highly correlated include V10, V12, V14, V16, and V17. These values were capped by efficiently replacing extreme values with other close values of the variable by determining the minimum and maximum range using the mean and standard deviation. This project adopts Synthetic Minority Oversampling Technique (SMOTE) [15] which creates data samples from the minority fraud class in our dataset along with an undersampling strategy to reduce the number of data samples belonging to the legitimate class. This can eliminate the bias and noise induced by a SMOTE-only approach.

3.2   Classification Algorithms

This project investigates state-of-the-art machine learning algorithms including Logistic Regression, K-Nearest Neighbours, and Random Forest for credit card fraud detection. Figure 2 illustrates Logistic Regression's feature ranks measured using the "correlation coefficient". The results indicate that V2, V4, and V11 have positive importance scores. The K-Nearest Neighbour algorithm in this study uses Euclidean distance to measure similarities. The K value is set to 5 empirically. Random forest is usually less sensitive to changes made in training data and reduces the overfitting of the model to a greater extent [9]. Figure 3 demonstrates the feature importance plot generated by the random forest classifier model. The most important features are V17, V12, V14, V10, V11, and V3.

3.3   Adversarial Attack on Tabular Data

Adversarial data samples are generated using an adversarial algorithm whose primary goal is to create a data sample similar to the input sample by making

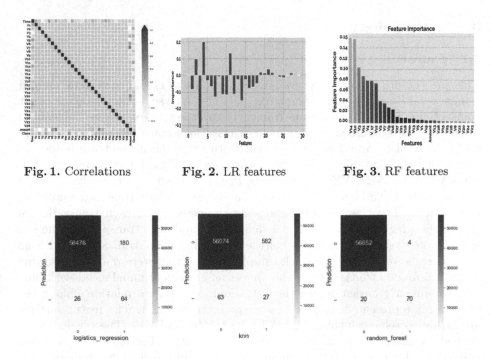

Fig. 1. Correlations   **Fig. 2.** LR features   **Fig. 3.** RF features

Fig. 4. Confusion matrix indicates algorithm performance across different classifiers

infinitesimal perturbations which lead to misclassification. This study employs evasion attacks [17] to generate adversarial samples on tabular data by inducing minimal changes to the input fed to the classifier thereby obtaining an incorrectly classified result. The adversarial generation by Lowprofool revolves around the computation of a feature importance vector for each input sample by computing lp-norm. The parameter p of lp-norm is set as 2, thereby computing a Euclidean distance while generating the feature importance vector [12]. The manipulated input sample are steered towards the opposite target class ensuring that manipulations are induced into less relevant features and are unobservable by the fraud detection system. The reliability of an adversarial attack is often evaluated using the metric referred to as success rate, which is the percentage of incorrect predictions.

4   Experimental Results and Observation

Model performance is tested with three different classifiers. Table 1 shows how novel SMOTE with undersampling had improved the fraud class performance for Logistic Regression. The overall system performance is shown in Table 2. Figure 4 illustrates the confusion matrix generated for Logistic Regression, K-nearest neighbors, and Random Forest algorithms. It is observed that Random Forest exhibits better results compared to K-nearest neighbors and Logistic Regression. The Random Forest algorithm correctly predicts 56652 legal transactions and 70 illegal transactions. The second-best performer is the Logistic Regression detecting 64 illegal transactions. The LowProFool algorithm was able to mislead the classifier with a high fooling rate. The results of the original prediction were compared with the prediction made using the adversarial samples. Table 3 shows the performance of the Logistic Regression algorithm on adversarial samples for the fraud class. Result demonstrates that many data samples that were initially classified as illegal transactions (1) are converted to legitimate transactions (0) with the help of the lowprofool approach.

Table 1. Impact of SMOTE sampling on model performance

Class	Precision	Recall	F-score
1 (fraud)	0.15	0.63	0.24
0 (legal)	1.00	0.99	1.00
1(fraud) - SMOTE	0.84	0.58	0.68
0 (legal) - SMOTE	0.99	0.99	1.00

Table 2. Model performance metrics

Metrics	LR	KNN	RF
Precision	0.9980	0.9972	0.9994
Recall	0.9932	0.9856	0.9995
F1-score	0.9954	0.9912	0.9994
Accuracy	0.9932	0.9856	0.9995
AUC	0.8246	0.6211	0.8832

Table 3. Performance metrics with adversarial samples for class 1 (fraud)

Model	Precision	Recall	F1score
Real samples	0.15	0.63	0.24
Lowprofool adversarial samples	0.0098	0.0017	0.0039

5   Conclusion

This study aims to investigate the robustness of machine learning algorithms against unforeseen adversarial attacks in credit cards. It evaluates the performance of Logistic Regression, k-nearest neighbors, and random forest algorithms on a credit card transaction dataset to identify illegal transactions followed by generating unobservable adversarial samples by making infinitesimal changes to input and eluding the classifier with a high success rate. Primary results can be utilized to evaluate the robustness of classification algorithms and the emerging need for suitable defensive techniques in financial fraud detection models.

References

1. Sailusha, R., Gnaneswar, V., Ramesh, R., Rao, G.: Credit card fraud detection using machine learning. In: 2020 4th International Conference on Intelligent Computing And Control Systems (ICICCS), pp. 1264–1270 (2020)
2. Widmer, G., Kubat, M.: Learning in the presence of concept drift and hidden contexts. Mach. Learn. **23**, 69–101 (1996)
3. Abdallah, A., Maarof, M., Zainal, A.: Fraud detection system: a survey. J. Netw. Comput.Appl. **68**, 90–113 (2016)
4. Awoyemi, J., Adetunmbi, A., Oluwadare, S.: Credit card fraud detection using machine learning techniques: A comparative analysis. In: 2017 International Conference on Computing Networking And Informatics (ICCNI), pp. 1–9 (2017)
5. Khatri, S., Arora, A., Agrawal, A.: Supervised machine learning algorithms for credit card fraud detection: a comparison. In: 2020 10th International Conference on Cloud Computing, Data Science Engineering (Confluence), pp. 680–683 (2020)
6. Wang, H., Bah, M., Hammad, M.: Progress in outlier detection techniques: a survey. IEEE Access. **7**, 107964–108000 (2019)
7. Papernot, N., et al.: Technical report on the cleverhans v2. 1.0 adversarial examples library. ArXiv Preprint ArXiv:1610.00768 (2016)
8. Azhan, M., Meraj, S.: Credit card fraud detection using machine learning and deep learning techniques. In: 2020 3rd International Conference on Intelligent Sustainable Systems (ICISS), pp. 514–518 (2020)
9. Gupta, A., Raghav, A., Srivastava, S.: Comparative study of machine learning algorithms for Portuguese bank data. In: 2021 International Conference on Computing, Communication, And Intelligent Systems (ICCCIS), pp. 401–406 (2021)
10. Cheng, M., Yi, J., Chen, P., Zhang, H., Hsieh, C.: Seq2sick: evaluating the robustness of sequence-to-sequence models with adversarial examples. Proc. AAAI Conf. Artif. Intell. **34**, 3601–3608 (2020)
11. Huang, S., Papernot, N., Goodfellow, I., Duan, Y., Abbeel, P: Adversarial attacks on neural network policies. ArXiv Preprint ArXiv:1702.02284 (2017)
12. Ballet, V., Renard, X., Aigrain, J., Laugel, T., Frossard, P., Detyniecki, M.: Imperceptible adversarial attacks on tabular data. ArXiv Preprint ArXiv:1911.03274 (2019)
13. Cartella, F., Anunciacao, O., Funabiki, Y., Yamaguchi, D., Akishita, T., Elshocht, O.: Adversarial attacks for tabular data: Application to fraud detection and imbalanced data. ArXiv Preprint ArXiv:2101.08030 (2021)
14. Ghamizi, S., Cordy, M., Gubri, M., Papadakis, M., Boystov, A., Le Traon, Y., Goujon, A.: Search-based adversarial testing and improvement of constrained credit scoring systems. In: Proceedings of the 28th ACM Joint Meeting on European Software Engineering Conference and Symposium on the Foundations of Software Engineering, pp. 1089–1100 (2020)
15. Dal Pozzolo, A., Caelen, O., Johnson, R., Bontempi, G.: Calibrating probability with undersampling for unbalanced classification. In: 2015 IEEE Symposium Series on Computational Intelligence, pp. 159–166 (2015)
16. Fernández, A., Garcia, S., Herrera, F., Chawla, N.: SMOTE for learning from imbalanced data: progress and challenges, marking the 15-year anniversary. J. Artif. Intell. Res. **61**, 863–905 (2018)
17. Nicolae, M., et al.: Adversarial Robustness Toolbox v1. 0.0. ArXiv Preprint ArXiv:1807.01069 (2018)

Anomaly Detection and Root Cause Analysis on Log Data

Daem Pasha, Ali Hussain Shah, Esmaeil Habib Zadeh, and Savas Konur(⊠)

Department of Computer Science, University of Bradford, Bradford BD7 1DP, UK
s.konur@bradford.ac.uk

Abstract. In this paper, we perform anomaly detection and root cause analysis on log data (system logs). Firstly, we employ a log parsing solution known as Drain (an online log parsing approach with fixed depth tree). We then present an anomaly detection approach that utilizes a decision tree model. This will be used to determine the anomalous devices in the log files. One benefit of decision tree models is that they are easily traceable, providing a contrast to most "black-box" solutions currently available in the industry. Finally, a sequential model using Keras is built to predict the root cause of a given issue.

Keywords: Root cause analysis · Anomaly detection · Log files · Machine learning

1 Introduction

Logging is a common practice in the IT industry and can provide useful information for anomaly detection. Logs keep the historical records of everything that happens in a system and can cover many types of events, e.g., transactional, error, and intrusion-based events.

Anomaly detection can be used to detect anomalous patterns in the logs. The problem with the current commercial anomaly detection solutions is that they are essentially a black box which makes it difficult to see what the algorithm is doing behind the scenes [3]. Another limitation is that they only focus on new/unique log events.

Root cause analysis (RCA) is useful considering that a single issue can cause a snowball effect leading to an influx of log records. RCA can be performed and used to determine the source of the issue without the need to trawl through thousands of log entries. A problem with the providers of these solutions, e.g., Zebrium, requires all your log data to be on their platform. This process can be costly as frequent cloud storage and data insertion can quickly increase the price.

In this paper, we propose a transparent anomaly detection method that utilizes Drain as log parsing (an online log parsing approach with fixed depth tree, which has a 51.85–81.47% improvement in run-time when compared with state-of-the-art online parsers) and a decision tree model for anomaly detection. One benefit of using decision tree models is that they are easily traceable, providing a contrast to most "black-box" solutions currently available in the industry. We will also look at other important issues such

M. Bramer and F. Stahl (Eds.): SGAI-AI 2022, LNAI 13652, pp. 333–339, 2022.
https://doi.org/10.1007/978-3-031-21441-7_27

as the frequency of the events to determine an anomalous appliance. We also use a sequential model using Keras to predict the root cause of a given anomaly. Our proposed solution is independent from any storage platform making it much more cost-effective and integrable with existing architecture.

2 Methodology

2.1 Data

The datasets used for this solution mainly contain log files and some network traffic metric data (see Table 1) [4]. The root cause analysis data file is used to train the RCA model. All these datasets have been obtained from a network traffic management company.

Table 1. Dataset description.

Name	Type	Train/test	Size	Anomaly:normal ratio
Syslogs (Linux system logs)	Log file	50/50	944	148:796
Root cause analysis data	Log file	50/50	1000	N/A

2.2 Methodology Outline

Fig. 1. Overall method diagram.

In the first stage, the *log processor* (Fig. 1) takes raw, unstructured logs and converts them into a consistent and structured format. For this process, we use Drain [1] which takes the log files and a template string (e.g., <Date> <Appliance> <Message>) as input and returns a CSV file with the data split into individual columns as output.

The output from the log parser is then fed into the *machine learning* module (Fig. 1) which utilises a decision tree model to determine anomalous patterns in the log files. We then output a list of anomalous appliances by utilising the TF-IDF measure (Sect. 2.4). Finally, we take into consideration multiple log files and metrics and pass them into a sequential model to determine the root cause of the failure.

2.3 Log Parsing

Drain is an open-source log parser that can parse logs with high accuracy and speed [2]. It categorizes logs by assigning them to a template and then extracts the parameters from the logs, making it very useful for machine learning. Drain also streams logs as it parses them. This means it does not require an offline training step and it is not limited by memory.

When a new log arrives, Drain uses regular expressions to pre-process the log. These regular expressions are provided by the system experts in terms of domain knowledge. We can then construct a tree and decide on the best group, based on the length of the logs. If the group does not exist, a new group is created [2].

Next, Drain further groups these logs by picking the first word from the log, for example, all words beginning with "Receive" are placed into the same group [1]. Finally, at the leaf node we see a list of different log groups and the log is placed in the most closely related group.

Table 2. MySQL log parser results.

Metric	Value
Precision	1.0
Recall	1.0
F-measure	1.0

Table 3. Syslogs log parser results.

Metric	Value
Precision	0.984
Recall	0.755
F-measure	0.992

Tables 2 and 3 show the F-measure values obtained from these log files, both of which come from live environments. This shows a good potential for our approach.

2.4 Anomaly Detection

For anomaly detection, we use the decision tree algorithm. This is because the decision tree model is much more interpretable as the thought process in the previous nodes leading up to the anomaly [3]. This will provide much more detail and insight which will be useful when diagnosing potential issues with the output.

To determine the best possible split for the tree, the model makes use of the Gini index. The next step is to split the data into the train and test datasets. His is a way to evaluate the performance of a model by using them to make predictions on data not involved in the training process. For the syslogs dataset, a train-test split of 50/50 has been selected. The train dataset is used to fit the model whilst the test dataset is used to test the model. This prevents bias as the same data is not being used twice, which could cause overfitting.

Next, we make use of a technique called *fit transform* to convert our dataset into something usable by the model. In this case for the decision tree, we will need to convert them into their numerical representation [5]. This process is called *text vectorization*.

To determine whether an appliance is anomalous we make use of a numerical statistic called TF-IDF (Term frequency-inverse document frequency). TF will increase proportionally, whereas IDF offsets that number. Events that are common for every block/appliance do not rank as high, however, an event that occurs multiple times in one block/appliance but does not occur in others would rank higher [6].

Finally, we can obtain the F-measure score for the model which can be used to determine the accuracy and reliability of the model.

Table 4. Syslog anomaly detection accuracy results.

Metric	Value
Precision	0.6
Recall	1.0
F-measure	**0.75**

Table 5. Decision tree parameters.

	Value
Max depth	∞
Criterion	Gini
Min sample split	**2**

Table 4 shows the results of the anomaly detection when applied to network traffic monitoring data. Table 5 shows the decision tree parameters. An F-measure score of 0.75 is desirable in this scenario as the dataset is only 1000 lines. In a real-world scenario, the dataset would be consuming a lot more data, which is expected to increase the accuracy as there is more train data.

2.5 Root Cause Analysis

For root cause analysis, we take our anomalous appliances from the anomaly detection and combine them with other sources of information (i.e., other log files or metric data). The more datasets there are, the more accurate the prediction is.

To classify the data, we need to convert our list of root cause outcomes (e.g., "MEM-ORY_ISSUE") into numerical values. This is a crucial step to obtain good results from our data [7]. A label encoder is used to fit and transform the root cause outcomes into numerical values. For this implementation, the Sequential model is used from the Keras framework. This is a machine learning model that is built up of many neural network layers.

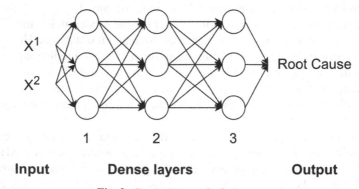

Fig. 2. Root cause analysis process.

Figure 2 shows the RCA process. Firstly, the input layer takes the values from the dataset (either 1 or 0). We then apply two dense layers with a ReLU (Rectified Linear

Unit) activation function; these layers have 128 neurons and take each of the previous inputs in.

Finally, we apply a dense layer with the SoftMax activation; this converts the inputs from the previous dense layer and makes a categorical prediction based on the number of root cause classes.

Table 6. Input data/parameters for RCA model.

Parameters	Value
Amount of data	148 lines
Number of categorisation classes	4
Epoch	20
Batch size	100
Validation split	50%
Optimizer	adam
Learning rate	0.01

Table 7. Results of RCA model after training on network dataset.

	Train	Test
Epoch	Acc.	Acc.
1	0.40	0.63
2	0.66	0.65
...	...	...
12	0.79	0.78
13	**0.80**	**0.78**

Table 6 shows the input parameters fed to the RCA model and Table 7 shows the results of the RCA solution after being trained with 13 epochs on 1000 lines of data with a 50% split ratio. In the future, this will be trained on a larger dataset which is likely to improve the accuracy. Figure 3 shows the class distribution for the four potential categories (root causes).

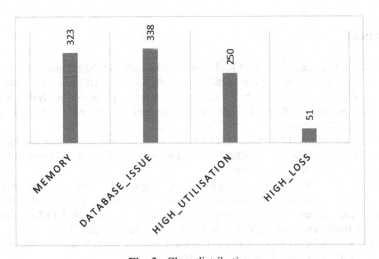

Fig. 3. Class distribution.

3 Conclusion and Future Work

This paper outlines a process that can be used to transform a number of logs into a much smaller and more useful output using three main components: log parser, anomaly detection, and root cause analysis.

The log parser is very effective and accurate with an F-measure score of 0.99 when applied to the syslogs dataset (Table 3). It also has some capabilities to detect and automatically parse log templates by checking the similarity threshold between them.

The anomaly detection algorithm is also effective in discovering anomalies as well with an F-measure score of 0.75 when applied to the syslogs dataset (Table 4). It is also easily viewable due to the transparent nature of the decision tree model. This helps when understanding the logic behind the decision. The use of a rule-based labeling system also greatly decreases the initial time taken to collect and prepare the data allowing for the use of a supervised learning algorithm without the initial delay that comes with data processing.

Root cause analysis has an accuracy score of 0.78 for the train dataset (Table 7), this is a good result for the current stage. Overall, there is a strong foundation for root cause analysis. The log parsing, anomaly detection, and root cause models show good results when applied to real-world datasets.

In future, we will consider the feasibility of our approach in very large datasets. In particular, we will apply our approach to use cases requiring high volume of real-time data traffic and logs such as autonomous vehicles [8], smart manufacturing [9], and ubiquitous systems [10, 11] and as well as scientific software systems [12, 13].

Acknowledgements. The authors acknowledge Innovate UK [KTP012139] and EPSRC (EP/R043787/1).

References

1. He, P., Zhu, J., Zheng, Z., Lyu, M.R.: Drain: an online log parsing approach with fixed depth tree. In: 2017 IEEE International Conference on Web Services (ICWS), pp. 33–40
2. He, S., Zhu, J., He, P., Lyu, M.R.: Experience report: system log analysis for anomaly detection. In: 2016 IEEE 27th International Symposium on Software Reliability Engineering (ISSRE), pp. 207–218
3. He, P., Zhu, J., He, S., Li, J., Lyu, M.R.: An evaluation study on log parsing and its use in log mining. In: 2016 46th Annual IEEE/IFIP International Conference on Dependable Systems and Networks (DSN), pp. 654–661
4. Zadeh, E., Amstutz, S., Collins, J., Ingham, C., Gheorghe, M., Konur. S.: Automated contextual anomaly detection for network interface bandwidth utilisation: a case study in network capacity management. In: Proceedings of 11th Int. Conference on CECNet, Frontiers in Artificial Intelligence and Applications, vol. 345,pp. 659–666 (2022)
5. Kumari, A., Shashi, M.: Vectorization of text documents for identifying unifiable news articles. Int. J. Adv. Comput. Sci. Appl. **10**, 305 (2019)
6. Salton, G., Buckley, C.: Termweighting approaches in automatic text retrieval. Inf. Process. Manage. **24**(5), 513–523 (1988)

7. Sola, J., Sevilla, J.: Importance of input data normalization for the application of neural networks to complex industrial problems. IEEE Trans. Nucl. Sci. **44**, 1464–1468 (1997)
8. Badue, C., et al.: Self-driving cars: a survey. Expert Syst. Appl. **165**, 113816 (2021)
9. Konur, S., et al.: Towards design and implementation of Industry 4.0 for food manufacturing. Neural Comput. Appl. 1–13 (2021)
10. Arapinis, M., et al.: Towards the verification of pervasive systems. Electron. Commun. EASST **22** (2010)
11. Konur, S., Fisher, M., Dobson, S., Knox, S.: Formal verification of a pervasive messaging system. Formal Aspects Comput. **26**(4), 677–694 (2013)
12. Blakes, J., et al.: Infobiotics workbench: A P systems based tool for systems and synthetic biology. Appl. Membr. Comput. Syst. Synth. Biol. Emerg. Complex. Comput. **7**, 1–41 (2014)
13. Bakir, M., et al.: Extended simulation and verification platform for kernel P systems. Int. Conf. Membr. Comput. LNCS **8961**, 158–178 (2014)

Developing Testing Frameworks for AI Cameras

Arkadiusz Herdzik and Carl James-Reynolds(✉) (iD)

Middlesex University, London NW4 4BT, United Kingdom
C.James-Reynolds@mdx.ac.uk

Abstract. It is possible for inexpensive cameras to include AI based features such as face recognition. However, a test framework for such cameras is required that will allow comparison of accuracy under differing conditions. This will then lead to the improvement of training data and algorithms.

A simple test framework has been developed and partially evaluated by testing multiple head/face accessories under different lighting conditions. Six participants took part and 300 pictures using a Huskylens were taken under a range of conditions. It was found that the camera could detect faces at a reasonable level of accuracy during 'middle of the day' lighting conditions, with or without head accessories. However, it delivers significantly lower detection rate with accessories that cover greater parts of the face and under green light.

There is still a need to further investigate this area of study with a higher number of participants in a more controlled environment. It is anticipated that better testing frameworks will lead to better algorithms, training data and specifications for users.

Keywords: Face recognition · Test framework · AI camera

1 Introduction and Background

A test framework for face recognition technology is required in order to ensure that users can make informed choices for real life critical scenarios.

AI devices have become easily available for purchase [1] and offer a range of different possibilities including, but not limited to, automating or improving tasks conducted by humans in day to day lives [2]. Mobile phone facial biometric security and Automated Border Control Systems (also known as E-Gates) are examples of what can be achieved using algorithms and data sets for training. As another example biometric approaches for security, can be used, as each person's biometrics are unique to that specific individual and face characteristics can quickly be detected [3].

With technology such as E-Gates, it is generally acceptable for the system to be inaccurate at verifying the identity of a person, and there is intervention in the form of an immigration officer that will take control [4]. This not the case with other uses of biometrics such as those in mobile phones or door entry systems where there is no human activity that monitors what the system does and its accuracy. This raises a question whether security systems and other AI tools are secure enough to be trusted when deployed for mass use.

© The Author(s), under exclusive license to Springer Nature Switzerland AG 2022
M. Bramer and F. Stahl (Eds.): SGAI-AI 2022, LNAI 13652, pp. 340–345, 2022.
https://doi.org/10.1007/978-3-031-21441-7_28

There are a wide variety of strategies for implementing face recognition, which makes the need for standards in testing even more important. Some [5] use facial features, but omit hair, using luminance as the source of information; others [6] use depth as an additional variable which increases accuracy. Using a depth sensor such as the one of a Microsoft Kinect [7] is primarily needed to define the area that separates the human and the background. Researchers [8] have emphasised the importance of increasing the number of iterations for the training model to improve accuracy. Because there is such a wide range of strategies and algorithms, these are not explored, however there are many reviews of this area [9–11].

A test framework needs to consider a number of factors:

- Environmental Factors

  - Light Colour and Intensity
  - Light Direction

- Positional Factors

  - Angle and Distance of camera to face

- Human Factors

  - Ethnicity
  - Hair Styles
  - Head Coverings
  - Face Coverings
  - Make-up
  - Gender
  - Age
  - Attempts to "cheat" the system

It may be that some factors can be kept as constants, so that subjects are asked to be a specified distance from the camera and to look straight into the lens, or to remove face coverings. In real life scenarios, it is not always possible to guarantee lighting conditions and some of the "Human Factors", such as make-up, may change over time.

In order to explore the framework, a test apparatus was developed, consisting of a picture frame with a NeoPixel LED Strip [12] placed around the inside border of the frame, pointing at the subject. An Arduino Uno [13] was used to control the LEDs to allow for colour and light direction to be changed. The frame was kept one metre from the camera.

The camera used for evaluation was Huskylens [14] (Zhiwei Robotics, 2022) developed by DFRobot. It contains a 2.0 megapixel camera; it doesn't contain a depth sensor and relies primarily on an already existing hard coded algorithm. There is an option of changing the threshold for face detection, but there is no publicly available information about how this works.

Figure 1. Shows the schematic of the testing system. The NeoPixel LED strip was placed inside a picture frame (facing the subject) and the process of taking the images was automated with each subject being illuminated from the top, bottom and sides using different colours. This was simplified to red, green and blue, but the colour range could easily be extended. The subject was one metre from the camera as shown in Fig. 2. Two Arduino libraries were used: Huskylens [14] which is for the Huskylens camera and the Adafruit NeoPixel library was used for the addressable RGB strip. The automation of the process made testing simpler and more reliable.

For each subject 60 passport style photos were taken. During the testing, pictures of participants were stored within micro-SD card and subsequently stored securely in the cloud.

Using observational technique, each image was checked to determine whether the Huskylens detected a face within the picture, and the result was recorded.

There can be situations where there is no border at all, indicating that although there is a face in the image, the Huskylens is unable to distinguish whether it is a face or part of the background.

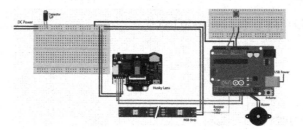

Fig. 1. Schematic of apparatus

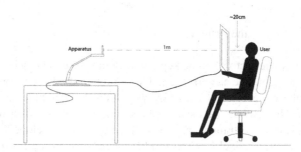

Fig. 2. Setup of equipment

2 Test Results and Findings

There were total of 6 participants of which 3 were males and 3 females.

The main results are shown in Fig. 3. It can be clearly seen that performance of the face recognition was best under red light and worst under green, which is surprising as green contributes the most to luminance. Unsurprisingly facemasks had a significant impact on performance, whilst hats had little impact, except in one case where the hat obscured the face. The camera detected a face, but could not identify it, as in Fig. 4. Glasses generally reduced detection rates, but typically only by 1/6. It was noted that in tests with the female participants wearing make-up that detection rates reduced, however due to the low number of participants, it is difficult to assign any significance to this. Across all tests except those with red light and no accessories, males were twice as likely to be detected as females.

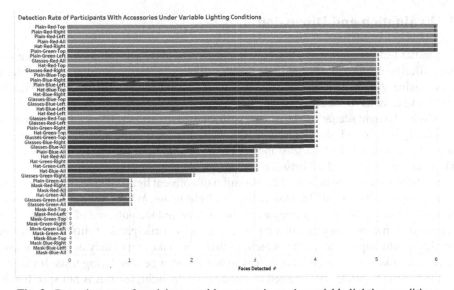

Fig. 3. Detection rate of participants with accessories under variable lighting conditions

While there is a low number of participants within this testing, 48 different light scenarios/types of accessories were used per participant.

Through the observation of tests that were run, it has been seen that the camera used seems to mostly focus on mouth, nose, and eyebrows as its reference point while eyes not as much. The detection rate with glasses was relatively good but another test that could have been carried out would have been with an eye patch to see if eyes do really make a difference.

Fig. 4. Example of output showing recognition of a face, but not identity

3 Evaluation and Discussion

The initial tests suggest that a testing framework would be a useful tool, as we can see that differing conditions have an impact of the efficacy of the recognition system. Many inexpensive "AI" cameras indicate that they work under "good" light conditions without this being clear as to the exact meaning of "good".

Under daylight scenarios, the camera performed as expected and facial features were accurately recognised, the colour green has been the most problematic for the camera while the colour red had the least impact on all results for different accessories worn. The tests were all carried out between 2:00pm and 4:00pm in the same room, However, it would be more accurate to control the variation of ambient light when testing the camera on participants. This could be achieved with a light meter. What has been learned from this project is that light really does affect the quality and the outcome of the data being collected. It has been noticed that taking pictures of participants at different times of the day would impact the results as pictures that were taken on cloudy or late hour days were more likely to cause the Huskylens to not detect a person during tests. It may be that the Huskylens uses an infra-red component of the light, but this is not specified in the documentation.

This work has been limited by a low number of subjects and could be improved with a wider range of ages and ethnicity. Different age scales for genders could have resulted in bias of the data results which could be the reason of the camera being more likely to detect males than females as males were within a similar age in the test whilst there was greater variation in the ages of the female participants. With a greater number of subjects, it would be possible for example to calculate an accurate recognition rate or other appropriate metric for "AI" Camera systems [15], and a potential user would use the metric best suited to their application.

The approach used could easily be adapted to ensure the subject was within the one metre range and a servo-motor could provide some small changes of camera angle.

Considering that some people use eyebrow pencils to draw or change the shape of their current eyebrows and use different coloured lipstick, this could become part of the test as the camera could potentially consider the participant as another person if their facial features or other parts surrounding the face were to slightly change.

It would also be appropriate to see if a camera could detect a photograph of a face, as it is important to ensure that a subject is present and not just their image.

There is a growing awareness of a need for transparency in AI systems, and this extends to accurate and detailed specifications that will allow users to determine if the equipment is fit for the intended task. Using a standardized test framework would assist with this, as it is independent of the Face Recognition technology used.

References

1. Shabbir, J., Anwer, T.: Artificial Intelligence and its Role in Near Future. arXiv:1804.01396 [cs] [Preprint]. Available at: http://arxiv.org/abs/1804.01396 (2018). Accessed: 29 December 2021
2. Donepudi, P.K.: Application of artificial intelligence in automation industry. Asian J. Appli. Sci. Eng. **7**(1), 15 (2018)
3. Kaur, P., et al.: Facial-recognition algorithms: A literature review. Med. Sci. Law **60**(2), 131–139 (2020). https://doi.org/10.1177/0025802419893168
4. Labati, R.D., et al.: Biometric recognition in automated border control: a survey. ACM Comput. Surv. **49**(2), 1–39 (2016). https://doi.org/10.1145/2933241
5. Sharif, M., Javed, M.Y., Mohsin, S.: Face Recognition Based on Facial Features, p. 8. (2012)
6. Chen, Y.-L., et al.: Accurate and Robust 3D Facial Capture Using a Single RGBD Camera. In: 2013 IEEE International Conference on Computer Vision. Sydney, Australia: IEEE, pp. 3615–3622 (2013). https://doi.org/10.1109/ICCV.2013.449
7. Cong, R., Winters, R.: How It Works: Xbox Kinect. [online] Jameco.com. Available at: https://www.jameco.com/jameco/workshop/howitworks/xboxkinect.html (2019). Accessed 12 Jan. 2022
8. Sunil, A., et al.: Usual and unusual human activity recognition in video using deep learning and artificial intelligence for security applications. In: 2021 Fourth International Conference on Electrical, Computer and Communication Technologies (ICECCT). Erode, India: IEEE, pp. 1–6 (2021). https://doi.org/10.1109/ICECCT52121.2021.9616791
9. Adjabi, I., et al.: Past, Present, and Future of Face Recognition: A Review. Electronics **9**(8), p. 1188 (2020). Available at: https://doi.org/10.3390/electronics9081188
10. Kortli, Y., et al.: Face Recognition Systems: A Survey. Sensors **20**(2), 342 (2020). Available at: https://doi.org/10.3390/s20020342
11. Lal, M., et al.: Study of Face Recognition Techniques: A Survey. Int. J. Adva. Comp. Sci. Appli. **9**(6) (2018). Available at: https://doi.org/10.14569/IJACSA.2018.090606
12. Burgess, P.: Adafruit NeoPixel Überguide (2013). [online] Adafruit Learning System. Available at: https://learn.adafruit.com/adafruit-neopixel-uberguide/arduino-library-use
13. The Arduino Uno: https://docs.arduino.cc/hardware/uno-rev3. Accessed: 20 June 2022
14. Gravity: HUSKYLENS - An Easy-to-use AI Machine Vision Sensor. Available at: https://wiki.dfrobot.com/HUSKYLENS_V1.0_SKU_SEN0305_SEN0336. Accessed: 6 June 2022
15. Sundaram, M., Mani, A.: Face recognition: demystification of multifarious aspect in evaluation metrics. In: Ramakrishnan, S. (ed.) Face Recognition - Semisupervised Classification, Subspace Projection and Evaluation Methods. InTech (2016). Available at: https://doi.org/10.5772/62825

Time is Budget: A Heuristic for Reducing the Risk of Ruin in Multi-armed Gambler Bandits

Filipo Studzinski Perotto[(✉)], Xavier Pucel, and Jean-Loup Farges

ONERA - The French AeroSpace Lab, DTIS - Information Processing and Systems
Department, 2 Avenue Edouard Belin, 31055 Toulouse, France
filipo.perotto@onera.fr
https://www.onera.fr

Abstract. In this paper we consider *Multi-Armed Gambler Bandits* (MAGB), a stochastic random process in which an agent performs successive actions and either loses 1 unit from its budget after observing a *failure*, or earns 1 unit after a *success*. It constitutes a survival problem where the *risk of ruin* must be taken into account. The agent's initial *budget* evolves in time with the received rewards and must remain positive throughout the process. The contribution of this paper is the definition of an original heuristic which aims at improving the probability of survival in a MAGB by replacing the time by the budget as the factor that regulates exploration in UCB-like methods. The proposed strategy is then experimentally compared to standard algorithms presenting good results.

Keywords: Multi-armed bandits · Risk of ruin · Safety-critical systems

1 Introduction

Multi-Armed Bandits (MAB) constitute a classic framework to model online *sequential decision-making* while facing the *exploration-exploitation dilemma* [11,16]. A MAB is typically represented by an agent interacting with a random process. At each successive round t, the agent chooses an action A_t to perform among k possible actions and receives a corresponding reward R_t. The agent must estimate the reward functions associated to each action by sampling them. Rewards resulting from a same action are independent but identically distributed, and do not give any information about other actions. In that standard version, budget and risk are not taken into account. The objective is to maximise the expected future sum of rewards [1]. Different methods and guarantees have been proposed in the literature depending on the available information and on the assumptions on the reward distributions [3,8].

Survival Multi-Armed Bandits (SMAB) [13,14] and in particular *Multi-Armed Gambler Bandits* (MAGB) [12] are recent extensions of the standard

M. Bramer and F. Stahl (Eds.): SGAI-AI 2022, LNAI 13652, pp. 346–352, 2022.
https://doi.org/10.1007/978-3-031-21441-7_29

MAB problem in which the agent has a budget that must remain positive throughout the process, otherwise the agent is ruined. An initial budget $B_0 = b$ evolves with the received rewards while the agent is alive, so as $B_t = B_{t-1} + R_t$ if $B_{t-1} > 0$, otherwise $B_t = 0$, the agent is ruined and the process no longer evolves. In that scenario, the agent can either increase the probability of running the process indefinitely, becoming infinitely rich, or inversely, can increase the probability of ruin, until eventually running out of budget, which means that maximising the sum of rewards requires reducing the chances of being ruined.

This paper focuses on MAGB problems [12], where the rewards are limited to two values, $+1$ and -1, and the initial budget is a positive integer. When occasionally $B_t = 0$ is achieved for the first time, the agent is ruined. The rewards are drawn from underlying stationary Bernoulli distributions. Formally, $\{k \in \mathbb{N} \mid k \geq 2\}$ is the number of actions, $\{b \in \mathbb{N} \mid b > 0\}$ is the initial budget, $\{p_i \in \mathbb{R} \mid 0 \leq p_i \leq 1\}$ is the probability of *success* after executing action i, which returns reward $+1$, and $1 - p_i$ is the complementary probability of *failure*, with reward -1. It means that $X_t \sim Bern(p_i)$ and $R_t = 2X_t - 1$ for $A_t = i$. The expected mean reward of action i is $\mu_i = 2p_i - 1$.

There are few results concerning SMAB and MAGB into the literature [12–14], and the definition of an optimal algorithm is still an open problem. Related extensions like *Risk Averse* [4,7,15,18], and *Budgeted* MAB [2,6,20], even if sharing similar concerns, cannot be reduced to the survival setting [13,14].

2   Standard MAB Algorithms

Lets assume that the agent always plays each action once at the beginning of the process, so as $A_t = t$ for $1 \leq t \leq k$, in order to provide the decision algorithm with a first observation of them. Empirical-Means is a greedy algorithm which successively chooses the action with the best estimated mean reward, $A_{t+1} = \arg\max_i \frac{S_{i,t}}{N_{i,t}}$, where $N_{i,t}$ is the number of times the action i had been performed until round t, and $S_{i,t}$ is the sum of received rewards due to that action. That strategy is sub-optimal since no systematic exploration is performed, then it may not converge to the best action.

Exploration can be performed by introducing some non-determinism on the decision. ε-Greedy is a naive algorithm which chooses either the action with best estimated mean reward with probability ε, a hand-tuned parameter, or a random action otherwise. That strategy is sub-optimal since the exploration rate remains constant throughout the process [5,19].

The standard approach for solving the exploration-exploitation dilemma is the *optimism in the face of uncertainty*. An intelligent exploration can be made by statistically controlling the confidence on the estimates. With similar mean reward, less explored actions should be preferred. UCB1 [1] chooses, at each time t, the action that maximises the estimated mean plus the maximum estimation error given by a confidence bound that progressively increases over time, so as:

$$A_{t+1} = \arg\max_{1 \leq i \leq k} \left[\frac{S_{i,t}}{N_{i,t}} + \sqrt{\frac{\alpha \ln(t)}{N_{i,t}}} \right], \tag{1}$$

where α is the parameter regulating exploration. That strategy is asymptotically optimal if α is sufficiently high.

Estimating the parameters of a Bernoulli bandit corresponds to estimating the parameters of a binomial distribution. The binomial distribution represents the probability of a given number of successes on a sequence of Bernoulli trials when the parameter is known. The probability of having x successes in n trials, given p is $\mathbb{P}(x \mid p, n) = \text{Bin}(p, n) = \binom{n}{x} p^x (1-p)^{(n-x)}$. In a Bayesian approach, the beta distribution corresponds to the conjugate prior for the binomial distribution. Assuming a uniform prior, the posterior density function for p is given by $f(p \mid x, n) = \text{Beta}(x+1, n-x+1) = p^x(1-p)^{n-x}(n+1)\binom{n}{x}$. Bayes-UCB [9] is an improved UCB-like method designed for Bernoulli bandits that is also asymptotically optimal. It chooses the action that maximises the $1 - \frac{1}{t}$ quantile from the Beta posterior:

$$A_{t+1} = \arg\max_{1 \le i \le k} \left[Q_{1-1/t}\big(\text{Beta}(X_{i,t}+1, N_{i,t}-X_{i,t}+1)\big) \right]. \tag{2}$$

Finally, Thompson-Sampling is another optimal Bayesian algorithm [10]. At each round, it draws a sample from the posterior of each action to decide which one to choose. This allows a non-optimal action to be sampled with a varying frequency, which dynamically balances exploration as the posterior becomes more precise:

$$A_{t+1} = \arg\max_{1 \le i \le k} \left[V_{i,t} \sim \text{Beta}(X_{i,t}+1, N_{i,t}-X_{i,t}+1) \right]. \tag{3}$$

3   Our Contribution: The Gambler Methods

In a MAGB, the probability of being ruined by always performing action i is $\left(\frac{1-p_i}{p_i}\right)^b$ if $p_i > \frac{1}{2}$, and 1 if $p_i \le \frac{1}{2}$ [12]. The expected duration of the game is $\frac{b}{1-2p_i}$ if $p_i < \frac{1}{2}$, and ∞ if $p_i \ge \frac{1}{2}$. It means that, in a MAGB, the action with highest mean presents the best life expectancy and the best survival probability, independent of the current budget, and then, like in the classic MAB, the action with maximal mean reward is the optimal action, to which optimal methods must asymptotically converge. However, when exploring, the agent must consider the remaining budget and the estimated parameters of each action in order to compare the estimated ruin probabilities associated to them.

In this paper, we suggest a heuristic modification that can be applied to UCB-like methods, which consists in replacing t for B_t into the considered equations. The intuition is that, for maximising the chances of survival, the lowest is the budget, the more the agent must favour exploitation over exploration in order to increase its budget and avoid ruin. In contrast, the higher is the budget, the more the agent should prefer a classic optimal strategy.

In this way, the Gambler-UCB method modifies UCB1 (Eq. (1)) by adding $\sqrt{\frac{\alpha \ln(B_t)}{N_{i,t}}}$ instead of $\sqrt{\frac{\alpha \ln(t)}{N_{i,t}}}$ to the estimated mean:

$$A_{t+1} = \arg\max_{1 \le i \le k} \left[\frac{S_{i,t}}{N_{i,t}} + \sqrt{\frac{\alpha \ln(B_t)}{N_{i,t}}} \right], \tag{4}$$

and the `Gambler-Bayes-UCB` method modifies `Bayes-UCB` (Eq. (2)) by taking the $1 - 1/B_t$ quantile from the beta posterior, instead of the $1 - 1/t$ quantile proposed on the original method:

$$A_{t+1} = \arg\max_{1 \leq i \leq k} \left[Q_{1-1/B_t} \left(\text{Beta}(X_{i,t} + 1, N_{i,t} - X_{i,t} + 1) \right) \right]. \qquad (5)$$

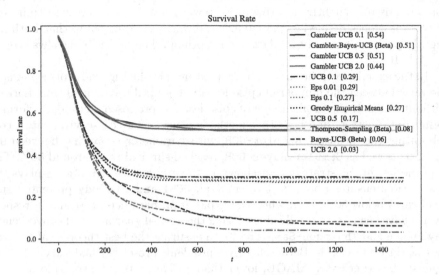

Fig. 1. Survival rate, i.e. the proportion of episodes in which the agent reaches the time-horizon $h = 1500$ without ruin in $n = 200$ episodes.

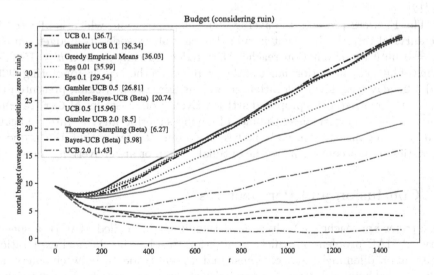

Fig. 2. Budget progression as a function of time, averaged over $n = 200$ episodes.

4   Experimental Results

The proposed algorithms, Gambler-UCB (Eq. (4)) and Gambler-Bayes-UCB (Eq. (5)) have been compared to classic and state-of-the-art MAB algorithms like UCB1 [1], Bayes-UCB [9], and Thompson-Sampling [10], but also with naive methods like Empirical-Means and ε-Greedy [17]. The experimental scenario presents $k = 10$ actions, the first 8 of them parameterised by $p_1 = ... = p_8 = 0.45$, which corresponds to a slightly negative mean reward, leading the agent to ruin, and the two last ones defined as $p_9 = 0.525$ and $p_{10} = 0.55$, meaning that both are slightly positive, but only the last one is optimal. The initial budget was set to $b = k = 10$.

In the experiences, the survival rate, presented in the Figure 1, corresponds to the ratio between the number of episodes running until the defined time-horizon without ruin over the total number of episodes. The proposed methods performed significantly better than the other methods considering the survival rates, corroborating the intuition. Gambler-UCB, with parameter α varying between 0.1 and 2.0, as well as Gambler-Bayes-UCB, reached survival rates around 50%. The hypothetical oracle strategy (not shown in the graphic), which always plays the best action, ensures about 80% of survival. UCB1 and ε-Greedy presented survival rates below 30%, even when the exploration parameters (α and ε, respectively) have been set to small values, losing theoretical guarantees of convergence. Bayes-UCB and Thompson-Sampling, both ensuring the best theoretical guarantees against the classic Bernoulli MAB problem, presented bad survival rates against the experienced MAGB, lower than 10%, due to intense exploration in the initial rounds. The greedy Empirical-Means method performs as well as the standard methods, reaching almost 30% of survival, corroborating the findings on [12].

The Figure 2 presents the average budget progression, which is affected by the survival rate. If the agent is ruined during an episode, its budget remains $B_t = 0$ until the simulation reaches the predefined time-horizon $h = 1500$. In terms of budget, the performance of the proposed methods is disappointing. UCB1 and ε-Greedy with low exploration, as well as Empirical-Means, presented the best performance on the proposed setting. Even if one instance of Gambler-UCB reaches similar performance, the fact of having superior survival rates indicates that it is making sub-optimal choices too often. It means that the proposed heuristics are not converging to the optimal action, or are converging too slowly.

5   Conclusion and Perspectives

This paper approaches a Multi-Armed Bandit setting called MAGB, a specific survival MAB problem, in which, in addition to solve the classical exploration-exploitation dilemma, the agent must find a good trade-off between safety and risk to avoid ruin, still trying to maximise the sum of rewards. Two algorithms have been proposed, Gambler-UCB and Gambler-Bayes-UCB, modifying respectively UCB1 and Bayes-UCB by replacing the time by the budget as the parameter that regulates exploration. The new methods presented good results in experimental simulations considering the survival rate, but are apparently sub-optimal in terms of convergence to the best action. Both methods are the result of a simple and intuitive heuristic, that seems to be efficient for preserving the agent alive during the initial rounds of the process, when it is more vulnerable to ruin, but the modified equations do not ensure gradative convergence to the best action. The results are nevertheless very promising, and the proposed heuristics should be the subject of theoretical analyses in future works, in order to find the necessary adjustments for ensuring optimality.

References

1. Auer, P., Cesa-Bianchi, N., Fischer, P.: Finite-time analysis of the multiarmed bandit problem. Mach. Learn. **47**(2–3), 235–256 (2002)
2. Badanidiyuru, A., Kleinberg, R., Slivkins, A.: Bandits with knapsacks. J. ACM **65**(3), 13:1-13:55 (2018)
3. Bubeck, S., Munos, R., Stoltz, G., Szepesvári, C.: X-armed bandits. JMLR **12**, 1655–1695 (2011)
4. Cassel, A., Mannor, S., Zeevi, A.: A general approach to multi-armed bandits under risk criteria. In: Proceedings of the COLT 2018, pp. 1295–1306 (2018)
5. Cesa-Bianchi, N., Fischer, P.: Finite-time regret bounds for the multiarmed Bandit problem. In: Proceedings of the 5th ICML, pp. 100–108. Morgan Kaufmann (1998)
6. Ding, W., Qin, T., Zhang, X., Liu, T.: Multi-armed bandit with budget constraint and variable costs. In: Proceedings of the 27th AAAI (2013)
7. Galichet, N., Sebag, M., Teytaud, O.: Exploration vs exploitation vs safety: risk-aware multi-armed bandits. In: Proceedings of the 5th ACML, vol. 29, pp. 245–260. PMLR (2013)
8. Garivier, A., Hadiji, H., Ménard, P., Stoltz, G.: KL-UCB-Switch: optimal regret bounds for stochastic bandits from both a distribution-dependent and a distribution-free viewpoints. CoRR abs/1805.05071 (2018)
9. Kaufmann, E., Cappé, O., Garivier, A.: On Bayesian upper confidence bounds for bandit problems. In: Proceedings of the 15th AISTATS, pp. 592–600 (2012)
10. Kaufmann, E., Korda, N., Munos, R.: Thompson sampling: an asymptotically optimal finite-time analysis. In: Proceedings of the 23rd ALT, pp. 199–213 (2012)
11. Lattimore, T., Szepesvári, C.: Bandit Algorithms. Cambridge University Press, Cambridge (2020)
12. Perotto, F.S.: Gambler bandits and the regret of being ruined. In: Proceedings of the 20th AAMAS, pp. 1664–1667 (2021)
13. Perotto, F.S., Bourgais, M., Silva, B.C., Vercouter, L.: Open problem: risk of ruin in multiarmed Bandits. In: Proceedings of the COLT 2019, pp. 3194–3197 (2019)
14. Riou, C., Honda, J., Sugiyama, M.: The survival bandit problem (2022). https://doi.org/10.48550/ARXIV.2206.03019
15. Sani, A., Lazaric, A., Munos, R.: Risk-aversion in multi-armed bandits. In: Proceedings of the 26th NIPS, pp. 3284–3292 (2012)
16. Slivkins, A.: Introduction to multi-armed Bandits. Found. Trends Mach. Learn. **12**(1–2), 1–286 (2019)
17. Sutton, R., Barto, A.: Introduction to Reinforcement Learning. MIT Press, Cambridge (1998)

18. Vakili, S., Zhao, Q.: Risk-averse multi-armed bandit problems under mean-variance measure. J. Sel. Top. Signal Process. **10**(6), 1093–1111 (2016)
19. Vermorel, J., Mohri, M.: Multi-armed Bandit Algorithms and Empirical Evaluation. In: Gama, J., Camacho, R., Brazdil, P.B., Jorge, A.M., Torgo, L. (eds.) ECML 2005. LNCS (LNAI), vol. 3720, pp. 437–448. Springer, Heidelberg (2005). https://doi.org/10.1007/11564096_42
20. Xia, Y., et al.: Finite budget analysis of multi-armed bandit problems. Neurocomputing **258**, 13–29 (2017)

Two-Phase Open-Domain Question Answering System

Vysakh Prasannan, Shahin Shemshian, Arinc Gurkan,
Lakshmi Babu Saheer[(✉)], and Mahdi Maktabdar Oghaz

Anglia Ruskin University, CB1 1PT, Cambridge, UK
{vp405,ss2817,ag137}@student.aru.ac.uk,
{lakshmi.babu-saheer,mahdi.maktabdar}@aru.ac.uk

Abstract. Text-based Internet content is increasing at a very rapid rate
day by day. As a result, even the best search engines are struggling to
retrieve the exact expected results of users' queries. On many occasions,
the users' expected result is embedded and scattered in a number of
different documents and conventional search engines are unable to pin-
point it. To address this shortcoming, this study proposes a two-phased
question answering system that utilizes a K-means clustering algorithm
alongside the T5 deep encoder-decoder model to formulate a concise
short answer to users' queries. The proposed system has been trained
using the Kaggle QA and SQuAD datasets and achieved the maximum
F1-score of 0.564 and a minimum loss of 8.56.

Keywords: Natural language processing · NLP · K-Means ·
Information retrieval · TF-IDF · Encoder-Decoder · Question
answering system

1 Introduction

Mainstream information retrieval systems allow users to find a list of documents
that might be associated with the searched terms and they leave it to the user
to extract the desired information from the list. However, a Question Answering (QA) system enables users to access knowledge in a more intuitive way and
formulate relevant responses in concise sensible wordings [1]. The primary goal
of a typical QA system is to formulate answers to questions as opposed to most
search engines and information retrieval systems that only return best-matching
articles that may or may not contain the desired results [1,2]. QA systems are
widely categorized into two groups: open-domain QA and closed-domain QA
systems. Open-domain QA systems are built to provide answers regardless of
the question's domain. Such a system tries to find the answer to the given question in the related documents or resources which are available and will return
the exact answer to the question after analyzing the related document contents.
Closed-domain QA systems differ from open-domain systems in a way that the
domain from which the question comes will be predefined and prefixed and the

© The Author(s), under exclusive license to Springer Nature Switzerland AG 2022
M. Bramer and F. Stahl (Eds.): SGAI-AI 2022, LNAI 13652, pp. 353–358, 2022.
https://doi.org/10.1007/978-3-031-21441-7_30

answer is only limited to the documents to which the system has access to [3]. Closed-domain QA systems can be perceived as an easier task as NLP systems can formulate domain-specific knowledge in ontologies. Also, they are usually limited to a certain type of questions such as descriptive questions rather than procedural [4,5]. Having said that, this research aims to design and develop an open-domain QA system using a pre-trained Text-to-Text Transfer Transformer Model (T5). T5 is a multi-task encoder-decoder model which pre-trained on a range of unsupervised and supervised tasks for text-to-text resolution. The proposed model also features a clustering module that clusters the input documents and users' queries into different categories based on their similarities measured by TF-IDF vectorization algorithm. The main contribution of this model is the novel two-phased unsupervised open-domain QA System capable of retrieving and modeling accurate results to given queries within the scope of the training datasets with reasonable accuracy. The next section of this manuscript investigates the state-of-the-art QA literature in more detail.

2   Literature Review

Text-based QA is one of the most well-known challenges in NLP and many studies have attempted to address it to this day. OpenAI developed GPT3 which is one of the most powerful QA models [6]. This model with over 175 billion parameters is the largest pre-trained NLP model. However, it is not open-source and publicly available. BERT (Bidirectional Encoder Representations from Transformers) is another mainstream NLP QA system [7]. It uses Bidirectional Transformers with 340 million parameters in its larger version. Unlike GPT3, BERT allows fine-tuning and customization. Raffel *et al.* [8] presented a new model called Text-to-Text Transfer Transformer(T5) which is easier to fine-tune and takes simple strings as input and output and unlike other models takes advantage of both encoder and decoder. It also introduces its own dataset (Colossal Clean Crawled Corpus - C4) which gets larger over time to train the model better. A study by Lende and Raghuwanshi [9], offers an open domain QA system that starts with pre-processing and then uses keyword extraction to retrieve relevant documents based on the question. Finally, it extracts the predicted answer from input documents. This study predicted 68 percent of the answers correctly. Although they achieved a good result for the closed-domain QA system, the result for the open-domain QA system was undesirable.

Another study by Mishra *et al.* [10], offers a close-domain QA system that answers users' questions on geographical topics. This study used different types of pre-processing operations that include noise removal, tokenization, and sentence splitting. This system has three main elements: question, document, and answer processing. The goal of the question processing part is to identify the question sub-type and the expected answer type. Based on the user query, passage retrieval finds related context. Possible answers are produced in the data retrieval part to create an input pool for the Answer extraction module. The system ranks possible answers based on the relevance to the user query. Although this study mainly investigates close-domain systems, it achieved an underwhelming average accuracy of 80%. Using more advanced NLP algorithms (e.g. T5), this problem could be mitigated. Kwok *et al.* [11] developed a QA system that extracts information on the web for finding answers to users' questions. This is one of the most common approaches in open-domain QA systems. Another web-based QA system proposed by Brill *et al.* [12] converts the user's question into a search engine query based on a set of predefined rules and retrieves the relevant search results accordingly. Once the relevant pages were retrieved it uses a series of n-grams to find the best answer related to the question from the pages retrieved.

3   Dataset Structure

The proposed model has been trained and tested using two different datasets. The first dataset is sourced from Kaggle's QA competition collected by a research team at Carnegie Mellon University between 2008 and 2010 [13]. This dataset consists of both questions and answers in different documents and it is divided into 3 parts based on students as S08, S09, and S10. This dataset consists of nearly 690,000 words worth of cleaned text from Wikipedia that was used to generate the questions. This dataset is particularly used for document clustering, rank-based retrieval of the relevant document, and testing of the T5 model. Besides, Kaggle's QA competition dataset, this study benefits the SQuAD (The Stanford Question Answering Dataset) dataset which has been used to train the T5 model [14]. This dataset which is considered to be the benchmark for QA studies consists of 107,785 question-answer pairs sourced from almost 536 different wikipedia articles.

4   Methodology

The proposed QA system architecture is divided into two major components. The first component primarily aims to find the relevant top-ranked documents from the dataset based on the domain from which the question is sourced. This component itself is divided into two sub-component. The first sub-component aims to cluster the input documents based on the domain of the documents using an unsupervised K-Means clustering algorithm. The second sub-component retrieves the top 10 documents related to the questions taken from the cluster that related to the domain of the question. The second component is the actual QA system which uses the T5 model to predict and generate the answer to the question using the retrieved documents from the first component. Both components have been trained and evaluated separately. Figure 1 shows the overall architecture of the proposed QA system. We have employed a series of standard pre-processing and vectorization processes to prepare the input document for clustering operations. The pre-processing includes the removal of the stop-words, punctuation, and stemming which converts words into the root form for better uniformity. The TF-IDF (Term Frequency-Inverse Document Frequency) vectorization algorithm has been used to quantify the importance or relevance of words in a given document relative to all documents in our dataset [15]. This converts the input document to a feature vector constructed based on the term frequencies. TF-IDF vector which represents the importance of each word in a particular document used for the clustering of the documents into different domains and for the retrieval of top-ranked documents from the cluster. The second component of the proposed model (T5 model) only benefits tokenization as stop-words removal and stemming could result in information loss in the output. Following the pre-processing and vectorization (TF-IDF) processes, the proposed model uses the K-means algorithm in order to cluster the input vectorized document into different clusters based on the TF-IDF similarity scores. The Kaggle QA competition dataset [13] is used for training of the K-means clustering algorithm. As a result, a total of 150 documents are optimally divided into 5 different clusters.

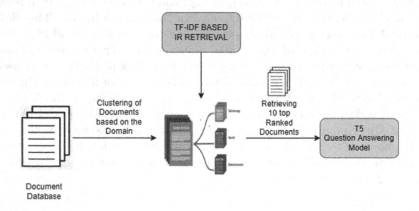

Fig. 1. Architecture of open-domain QA system

Cluster 0 with a total of 50 documents is the most populous while cluster 2 with only 15 documents is the most sparse cluster. We also have identified the top 10 frequent words in each cluster as demonstrated in Table 1. After the documents clustering process, the same K-means algorithm is used to identify the most appropriate cluster for the question. Similar to the training process, TF-IDF is used to vectorize the questions and documents. The similarity scores have been used to retrieve the top 10 relevant documents. These documents will be fed to the T5 model to predict and generate the appropriate answer. The T5 encoder-decoder model has been employed to predict and generate the answer to the question from the top 10 Retrieved Documents [8]. The architecture of the T5 model is consisting of 768 hidden layers with around 222 million trainable parameters which makes it computationally expensive to train from scratch. Hence, we used weights from a pre-trained T5 model that was trained using the SQuAD dataset [14] with the training and validation split of 95 to 5 percent.

Table 1. Top 10 frequent words in each document cluster

Cluster Name	Most Frequent Words
Cluster 0	countri, univers, offici, region, popul citi, spoken, dialect, languag, the
Cluster 1	play, tone, sound, vibrat, player, pitch music,string,tune,instrument
Cluster 2	radioact, phosphoresc, avogadro, volta, paper uppsala, experi, he, becquerel, celsiu
Cluster 3	eat, mammal, hunt, predat, prey,anim male, the, femal, speci
Cluster 4	john, friend, jame, portrait, life father, the, work, hi, he

5   Result Analysis

Both components of the proposed model have been tested and evaluated separately. To test the accuracy of the first component (clustering and document retrieval) we used the Kaggle QA dataset that includes the question and answer along with the document which contains the answer. To measure the accuracy of the first component, we have compared the answer's document ID (ground-truth) with the ID of the retrieved document. The experiment result shows the proposed document retrieval algorithm has achieved a total accuracy of 70 percent. The performance of the T5 model has been measured using the loss and F1-score values. Experiment results show that the proposed model achieved the maximum F1-score of 0.564 and a minimum loss of 8.56. Table 2 shows an example question that is randomly taken from the Kaggle dataset and fed into the proposed model along with the ground-truth and the answer generated by the proposed model.

Table 2. Qualitative example of the proposed model performance

Topic	Jakarta
Question	Is the most important river the Clliwung River
Expected Answer	Yes
Predicted Answer	Yes

6   Conclusion

This study attempted to design and develop an intuitive QA system with the goal of enabling users to access knowledge in a more intuitive way and formulates relevant responses in concise words as opposed to most search engines and information retrieval systems that only return full documents or best-matching articles that may or may not contain the desired results. The proposed QA system consists of two major components including a clustering and document retrieval model that returns the most relevant documents and a T5 encoder-decoder model that predicts and generates the answer to the question. The proposed QA system achieved a maximum F1-score of 0.56 and a minimum loss of 8.56. Although the results are far from ideal, this study shows the feasibility of the design and development of such a system using publicly available datasets and models.

References

1. Dwivedi, S., Singh, V.: Research and reviews in question answering system. Procedia Technol. **10**, 417–424 (2013)
2. Pundge, A., Khillare, S., Mahender, C.: Question answering system, approaches and techniques: a review. Int. J. Comput. Appl. **141**, 0975–8887 (2016)
3. Chen, C.: Neural network models for tasks in open-domain and closed-domain question answering (2020)
4. Arbaaeen, A., Shah, A.: Ontology-based approach to semantically enhanced question answering for closed domain: a review. Information **12**, 200 (2021)
5. Ravichandran, D., Hovy, E.: Learning surface text patterns for a question answering system. In: Proceedings Of The 40th Annual Meeting Of The Association For Computational Linguistics, pp. 41–47 (2002)
6. Brown, T., et al.: Language models are few-shot learners. Adv. Neural. Inf. Process. Syst. **33**, 1877–1901 (2020)
7. Devlin, J., Chang, M., Lee, K.,Toutanova, K. BERT: pre-training of deep bidirectional transformers for language understanding. arxiv Preprint arxiv:1810.04805 (2018)
8. Raffel, C., et al.: Others Exploring the limits of transfer learning with a unified text-to-text transformer. J. Mach. Learn. Res. **21**, 1–67 (2020)
9. Lende, S., Raghuwanshi, M.,:Question answering system on education acts using NLP techniques. In: 2016 World Conference On Futuristic Trends In Research And Innovation For Social Welfare (Startup Conclave), pp. 1–6 (2016)
10. Mishra, A., Mishra, N., Agrawal, A.: Context-aware restricted geographical domain question answering system. In: 2010 International Conference On Computational Intelligence And Communication Networks, pp. 548–553 (2010)
11. Kwok, C., Etzioni, O., Weld, D.: Scaling question answering to the web. In: Proceedings of the 10th International Conference On World Wide Web, pp. 150–161 (2001)
12. Brill, E., Dumais, S., Banko, M.: An analysis of the AskMSR question-answering system. In: Proceedings of the 2002 Conference on Empirical Methods in Natural Language Processing (EMNLP 2002), pp. 257–264 (2002)
13. Smith, N., Heilman, M., Hwa, R.: Question generation as a competitive undergraduate course project. In: Proceedings of the NSF Workshop on the Question Generation Shared Task and Evaluation Challenge, pp. 4–6 (2008)
14. Rajpurkar, P., Zhang, J., Lopyrev, K., Liang, P.: SQuAD: 100,000+ questions for machine comprehension of text. arXiv Preprint arXiv:1606.05250. (2016)
15. Luhn, H.: The automatic creation of literature abstracts. IBM J. Res. Dev. **2**, 159–165 (1958)

Have a Break from Making Decisions, Have a MARS: The Multi-valued Action Reasoning System

Cosmin Badea$^{(\boxtimes)}$ (iD)

Imperial College London, London SW7 2AZ, UK
cb2610@imperial.ac.uk

Abstract. The Multi-valued Action Reasoning System (MARS) is an automated value-based ethical decision-making model for agents in Artificial Intelligence (AI). Given a set of available actions and an underlying moral paradigm, by employing MARS one can identify the ethically preferred action. It can be used to implement and model different ethical theories, different moral paradigms, as well as combinations of such, in the context of automated practical reasoning and normative decision analysis. It can also be used to model moral dilemmas and discover the moral paradigms that result in the desired outcomes therein. In this paper we give a condensed description of MARS, explain its uses, and comparatively place it in the existing literature.

Keywords: Mathematical models for AI · Logics for AI · Multi-criteria decision-making · AI ethics · Value alignment · Intelligent agents · Expert and knowledge-based systems

1 Introduction and Background

What is the right thing to do in any given situation? Even though all of us face some instance of this question often, as a society we have not yet reached a consensus about morality, let alone about a formalization thereof [2]. These days, however, finding an automated approach to moral reasoning is getting more urgent than ever. Autonomous agents are already being used in applications such as self-driving cars, drones, trading applications and manufacturing [10]. Some researchers are working on extending the systems' abilities at a fundamental level [2] and on exploring their potential in new fields such as search-and-rescue or patient and health care [4, 8, 17].

Artificially intelligent (AI) agents are by their very nature designed to react differently in different situations. As the situations could be infinitely many, it seems impossible to define adequate responses to all of them *a priori,* and even when we could (in limited domains), the Interpretation Problem [2] means that our symbolic representations may be misinterpreted. How, then, can we ensure that an artificial agent's actions are in line with the moral values of the society which it is embedded in, to obtain moral or safe agents? This is the main challenge in value alignment and machine ethics ([6, 23]). As

© The Author(s), under exclusive license to Springer Nature Switzerland AG 2022
M. Bramer and F. Stahl (Eds.): SGAI-AI 2022, LNAI 13652, pp. 359–366, 2022.
https://doi.org/10.1007/978-3-031-21441-7_31

part of answering this, we address the question: **Given the relevant circumstances, how should an AI agent automatically choose between different actions based on their underlying moral significance?**

It has been argued that we should build moral agents with inbuilt moral paradigms [2, 17], allowing them to be explicit moral agents [21], and MARS helps do that (although we can also build implicit moral agents with it). For brevity, we omit a discussion of the most important moral theories for AI Ethics, suffice it to enumerate them as being *Virtue Ethics* [9], *Consequentialism* (and its formulation *Utilitarianism* [22]), and *Deontology* [1]. We argue for their pros and cons elsewhere [2–4, 17].

Within the field of machine ethics, two different approaches to engineering moral decision-making have emerged: the top-down encoding of ethical theories and the bottom-up design of systems which aim at a specified goal [12, 24].

Bottom-Up Approaches. Systems built on this approach include the similarly-built *GenEth* [7], *EthEl* [5], *MedEthEx*, case-based reasoners such as *Truth-Teller* [18] and *Sirocco* [19] and of course learning-based systems relying on, for instance, Recurrent Neural Networks [16] to learn the moral permissibility of actions.

Top-Down Approaches. Most relevantly here, [13] explores ways of making automated ethical reasoning formally verifiable, and [20] investigates both the individual and collective realms of ethics.

2 The Multi-valued Action Reasoning System (MARS)

We illustrate the system using the example of *Hal the diabetic*, as in [11]: Hal, a diabetic urgently in need of insulin, has lost his supply through no fault of his own. Carla, another diabetic, has insulin. Hal can take it from her house, without her permission or knowledge. Knowing that Carla has diabetes, is he justified in taking it?

To model this dilemma, we need a way of representing Hal's options. In MARS, an **action** a_i is a process that can be selected by an agent in a decision problem. Semantically, choosing an action means electing to perform the corresponding act. We assume there is a finite number of mutually exclusive actions available, and we denote the set of actions $A = \{a_1, a_2, \ldots a_n\}$. Only one of the actions can be performed by the agent, its occurrence implying the non-occurrence of all others. In Hal's case, following [11], we set $A = \{$"take insulin", "don't take insulin"$\}$.

Values and Impact Functions. Given these actions, we need a way of assessing them through the lens of an agent's moral paradigm. Values have been [6] suggested as a suitable basis for ethical reasoning and we strongly believe in the arguments for using a value-based approach which we extensively make elsewhere [2, 17]. An action can be analyzed in terms of relevant values, and a moral theory can also be represented in terms of values, given a suitable technical framework, such as MARS. Our concept of values aims to be as general as possible, so that we can model different philosophical approaches. That means the chosen values could be of myriad sorts: reasons for or against performing actions, consequences, intentions, duties, principles, rules, virtues, states of affairs to obtain, possible worlds or features of such etc.

In MARS, a **value** v_i is a concept of (moral) significance. Values are the first input for MARS, and the (finite) set of values we denote V. Thus, $V =$ {"Hal's life", "Carla's life", "Property"}. Taking the insulin would save Hal's life, but endanger Carla's, while not taking it could be done to respect her property rights, hence our values.

To talk about the impact that actions have on values, we use the concepts of *promotion* and *demotion* ([6, 7, 15]). In MARS, we say that action a **promotes** (or **demotes**) value v to mean that performing this action is **in** (or **against**) the spirit of the value. The sets of values that are promoted and demoted by action a respectively are $V_a{}^+$, and $V_a{}^-$. We avoid restricting ourselves to particular paradigms, which would happen if promotion meant "increasing the quantity of v after performing a" (might be used for a utilitarian approach [14]). For Hal's action "take insulin", $V_a{}^+ =$ {"Hal's life"} and $V_a{}^- =$ {"Carla's life", "Property"}.

We can now define a function $I_a: V \rightarrow \{-1, 0, 1\}$ in (1) which evaluates the impact that performing a given action a will have on the set of values V. We call this the **impact function**. It allows us to obtain a numerical evaluation of how much a given action promotes or demotes a certain value, which we call the **impact coefficient** of the action with regards to the value (2). This will later enable us to compare actions.

$$I_a(v) = \begin{cases} 1, & \text{if } v \in V_a^+ \\ -1, & \text{if } v \in V_a^- \\ 0, & \text{otherwise} \end{cases} \tag{1}$$

$$i_a^v := I_a(v) \tag{2}$$

$$\left(i_a^{v_1}, i_a^{v_2}, \ldots, i_a^{v_m}\right), \text{ where } m = |V| \tag{3}$$

Every action promotes, demotes, or has no impact upon every value. We can extend this function to a larger target set, such as $\mathbb{Z}$ or $[-1, 1] \subset \mathbb{R}$, to account for various degrees of promotion and demotion (discrete, continuous).

Now we can define a convenient way of representing actions in terms of their promotion/demotion of the values in V, named the **impact representation** of an action, as the tuple consisting of all the impact coefficients it has on all the values (3). For example, we get the representation $a_1: (1, -1, -1)$ for action a_1 (taking the insulin) which promotes the first value, Hal's life, and demotes the others. Thus, we can evaluate an action based on the value set given.

Moral Paradigms: Strata with Values. We now have a way of representing actions in terms of their promotion and demotion of relevant values. To make an ethical decision, we also need a way of comparing these actions. Thus, the second input for MARS is a **moral paradigm** which is an expression of what is considered important and the basis for making ethical decisions.

In MARS, the *qualitative difference between values* is modelled using a stratified ordering of values. This qualitative differentiation between values is a central feature of MARS. Using it, one can represent the idea that an action promoting a particular value should always be preferred over an action that promotes lesser values; regardless of the number of lesser values or the amount that they are promoted in. This is crystallized in the concept of **strata** which are abstract layers made up of groups of values that are qualitatively more important than others. For instance, we might have "Life" in a higher stratum, wanting any action that saves someone's life to be preferred over actions that involve less important values. An advantage of this stratified approach is that we can model situations in which there is no total order over the values, a limiting assumption which previous work has often relied on [11, 13].

A stratum S_i, $i \in [1, k]$, is a subset of the values in V. We define $S = (S_1, S_2, ..., S_k)$ to be the set of all k strata. This is an input to MARS. S_i is a partition of V, so every value in V belongs to exactly one stratum. We define a relation $>_S$ on strata that helps us enumerate the ordered strata from top to bottom. The higher the stratum, the more important are the values therein. Importantly, note that values being in the same stratum does not necessarily make them equally preferred. This relation has the following properties: Irreflexivity, Asymmetry, Transitivity, Completeness – it is a total order.

We can thus directly express the qualitative difference between values in different strata, given by the relation $>_V$, making a value v qualitatively more important than v' *if and only if* (*iff*) v is in a higher stratum than v'. This relation has the following properties: Irreflexivity, Asymmetry, Transitivity, Transitivity of incomparability. It is therefore a strict weak ordering. Moral paradigms given as input to MARS may be:

A *selfish version of Hal* might value his own life strictly more than Carla's: • Stratum 1: Hal's Life; • Stratum 2: Carla's Life; • Stratum 3: Property	An *egalitarian Hal*, however, might value both of their lives similarly: • Stratum 1: Hal's Life, Carla's Life; • Stratum 2: Property

2.1 Evaluation Models

Given an ordering of values in strata and a set of available actions represented by their impact on those values, let us now consider how MARS selects the ethically preferred actions. This part of MARS, the evaluation algorithm or model, is the last parameter. Values in higher strata are qualitatively more important than those in lower strata, but values within a stratum could still be compared and evaluated against one another, and this is what we describe in this section. For brevity, we illustrate MARS using three of our evaluation models, described below. Note that different models yield different semantics for the system and can lead to vastly different results. We consider this to be a strong point to MARS, as it is agnostic to the underlying ethical paradigm and can thus flexibly cater to many vastly different ethical standpoints.

Global Maximum Model. To begin with, let us only consider the most important features of each action and assume a total order. We can thus compare actions based on the most important value that the actions impact upon differently. The preference relation on actions is thus defined in the following way (4): $a_1 \succ_A a_2$ iff there is a value for which a_1 has a higher impact coefficient than a_2 and all values that are higher than it in the moral paradigm are "tied" between the two actions, in that they have the same impact upon them:

$$a_1 \succ_A a_2 \Leftrightarrow \exists v \in \mathcal{V}.i_{a_1}^v > i_{a_2}^v \wedge \forall v' \in \mathcal{V}.\left(v' \succ_V v \rightarrow i_{a_1}^{v'} = i_{a_2}^{v'}\right) \quad (4)$$

When applying this algorithm to selfish Hal, the action a_1 "take insulin" is preferred, as its impact coefficient for the value in the topmost stratum ($i_{a_1}^{v_1}$) is 1, while the correspondent ($i_{a_2}^{v_1}$) is -1 for action a_2. However, the above model is insufficient to deal with actions with the same impact coefficient in the highest stratum.

Additive Model. This model is based on the intuition that all impact coefficients in a stratum should be considered when evaluating an action. One possible approach to achieving this is to aggregate the impact coefficients within strata. The sum of impact coefficients of an action for a given stratum is one method of evaluating which of the actions are morally preferred [14, 15], based on these having a more positive impact upon more of the values that we care about. The preference relation on actions here defines (5) $a \succ_A a'$ iff there is some stratum in which the preferred action has more of an impact, measured additively in terms of impact coefficients on the values in that stratum, than the other actions, and all the corresponding strata before it were "tied":

$$a \succ_A a' \Leftrightarrow \exists k \in [1, |\mathcal{S}|]. \sum_{v \in S_k} i_{a'}^v < \sum_{v \in S_k} i_a^v \wedge \forall l \in [1, k-1]. \sum_{v \in S_l} i_{a'}^v = \sum_{v \in S_l} i_a^v \quad (5)$$

Let us consider how this model could be applied to find a preferred action according to egalitarian Hal's moral paradigm. As the sum of impact coefficients is the same for both actions in the first stratum, but the action "don't take insulin" has a higher sum in the second stratum, egalitarian Hal will not take the insulin.

Note that this model gives rise to an impact representation of actions evaluated according to the moral paradigm, consisting of this additive aggregation of values within in each stratum. One can then see that an equivalent way of comparing actions is comparing these evaluations using a lexicographic ordering. In the above example "Take insulin" could thus be seen as $(0, -1)$ and "Don't take insulin" could be seen as $(0, 1)$. This representation makes it easier to see why the second action is preferred.

Weighted Additive Model. The additive model can be extended by weighing impact coefficients differently. This would model a moral paradigm in which two values in the same stratum are comparable, but not equally important, giving us a way of quantitatively differentiating them. Furthermore, Dancy suggests that the importance of features that are morally relevant might change depending on the situation [14]. Thus, we can use this concept of weights to elegantly model this changing importance of the different values. We define weights $w^v \in R, v \in \mathcal{V}$, associated with the impact coefficients $i_a^v, \forall a \in A$, and define the preference relation $\succ_A$ for this model as in (6).

$$a \succ_A a' \Leftrightarrow \exists k \in [1, |\mathcal{S}|]. \sum_{v \in S_k} w^v i_{a'}^v < \sum_{v \in S_k} w^v i_a^v \\ \wedge \forall l \in [1, k-1]. \sum_{v \in S_l} w^v i_{a'}^v = \sum_{v \in S_l} w^v i_a^v \quad (6)$$

$$a \in \mathcal{P} \Leftrightarrow \nexists a' \in A.a' \succ_A a \quad (7)$$

Preferred Actions Set. So far, we have shown how we can do pairwise comparison of actions. But what of our final answer, the actions that are preferred? Our semantics for a **preferred actions** set P, the set of actions which are preferred over all available actions, is that an action a belongs to P iff there is no other action which is preferred to it (7). Note that there might be several actions in this set.

Alternative Models. For brevity, we shall only mention some of the other evaluation models we have for MARS. *Minimal Number of Negative Impact Coefficients:* We prefer actions which demote as few values as possible, violations in higher strata being deemed more important than violations in lower strata. *Minimal Sum of Demotions:* We prefer actions with minimal sums of demotion. *Stratum Satisfaction and Violation:* What if there are several ways of promoting a value? Promoting one value then satisfies the entire stratum, and adjacent values are no longer considered.

Enjoying MARS: A Workflow

1. Establish a scenario to model. Establish what the available actions A are. Decide which values or features the decision depends on. Such features could be intentions, reasons, desirable consequences etc. These values make up the set V.
2. Establish which values are of comparable importance and which are qualitatively more important than others. This will yield the ordering of values in strata, S.
3. Decide how the actions impact upon the values. Is performing a given action "in the spirit of" a value? If so, the impact coefficient for that pair should be 1. If it acts "against the spirit" of the value, then it should be a −1. If the value is irrelevant to the action, it is a 0. Thus, we obtain the impact functions in I.
4. Select an evaluation model to compare the actions against each other. Do we want values in the same stratum to be counted or added up, or weighted and compared against each other? Do we want to select actions that have the highest number of good impact coefficients, or the least negative impact coefficients?
5. Apply the evaluation model to obtain the set of preferred actions P. These are the actions one can perform, given the stratified moral paradigm used as input.

Related Work, Comparisons, Limitations. Firstly, the *GenEth* system by Anderson et al. uses a similar action representation to ours [7]. In their work, a bottom-up approach of learning ethical principles is presented. We, on the other hand, introduce a top-down approach. As such, the systems offer the respective advantages and disadvantages of these strategies, and we agree that a combination of top-down and bottom-up may be necessary to create moral artificial agents [12]]. The advantages of top-down systems such as ours are: allowing for an *a priori*, explicit, encoding of principles, potentially helping with explainability of the decision-making process, and verification of the system before it is employed. On the other hand, encoding moral paradigms and making the connection between abstract principles and rules or implementation is very hard, presenting a significant obstacle.

Dennis et al. [13] propose a hybrid system implementing both a component to interact with the environment to obtain knowledge about the actions, as well as a discrete decision-making component. The ethical policy provided to the agent in their system consists of a total order over the ethical principles. Our system, in contrast, does not require a total order of values, thanks to the stratified structure of the moral paradigm, thus allowing us to encode more varied moral paradigms. This is useful when there is uncertainty about the way that the values ought to be ranked.

Pereira et al. [20] tackle automated ethical reasoning by using logic programming. We see our work as complementary to theirs, in that we do not directly address the same problem in the same way, and we do not focus on the underlying implementation and its properties but on the higher-level theory and model used for reasoning.

Finally, we have tested MARS using examples from the above, replicating the inputs used and checking to see if we can obtain the same results in terms of preferred actions, which, by selecting a suitable evaluation model, we do. There are improvements that can be made to our system, in line with the points we have made throughout, to be addressed in an extensive forthcoming paper on MARS. See you there!

References

1. Alexander, L., Moore, M.: Deontological ethics. In: Zalta, E.N. (ed) The Stanford Encyclopedia of Philosophy. Stanford University, winter 2016 edition (2016)
2. Badea, C., Artus, G.: Morality, Machines and the Interpretation Problem: [...]. Forthcoming in: AI XXXIX, LNAI. Springer, London, arXiv:2103.02728 (2022)
3. Bolton, W., Badea, C., Georgiou, P., Holmes, A., Rawson, T.: Developing moral AI to support antimicrobial decision making. Nat. Mach. Intell. (2022). https://doi.org/10.1038/s42256-022-00558-5
4. Post, B., Badea, C., Faisal, A., Brett, S.J.: Breaking bad news in the era of artificial intelligence and algorithmic medicine. AI Ethics (2022). https://doi.org/10.1007/s43681-022-00230-z
5. Anderson, M., Anderson, S.L.: Ethel: toward a principled ethical elder care robot (2008)
6. Anderson, M., Anderson, S.L.: Machine Ethics. Cambridge University Press (2011)
7. Anderson, M., Anderson, S.L.: January. GenEth: a general ethical dilemma analyzer. In: AAAI, pp. 253–261 (2014)
8. Andrade, A.O., et al.: Bridging the gap between robotic technology and health care. Biomed. Signal Process. Control **10**, 65–78 (2014)
9. Aristotle, R.W.D., Brown, L.: The Nicomachean Ethics. OUP, Oxford (2009)
10. Bekey, G., et al.: Robotics: State of the Art and Future Challenges. World Scientific (2008)
11. Bench-Capon, T.: Value based argumentation frameworks. arXiv preprint cs/0207059 (2002)
12. Charisi, V., et al.: Towards moral autonomous systems. arXiv:1703.04741 (2017)
13. Dennis, L., Fisher, M., Slavkovik, M., Webster, M.: Formal verification of ethical choices in autonomous systems. Robot. Auton. Syst. **77**, 1–14 (2016)
14. Dietrich, F., List, C.: What matters and how it matters: a choice-theoretic representation of moral theories (2016)
15. Feldman, F.: Utilitarianism, Hedonism, and Desert: Essays in Moral Philosophy. CUP (1997)
16. Guarini, M.: Computational neural modeling and the philosophy of ethics reflections on the particularism-generalism debate. Included in Anderson, 2011. Machine Ethics, p. 316 (2011)
17. Hindocha, S., Badea, C.: Moral exemplars for the virtuous machine: the clinician's role in ethical artificial intelligence for healthcare. AI and Ethics **2**, 1–9 (2021). https://doi.org/10.1007/s43681-021-00089-6

18. McLaren, B.M., Ashley, K.D.: Case-based comparative evaluation in truth-teller. In: Proceedings from the Seventeenth Annual Conference of the Cognitive Science Society (1995)
19. McLaren, B.M.: Extensionally defining principles and cases in ethics. Artif. Intell. **150**, 145–181 (2003)
20. Pereira, L.M., et al.: Programming Machine Ethics, vol. 26. Springer (2016)
21. Badea, C., Gilpin, L.H.: Establishing meta-decision-making for AI: an ontology of relevance, representation and reasoning. In: AAAI 2021, Fall FSS-21. arXiv:submit/4523302 (2021)
22. Sinnott-Armstrong, W.: Consequentialism. In Zalta, E.N. (ed) The Stanford Encyclopedia of Philosophy. Metaphysics Research Lab, Stanford University, winter 2015 edition (2015)
23. Wallach, W.: Machine Ethics and Robot Ethics. Ashgate Publishing (2016)
24. Wallach, W., Allen, C., Smit, I.: Machine morality: bottom-up and top-down approaches for modelling human moral faculties. AI & Soc. **22**(4), 565–582 (2008)

Author Index

Printed in the United States
by Baker & Taylor Publisher Services